THE NIGER AND ITS NEIGHBOURS

THE NIGER AND ITS NEIGHBOURS

Environmental history and hydrobiology,
human use and health hazards
of the major West African rivers

Edited by
A.T.GROVE
University of Cambridge, African Studies Centre, UK

A.A.BALKEMA / ROTTERDAM / BOSTON / 1985

In memory of Julian Rzóska

ISBN 90 6191 512 0

© 1985 A.A.Balkema, P.O.Box 1675, 3000 BR Rotterdam, Netherlands

Distributed in USA & Canada by: A.A.Balkema Publishers, P.O.Box 230, Accord, MA 02018

Printed in the Netherlands

Preface

Julian Rzóska originally proposed this book on the Niger. He saw it as being concerned with the ecology of the river and in particular with those features associated with its remarkable course, first towards the desert and then away from it through the Sahel, savanna and forest zones to the Atlantic. He invited me to contribute a chapter on the physical evolution of the Niger basin and the Chad and Senegal basins to east and west. Soon after, alas, his sight failed and he asked me if I would act as editor. Julian Rzóska died on 31st December 1984 while page proofs were being corrected.

We had already agreed to include material on the Senegal River and Lake Chad which share the Niger's genesis and as a result have similar faunal characteristics. As a geographer I was attracted to the idea of including a consideration of how people use the rivers and how the rivers affect people living by them, that is the interaction of man and water in West Africa. The Volta is a river which has attracted much attention in recent years both as a result of the construction of the Akosombo Dam in the mid-1960s and more recently the campaign against river blindness (*Onchocerciasis*), so it was decided to include this river as well. Then Jack Talling suggested the title which has been adopted, *The Niger and its Neighbours*.

The shape of the book is thus readily explained. Part One is, I believe, much as Julian Rzóska had originally visualised the book. It includes a contribution on the biology of the river systems by Dr. Rosemary Lowe-McConnell. Part Two brings together material on the human geography of the riverine areas. I have outlined the history of the river peoples and traditional modes of life, dwelling particularly on those areas where people are most dependent on water, that is on the alluvial plains constructed by rivers as deltas and floodplains under the varying climatic conditions and sea-levels of the Late Quaternary. Bill Adams who has investigated the consequences of river control schemes in Nigeria provides a chapter on the impact of such schemes on the environment and people. Nick Chisholm and Jean Grove direct attention to the Lower Volta. Finally, in Part Three, David Molyneux and his collaborators, Frank Walsh, David Brown and

Chris Wright discuss three of the main health hazards to which riverside dwellers are exposed and the measures being taken to cope with them. Wright, sadly, died on 19th June 1983, soon after his contribution to this volume had been written.

In the tropics, with high temperatures throughout the year and great water losses by evaporation, rivers and lakes are particularly valuable resources. Populations in West Africa are increasing at rates of about 3% annually and dependence on imported foodstuffs is increasing at a similar rate. The future well-being of millions of people depends on optimal use being made of rivers and lakes as sources of water for domestic purposes, for livestock, for irrigating farmland and grazing, for supplying towns and factories and disposing of their wastes, and as waterways for boats.

River control works started about 1950 with schemes at Richard Toll alongside the Senegal River and at Markala (Sansanding) in the Inland (Central) Niger delta. The Volta River (Akosombo Dam) Project followed and construction on the Niger of the Kainji Dam was completed in 1968. Dams have since been completed on the Sokoto in north-west Nigeria, on the Gongola tributary of the Benue and on the Nigerian feeders of Lake Chad. Other schemes are under way.

The Sahelian drought of 1968-1974 following the wet years of the 1950s and early 1960s not only indicated the possible range of variation of rainfall and river discharge, it also drew attention to the poverty of the zone and its lack of man-made and natural resources. The need to make the best possible use of the rivers was evident. International river basin commissions have been constituted which are in a position to oversee the development of West Africa's water resources. It is vitally important that they give good advice and that the individual countries concerned make the right decisions.

The decade 1975-84 has seen the rainfall deficits in the interior of West Africa accentuated. At present it is impossible to tell when or if conditions will return to those of the 1950s and 1960s or whether the new drier mode will persist.

I would like to express my appreciation of the kindness and patience of the contributors to this volume. My grateful thanks go to Arthur Shelley and Ian Gulley of the Cambridge University Geography Department and to my daughter Jane Powell for drawing the maps and diagrams and to Dennis Blackburn for the photographic work.

Finally I would extend my good wishes to the members of the British Hovercraft Expedition of 1969-70, especially to its leader David Smithers who gave me the opportunity to travel by water from the Atlantic to Lake Chad, just before the current dry period began.

A.T. Grove

Cambridge
January 1985

Contents

PART TWO: HUMAN USE

Part One
Environmental change and hydrobiology

A.T.GROVE
African Studies Centre, Free School Lane, Cambridge

The environmental setting

1.1 LATITUDINAL ZONATION AND RIVER REGIMES

West Africa lies between the Sahara and the Gulf of Guinea, like a
peninsula running westwards from the watershed between the Nile and
Chad drainage systems. The main sources of its rivers are in the high
rainfall areas quite close to the coast. From the highlands in the interior
of the Ivory Coast and the Republic of Guinea, the headwaters of the
Upper Niger and Senegal run north before turning away from the desert.
The Senegal curves west and finally south to reach the sea near St Louis.
The Niger wanders across the plains of an inland basin at an elevation of
270 to 250 m between Ségou and Tombouctou before heading east to
Tossaye where it leaves the Inland or Central Basin and follows an
angular course to its marine delta on the Bight of Biafra. The main
headwaters of the Benue, Logone and Chari, all rising on the Adamawa
Plateau in the east, also run towards the north. The Benue turns away to
the west and joins the Niger at Lokoja; the Logone and Chari traverse
gently sloping plains at about 300 m and enter Lake Chad, the surface of
which is at between 278 and 283m (Figure 1).

The two main highland source regions are ancient bulges of the
continental crust. Between them lie the troughs of the lower Niger and
Benue controlled by faulting associated with the separation of Africa and
South America in Mesozoic times. Further west is the basin of the lower
Volta occupying a saucer-shaped set of Palaeozoic rocks. North of
latitude 10° N greater structural basins extend into the Sahara, preserving
marine and continental sedimentary rocks of Mesozoic and later age and
forming the catchments of the lower Senegal, middle Niger and Chad
(Figure 11).

Because of the high temperatures, evaporation is great and flow in the
rivers represents the small difference between rainfall and evaporation
losses. A small volume of water escapes from the Chad basin at times
when Logone floodwaters spread westwards to reach the Mayo
Kebbi tributary of the Benue; all the rest of the rain falling on the basin is
evaporated. In general, little water is contributed to the major rivers from

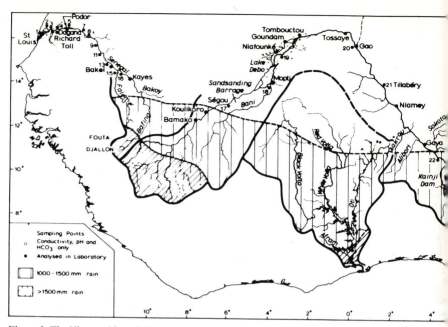

Figure 1. The Niger and its neighbours derive a high proportion of their discharge from the limited areas in their catchments receiving more than 1500 mm of rain annually. Points marked along the Senegal and Niger are places where river water was sampled by the author in 1969. The extent of the Early Holocene lake in the Chad basin is indicated.

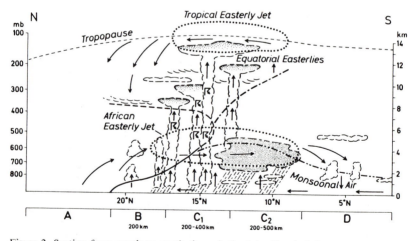

Figure 2. Section from north to south through the Inter-Tropical Convergence Zone in August when it is in its most northerly position; about 21°N at the surface. At this time of year there is little or no rain in Zone A, isolated storms in B, longer storms in C1, prolonged monsoonal rain in C2 and a pause in the rains in D (modified from Maley 1981).

4

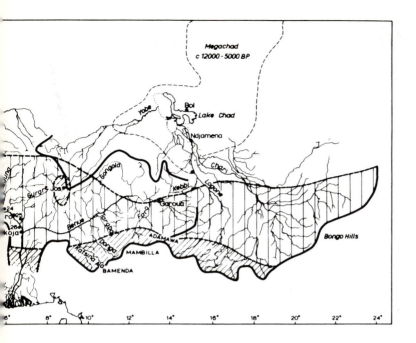

those areas where the annual rainfall is less than 1000 mm. Flow in the mainstreams is largely derived from the Guinea and Cameroun source areas where mean annual rainfall totals exceed 1500 mm. Near the Nigeria-Cameroun frontier, high rainfall contributes such a large volume of water to the Benue that at Lokoja its discharge exceeds the flow of the Niger.

The rain is derived from moist equatorial air moving inland from the Atlantic and undercutting dry easterly air that occupies the Sahara for much of the year. An ill-defined front between the two air masses, declining towards the north, is called the Inter-Tropical Convergence Zone (ITCZ). Most of the rain is the result of convectional activity and uplift of moist air, added by passage over highlands, well to the south of the ground position of the ITCZ and where the depth of moist air exceeds 2000 m. From November to February the ITCZ lies in the vicinity of the Guinea coast and little rain falls over West Africa. The ITCZ moves slowly north to reach the southern margin of the Sahara in August and then retreats more rapidly south (Figure 2).

The rainy season in the north is confined to the period June to September. Where the mean annual precipitation is less than 400 mm, the

5

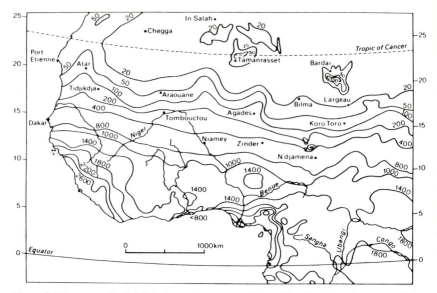

Figure 3. Mean annual rainfall isohyets in mm over West Africa showing values generally increasing towards the south except in the vicinity of the Volta delta where rainfall at the coast is less than 800 mm.

rain falls mainly in local thunderstorms associated with the passage of Easterly Waves (Ojo 1977). South of the Sahel longer periods of rain lasting several hours cover extensive areas. South of the Sudan zone, with mean annual totals exceeding 1000 mm, spells of monsoonal rain may last for a day or two and the sky is overcast for much of the rainy season (Figure 3).

The decrease in the amount of rain and the length of the rainy season from the Gulf of Guinea towards the Sahara gives a remarkably regular latitudinal arrangement of the climatic belts and vegetation zones (Figure 4).

Natural plant assemblages and agricultural opportunities vary from south to north (Figure 5). Rain forest in the south has been extensively replaced by oil-palm woodland consisting largely of trees that have been selectively preserved because of their usefulness to man. In the course of the last one hundred years, coffee and cocoa have been planted in areas with 1400–2000 mm of rain; rubber plantations have been established in wetter areas.

The staple foods in the forest lands are cassava, yam, cocoyam, plantain and maize. Further north, in the Guinea zone of tall savanna woodland, maize and sorghum are more important foodstuffs than root crops. Northward again in the Sudan and Sahelian zones, which occupy such a large part of the interior basins, millet, sorghum and pulses are the chief food crops, while groundnuts and cotton are grown largely for sale. Much of this

6

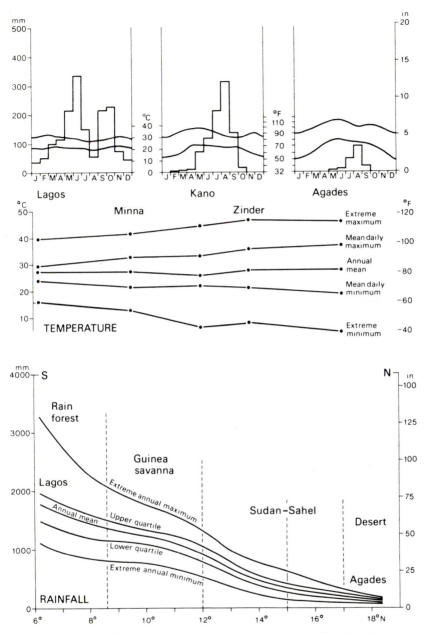

Figure 4. The length of the rainy season and the amount of rain falling diminish inland from the coast towards the desert interior while the daily and seasonal ranges of temperature increase inland (Grove 1977).

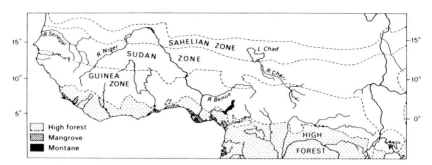

Figure 5. Latitudinal zonation of the biomes corresponding with the diminishing rainfall from the Gulf of Guinea towards the Sahara.

drier country is outside the range of the tsetse-fly and cattle, owned by sedentary villagers as well as by pastoralists, are numerous. Cattle, goats and sheep graze and browse on the uncultivated land and also feed on crop residues, both stubble and the bran remaining after milling or grinding. Fulani pastoralists lead their herds to the well-watered highland source areas of the major rivers. Northwards into the desert, sheep, goats, donkeys and camels are largely in the hands of Moorish, Touareg and Tibou pastoralists and cultivation is confined to irrigated oases.

A break in the rainy season in August is commonly a feature of the climate close to the Gulf of Guinea when the ITCZ is far to the north. The pause increases in length westwards from the Niger Delta and eastwards from the Ivory Coast. On the Accra Plains and Volta Delta it lasts from July into September and mean annual totals are only 750 mm, less than anywhere else in Ghana. This anomalous coastal dry zone, the southern intensification of a relatively dry meridional belt within the loop of the Niger, effectively separates one high rainfall region in south-east Nigeria and west Cameroun from another lying behind the Windward Coast of Sierra Leone and Liberia. A broad tongue with reduced rainfall extends south to the Bouaké (Baoulé) region of Ivory Coast but fails to reach the coast. The main tributaries of the Volta flow south across this Bouaké tongue and unite to form the Volta mainstream now submerged by the Volta Lake. High rainfall and high forest reach the Lake above the Akosombo Dam; to the south, the lowest reaches of the river traverse semi-arid, grassy coastal plains.

Most West African rivers are at or near their lowest levels at the end of the dry season about April, when channels in the north are dry and most of the main rivers can be forded. Then come the first rains, thunderstorms locally called tornadoes, associated with the westerly passage of frontal systems called Easterly Waves. The larger rivers begin to rise in June and in the headwaters peak discharges are in August. As the flood waves pass downstream, maximum levels are reached on the lower Benue in September and on the Lower Senegal, Volta and Logone-Chari in

October (Ledger 1969). The input of water to Lake Chad exceeds evaporation losses from July until December and the lake normally reaches its highest levels at the end of the year. Similarly, the floodwaters of the Upper Niger spread over the alluvial plains of the Inland Delta downstream of Ségou in the last quarter of the year, come together again near Tombouctou and eventually spill over the sill downstream of Bourem at Tossaye where maximum discharges usually occur in January (Figure 40). The floodwater, cleared of silt in its passage of the Inland Delta and called the Black Flood, reaches Gao in November and enters the Kainji reservoir a week or two later; it continues to flow until April when the local dry season is most intense and local stream discharges are lowest.

1.2 SOURCES OF INFORMATION

The environmental setting of the rivers is well portrayed on maps published by the Organisation of African Unity (OAU) in the International Atlas of West Africa. Topographical maps are available for all the river basins on a scale of 1:250,000 and for most parts on larger scales still. Maps showing geology, soils and other environmental conditions have been published by national survey departments, by the Institut Geographique National and CNRS in Paris, and by the Directorate of Overseas Surveys and the Land Resources Division of the U.K. Overseas Development Administration.

Geographical texts dealing with riverine environments in West Africa include Morgan & Pugh (1969) and Harrison-Church (1980).

Hydrological data are published by ORSTOM and in particular reference should be made to the Hydrographical Monographs of the Niger, Senegal, Logone, Chari and Lake Chad. A great deal of information about the hydrological and sedimentary characteristics of the Lower Niger and Benue was brought together by NEDECO (1959) in *River studies and recommendations on improvement of Niger and Benue.* ORSTOM, in conjunction with Electricité de France maintains a list of hydrological publications categorised according to country and mention should be made of Rodier (1963). Many reports by international and commercial organisations are in mimeographical form and not always easily accessible.

1.3 THE VARIABILITY OF RAINFALL AND RIVER FLOWS

1.3.1 *The instrumental record*

The headwaters of the rivers respond to individual storms by rising and falling rapidly. On the larger rivers the occurrence of seasonal flood peaks and troughs is more clearly apparent. The peaks vary in their timing from

9

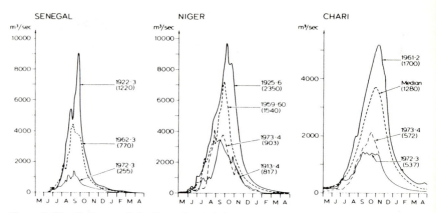

Figure 6. The discharge of the Senegal at Bakel, the Niger at Koulikoro and the Chari at N'djamena showing the great range between wet and dry years, especially in the case of the Senegal.

year to year by two or three weeks. The interannual variability in the height of the peaks and annual discharge is very great.

Evaporation losses are always high and the potential evaporation increases in years with deficient rain because of reduced cloudiness and atmospheric humidity in such dry years. The depth of evaporation from measuring pans on Lake Chad increases from 1850 mm in wet years to 2150 mm in dry ones. On the other hand, total volumetric evaporation losses are greater in wet years because the extensive areas flooded present wide evaporative surfaces whereas in dry years water is more confined to channels. In the main source areas of the rivers the mean percentage variability of the rainfall is moderate; it increases towards the Sahara.

The effects on river discharges of rainfall departures from the mean are accentuated by the high evaporation and evapotranspiration losses. In the case of the Niger at Koulikoro the rainfall over the catchment upstream varies more than 250 mm above or below the mean of 1650 mm, i.e. by about 15%, one year in ten whereas the annual discharge at Koulikoro varies from the mean of 45 km^3 by about 15 km^3, i.e. by about 33%, one year in ten. On the Senegal river at Bakel, where the mean annual discharge is about 22 km^3, annual discharge values between 1903 and 1979 have varied from 8.2 km^3 in 1972 and 8.5 km^3 in 1913 to 38.8 km^3 in 1906 and 39.3 km^3 in 1924, i.e. from almost double to less than a half of the mean. Such values reflect and magnify the variability of the rainfall in the source areas of the Fouta Djallon as well as in the Sudan zone.

The occurrence of wet and dry years is not randomly distributed in either space or time. Maps of negative and positive rainfall departures from the mean show that large contiguous areas are commonly affected by either deficiencies or surpluses in individual years, with a latitudinal zonation often apparent in the distribution patterns (Grove 1973;

10

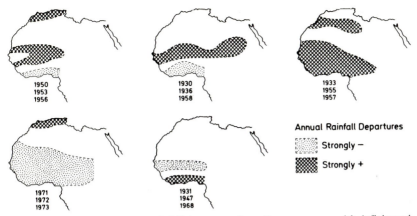

Figure 7. In years with strong rainfall departures from the mean, areas with deficits and surpluses are commonly arranged in latitudinal bands (derived from Nicholson 1981).

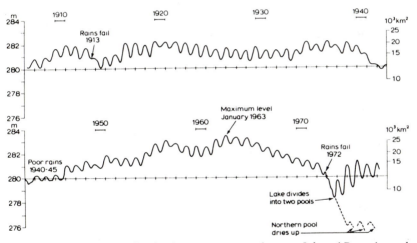

Figure 8. Lake Chad normally rises by a metre or two between July and December and then falls by a similar amount. The Lake's level and extent increased in the mid-1950s and then a decade later began to diminish, reaching very low values in the mid-1970s that persisted into the 1980s (from Grove 1978).

Nicholson 1981; Figure 7). As a result the Niger and its neighbours tend to respond in the same way in individual years; for example, 1913 and 1972 were both years of unusually low discharge of the Senegal, Niger, Logone-Chari and also of the Nile and Volta, all of which have their headwaters in the same latitudinal zone.

The spatial correlation is accompanied by temporal clustering of wet and dry years. The drought years that affected Sahel and Sudan between

11

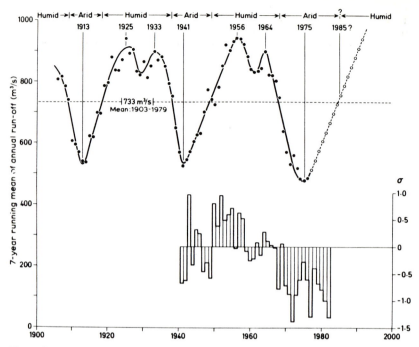

Figure 9. Seven-year running means of Senegal river discharge from 1903 to 1979 display a remarkably regular oscillation (Faure & Gac 1981a). They are compared here with normalised rainfall departures for Sahel/Sudan given by Lamb (1982). The contrast between the wet 1950s and the dry 1970s is clear. It is far from certain that river discharge and rainfall values will follow the upward trend extrapolated into the 1980s and early 1990s from the Senegal discharge records.

1968 and 1974 have already been mentioned. Other groups of dry years affected much of the same zone in the second and fifth decades of this century. Lake Chad acts as an accumulator of positive departures from the mean of Logone-Chari discharge, rising in response to runs of wet years, falling with successive years of drought (Figure 8).

Diagrams prepared by Faure & Gac (1981a), plotting seven-year running means of the Senegal's annual discharge at Bakel from 1903 to 1979, bring out a remarkable regularity in the river's discharge in the course of this century. Low values appear for the period 1909–1919 and 1938–49 with twin peaks in 1925 and 1933 and also in 1956 and 1964 (Figure 9). The seven year running means of the annual discharge values of the Upper Niger and Logone-Chari produce strikingly similar oscillations.

Faure and Gac were tempted to extrapolate the Senegal curve into the 1980s and predicted that the river discharge, and by implication the rainfall, could be expected to be restored to the long-term mean by 1985,

12

Table 1. April-October rainfall departure statistics for subsaharan West Africa 1941-82 (Lamb 1983).

Year	1941-74 base Average of all station departures (σ)	Fraction of stations with departure $\geqslant -1.0\ \sigma$ (if all-station average is negative) or $\geqslant +1.0\ \sigma$ (if all-station average is positive)	Fraction of stations with departure $\geqslant -0.6\ \sigma$ (if all-station average is negative) or $\geqslant +0.6\ \sigma$ (if all-station average is positive)
1941	−0.67	4/14	7/14
1942	−0.63	7/14	8/14
1943	+0.96	9/14	11/14
1944	−0.34	5/14	5/14
1945	+0.32	3/14	3/14
1946	+0.25	1/14	3/14
1947	−0.46	3/15	7/15
1948	−0.30	4/15	7/15
1949	−0.58	5/14	7/14
1950	+0.80	8/20	13/20
1951	+0.38	5/20	10/20
1952	+0.95	7/19	13/19
1953	+0.50	5/19	8/19
1954	+0.60	7/20	10/20
1955	+0.72	5/20	9/20
1956	−0.03	3/20	7/20
1957	+0.63	7/20	11/20
1958	+0.52	6/20	9/20
1959	−0.08	4/20	7/20
1960	−0.25	3/18	4/18
1961	−0.22	1/20	4/20
1962	+0.09	3/20	5/20
1963	−0.15	2/20	5/20
1964	+0.28	4/20	7/20
1965	+0.11	1/20	6/20
1966	+0.03	5/20	7/20
1967	−0.02	2/20	5/20
1968	−0.78	7/20	14/20
1969	+0.06	3/20	6/20
1970	−0.72	8/20	13/20
1971	−0.88	9/20	15/20
1972	−1.39	17/20	19/20
1973	−0.91	13/18	16/18
1974	−0.60	7/16	10/16
1975	−0.27	3/20	8/20
1976	−0.62	7/20	10/20
1977	−0.42	13/18	15/18
1978	−0.42	5/20	10/20
1979	−0.70	8/20	14/20
1980	−0.80	9/20	13/20
1981	−1.00	9/20	15/20
1982	−1.30	15/19	16/19

with another long drought period to be expected about 2005 AD. There are some leaps in the argument. The discharge of the Senegal at Bakel is a function of the rainfall in the Sudan zone and further south in the Guinea highlands. However, Palutikoff et al. (1981) have found a correlation coefficient of 0.76, significant at the 0.1% level, between the runoff figures and normalised annual rainfall departures for the Sahel. The runoff data is thus an acceptable substitute (proxy) for Sahelian rainfall. Spectral analysis confirmed the existence of a strong thirty-year cycle in the discharge record. Of course, the fact that such a cycle was repeated 2½ times between 1903 and 1979 does not imply the existence of an oscillation that can be extended into the future. Such cycles are inclined to cease in a disconcerting fashion soon after they have been identified. It would be unwise therefore to base river control and other policies on predictions of the kind suggested by the supposedly cyclic behaviour of the Senegal. It must also be borne in mind that the behaviour of the rains and the rivers they feed can be quite different in successive years. The discharge of the Senegal in 1967 was 32.7 km^3; in 1968 it was only 12.5 km^3.

Figures presented by Lamb (1982 and 1983) make it clear that the Sahelian drought of the years around 1970 persisted into the 1980s. From 1978 to 1982 drought became increasingly severe in each successive year (Figure 9). Four of the eight years 1975–82 received substantially less rain than the better-known drought years of the 1940s and by 1983 a quarter of a century had elapsed since the last period of abundant rain, in 1950–58.

Annual rainfall predictions of a probabilistic nature, based on the recurrence intervals or return periods of events of different magnitudes, calculated from the instrumental records, are of limited value because they depend on the long-term mean remaining constant. In fact there are steps up and down in long term means, such as the step down that affected much of tropical Africa at the end of the last century (Kraus 1954).

East African lake levels and the discharge of the Nile into Egypt were well above twentieth century mean values for the last three decades of the nineteenth century; for the next sixty years they were much lower and then in 1961 they suddenly increased and remained high for several years (Kite 1981). Such shifts, which are of great importance for water storage, hydro-electric power generation and the supply of water for irrigation projects, are at present quite unpredictable.

1.3.2 *The historical record*

Until the beginning of the twentieth century, records of river flow and rainfall in West Africa are very scanty indeed. Reconstructing environmental change over a longer period involves resorting to a variety of sources including accounts of early travellers, the incidence of famines supposedly caused by drought, and analogues with neighbouring regions. It is a hazardous field of study where it is difficult to distinguish the short-

Table 2. Variations in discharge of the Nile at Aswan, the Senegal at Bakel, The Chari at N'djamena and the Niger at Koulikoro as percentages of the 1933-45 mean (*Monographie Hydrologique du Bassin du Niger* 1970).

Year	Nile	Year	Nile	Senegal	Niger	Year	Nile	Senegal	Chari	Niger
1870	–	1900	103	–	–	1930	91	119	–	152
1871	137	1901	107	–	–	1931	95	107	–	132
1872	142	1902	85	–	–	1932	104	111	–	134
1873	118	1903	115	90	–	1933	101	120	105	124
1874	148	1904	101	104	–	1934	111	98	117	111
1875	142	1905	86	123	–	1935	119	167	92	110
1876	142	1906	113	174	–	1936	108	177	136	128
1877	100	1907	85	74	86	1937	99	91	85	98
1878	168	1909	129	108	92	1938	124	113	122	111
1879	168	1909	129	127	146	1939	92	79	104	102
1880	140	1910	119	95	96	1940	81	61	79	89
1881	122	1911	101	76	120	1941	78	58	67	93
1882	115	1912	87	80	98	1942	102	61	91	76
1883	136	1913	56	49	63	1943	97	94	104	90
1884	122	1914	103	59	70	1944	89	45	93	75
1885	125	1915	85	81	103	1945	96	135	101	93
1886	118	1916	139	97	105	1946	–	105	131	114
1887	145	1917	135	86	109	1947	–	92	–	97
1888	98	1918	99	146	137	1948	–	92	117	123
1889	118	1919	95	76	106	1949	–	74	102	105
1890	140	1920	102	118	93	1950	–	166	126	112
1891	135	1921	94	61	79	1951	–	122	99	157
1892	148	1922	104	176	109	1952	–	104	108	126
1893	141	1923	106	108	117	1953	–	91	111	147
1894	153	1924	106	188	165	1954	–	154	135	155
1895	155	1925	83	120	177	1955	–	152	148	155
1896	150	1926	104	74	130	1956	–	137	125	106
1897	126	1927	89	154	146	1957	–	149	105	154
1898	135	1928	97	148	163	1958	–	159	101	118
1899	195	1929	126	144	156	1959	–	114	114	119
						1960	–	90	123	128
						1961	–	136	152	97
						1962	–	109	145	142
						1963	–	94	122	–
						1964	–	137	115	–

lived event from longer-term departures from the mean (Maley 1981; Nicholson 1980).

There are similarities in the discharge of the Nile, the behaviour of West African rivers and the level of Lake Chad where these records overlap in this century (Table 2). In the latter part of the nineteenth century, the flow of the Nile was well above the mean for the first half of this century and there is good reason to suppose that Lake Chad was enlarged for Nachtigal relates that in 1874 it overflowed 180 km along the Bahr-el-Ghazal, the channel leading down into the Djourab of Borkou

15

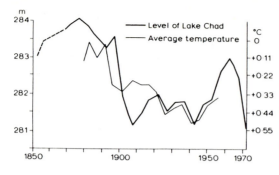

Figure 10. The shrinkage of Lake Chad at the end of the last century corresponds with an increase in temperatures in low latitudes of about 0.3°C (Mitchell 1961) which Maley (1973, 1981) suggests may have been associated with decreased cloudiness.

(Nachtigal 1971). Maley (1973, 1981) has compared the variations in the level of Lake Chad since 1850 with annual temperatures between 30° N and 30° S, from which it would seem that lake level fell when temperatures between the tropics increased (Figure 10).

In the middle of the nineteenth century Lake Chad was lower. Overweg who voyaged on the lake in 1851 reported it had been lower still a century earlier, so low that a raiding party from Makkiri had been able to invade and plunder all Bidummaland, including the sandridges that form islands when the lake is at its mean twentieth century level. About the same time Barth (1965) was told by the local people that an old man was still alive who in his youth, presumably about 1790–1800, had been taken by boat along the Bahr-el-Ghazal from Lake Chad to Borkou. Yet Denham who made a circuit of the lake in 1823, directs attention to a high stand said to have occurred early, not late, in the eighteenth century (Denham et al. 1831). Confusion is likely to arise from depending too heavily on the remarks made to early travellers by local informants. Furthermore, events of recent years make it clear that Chad can rise to the level of the Bahr-el-Ghazal, as it did in 1963, and then fall to an extremely low level in little more than a decade (see Carmouze et al. 1983).

Records of famines in Borno from 1744–47 and in the Niger Bend area about 1736–58 are believed to be the results of severe droughts. Nicholson (1980) sees them as indicating an extremely arid phase within a dry period that began about 1680 and reached a climax about 1829–39.

Conditions in the Sahel/Sudan in the sixteenth century, especially in the Inland Niger Basin, were so prosperous that it is scarcely conceivable severe droughts could have been prevalent at that time. Niger floods seem to have been higher, wheat was grown extensively, and trade prospered. This was the period before the Moroccans conquered Tombouctou in 1591 and it is possible that those who opposed the invaders have exaggerated the preceding prosperity which in any case may be largely attributable to stable political conditions. However, Borno has also been described as having been a peaceful and prosperous state at this time (Urvoy 1949). Maley (1973) envisages Lake Chad as rising in the sixteenth century and remaining at a high level for much of the following century in

16

response to plentiful rains in the Sudan-Guinean source areas of the Chari and Logone.

A thousand years ago the southern margins of the Sahara seem to have been less arid than they are today. Large towns were already established by that time in areas where cultivation is scarcely possible without irrigation. They were no doubt heavily dependent on long distance trading in gold, ivory, salt and Mediterranean manufactures, yet it seems unlikely that they would have been such thriving centres had rainfall been as low as it is now. Al Muhallabi writing in the second half of the tenth century described Zaghawa people as living a sedentary life in a part of Kanem where the mean annual rainfall today is only 50-100 mm. Ibn Said wrote that when Ibn Fatima visited Kanem early in the thirteenth century there was such a strong flow of water along the Bahr-el-Ghazal he supposed it to be a tributary of the Nile (Hopkins 1981).

Between the thirteenth and sixteenth century there may have been some desiccation. Toubou pastoralists shifted south into Kanem; Awdaghast in the western Sudan, which is believed to have sheltered some 5000 people, was abandoned.

It is of some interest and possible importance to conclude that signs of climatic deterioration on the south side of the Sahara, with reduced rainfall in the vicinity of the Niger bend and Lake Chad, are apparent in the latter part of the thirteenth century and that, after a period of amelioration, aridity and droughts returned in the seventeenth and eighteenth centuries. These dry periods in the Sahel were also times of climatic deterioration in western Europe, commonly referred to as the Little Ice Age. It is possible that there have been shifts in the atmospheric circulation that have affected both parts of the world at about the same time; there are, however, few signs that the Sahel/Sudan droughts around the years 1913, in the 1940s, and again in the 1970s are related to climatic events in Europe in any simple way.

Fluctuations of climate over time periods of decades and centuries are still mysterious; credible and reliable predictions are as yet unattainable and past records, though indicative of the range of variation that can be experienced, provide little guidance as to the timing or the recurrence intervals of future climatic and hydrographic events.

1.4 THE ENVIRONMENT AND DEVELOPMENT

The drought of the early 1970s attracted the world's attention to the Sahel. The people there are amongst the poorest in the world and their dependence on their physical environment for sustenance is direct. It is quite understandable that in these circumstances attention should have been directed towards the rivers of the Sahelian zone where the Senegal and Niger and Lake Chad have until recently risen and fallen from season to season and year to year without any form of control by man. Now they are being seen as valuable sources of water for large-scale irrigation agriculture and numerous dams are being built across headwaters and mainstreams.

At the same time that the people of the Sahel were struggling to survive a natural disaster, people in Nigeria in the early 1970s were emerging from a Civil War to find that the oil and gas of the Niger Delta constituted an even greater natural bonanza than they had imagined. The life of the oil-fields is estimated to be only a few decades. The proceeds have to be distributed and invested to the benefit of northern Nigerians as well as those living in and near the Delta. Again large-scale irrigation schemes are seen as a means of investing productively and visibly to provide foodstuffs for a country with a rapidly growing population and increasing reliance on imported foodstuffs.

Falls and gorges on West African rivers, commonly quite close to the coast, provide opportunities for dam construction, for water storage and generating electricity. Ambitions to industrialise on a basis of cheap power have stimulated a number of projects on the major rivers over the last two decades. Quite suddenly, then, the rivers of West Africa are being harnessed and their waters put to work by engineers and agriculturalists from western industrial countries. The intention is in many respects admirable, but the procedures adopted and the outcome are not always as beneficial for the local people as had been intended.

The riparian environment is a complex one with special advantages so far as variety of resources is concerned and special problems, especially disease hazards, associated with the presence of water and with soils remaining moist through the dry season. A variety of peoples with different languages and cultures, and differing attitudes to land and water and food, have come to exploit the various components of the environment for their own particular purposes. Now the scene is changing and local people are rarely involved in the decisions being made deliberately to change their environment or to carry out engineering operations that may incidentally and inadvertently modify the resource base and disease risks. The costs attached to river control works include not only construction expenses but also the trials endured by the people who are disturbed. In Western countries such costs are borne by the state which compensates those who are displaced or are otherwise incommoded by river impoundment. In regions like West Africa, where the costs may include the spread of diseases such as schistosomiasis, compensation is much less adequate and effective.

Now that water is becoming a scarce resource in West Africa, it is being recognised that river control for the benefit of one area almost invariably means that it is to the detriment of other areas upstream or downstream or both. International organisations have been established to advise and to plan if not to determine the nature of river development projects. National bodies have also been set up to organise river basin development. Sources of information are scattered and one of the objects of the chapters that follow is to bring together some of this material in a form that is accessible to the non-specialist.

18

1.5 REFERENCES

Barth, H. 1965. *Travels and discoveries in North and Central Africa, being a journal of an expedition undertaken under the auspices of H.B.M's government in the years 1849-55* (facsimile). London: Cass.

Bouchardeau, A. 1968. *Monographie hydrologique du Logone.* Service hydrol. Paris: ORSTOM.

Carmouze, J.P., J.R. Durand & C.L. Lévêque (eds.) 1983. Lake Chad: Ecology and productivity of a shallow tropical ecosystem. *Monographiae Biologicae* 53. The Hague: Junk.

Denham, D., H. Clapperton & W. Oudney 1831. *Travels and discoveries in northern and central Africa in 1822, 1823 and 1824* (4 vols.). London: Murray.

Faure, H. & J.-Y. Gac 1981a. Will the Sahelian drought end in 1985? *Nature* 291: 475-8.

Faure, H. & J.-Y. Gac 1981b. Senegal River runoff. *Nature* 293: 414.

Grove, A.T. 1973. Desertification in the African environment. In D. Dalby & R.J. Harrison Church (eds.), *Drought in Africa.* London: SOAS, Centre for African Studies.

Grove, A.T. 1978. Geographical introduction to the Sahel. *Geogr. J.* 144: 407-415.

Harrison Church, R.J. 1980. *West Africa.* London: Longman.

Hopkins, J.F.P. 1981. *Corpus of early Arabic sources for West African history.* Cambridge: Cambridge University Press.

Hurst, H.E., R. Black & Y.M. Simaika 1965. *Long-term storage.* London: Constable.

Kite, G.W. 1981. Recent changes of level of Lake Victoria. *Hydrological Sciences Bull.* 26: 234-43.

Kraus, E.B. 1955. Secular changes of tropical rainfall regimes. *Quart. J. Roy. Met. Soc.* 81: 138-210.

Lamb, P.J. 1982. Persistence of Subsaharan drought. *Nature* 299: 46-48.

Lamb, P.J. 1983. Subsaharan rainfall update for 1982: continued drought (submitted for publication).

Ledger, D.C. 1969. The dry season flow characteristics of West African rivers. In M.F. Thomas & G.W. Whittington (eds.), *Environment and Land Use in Africa.* London: Methuen.

Maley, J. 1980. Les changements climatiques de la fin du Tertiaire en Afrique: leur conséquences sur l'apparition du Sahara. In M.A.J. Williams & H. Faure (eds.), *The Sahara and the Nile.* Rotterdam: Balkema.

Maley, J. 1981. *Etudes palynologiques dans le bassin du Tchad et Paléoclimatologie de l'Afrique nord-tropicale de 30,000 ans à l'époque actuelle.* Paris: ORSTOM.

Mitchell, J.M. 1961. Recent secular changes of global temperature. *Annals New York Acad. Sc.* 95: 235-250.

Morgan, W.B. & J.C. Pugh 1969. *West Africa.* London: Methuen.

Nachtigal, G. 1971. *Sahara and Sudan (vol 4, Wadai and Darfur).* (Trans. by A.G.B. & H.J. Fisher) London: Hurst.

NEDECO 1959. *River Studies and recommendations on improvement of Niger and Benue.* Amsterdam: North-Holland.

Nicholson, S.E. 1980a. The nature of rainfall fluctuations in sub-tropical West Africa. *Mon. Weather Rev.* 109: 2191-2208.

Nicholson, S.E. 1980b. Saharan climates in historic times. In M.A.J. Williams & H. Faure (eds.). *The Sahara and the Nile.* Rotterdam: Balkema.

Nicholson, S.E. 1981. Rainfall and atmospheric circulation during drought periods and wetter years in West Africa. *Monthly Weather Review* 109: 2191-2208.

Ojo, O. 1977. *The climates of West Africa.* London: Heinemann.

Palutikof, J.P., J.M. Lough & G. Farmer 1981. Senegal River runoff. *Nature* 293: 414.

Rodier, J. 1963. *Bibliography of African Hydrology.* Paris: UNESCO.

Urvoy, Y. 1949. Histoire de l'empire de Bornou. *Mém. de l'Inst. Francais d'Afrique Noire* 7.

A.T.GROVE
African Studies Centre, Free School Lane, Cambridge

The physical evolution of the river basins

2.1 INTRODUCTION AND SOURCES OF INFORMATION

The major relief features of West Africa are the outcome of earth movements over a long period of time involving the movement of tectonic plates and the separation of West Africa from Brazil in the early Mesozoic. Uplift near the coast and downward movements in the interior and especially in the rifts occupied by the lower Niger-Benue, have been accompanied by erosion of the crystalline highlands and intermittent sedimentation in the basins and troughs. Long-continued weathering of the upland surfaces and removal of soluble material has left behind the less mobile constituents of the original rocks in the form of ferruginous duricrusts.

The detailed modelling of the landscape has been effected in the Quaternary period, the last two or three million years of the earth's history which have seen the multiple glaciation of middle latitude land masses, especially on either side of the North Atlantic. Associated climatic changes brought alternations of wetter and drier conditions than those of the present day to tropical Africa. In the wetter millennia, great lakes formed in the Chad basin; in the drier millennia, extensive dunefields extended south from the Sahara. Such environmental oscillations have greatly modified the relief and soils of the basins of the Niger and its neighbouring rivers in the last 50,000 years. Fluvial networks have alternately expanded and contracted with important consequences for the distribution of the riverine fauna and flora. Load/discharge relationships have varied thereby causing sedimentation and downcutting cycles and shaping alluvial plains alongside the rivers.

French geographers and geologists such as Chudeau (1913) and Tilho (1910–14) recognised the evidence for climatic change in the course of their exploratory journeys. Falconer (1911) brought together the findings from a number of geological traverses that threw light on the evolution of the Niger-Chad watershed. The first attempt to take an overview of the Niger basin as a whole was from Urvoy (1942).

After World War 2 Tricart (1961, 1965) was the moving spirit, exploiting newly available air photographs to analyse the components of the relief of the Inland Niger Delta and the coast of Senegal. His lead was followed by Gallais (1967a, b) in Mali and by Michel (1968, 1973) in Senegal. In the Chad basin, Pias & Guichard (1957) recognised the former shoreline of Chad running from Bongor north-west into Nigeria and mapped the associated sediments (Pias 1970). A chronological base for the late Quaternary events began to be laid by Faure et al. (1963) with their radiocarbon dates for lake deposits north of Lake Chad. More detailed studies of the Quaternary stratigraphy of the Chad basin were made by Servant (1973), Servant & Servant (1970, 1980), by S. Servant-Valdary (1977) who directed her attention to the diatomites, and by Maley (1981) who examined the pollen in cores. In the anglophone areas, Grove (1958, 1959), Grove & Pullan (1963) and Grove & Warren (1968) drew attention to the great size of Lake Chad in the Early Holocene and the extension southwards of Saharan dunes in the Late Pleistocene.

2.2 THE OLDER RELIEF FEATURES

2.2.1 *Erosion forms*

Many of the prominent escarpments and plateaus forming the watersheds between the river basins are composed of ancient sandstones of Palaeozoic and earlier ages, gently folded and uplifted. They outcrop widely in Tibesti, at the northern margins of the Chad basin, overlying granites and phyllites and supporting Late Cenozoic lavas and ignimbrites. The Niger near Mopti is overlooked from the east by a sandstone plateau, bounded by faults and flexures, the Bandiagara Plateau, which is prolonged north-east by the plateau of Gandamia and the residual buttes of Hombori. Sandstones and shales forming the lower Volta basin outcrop in strong, outward-facing escarpments which overlook the plains declining south to the coast of south-east Ghana (Figure 11).

The Mesozoic rocks of West Africa include marine beds that were laid down when shallow seas spread south from what is now the Sahara while the Niger and Benue troughs were still marine gulfs extending into what are now the Sokoto and Chad basins. There was probably never any continuous north-south seaway across West Africa to Tethys in the Mediterranean region but a hundred million years ago the highlands of Tibesti, Aïr and Hoggar, which now limit the river basins on the north, were great islands or peninsulas rising from shallow Cretaceous seas. The Futa Jalon and other highlands extending east to form the *Guinea dorsale* between the Guinea Republic and Liberia were relatively uplifted so that the region of the Craton Eburnéan was rejuvenated while the basin of Taoudeni to the north was downwarped.

Ancient highlands in the source areas of the rivers, the Futa Jalon, Guinea dorsale and Adamawa, remained relatively unchanged during the Cenozoic period. They preserve remnants of ancient land surfaces as

22

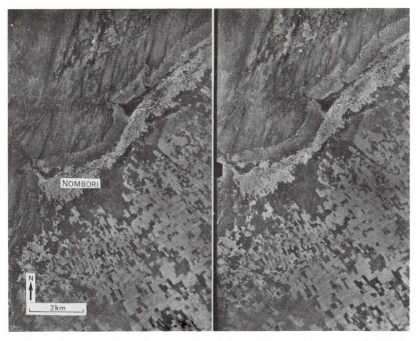

Figure 11. A stereoscopic pair of air photographs showing the sandstone Bandiagara Plateau, top left, bordered by a southeast-facing scarp and a valley at the scarpfoot. Cultivated plains stretch away to the east and south where eolian sands were shaped into low dunes running ESE-WSW by the winds about 15,000 years ago.

dissected erosional plains that correspond with erosion surfaces believed to have been formed in early Mesozoic times when Brazil and West Africa were still in contact. Later surfaces at lower levels can be distinguished, though not with precision, separated by escarpments where resistant rocks outcrop. Dating such surfaces is still largely a matter of conjecture in West Africa.

From the erosional plains cut across the older rocks and carpeted with the products of weathering, rock domes and inselberg complexes emerge, in many cases the altitudes of their summits corresponding with those of erosion surfaces on nearby upland plains. Such rock masses are believed to be residual features, the products of successive cycles of deep weathering followed by stripping away of the weathered layer as the result of periods of stability interrupted by changes of climate and base level (Thomas 1974). The majority of the inselbergs are formed of very old granites and gneisses and the settings of the rock domes indicate that the forms themselves are ancient. Inselbergs rising above the plains in the vicinity of Katsina, for instance, are surrounded by Cretaceous sedimentary rocks and it seems likely that they were once buried beneath

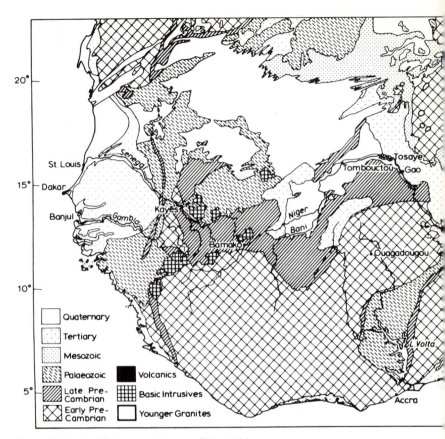

Figure 12. A simplified geological map of West Africa.

these sediments and have been exhumed with the removal of the Cretaceous sedimentary cover in Late Cenozoic times. Granites of the Jos Plateau and Aïr intruded in Jurassic times, 'Younger Granites', form koppies made up of cuboidal blocks, overlooking plains developed in less resistant gneisses and schists.

Sedimentary strata that accumulated in relatively depressed regions towards the end of the Mesozoic era and in the Early Tertiary include great thicknesses of sandstones similar in general appearance to those of Palaeozoic age from which they may have been in part derived, but containing fossil wood. They produce landscapes of extensive plains where they are horizontally disposed, or long ridges where the beds are tilted or folded as on the north side of the Benue valley near Numan. Shales and limestones accumulated in the Chad basin and also in the vicinity of the lower Senegal, Gambia and Niger rivers. Many of these rocks are important economically, yielding not only water, coal,

24

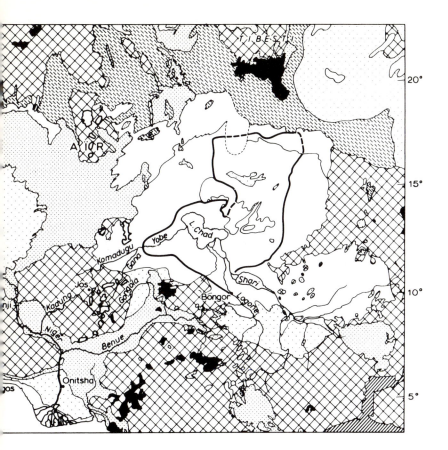

phosphate and raw materials for making cement, but also, in the region of the Niger Delta, providing reservoirs of petroleum.

2.2.2 *The products of weathering*

Early in the Tertiary period, about 60 million years ago, West Africa is believed to have been situated about 15° further south than at present (Figure 13). World climates were less strongly differentiated than they are now and a greater proportion of the region was capable of supporting forest. Under the hot, humid conditions, rock weathering was accompanied by the breakdown of silicates in the crystalline rocks, the removal of the more soluble substances in solution, and the accumulation of residues consisting largely of the oxides and hydroxides of iron and aluminium plus quartz. Such substances which are common in the clayey weathered layers of the humid tropics at the present day were converted

25

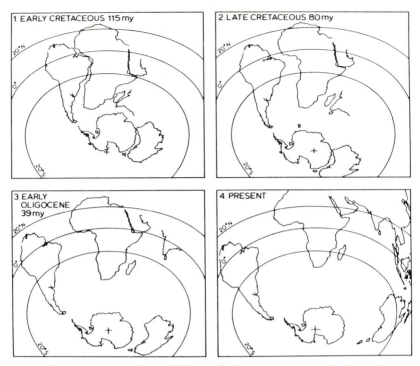

Figure 13. The changing position of Africa in relation to the equator and other continents. in the course of the Tertiary era West Africa has moved north throuth about 15° (from Norton & Sclater 1979).

over time into hard masses of low grade iron-ore and bauxite. These indurated residual deposits, commonly called duricrusts, appear in the landscape as superficial incrustations somewhat resembling thin sheets of volcanic lavas and responding in a similar way to long-continued erosion. They are typically found covering the interfluves of upland plains or outcropping on the lower slopes of gently sloping piedmont plains called glacis by French geomorphologists.

Since duricrusts are slaglike, pisolitic or vermicular in structure and fractured by tree roots and marginal undercutting, water sinks into them rather than running over the surface and emerges in zones of seepage or in springs at the edges of the duricrust sheets. The margins are steep slopes, locally undercut by spring sapping and mantled by blocky debris released by breakdown of the edges of the resistant duricrust 'caprock'.

Quite commonly it is possible to identify two or three levels in the landscapes of the erosional upland plains. The crests of mesas or buttes, rising a few metres or some tens of metres above the general level of the plains are capped by a thick layer of duricrust, sometimes termed primary laterite. At lower levels, duricrusts derived in part from the older material

26

at higher levels veneer glacis and terraces overlooking the main drainage lines. Close to modern streams are lightly indurated surfaces covered in some cases by aeolian and waterlaid sediments.

The age of the duricrusts is very uncertain. Some are interbedded with Early Tertiary rocks and are certainly millions of years old; others have formed much more recently in sediments overlying terrace gravels and have been known to contain hand-axes. Exposures are commonly observed along main roads, in cuttings or where material has been excavated and used for road or other construction purposes. On air photographs ferricrete commonly has a distinctive appearance, dark in tone because of the lack of cultivation, with a sprinkling of white dots marking termite heaps that have been eroded, spreading pale sediments over the surrounding duricrust. Fortunately for West African agriculture, extensive areas of such material that would have been scarcely cultivable were covered by blown sand to a depth of several meters when desert conditions extended several hundreds of kilometers further south than today in the Quaternary era.

In many areas duricrusts are lacking; west of the lower Niger in Yorubaland for example, the weathered layer is commonly a few metres thick, deeper on the minor watersheds than near the rivers and forming a useful aquifer which can be tapped by shallow wells. East of the lower Niger and north of the Niger Delta, and also in parts of the middle Gongola valley, poorly consolidated sandstones, shales and clays form rolling upland country. The sandstones have been altered to a depth of several metres, being stained a bright red either by percolating solutions or by the breakdown within the weathered layer of minerals containing iron. Within about 200 km of the coast in south-east Nigeria where the annual rainfall exceeds 2000 mm the coloration is yellow rather than red.

2.2.3 The geomorphology of dam sites

In the highlands, rivers have been the main agents of erosion removing products of decay to the oceans or to interior basins, carrying their loads in solution and in particulate form. The highlands have also been the scenes of volcanic activity. Cameroon Mountain marking the south-east corner of West Africa is a volcano rising to over 4000 m which is still active on occasions. Extensive lava plateaus and ridges extend north-east over the highlands of West Cameroun in the vicinity of Bamenda and as far as the Adamawa Plateau at the sources of the Benue and Logone. On the northern side of the Benue valley smaller spreads of lava occupy parts of the Jos Plateau, the Longuda Plateau west of the Gongola valley, and the Biu Plateau between the Gongola and Hawal valleys.

Rivers flowing across the 'new' surfaces presented by the lava flows and also by sedimentary plains of accumulation have in some cases incised their channels and thereby superimposed their courses across older buried land surfaces and rock structures. Where the older rocks are inclined, drainage patterns superimposed in this way do not conform with the old

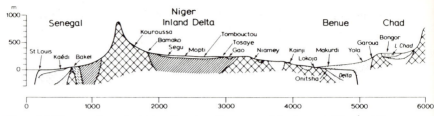

Figure 14. Diagramatic geological section along the course of the Senegal, Niger and Benue rivers and across the Chad basin. The symbols for the rocks are the same as for Figure 12.

Figure 15. The Volta dam under construction in 1963.

structural pattern but streams cut across resistant outcrops giving gorges such as those on the Gongola at Kiri and Dadin Kowa where the river cuts across dipping Mesozoic sandstones. Such gorges provide convenient sites for damming rivers, with hard rock close to the surface and the possibility provided for a small structure to impound a large volume of water. Beaudet et al. (1981) regard the gorge at Tossaye (Touassa) at the eastern edge of the Inland Basin of the Niger as being essentially the outcome of the river being superimposed onto a layer of resistant oolitic sandstone.

Other dam sites occur near 'fall lines' where rivers descending from crystalline uplands to sedimentary plains have cut headwards to produce rapids and water falls. The Niger at Kainji is one such example (Figure 14). The Akosombo Dam on the Volta is situated in a gorge where the river leaves a sandstone and shale basin that occupies much of south-eastern Ghana and cuts across an intrusive dyke complex that forms the Akwapim Hills. From the coast west of Accra they are prolonged for hundreds of kilometres NNE as the Togo and Atakora ranges which

28

reach the Niger where it forms a W in the south-west corner of the Niger Republic, providing another possible but rather remote dam site.

When the Volta was diverted through a tunnel in the early stages of constructing the Akosombo Dam, a circle about a metre in diameter with a cup-shaped hollow in its centre was exposed, inscribed in a rock-face in the gorge about 9 m below river level. It appeared to be man-made and seemed to imply that a vertical displacement of at least 9 m had affected the dam site since the circle was engraved. (Thompson 1975). The dam is known to lie in an active fault-zone and Accra was badly shaken by an earthquake in 1938. There is an alternative less worrying explanation for the engraving as will appear later (see p. 37); nevertheless, with such a large load imposed by the lake, occasional seismic activity in the vicinity of the dam may be expected.

2.3 LATE QUATERNARY LANDFORMS

2.3.1 *Alternating drier and wetter climates*

Cores drilled in deep ocean floor sediments off the coast of Saharan Africa provide evidence that the desert was already in existence by Mid-Tertiary times (Sarnthein & Diester-Haas 1977; Street 1981). Layers of stained and frosted grains of quartz sand in the cores are believed to consist of dune sands. It has been argued that at times when sea-level was low in middle and late Cenozoic times, continental dunes were prolonged across the continental shelf under the influence of easterly winds and the sand blown into the sea sludged down the continental slope in turbidity flows to reach the deep sea plains. The sandy accumulations forming the ergs or sand seas of the Sahara are therefore considered to have been in existence for millions of years. However, the surface features of the bare dunes and of the vegetated, 'fixed' dunes or Qoz of the Sahel and Sudan zones have been acquired over a much shorter period of time.

Within the last 120,000 years that have elapsed since the Last Interglacial period, when conditions were as warm as they are at the present day, the Sahara has been much less arid in at least two periods each lasting for several thousands of years. In the intervening dry periods, desert conditions and active dunes have extended 500 km south of their present limits. The evidence for desert expansion is in the form of great linear systems of sand mounds, regularly disposed across enormous tracts of country. They are more easily recognisable on air photographs and satellite imagery than on the ground. In the Sudan zone the former dune ridges, now rounded and vegetated, are very largely under cultivation. The signs of former greater water action appear in the landscapes of the southern Sahara in the form of integrated drainage systems extending for hundreds of kilometers from the desert mountains, Tibesti, Aïr and Hoggar across barren wastes. Those originating in Aïr join together to form very broad wadis called dallols in western Niger and eastern Mali that run down to the Niger between Tossaye and Kainji. On the plains bordering eastern Tibesti, gravel ridges mark old river courses where the relief has been inverted; the coarse gravels of the channel lag deposits remain in place as sinuous ridges while adjacent finer grained sediments have been blown away by the wind. Today the desert wadis are dry, except on rare occasions when storms of unusual intensity bring heavy rain to the source areas; they rarely if ever contribute to the discharge of the great rivers. But as recently as 5000 years ago many of them were occupied by running water, at least seasonally, and active drainage networks were more symetrically disposed about the Senegal, Niger and Lake Chad than they are at the present day.

The evidence of alternating conditions, at times wetter and at other times drier than now, is most clearly displayed in the landscape in the vicinity of Lake Chad (Figure 16). All along the eastern side of the lake are long, narrow, sandy islands, running NNW-SSE, separated by channels which become narrower, shallower and obstructed by reed beds towards the eastern shore. The islands are the flattened tops of sharp-crested dunes, ridges that were developed at right angles to the prevailing ENE winds of the dry season at a time when the Logone and Chari terminated much further south and the lake floor was dry. Far away from the existing lake, hollows between the rolling grass-covered dunes are floored by lake deposits several metres thick, containing diatom and gastropod remains and fish-bones. They accumulated on the floor of a

Figure 16. Lake Chad is shown at the top as it was in January 1973 when there was still open water in the northern as well as the southern basin. The archipelago on the northern and eastern sides has been formed by dunes which run at right angles to the winds that shaped them being flooded by the Early Holocene and current lake. The satellite image on the left, showing the southwest corner of the lake as it was in January 1973, can be compared with another image from January 1976 by which time much of the floor was dry.

30

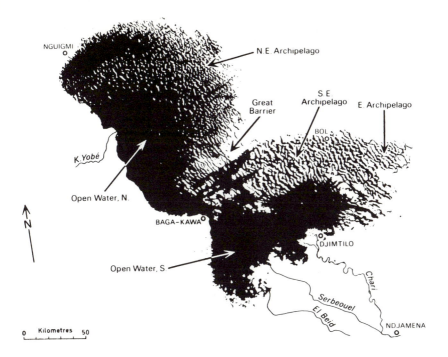

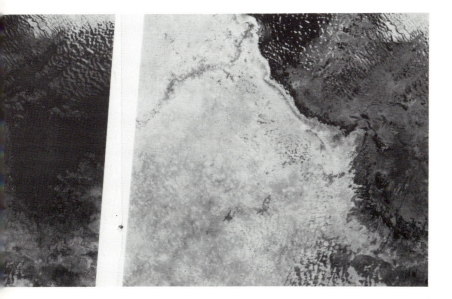

31

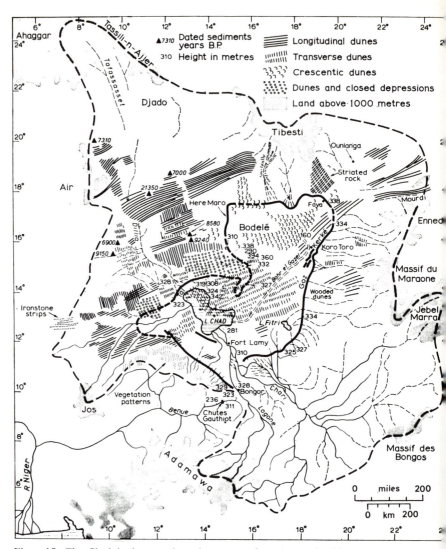

Figure 17. The Chad basin occupies a large part of northcentral Africa between the Congo/Zaire basin in the south and Tibesti in the north. The southern limit of mobile dunes at the present day lies at about 16°N. ENE winds in the Late Pleistocene shaped dunes as far south as 11°N. In the Early Holocene a great lake in the Bodélé depression extended south as far as Bongor where water was able to escape westwards to the Benue and the Atlantic. In this wet period almost the whole of the Chad basin was outside the limits of the desert (Grove & Warren 1968).

32

very much more extensive Lake Chad, Megachad it was called by Moreau (1963), the surface of which stood 50 m above the level of the present lake at an elevation of 330 m above sea-level (Figure 17). Megachad extended north-east occupying the Bodélé depression where it was over 150 m deep; at the southern corner its waters spread westwards from the Logone-Chari delta of the time, in the vicinity of Bongor, to overflow down the Mayo Kebbi to the Benue and Atlantic, in some years no doubt in great volume. Water still follows the same route when the Logone in flood reaches its peak levels and spills across the plains. As late as 1947 it was feared by Tilho (1947) and others that the Benue might capture the Logone and deprive Lake Chad of a main supply of water, but greater knowledge of the history of climate and the hydrography of the region has dispelled such fears (Carmouze *et al.* 1983).

2.3.2 *Ancient dune fields and Late Pleistocene climates*

Dunes are not readily dated by isotopic methods for they consist almost entirely of quartz sand and contain little organic material. Perhaps thermoluminescent techniques will provide chronologies for them in the future. At present reliance has to be placed on dates given by organic remains within them such as the thin lenses of calcareous sediments some tens of metres below the surface of rolling sand hills near Lake Chad which have given values of about 40,000 BP. Dune sands in the Niger Republic and near Richard Toll on the Lower Senegal are also suspected to be about 40,000 years old. However, radiocarbon dates as early as this are liable to be misleading because even very slight contamination with modern carbon, brought in for instance by percolating water, can result in isotope analysis giving ages of 30,000 to 40,000 years to materials which are in fact much older.

Aridity in the southern Sahara seems to have been interrupted about 25,000 to 20,000 years ago. Dates of lacustrine material within this time range were obtained from Fachi (21340 BP) in the northern part of the Chad basin by Faure et al. (1963) and also from the Chemchane depression in what is now an extremely arid part of southern Mauritania. Thomas & Thorpe (1980) have described fluvial sediments in the Yengema and Tongo areas of Sierra Leone indicating episodes of scouring with gravel entrainment alternating with what appear to have been stable forested conditions and clay accumulation in river channels 28,000 to 20,000 years ago. They interpret the evidence as indicating short-lived periods of alternating greater precipitation and greater aridity than at the present during those eight millennia.

Prolonged aridity seems to have returned to the interior of West Africa about 20,000 BP and to have persisted there until about 12,000 BP. It seems likely that most of the dunefields at the southern margins of the Sahara, both active and vegetated, were shaped about this time. They include the great longitudinal red dunes of the ancient erg of north-east Nigeria, to the west of Lake Chad, which were partially inundated by

Megachad between 12,000 and 4,500 BP, as were the transverse dunes of Kanem on the east side of the lake. Both systems would seem to be of Late Pleistocene age. The longitudinal dunes of the Sokoto coversands described by Sombroek & Zonneveld (1971) are comparable in every way with those of Borno. The fixed dunes between Zinder and Niamey mapped as 'erg recent' by Bocquier & Gavaud (1964) and those in Senegal attributed to the 'Ogolian 11' regression by Michel (1973) are similar.

The sand composing the fixed dunes consists of grains between 100 and 200 μm in diameter, most of it being fine rather than coarse sand, with the proportion of clay less than 10% and normally nearer 5%. The heavy mineral assemblages indicate that much of the sand has been derived from local rocks no more than a few tens of kilometres away. However, some of the more worn and well-sorted sand is probably derived from a greater distance, possibly from basins in the northern Sahara, driven across the bare desert surface by northerly and north-easterly winds (Mainguet et al. 1980).

On the Chad-Niger watershed south-east of Katsina, and further north towards Aïr in the Niger Republic, blown sand is banked against the eastern sides of rocky hill ranges rising sharply some tens or a few hundred metres above the plains. On their leeward sides, linear strips of lateritic ironstone are exposed at the surface, running WSW or W for a hundred kilometres or more with remarkable regularity. On either side of these strips, which remain uncultivated, are deep soils developed on the sands that were blown through gaps between the hills and are now vegetated or cultivated (Grove & Pullan 1963). Near Kazaure, north of Kano, shallow hollows immediately to leeward of the hills are occupied by lakes, at least in the rains and for some months afterwards. Larger lakes occupy basins on the west sides of rocky hills near the Niger west of Tombouctou, the largest being Lake Faguibine (Figure 18).

On the western side of the Hausaland erg, in the vicinity of Zaria, soils are derived from fine sand and silts similar to loess. This material was sorted out from the coarser material by the wind and carried further west in suspension rather than saltation, before settling out (McTainsh & Walker 1982). It is less liable to disturbance by wind action at the present day than are the sandy soils further east and north but is inclined to become compacted at the surface, giving high rates of runoff leading to the formation of large gullies.

South of the Niger bend, sand was swept WSW and shaped into linear dunes that curve south-west as they approach the eastern side of the Bandiagara plateau so as to trespass into the northernmost part of the Volta basin. These dunes appear to have obstructed the course of a river that formerly ran north-east into the Niger; presumably, when wetter conditions returned and it began to flow again, it found an easier route southwards and was thus diverted to become a headwater of the Volta as the Sourou river (Figures 11 and 40).

The Niger itself was obstructed by dunes well upstream of Tombouctou possibly on more than one occasion in the Late Quaternary, but dating of

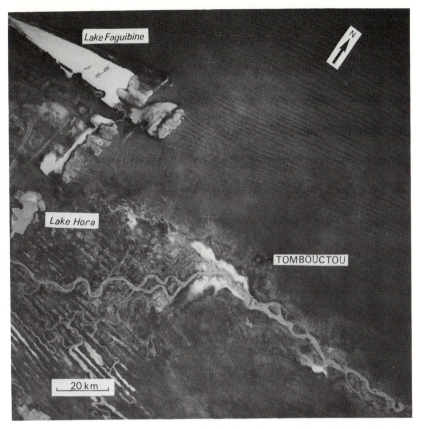

Figure 18. The Niger running northeast across ancient dunes and then changing direction near Tombouctou to run parallel with them. The wedge-shaped Lake Faguibine, top left, is in the lee of rocky hills; other smaller lakes are similarly disposed to the south of it. The ancient dune lines can be seen to diverge on the windward side of the hills (Skylab).

the dunes is uncertain. There are many signs in the form of ancient drainage channels that rivers have escaped northwards from the Ségou basin into desert depressions to the north. Chudeau (1913) recognised a channel running north past Tombouctou and air photographs enabled Palausi (1955) and Kervran (1959) to trace it from the Niger at Kabara (the port for Tombouctou) into the Azaouad depression. Further upstream Furon (1929) identified three ancient channels, the Nara, Fodéré and Ourkem which appear to have carried Niger water from the Macina area into the Hodh depression. Urvoy (1942) was inclined to think that these channels were active during the last pluvial which he correlated with the Wurm glaciation. Tricart (1959) recognised that the glacial periods were associated with greater aridity on the south side of

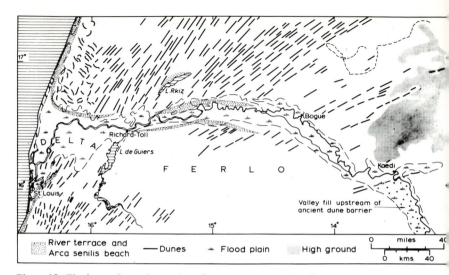

Figure 19. The lower Senegal ceased to flow downstream of Kaédi for several millennia in the Late Pleistocene; its course was obstructed by dunes shaped by winds from the ENE (Grove & Warren 1968).

the Sahara and argued that the linear dunes running across the alluvial plains between Mopti and Tombouctou had been constructed by the wind during the Riss and Wurm. This alpine glacial terminology is now recognised to be misleading and it is evident that the dune and lacustrine features of the Niger basin are much younger than Tricart suggested.

Linear dunes running ENE to WSW in southern Mauritania have been shown by Michel (1973) to have obstructed the course of the Senegal at Kaédi between 20,000 and 12,000 years ago (Figure 19). They can be traced almost as far south as Dakar and it is suspected that they extended across the continental shelf which at this time was partly exposed. In the Ségou basin of the Niger the massive dunes running westwards from the north end of the Bandiagara Plateau are likely to have formed about the same time and may have been reactivated on one or more occasions in the Holocene.

Under the drier conditions in West Africa towards the end of the Pleistocene, runoff and river discharge must have been much less than at present. Today, contributions to river flow are slight where the mean annual rainfall is less than 750 mm. With isohyets displaced 400 to 500 km towards the equator only rivers to the south of latitude 10° N would have maintained a considerable discharge. In Sierra Leone no dateable woody material has been found in the Yengema and Tongo river sediments for the period between 20,000 and 12,500 BP. Thomas and Thorpe (1980) presume that conditions in and around the river channels were too dry for the growth of large trees and that, deprived of a forest cover, weathered

36

material was stripped from hillsides and spread across valley floors by seasonal sheetwash to form glacis surfaces. It is possible that the lower Volta river at the end of the dry season dried up completely, exposing the rock wall in the gorge at Akosombo and thereby allowing people to engrave the circle mentioned earlier (p. 29).

The shift in the rainfall belts caused the biomes, the climatically determined vegetation zones and the living creatures inhabiting them, to shift south in the Late Pleistocene so that Sahelian plant assemblages occupied what is now savanna, and rain forest was confined to the wettest areas of present day West Africa (Hamilton 1976). On Cameroon Mountain one might visualise montane forest reaching down to less than 1000 m on account of lower mean temperatures than those of today, with evergreen forest persisting close to sea-level. In places like southern Ghana the forest may not have been continuous but restricted to places where soil water conditions were favourable. The evidence for such conjectures comes particularly from Lake Bosumtwi, which lies in a circular meteorite caldera within the forest zone of southern Ghana, to the south-east of Kumasi. Sediment cores from the bed of the lake have yielded very little tree pollen before 10,000 BP. However Talbot & Hall (1981) have found leaf impressions in laminated silts laid down by a stream that enters the caldera from the north, overlying a layer of charcoal which has been dated 12060±130 BP. The leaves are of semi-deciduous forest species, many of them trees that can only regenerate in forest gaps. At about the same time, towards the end of the Pleistocene, southern Ivory Coast was also characterised by open forest (Assemien et al. 1970).

Late Pleistocene aridity in West Africa and much of the rest of the tropical world coincided with the waning stages of the Last Glaciation when the great ice sheets of North America and northern Eurasia, having reached their maximum extents about 18,000 years ago, were shrinking. In winter, sea-ice around Antarctica extended 8° nearer the equator than now; cold upwelling water of the Benguela current spread further north, and surface waters over parts of the Gulf of Guinea in August were more than 4° C cooler than they are now (Van Zinderen Bakker 1982). In the North Atlantic, sea-ice extended south in winter as far as a line from Brittany to New York and cold water spread down the coast of Morocco to cross the Tropic of Cancer. This chilling of the surface waters of the Atlantic off West Africa not only reduced evaporation from the ocean surface and the supply of precipitation over the continent, it must also have increased the stability of air moving inshore and reduced rainfall in what are now the humid coastlands of the Gulf of Guinea.

The continental ice-sheets on either side of the North Atlantic locked up 40 million km^3 of water from the ocean basins in the last glacial period and as a result, the surface of the sea was lowered by about 100 m and then, as the ice melted away, rose to near present levels between 15,000 and 7,000 BP. Except in the vicinity of Sierra Leone, the continental shelf around West Africa is narrow and so rivers flowing towards the coast, particularly across the less resistant sedimentary rocks, cut down deeply

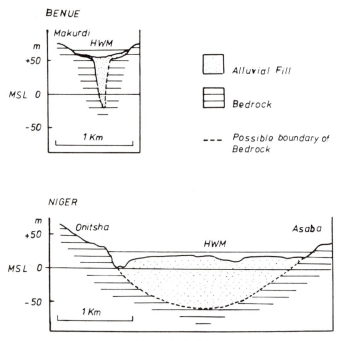

Figure 20. Boreholes drilled into the bed of the Benue at Makurdi and the Niger at Onitsha penetrated over 40 m of alluvial fill without reaching bedrock. The buried channels are believed to have been excavated at times of lower sea-level when ice-sheets were much larger than at present (after NEDECO 1959).

as they had probably done in earlier glacial periods. The Volta below Akosombo has an extremely accidented longitudinal profile (Figure 73) cut into hard rock and does not seem to have been affected in this way; as we have noted, its flow was probably very restricted in the Late Pleistocene. But a deep channel discovered under the lower Benue when drilling was carried out before the erection of the bridge at Makurdi is known to extend as far upstream as Yola (Figure 20). In the Senegal, an old channel lies 38 m below sea level at Rosso and 15 m below as far upstream as Bogué 230 km from the coast (Michel 1980). At the mouth of the Gambia river too the rock bed is more than 38 m below sea-level.

2.3.3 End Pleistocene/Early Holocene pluvial conditions

Between about 12,500 and 4,500 BP lake levels were high in tropical Africa and in other parts of the world in low latitudes (Street and Grove 1979). There were intervals possibly lasting several centuries, about 10,000 BP and again about 7,500 BP, when lake levels were low, but for most of the first half of the Holocene period and the extreme end of the

38

Pleistocene period conditions were wetter than they had been in the preceding eight millennia or have been since.

Some ice persisted in northern Eurasia and Hudson's Bay until about 8,000 years ago and sea-level was still depressed in the early part of the pluvial period; this was probably the time when some rivers excavated or re-excavated their deep channels. Temperatures in the southern oceans rose to levels a degree or two higher than at present about 9,500 years ago; the 'altithermal' in North America and the 'Atlantic' warm period in north-west Europe came later about 7,500 to 4,500 BP. This Early and Middle Holocene, which can be regarded as the peak of an interglacial, saw an extension of wetter conditions over West Africa, including the Sahara, before current greater aridity set in about 4,500 years ago.

A possible explanation for the pluvial which has been considered by Kutzbach (1981) is the relative position of the earth and the sun at that time. The earth 10,000 years ago was closer to the sun in the northern summer than it is now. As a result, the radiation received in low latitudes north of the tropic was some 7% greater from May to August, thereby enhancing the monsoonal inflow of moist air and, according to a simulation model experiment, increasing rainfall by some 10% in West Africa.

The great size of the pluvial lakes in low latitudes suggests that the rainfall in Holocene times was in fact much more than 10% greater than at present. In particular the enormous extent of Megachad must be appreciated. It occupied an area of 330,000 km^2, ten times the extent of Late Pleistocene Lake Bonneville in the south-west USA. Waves generated by north-east winds formed a barrier beach about 12 m high which runs across Borno from Geidam on the Yobe river to Maiduguri and Bama and then across the northern tip of the Cameroun Republic to Yagoua on the Logone, a distance of some 400 km. Rivers rising on the watershed with the Niger, between the Jos Plateau and Aïr, formed swamps and lagoons to the south-west of the barrier beach and three of them, the Yobe, Ngadda and Yedseram, penetrated the barrier and laid down extensive deltaic fans of sediment. A much greater delta formed jointly by the Logone and Chari stretched east of N'djamena and Bongor. At the southern edge of the present lake, pinnacles of rhyolitic rock called Hadjer el Hamis project through the alluvium east of the Chari (Figure 21); caves developed in them, 40 m above the plains, mark the ancient level of Megachad. Other deltaic features on the north side of Megachad, at Angamma west of Faya, accumulated between 10,000 and 6,000 BP, and extensive spreads of alluvium occupying hollows to the north of Ounianga show that rivers from Tibesti contributed to the supply of Megachad.

Various attempts have been made to calculate the hydrographic balance of Megachad and its basin, but there are considerable discrepancies between the results. Kutzbach (1980), basing his calculations of water losses from the lake and its catchment on radiation inputs and the vegetation cover, calculated annual evaporation losses from the lake surface to have been 1250 mm. He then deduced that

Figure 21a. The Hadjer el Hamis rock pinnacles south of Lake Chad with caves about 40 m above lake level.

Figure 21b. A section in the 320-330 m barrier beach near Maiduguri displaying the steep bedding in the sands presumed to be the result of wave action.

40

average precipitation over the Chad basin in the early Holocene was 650 mm compared with 350 mm at the present day. The lake would then have received 650 mm of rain falling onto its surface and the equivalent of 600 mm from inflowing rivers. At present the mean annual discharge of the Logone and Chari, about 40 km^3, constitutes almost the entire input of river water into the lake; according to Kutzbach's calculations the rivers entering Megachad in the Early Holocene must have provided 245 km^3. Other hydrologists have argued that this is an underestimate because annual evaporation losses from Megachad would have been nearer 2,000 mm than 1250 mm; after all, temperatures 8,000 years ago were close to those of the present day and current annual losses from Lake Victoria, for instance, are about 1,500 mm. No doubt rivers from the Jos Plateau and Tibesti made much larger contributions than they do today, but even if they provided as much as 40 km^3, the discharge of the Logone and Chari must have been 5 times that of the present if we accept Kutzbach's conservative estimates. With flood levels several metres higher than now, the overflow from the Logone to the Benue in average years must have been large and in wet periods immense. As the source areas of the Senegal and Upper Niger are similarly disposed to those of the Logone and Chari in relation to the isohyets, and both rivers would have been supplied with water from the north flowing down tributaries which are now merely systems of desert wadis, their flows too may have been five times or more greater than at present.

When the rains returned to the southern Sahara and Sahel about 12,000 years ago with such dramatic results, sea-level was still about 30–40 m lower than at the present day. Flooding rivers backed up against the lines of dunes, cut them away and burst through the barriers that had been built up by the wind over several arid millennia. Great volumes of sand were swept down mainstreams to the coast. Cores from the Niger Delta show a twenty-fold increase in sedimentation rates about 11,500 BP; at the same time, decreased $^{18}O/^{16}O$ values from benthic foraminifera offshore point to greater discharges of freshwater from the Niger (Pastouret et al. 1978). Ample sediment supplies were made available along the coasts for building barrier beaches, fronting deltas and facing winds with maximum fetch over the oceans, when sea-level stabilised about 7000 years ago.

In the Early Holocene river valleys of the interior, sediment accumulated to form alluvial fills and broad floodplains that are now striking features of the lower Senegal and Benue. In Sierra Leone, gravels covered by deposits of lateral and vertical accretion point to strong fluvial activity between 12,500 and 7,500 BP according to radiocarbon dates of wood recovered from them (Thomas & Thorpe 1980). The rivers of the Sahel zone and southern Sahara were most powerfully affected by the wetter climates of the end-Pleistocene and Early Holocene. Channels that had been dry for thousands of years and are occupied today only by stormwater contributed large volumes to the mainstreams and formed large, fine-textured floodplains (Sellars 1981). Upstream of Tombouctou the Niger

Figure 22. At Tossaye the course of the Niger narrows where it cuts across a rock bar and spills out of the interior basin to which it was confined for several millennia between 20,000 and 12,000 years ago.

flooded the Ségou basin and it may well have been at this time that overflowing water spilled north towards the desert basins. Dunes were undercut and large levees built alongside river channels now emerge above the highest floods. Alluvium spread over the central parts of the basin downstream of Lake Debo blocked local tributaries draining Gourma and Goundam so as to create the lakes that persist in the relict hollows south and west of Tombouctou. Downstream of Tombouctou the Niger followed an ENE course with linear dunes running parallel to it on either side. It was a course which the river seems to have followed in earlier times, for it trenched old alluvium that now forms a high terrace and laid down river sediments that now form a low terrace, narrowing downstream to the rock sill at Tossaye (Figure 22).

It has been widely accepted that the existing angular course of the Niger bend was first acquired in the late Quaternary as the result of overflow from the Ségou basin some 12,000 years ago. However, recent examination of the landforms of the Niger valley upstream of Tossaye show its features closely resemble those of the Saharan valleys that reach the river downstream of Tossaye (Beaudet et al. 1977). The Tilemsi, Bosso and Maouri dallols are all shallow, trough-like valleys, several kilometres wide, cut into horizontally disposed rocks of the Continental Terminal. They are overlooked by convex hills a few kilometres in diameter and up to 30 m high, with crests mantled by duricrust a half to one and a half metres thick and bounded by concave slopes and two sets of glacis. The landscape either side of the Niger upstream of Tossaye displays the same old features and the dallols downstream are evidently the Niger's ancient left bank tributaries. Now they are giant wadis, lacking well-defined channels and floored by fine-grained sediments a few metres thick that were laid down by meandering rivers between 12,000 and 8,000 years ago when the rains were probably more evenly distributed through the year. The remains of Nile perch (*Lates niloticus*) as well as the bones of elephant, antelope and buffalo have been discovered in Holocene sediments far up the Tilemsi, on the flanks of the Adrar des Iforas at the southern margins of the Tanezrouft (Petit-Maire & Riser 1981). They emphasise the scale of climatic deterioration over the last 5,000 years. If the Tilemsi was such an active drainage way in the Early and Middle Holocene, then the northern tributaries of the Rima-Sokoto system must also have flowed strongly.

In the Senegal valley, as sea-level rose in the Middle Holocene, clayey sediments 2 to 5 m thick accumulated. During a drier phase about 7,000 BP, winds from the NNE reworked some of the earlier dune deposits and a second valley fill came into existence set within the earlier one. As sea-level continued to rise to reach a maximum, a metre or two above the present, the sea invaded the lower Senegal and Gambia converting them into long narrow estuaries (Figure 23). The Ogolian dunes were eroded, forming sandy beaches containing *Arca* (or *Anadara*) *senilis*, cockle shells dating to about 5500 BP. They can be traced as far upstream as Bogué, 230 km from the sea where climatic conditions were humid enough for

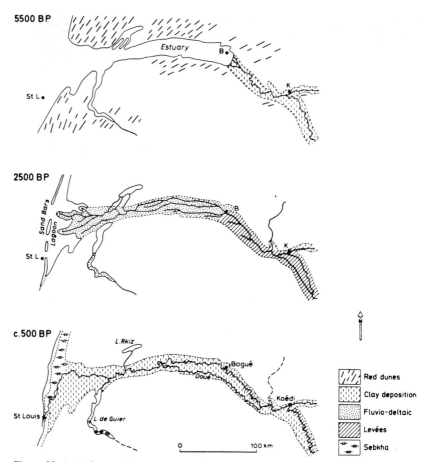

5500 BP

Estuary

B.

St L.

K

2500 BP

Sand Bars

Lagoon

St L.

B

K

c.500 BP

N

L.Rkiz

Bogué

Doué

Kaédi

St Louis

L. de Guier

Red dunes

Clay deposition

Fluvio-deltaic

Levées

Sebkha

0   100 km

Figure 23. In Holocene times, about 5,500 BP, the sea flooded the valley of the Senegal downstream of Bogué to form a beach of cockle shells (*Arca senilis*). Clayey sediments accumulating upstream were then buried beneath river levees as fluvio-deltaic sediments filled the estuary and blocked former tributary creeks, about 2500 BP, to form the lakes Rkiz and de Guier. Coastal sandbars formed a river mouth lagoon which was transformed into saline mudflats, a sebkha, when the coastal barrier became a continuous sandspit, and clays were deposited all along the lower valley floodplain (after Michel 1973).

mangrove swamps to form. At the same time in the Gambia, tides reached 200 km upriver as far as Georgetown.

2.3.4 *Late Holocene onset of current climates and delta development*

The last pluvial period in West Africa came to an end about 4500 BP. Since then climate and sea-level have fluctuated through quite a narrow range as compared with the wider ranging oscillations of the Late

44

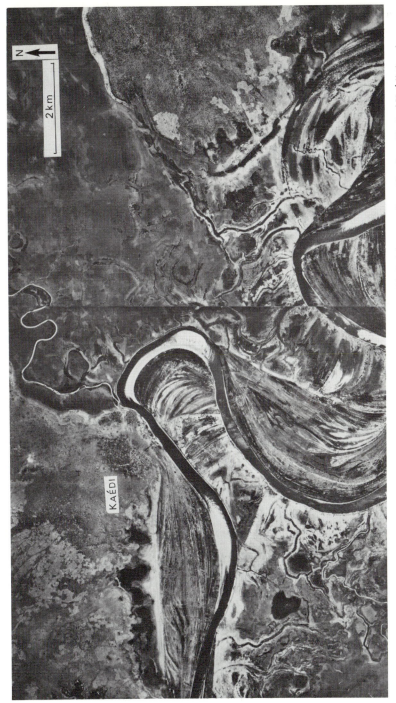

KAÉDI

N

2 km

Figure 24. Meanders of the Senegal, near Kaédi, bordered by levees increasing in age and in height away from the river. West of Kaédi they have created small lakes and to the east of the town a clayey, flat-floored basin across which the Gorgol tributary meanders.

45

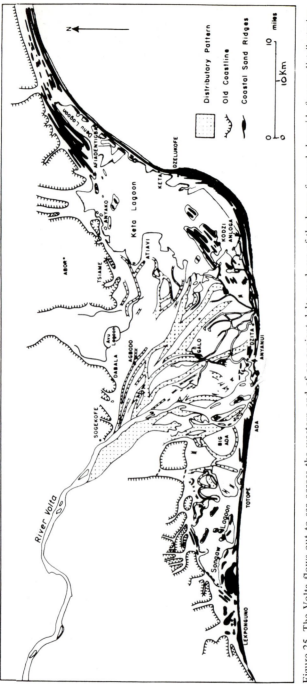

Figure 25. The Volta flows out to sea across the western end of an ancient delta made up of the levees formed alongside former distributaries, fronted by a coastal sandbar and with intervening lagoons.

46

Pleistocene and Early and Middle Holocene. Nevertheless the small-scale fluctuations involved are not insignificant, for they modified micro-topography and soils and have thereby influenced land use, irrigation potential and location of settlements alongside the rivers.

As lakes dried up or diminished in size about 4500 BP, desert conditions advanced towards the equator and fixed dunes on the southern edge of the Sahara were reactivated by winds from a more northerly quarter than those of the Late Pleistocene. On the plains of the coastal dry zone between Accra and the Volta delta, Talbot (1980) has shown that a blanket of sand was spread 30 km inland by SSW winds which he argues were stronger than those of the present day.

Lake Chad dried up about 4500 BP but by 3700 BP somewhat wetter conditions than those of the present returned, for a low mound can be traced at a height of 286 m crossing deltaic sediments between N'djamena and Hadjer el Hamis and running alongside the El Obeid (Ebeji) river to Mongonu. At this level of Chad, water flowed down the Bahr-el-Ghazal; the Djourab depression, now occupied by dunes and shallow salt pools, held a lake as much as 120 m deep that persisted for several centuries possibly to less than 2000 years ago. On the southern side of the 286 m ridge in Borno, and also in the N'djamena area, black firki clays 2 to 3 m thick were deposited in flat-floored lagoons; these clays, with high contents of illite and smectite, resemble those accumulating on the floor of the present lake.

At the mouth of the Senegal between 4000 and 2000 BP a series of barrier beaches was built across the river mouth by waves approaching from the NW thereby transforming the lower estuary into an extensive lagoon. Further upstream the river built systems of levees, the tops of which emerge above the highest floods of the present day (Figure 24). Downstream of Bogué, fine-grained sands and yellow silts accumulated successively further downstream to form an elongated delta that broadened below Richard Toll to block off a left-bank tributary thereby forming the Lac de Guier and filling in the coastal lagoon.

Many of the features of the Volta delta and Niger delta were acquired in the Holocene. Air photographs of the Volta delta show several low sandy ridges radiating from Sogekofe marking the positions of former radial distributaries of the river which now occupies a single channel. Between the ridges are lagoonal depressions now mainly fed by local rivers. The front of the delta was eroded on either side of the present river mouth and the modern barrier beach forming the delta front was built further east, seawards of earlier beach ridges, thereby encompassing the Keta lagoon. West of the delta a beach ridge surmounted by a fixed dune runs along the coast to Tema (Figure 25).

The long-term history of sedimentation in the region of the Niger delta involves three main depositional cycles, in the Middle Cretaceous, Paleoeocene times, and from the Eocene to the Holocene (Short & Stäuble 1967). Subsurface structures resulting from gravitational movements as the delta accumulated include 'rollover anticlines' in sandstones of the Agbada formation, belonging to the last of the depositional cycles, which provide reservoirs for oil and gas. This Agbada formation is overlain northwards by sandy beds of the Benin formation and in the Port Harcourt area by Afam clays of Miocene age.

During periods of low sea-level in the Pleistocene the Niger cut a deep gulf into its ancient delta, remnants of which form dry land, with some swamps, along the northern and eastern sides of the main freshwater swamps of the floodplain extending south of Onitsha into the central part of the delta. Within the Late Pleistocene gulf sands and shelly debris were laid down to depths exceeding 45 m at Onitsha (Figure 20). As sea-level rose at the end of the Pleistocene and in the Early Holocene, strand plain deposits were covered by sands brought down by the Benue and Niger. Over the last 6000 years, during which sea-level has not varied greatly, the delta floodplain has advanced across brackish water mangrove swamps

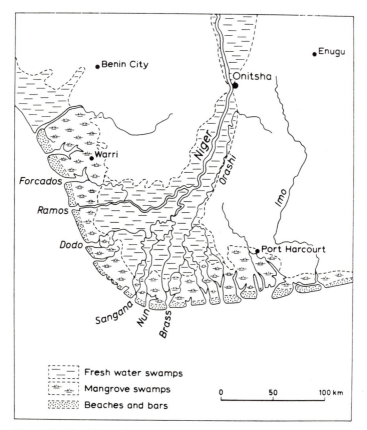

Figure 26. The Niger delta has extended seawards over the last 6000 years across the remains of an earlier delta into which it is embayed.

48

and the delta front beach ridges have been built up progressively further seawards, while the older beach ridges to the rear have been eroded by meandering mangrove swamp creeks (Figure 26).

2.3.5 Current morphological change

2.3.5.1 *Coastal change.* At the present time about two-thirds of the sediments delivered to the delta by the Niger are supplied by the Benue, amounting to about 24 million tonnes annually out of a total of some 38 million tonnes. Most of this material reaches the western delta front by the Forcados, Ramos-Dodo, Sangana and Nun, distributaries about 10 to 15 m deep which share most of the Niger discharge between them. Some of the fluvial sands accumulate alongside distributaries forming levees, with finer organic silts being deposited on the flats between the creeks. Sandbars tend to obstruct the mouths of the distributaries and under natural conditions velocities of floodwater over the bars as the tide ebbs can exceed 2 m sec^{-1}.

The sediment carried out of the river mouths is joined by material that has been carried eastwards by the warm, shallow Guinea current and by longshore drift where the coast runs west to east and waves under the influence of the prevailing winds approach from the south-west. Strandline sediments are thrown up into beach ridges by the heavy surf and ridges are built successively further seawards to form barrier islands, on average about 5 km wide and rising 2 to 4 m above mean sea-level. There are about 20 major barrier islands along the delta front, separated one from another by tidal channels; a barrier scarcely broken, except at Lagos and by a few rivers, with a lagoon behind it extends as far west as the Volta delta.

A narrow sandspit several kilometres long extends across the mouth of the Senegal diverting it to the south (Figure 27). From time to time it is broken through, the river eroding it from one side and the sea from the other. At Keta, on the front of the Volta delta, coast erosion has been the rule throughout the last half century and half the town has been destroyed; it is just conceivable that the Akosombo dam, by holding back sediment transported by the Volta has accelerated the process in recent years. At Lagos the seaward extension of breakwaters at the harbour mouth is certainly responsible for rapid coast erosion immediately to the east by holding up the eastward movement of sediment. The discharge of the Niger into the Atlantic takes place through a number of creeks which have varied greatly in the importance of their discharge over the years, largely as a result of natural processes of erosion and sedimentation in the channels. Now, dredging or construction works are playing an increasingly important part in erosion and aggradation along the Delta coast.

2.3.5.2 *The Central Niger Delta.* The Ségou basin of the middle Niger is far removed from the effects of variations of sea-level. Its Late Quaternary

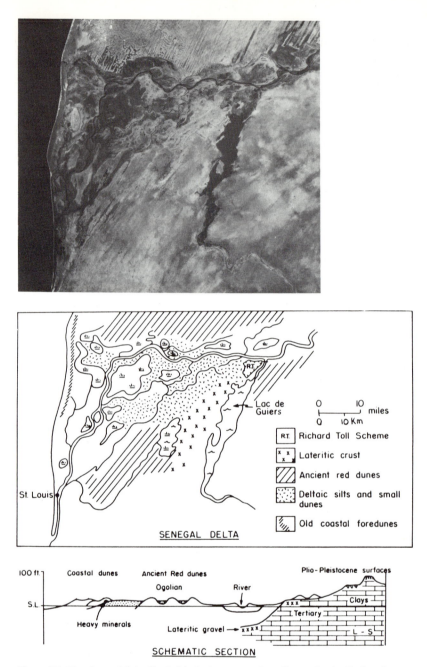

Figure 27. The Senegal delta lies behind a long coastal sandbar and spit. Shallow lagoons on either side of the river provide opportunities for irrigation which is expected to take place when a dam at Diama has been completed in order to exclude seawater. NASA-ERTS satellite image E-1213, 21 February 1973.

50

history has mainly involved climatic oscillations that seem to have resulted in great changes in river discharge from one millennium to another. The basin is not entirely immune to tectonic disturbance; Monod & Palausi (1958) pointed to emissions of volcanic lavas in recent times and there are signs of gentle subsidence of the basin floor in the Holocene immediately west of the Bandiagara Plateau with maximum river flow shifting successively towards the south-east. But the main dynamism of the central delta drainage has involved expansion of the distributary network, expanding lakes, and increased overflow at Tossaye in wet periods, alternating with reduced discharge and the extension of dunes from east-west across the lacustrine plain in dry ones. It is possible to distinguish today an upper delta occupying 7200 km² south-west of Kouakourou and Sofara, criss-crossed by the levees of numerous early and Middle Holocene diffluents. Towards the north a middle delta occupies a somewhat larger area. Further downstream still, immediately south of Lake Debo and the Niafounké dunes, is the lowest delta, 3900 km² where sedimentation continues to the present day (Figure 28). From Lake Debo the Issa Bar and the Bar Issa break through a series of about 20 linear dunes, each about a kilometre wide and 160 km long, and make their way to a confluence upstream of Tombouctou (Figure 28).

2.3.5.3 *Rivers on crystalline rocks*. Rivers flowing over crystalline rocks and interrupted by rockbars and rapids in the headwater areas provide ideal conditions for the breeding of *Simulium damnosum*, the black fly spreading river blindness (chapter 10).

Rapids and gorges formed by deeper localised incision are developed where rivers leave the crystallines and cut down into sedimentary formations. The Lagdo gorge of the Benue upstream of Garoua, is being dammed to provide storage with a view to evening out the discharge downstream and lengthening the season when the upper river is navigable.

On the Niger between Bamako and Koulikoro gradients over the rapids where the river leaves the crystallines exceed 50×10^{-5}, i.e. 0.5 m/km. A dam at Sotuba allows electricity to be generated and water to be led to an irrigation scheme 22 km downstream (Figure 29). From Koulikoro, river steamers operate for several months of the year as far as Ansongo. Further downstream, rapids between Labbezenga and Tillabéry impede navigation which remains difficult as far as the W gorge where the Atakora ranges reach the Niger. A gently sloping reach either side of the Sokoto confluence extends downstream past Yelwa to Lake Kainji where rocks which formerly outcropped to give the Bussa rapids are now submerged beneath Kainji lake. The Sokoto has a shallow box-like valley whereas the Kaduna and Gurara entering the Niger downstream of Kainji flow through minor canyons. The Niger skirts granite outcrops at Jebba and is then bordered by tabular plateaus until it joins the Benue at Lokoja. Below the confluence the Niger, apparently superimposed onto the end of a tongue of crystalline rocks extending east from Yorubaland, flows along a straight channel only about a kilometre wide in a rocky sector 50 km long.

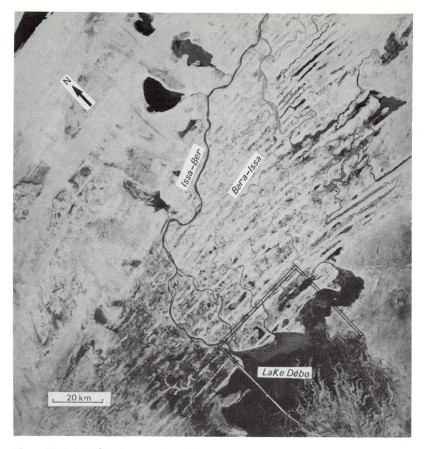

Figure 28. Lake Débo, bottom, is at the northern extremity of active sedimentation in the Inland Niger Delta. From the lake, Niger water escapes northwards across a number of fixed dunes and enters the lakes region of the delta (Skylab & Gallais 1967b).

2.3.5.4 *Rivers on sedimentary rocks*. Rivers flowing over sedimentaries of Mesozoic and Tertiary age, in the Benue and Lower Niger troughs, flow over their own alluvium. At times of low sea-level in the Pleistocene the Benue was probably well-supplied with water by its Cameroon tributaries and cut down 90 m or more. Then great thicknesses of sediment accumulated, as sea-level rose, to form broad floodplains several kilometres wide. The small scale relief of the floodplains is provided by old channels and levees left behind as rivers migrated laterally, shifting their positions a kilometre or more in the course of a century, judging from early charts. Soil textures and drainage conditions vary greatly over short distances according to this relief and when irrigation is contemplated, soil mapping requires large-scale air photographs and detailed ground checking.

52

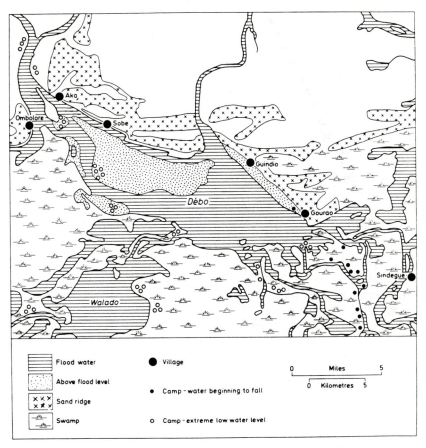

Flood water

Above flood level

Sand ridge

Swamp

● Village

● Camp - water beginning to fall

○ Camp - extreme low water level

0   Miles   5

0   Kilometres   5

Figure 28 (cont.).

For long stretches along the Benue the high water channel is almost straight, a kilometre or two wide and some 10 m deep. At high water, tributaries are ponded back by the mainstream and water spills over grassy plains for several kilometres either side of the channel, trees clustering on the better drained levees. By December, Benue water levels have fallen to reveal sandbanks 5 or 6 m high between which the low water channel winds, deepening near the steep banks, shallowing as it crosses to the other side of the high water channel (Figure 30).

Sandbanks are known to shift 300 m downstream in a year. Some colonised by shrubs and trees are more permanent features, notably at the mouths of major tributaries where local bank erosion has been promoted by weak material.

BAMAKO

2km

N

Figure 29. Below Bamako the Niger crosses the Sotuba rapids where, top right, the channel is very narrow and shallow in the dry season.

54

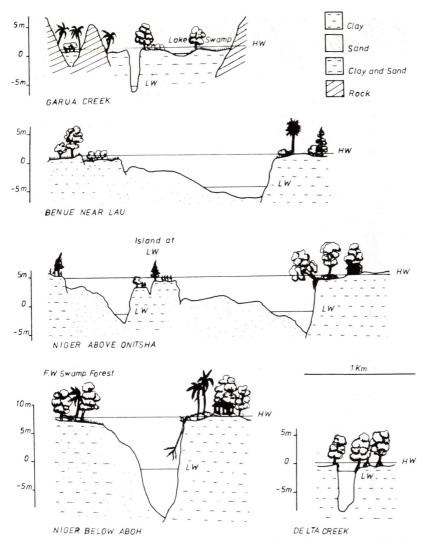

Figure 30. Cross-sections of the Benue and Niger and of a Niger delta creek (from NEDECO 1959).

Some tributaries are particularly important sources of sandy sediments. Alluvial tin mining on the Jos Plateau has involved the dumping of large volumes of overburden of mixed calibre into the headwaters of the Kaduna tributary of the Niger and also into various streams draining into Lake Chad. According to Sombroek and Zonneveld (1971) waves of sediment, not necessarily of natural origin, are moving down the Sokoto and Rima. Broad spreads of sediment progressing down the Ide Mili and

Figure 31. Gullies such as this one are incised into slopes underlain by a deep layer of red, weathered sandstones and clays of mid-Tertiary age between Awka and Orlu in south-east Nigeria. They carry heavy loads of sediment into the headwaters of the Mamu river which drains by the Anambra into the Niger near Onitsha. Such gullies are believed to have formed in this heavily settled area since the clearing of the forest for farming. Water runs off roads, market-places and other bare land and follows footpaths to the heads of the gullies, many of which are still actively eroding.

Anambra tributaries of the Niger are derived from great systems of gullies between Awka and Ekwulawbia (Figure 31).

NEDECO (1958) paid considerable attention to the great quantities of sediment transported by the Faro river which joins the Benue on its left bank (on the Cameroun-Nigeria frontier) and transforms it from a meandering into a braided river. A few kilometres below the confluence, the Wuro Boki sand flats, a major obstacle to river traffic, are built of sand from the Faro. The equally notorious Gamadio flats are possibly attributable to the gentle longitudinal gradient of the Benue below Numan, but the fact that they lie just downstream of the Gongola confluence may be significant.

2.3.5.5 *Meandering rivers*. Meandering stretches occur where longitudinal gradients are low and channels are cut into resistant clayey alluvium, notably below Aboh in the Niger delta, on the Taraba above its

56

confluence with the Benue, and between Garoua and the point where the Faro joins the Benue. The sand brought down by the Faro has accumulated near its confluence with the Benue so as to reduce the latter's gradient upstream to less than 13×10^{-5} and causing it to meander along a floodplain littered with lakes and overlooked by rocky cliffs. In its upper stretches the Faro also meanders, but only as far downstream as its confluence with the Deo. This river draining the Alantikas brings in the abundant sands that cause the Faro to braid and are eventually responsible for shoaling in the Benue.

2.3.5.6 *Creek systems.* Distributary networks of creeks meander through the coastal deltas of the Senegal and Niger and the inland deltas of the Chari-Logone (Cabot 1967) and Niger. For 150 km along the lower valley of the Senegal, from Vinding to below Podor, the Doué runs parallel to the mainstream and about 20 km south of it. The central delta of the Niger is much more complicated with a multiplicity of channels having

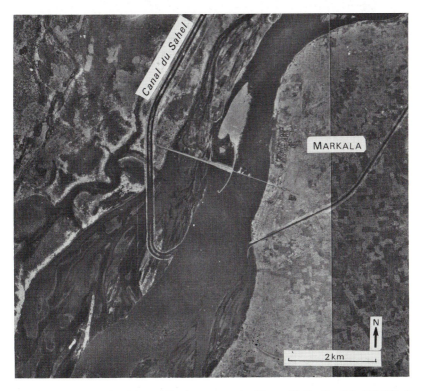

Figure 32. The Markala or Sansanding barrage on the Niger with the Canal du Sahel leading water to the north from the left bank and a narrow waterway for river craft on the right bank.

longitudinal gradients of as little as 1×10^{-5}, i.e. 1 cm/km. At Markala (Sansanding) an earthern barrage with a weir raises the level of the Niger by some 4 m to a height from which it can run along two ancient distributary channels, acting as canals to carry irrigation water (Figure 32). The north bank of the river as far as Ké-Macina is built up as an artificial dyke to allow controlled irrigation of rice fields behind it. From Diafarabé, the Marigot de Diaka leads a quarter of the Niger's water for 170 km across flooding alluvial plains to Lake Debo where it rejoins the mainstream which has been supplemented at Mopti by the Bani. McIntosh (1980) has described the Niger-Bani confluence as having shifted successively further downstream in recent centuries from Koa and Kolenge to Kouakourou.

Numerous lakes at the margins of the central delta are fed from the Niger, their receipts varying from year to year according to the level of the flood, but their evaporation losses always being in the neighbourhood of 2000 mm. Consequently they oscillate seasonally through vertical ranges of 1 to 3 m and move up and down from one decade to another through as much as 10 m. Cultivators frequently have to resite their cropland accordingly, moving up or downslope to avoid disaster. In recent decades small dams and sluices have helped to stabilise levels in the short term; but they can do little to counteract long-continued drought and low Niger discharges.

2.4 REFERENCES

Allen, J.R.L. 1965. Late Quaternary Niger delta, and adjacent areas: sedimentary environments and lithofacies. *Am. Assoc. Petroleum Geologists Bull.* 49: 547-600.
Assemien, P., J.C. Filleron, L. Martin & J.P. Taster 1970. Le Quaternaire de la zone littorale de Côte d'Ivoire. *Bull. Ass. Sénégal et Quatern. Ouest afr. Dakar* 25: 65-78.
Beaudet, G., R. Coque, P. Michel & P. Rognon 1977. Y-a-t-il eu capture du Niger? *Bull. Assoc. Géogr.* 445-6: 215-232.
Beaudet, G., R. Coque, P. Michel, & P. Rognon 1981. Reliefs cuirassés et évolution géomorphologique des régions orientales du Mali. *Z. Geomorph. N.F. Suppl. Bd.* 38, 38-62.
Blanck, J.P. 1968. *La boucle du Niger (Mali). Cartes géomorphologiques et notice; project d'aménagement.* Strasbourg: Centre Geogr. appliquée.
Bocquier, M. & M. Gavaud 1964. Etude pedologique du Niger oriental. *Rapport général : carte pédologique de reconnaissance 1:500,000, feuille Maradi.* Dakar-Hann: ORSTOM.
Cabot, J. 1961. *Les lits du Logone: étude géomorphologique,* Paris: SEDES.
Carmouze, J.P., J.R. Durand & C.L. Lévèque (eds.) 1983. Lake Chad: Ecology and productivity of a shallow tropical ecosystem. *Monographiae Biologicae* 53. The Hague: Junk.
Chudeau, R. 1913. La zone d'inondation du Niger. *Bull. de la Société de Géographie Commerciale* 35: 569-87.
Falconer, J.D. 1911. *The Geology and Geography of Northern Nigeria.* London: Macmillan.
Faure, H., E. Manguin & R. Nydal 1963. Formations lacustres du Quaternaire supérieur du Niger oriental. Diatomites et âges absolus. *Bull. Bur. Rech. Géol. Min.* 3: 41-63.
Furon, R. 1929. L'ancien delta du Niger. *Rev. de Géogr. Phys. et de Géol. Dyn.* 2: 265-274.
Gallais, J. 1967a. Le delta intérieur du Niger. *Mém de I.F.A.N.* 79 (2 vols.). Dakar.
Gallais, J. 1967b. Le delta intérieur du Niger et ses bordures: étude morphologique. *Mém et Doc Centre de la Documentation Cartographiques et Géographiques.* Paris: CNRS.

Grove, A.T. 1958. The ancient erg of Hausaland and similar formations on the south side of the Sahara. *Geogr. J.* 124: 528–33.

Grove, A.T. 1959. A note on the former extent of Lake Chad. *Geogr. J.* 125: 465–7.

Grove, A.T. & R.A. Pullan 1963. Some aspects of the Pleistocene palaeogeography of the Chad basin. In F.C. Howell & E. Bourlière (eds.), *African Ecology and human evolution.* London: Methuen.

Grove, A.T. & A. Warren 1968. Quaternary landforms and climate on the south side of the Sahara. *Geogr. J.* 134: 194–208.

Hamilton, A.C. 1976. The significance of patterns of distribution shown by forest plants and animals in tropical Africa for the reconstruction of upper Pleistocene palaeoenvironments: a review. *Palaeoecology of Africa* 9. Cape Town/Rotterdam: Balkema.

Kervran, L. 1959. Le cours fossile du Niger. *Notre Sahara* 10: 53–8.

Kutzbach, J.E. 1980. Estimates of past climate at paleolake Chad, North Africa, *Quaternary Research* 14: 2i0–223.

Kutzbach, J.E. 1981. Monsoon climate of the Early Holocene: climate experiment with the earth's orbital parameters for 9000 years ago. *Science* 214: 59–61.

McIntosh, S.K. & R.J. McIntosh 1980. *Prehistoric investigations in the region of Jenne, Mali.* Cambridge: Monographs in African Archaeology 2. Oxford: British Archaeological Reports.

McTainsh, G.H. & P.H. Walker 1982. Nature and distribution of Harmattan dust. *Z. für Geomorphologie* 26: 417–435.

Mainguet, M., L. Canon & M.C. Chemin 1980. Le Sahara: géomorphologie et paléogéomorphologie éoliennes. In M.A.J. Williams & M. Faure (eds.) *The Sahara and the Nile.* Rotterdam: Balkema.

Maley, J. 1981. Études palynologiques dans le bassin du Tchad et paléoclimatologie de l'Afrique nord-tropicale de 30000 ans a l'époque actuelle. *Trav. et Doc* 129. Paris: ORSTOM.

Michel, P. 1968. Genèse et évolution de la vallée du Sénégal, de Bakel à l'embouchure (Afrique Occidentale). *Z. Geomorphol, N.F.* 12: 318–349.

Michel, P. 1973. Les bassins des fleuvres Sénégal et Gambie. Etude géomorphologique. *Mém. ORSTOM* 63 (3 vols).

Michel, P. 1980. The southwestern Sahara margin: sediments and climatic changes during the recent Quaternary. *Palaeoecology of Africa* 12. Rotterdam: Balkema.

Monod, T. & G. Palausi. 1958. Sur la présence dans le région du lac Faguibine de venues volcaniques d'âge subactuel. *C.R. Acad. Sci. Paris* 246: 666–8.

Moreau, R.E. 1963. Vicissitudes of the African biomes in the late Pleistocene. *Proc. Zool. Soc. Lond.* 141: 395–421.

NEDECO 1959. *River studies and recommendations on improvement of the Niger and Benue.* Amsterdam: North Holland Publishing Company.

NEDECO 1961. *The waters of the Niger delta.* The Hague: ?

Palausi, G. 1955. Au sujet du Niger fossile dans la région de Tombouctou. *Revue de Géomorphologie Dynamique* 6: 217–8.

Pastouret, L., H. Chamley, G. Delibrias, J.C. Duplessis & J. Thiede 1978. Late Quaternary climatic changes in West Tropical Africa deduced from deep sea sedimentation off the Niger Delta. *Oceanolog. Acta* 1: 217–232.

Petit-Maire, N. & J. Riser, 1981. Holocene lake deposits and palaeoenvironments in central Sahara, northeastern Mali. *Palaeogeography, Palaeoclimatology, Palaeoecology* 35: 45–61.

Pias, J. 1970. Les formations sédimentaires tertiares et quaternaires de la cuvette tchadienne et les sols qui en dérivent. *Mém. ORSTOM* 43.

Pias, J. & E. Guichard 1957. Origine et conséquences de l'existence d'un cordon sableux dans la partie sud-ouest de la cuvette tchadienne *C.R. Acad. Sci. Paris* 244: 791–3.

Sarnthein, M. & L. Diester-Haas 1977. Eolian-sand turbidites. *J. Sed. Pet.* 47: 869–90.

Sellars, C.D. 1981. A floodplain storage model used to determine evaporation losses in the upper Yobe river, Northern Nigeria. *J. of Hydrology* 52: 257–268.

Servant, M. 1973. Séquences continentales et variations climatiques: évolution du bassin du

Tchad au Cénozoique Supérieur. Paris: Thèse d'Et. Université Pierre et Marie Curie.

Servant, M. & S. Servant 1970. Les formes lacustres et les diatomées du Quaternaire récent du fond de la cuvette tchadienne. *Rev. de Géogr. Phys. et de Géol. Dyn* 12: 63–76.

Servant M. & S. Servant 1980. L'environment Quaternaire du bassin du Tchad. In M.A.J. Williams & H. Faure (eds.), *The Sahara and the Nile*. Rotterdam: Balkema.

Servant-Valdary, S. 1977. *Evolution des diatomées et paléolimnologie du bassin tchadien au Cénozoique Supérieur*. Paris: Thèse d'Et. Université Pierre et Marie Curie.

Short, K.C. & A.J. Stäuble 1967. Outline of Geology of Niger Delta. *Am. Assoc. Petroleum Geologists Bull.* 51: 761–779.

Sombroek, W.G. & I.S. Zonneveld 1971. *Ancient dune fields and fluviatile deposits in the Rima-Sokoto basin (N.W. Nigeria)*. Soil Survey Paper No. 5, Wageningen: Netherlands Soil Survey Institute.

Street, F.A. 1981. Tropical palaeoenvironments. *Progress in Physical Geography* 5: 157–185.

Street, F.A. & A.T. Grove 1976. Environmental and climatic implications of Late Quaternary lake-level fluctuations in Africa. *Nature* 261: 385–90.

Street, F.A. & A.T. Grove 1979. Global maps of lake-level fluctuations since 30,000 BP. *Quaternary Research* 12: 83–118.

Talbot, M.R. 1980. Environmental responses to climatic change in the West African Sahel over the past 20,000 years. In M.A.J. Williams & H. Faure (eds.), *The Sahara and the Nile*, Rotterdam: Balkema.

Talbot, M.R. 1981. Holocene changes in tropical wind intensity and rainfall: evidence from south-east Ghana. *Quat. Res.* 16: 201–20.

Thomas, M.F. 1974. *Tropical geomorphology: a study of weathering and landform development in warm climates*. London: Macmillan.

Thomas, M.F. & M.B. Thorpe. 1980. Some aspects of the geomorphological interpretation of Quaternary alluvial sediments in Sierra Leone. *Z. Geomorph. N.F. Suppl. Bd.* 36: 140–161.

Thompson, T.F. 1970. Holocene tectonic activity in West Africa dated by archaeologic methods. *Geol. Soc. Am. Bull.* 81: 3759–3964.

Tilho, J. 1910–1914. *Documents scientifiques de la mission Tilho*. 1906–9 (3 vols.). Paris: Imp. Nat.

Tilho, J. 1947. *Le Tchad et la capture du Logone par le Niger*. Paris: Gauthier-Villars.

Tricart, J. 1959. Géomorphologie dynamique de la moyenne vallée du Niger. *Ann. Géogr. Fr.* 368: 333–343.

Tricart, J. 1961. Notice explicative de la carte géomorphologique du Delta du Sénégal. *Mém. B.R.G.M.* 8.

Tricart, J. 1965. Rapport de la mission de reconnaissance géomorphologique de la vallée moyenne du Niger. *Mém. I.F.A.N., Dakar* 72.

Urvoy, Y. 1942. Les bassins du Niger. Étude de géographie physique et de la paléogéographie. *Mém. I.F.A.N.,* Dakar 4.

Zinderen Bakker, Van, E.M. 1982. African palaeoclimates 18000 BP. *Palaeoecology of Africa* 15. Rotterdam: Balkema.

A.T.GROVE
African Studies Centre, Free School Lane, Cambridge

3

Water characteristics of the Chari system and Lake Chad

3.1 INTRODUCTION AND SOURCES OF INFORMATION

The Chad basin occupies over 1 million km² of the southern Sahara plus a similar area of savanna and forest extending south to the Congo (Zaire) watershed (Figure 17). The lowest portion of the basin in the Bodélé depression, at a height of only 160 m above sea-level, is believed to have been dry for the last 2000 years though it was the deepest part of Megachad in the Early Holocene. The present lake, 500 km to the south of the Bodélé depression and at a height of 278–283 m above sea-level, remains a vast sheet of water only a few metres deep. The only major African lake outside the Rift Valley region, Lake Chad was an object of great interest to early European travellers, most of whom reached it from the north after a long desert crossing and were much impressed by the freshness of its water; this is the quality with which we are mainly concerned.

Lake Chad has received in recent years the concentrated attention of a team of French scientists from ORSTOM, the Office de la Recherche Scientifique et Technique Outre-Mer. Climatic data and lake levels have been recorded systematically since 1954 and estimates of former levels have been carried back to 1895 (Figure 8). A hydrobiological laboratory was established in N'djamena, the capital of the Chad Republic, formerly Fort Lamy, in 1964 with the initial aim of studying the biological productivity of the lake. Subsequent investigations have included not only the populations and biomasses of several groups of organisms but also the operation of the lake basin as a geochemical and ecological system. They have gone far towards explaining how it is that the lake remains fresh in spite of a mean annual input of about 2.6×10^6 tonnes of dissolved substances annually. Gac's (1981) study of the geochemistry of the Chad basin, which includes a full bibliography, brings together recent researches in this enormous field laboratory in a masterly fashion.

Table 3. Characteristics of rivers and their loads and rates of river basin erosion (Gac 1981).

	Length (km)	Area (X10⁶km²)	Discharge (X10⁹m³)	Dissolved (X10⁶t)	Erosion (t/km²/y)	Conc. (mg/l)	Solids (X10⁶t)	Erosion (t/km²/y)	Conc. (mg/l)
World rivers									
Amazon	7025	6.30	5519	219	46	53	490	78	88
Orinoco	2600	0.88	1200	50	57	52	80	91	84
Mississippi	6800	3.27	580	130	40	223	307	94	530
Mekong	4023	0.80	577	60	75	105	345	430	600
Ganges	2700	0.97	488	76	78	208	520	536	1420
African rivers									
Zaire	4700	3.88	1200	37	9	31	50	13	42
Zambezi	2575	1.34	131	20	15	149	42	31	324
Niger	4184	1.13	195	9	8	48	28	25	127
Nile	6700	2.87	89	18	6	200	67	23	755
Senegal	1800	0.27	24	1	9	42	1	5	58
Chari	1300	0.33	40	2	1	59	3	10	87

3.2 THE RIVERS: THEIR PARTICULATE AND DISSOLVED LOAD

The main source area for the rivers entering Chad is the upland country at 800 to 1000 m extending eastwards from the lava-capped Adamawa Plateau in northern Cameroun to the crystalline highlands of the Central African Republic, where the mean annual rainfall is between 1200 and 1600 mm. Further east the altitude increases to 1600 m in the massif de Guera and to 3000 m in Jebel Marra in the Sudan Republic, but the rainfall diminishes to the east and north, and much of the water draining westwards is lost by evaporation from enormous swampy plains northeast of Sahr (formerly Ft Archambault) which are comparable in area to Lake Chad itself.

The flow of the headwaters in the south-west scarcely increases in volume below the 500 m contour, for northwards to the lake the annual evaporation from open water surfaces increases from 1200 mm to over 2000 mm and the mean annual rainfall diminishes from 1200 mm to less than 500 mm. On leaving the crystalline rocks, the rivers traverse sedimentary beds of Cenozoic age (Continental Terminal) that dip northwards and extend below the lake at a depth of a few hundred metres.

The dissolved solids in the waters flowing across the Continental Terminal past Moundou, Doba, Munda and Sahr, totalling 2.4×10^6t annually, are equivalent to 88% of the amounts finally delivered to Lake Chad, and the total particulate load at those points, 3.25×10^6t (1969-72 average), is considerably in excess of the amount of sediment finally arriving at the delta (Carmouze 1979). In their lower courses the Logone and the Chari, spilling over their banks as they rise in flood towards the end of the rainy season, lose about 15-40% of their discharge by evaporation, plus 15-35% of their dissolved load and 20-60% of their suspended load sediment. Some water from the Logone escapes at flood peaks over the left bank downstream of Lai and above Bongor, to follow the route westward which was taken thousands of years ago by water spilling from Megachad, and reaches the Benue river by way of the Mayo Kebbi. Downstream of Bongor, floodwaters spread over the Yaéré plains and the surplus escaping evaporation feeds the El Beid (Ebeji), a river which rises on the floodplain and crosses the northern projection of Cameroun to reach Lake Chad along the frontier with Nigeria (Figure 50). The spillage of floodwater from Logone and Chari over the plains retards and diminishes the floodpeak. On average a million tons of sediment are filtered out of the river water by the reeds and grasses annually and added to the Quaternary deposits south of the Lake.

At Batangafo where the Ouham, principle tributary of the Chari, leaves the crystalline rocks of the highland source area the particulate load is composed mainly of kaolinite 59%, illite 14%, felspars 6.5%, and quartz 10%. On the way to the confluence of Chari and Logone, the proportions and absolute amounts of all these constituents diminish and the proportion of smectites increases. The smectites are derived from the soils of the floodplains where they are synthesised from kaolinites deposited by the river combining with hydrous silica dissolved in the floodwaters (Carmouze 1976).

The Chari entering Chad in the dry season carries a solid load of little more than 25ppm. With the first rains, concentrations of suspended sediment increase rapidly to ten times that value, but as the rainy season progresses the plant cover protecting the slopes and covering the floodplains increases in effectiveness and at maximum discharge the water is fairly clear, with a white Secchi disc visible at a depth of 2 to 4 m. The total solid load brought to the confluence annually by the Logone is about 1×10^6t and by the Chari 1.4×10^6t. Almost 40% of this material consists of kaolinite, about 11% smectites, 11% illite and rather less than

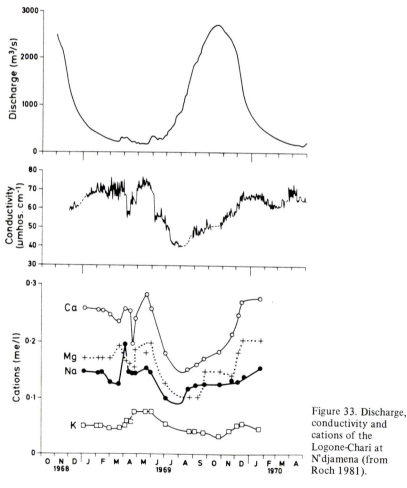

Figure 33. Discharge, conductivity and cations of the Logone-Chari at N'djamena (from Roch 1981).

Table 4. Mean chemical composition of Chari and Chad waters in 1967 (Carmouze & Pedro 1977).

Elements	Chari (mg/l)	Lake Chad (mg/l)	Coeff. of concentration
$Si(OH)_4$	22.2	46.7	2.1
CO_3H^-	31.5	247.7	7.8
Ca^{2+}	2.0	12.5	6.0
Mg^{2+}	0.9	6.2	6.6
Na^+	2.9	33.6	11.5
K^+	1.8	16.8	9.1
Total	61.5	36.3	5.9

10% quartz; in addition there is a good deal of organic matter and a few percent iron and aluminium oxides. The mean concentration of the suspended load, about 60ppm, is rather low by world standards (Table 3).

The concentration of the dissolved load of the Chari and Logone increases somewhat between the headwater regions, above 500 m, and the confluence as a result of spillage over the floodplains and evaporation. Electrical conductivities vary between 40 and 70 μmhos at 25° C with a mean solute load of about 42ppm dissolved ions and 25ppm silica (Figure 33). The lowest concentrations occur in the early rains when flow is derived from water that has run quickly over the surface. The residence time of soil water increases as the dry season progresses and river salinities reach maximum values in April and May. The prevalence of cations present is in the order Ca^{++}, Mg^{++}, Na^+ and K^+ throughout most of the river system with the exception of the Bahr Sara where Na^+ moves up to second place, and in the Lim and Pendé where it is first. Below N'djamena the values of the ions and silica in solution are as shown in Table 4.

The concentration of ions in solution is rather low, about a half the world average: the concentration of silica, it is important to note, is about one and a half times that in the average river.

3.3 LAKE CHAD

3.3.1 Water inputs and outputs

The L-shaped lake spreads over a remarkably flat plain that slopes extremely gently to the north where its floor is about 2 m lower than the floor near the point of entry of the Chari at Djimtilo. The water surface gradient to the north is accentuated by the annual increment of water entering from the south and the abstraction mainly by evaporation which greatly exceeds precipitation especially in the north. Furthermore, mean annual rainfall declines from about 600 mm at the south end of the lake to about 250 mm in the north. Movement of lake water is consequently northwards and also outwards towards the shores, the actual flow patterns being affected by the winds, which are SW from June to October and NE during the rest of the year, and by the morphology of the basin floor. A rise called the Great Barrier, only a few metres high, runs across the centre of the lake to separate a deeper northern basin from a shallower southern one. On the east side of the lake, the system of NW to SE dunes, formed at right angles to the dry season winds of the drier period of the Late Pleistocene, extend into the lake as low, linear sandy islands (Figure 16).

Under what are considered to be average conditions in this century, the lake is at a level of 282 m and occupies an area of about 20,000 km². When this is the case, evaporation from the surface constitutes about 94% of the water losses from the lake. The evaporation varies seasonally, being at a minimum in the humid cloudy period from June to September and again during the cool months with reduced solar radiation inputs from November to March. Such variations are overwhelmed by the seasonal oscillation of the inputs. Of the mean annual rainfall over the lake, amounting to 310 mm, a half falls in August; of the discharge of the rivers, constituting 87% of the water inputs to the lake, over a half arrives

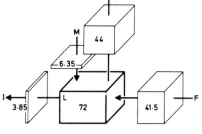

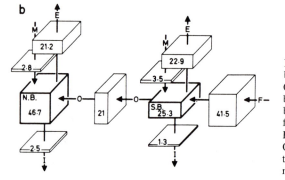

Figure 34. Mean water balance in km³ of a) Lake Chad and b) the northern basin (N.B.) and southern basin (S.B.). F: Chari inflow; E: Evaporation; M: Precipitation; I: Infiltration; O: Overflow from southern to northern basin (Carmouze 1979).

66

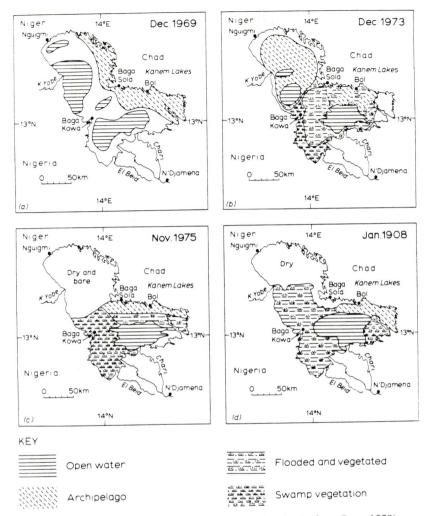

KEY

Open water	Flooded and vegetated
Archipelago	Swamp vegetation

Figure 35. Extent of Lake Chad at High, medium and low levels (from Grove 1978).

between August and October. The result is that the lake surface oscillates through a range of almost a metre, rising from July to December and falling from January to June (Figure 34).

From year to year the annual rate of evaporation from the lake surface varies from about 2250 to 2450 mm; the annual rainfall on it varies from little more than 100 mm to as much as 450 mm. But changes in the volume and extent of the lake from year to year are dominated not so much by local conditions as by annual variations in rainfall over the catchment of the Logone and Chari. These cause annual discharge into the lake to vary

67

from less than 20 to well over 50 km^3, the average being about 40 km^3. As the mean volume of the lake is only about 60 km^3, successions of a few wet years or dry years cause the lake to expand and contract rapidly.

At low states of Chad, resulting from a reduction in mean rainfall over the catchment by about 300 mm, the lake is confined to the basin south of the Great Barrier and the floor of the northern lobe dries out completely. At high states of the lake, caused by rainfall about 400 mm above the mean, open water extends across the Great Barrier, the northern pool is deeper and holds more than the south, and when the water reaches a level of 283 m it overflows along the Bahr-el-Ghazal for as much as 100 km. For most of this century the lake has stood between the extremes, with water usually moving freely from the southern basin to the northern basin. During the decade of the most detailed scientific observations, the lake fell from a high state in 1963 to its lowest recorded level in 1974 (Figure 35). From 1974 until 1985 it remained low and confined to the southern basin (Figure 8).

3.3.2 *The water chemistry of the lake*

The main studies of the chemistry and hydrobiology of the lake were carried out before the effects of the Sahel/Sudan zone drought of the 1970s had been severely felt and it is with this period, when Chad was standing at 282 m, that we shall be primarily concerned. The effects of longer term rise and fall of lake level are then considered.

It is apparent from measurements of the electrical conductivity that the Chari floodwaters enter the lake and extend northwards from July onwards each year in a tongue that broadens and lengthens across the southern basin and eventually reaches the northern lobe and the archipelago (Figure 36). So long as egress to the northern basin is available, the southern basin acts as a transit way, an extension of the river itself, with a mean residence time for the incoming water of only about 6 months. The northern basin on the other hand, which can contain twice the volume of the southern one, normally acts as the main storage basin, the mean residence time there being two years (Carmouze 1979).

The details of the flow patterns through the lake and the eventual fate of the ions and silica have been traced from analyses of the isotopic content of the water, ^{18}O, deuterium and tritium, its chemistry, the clay mineralogy of the lake floor materials and both the microscopic and large plants and animals living and dying in the lake (Roche 1973, 1975; Figure 36). Rain falling on the lake in July and August has a low δ^{18}O ratio. The floodwaters of the Chari have higher values, similar to that of the mean for ocean surface water, expressed in terms of SMOW (Standard Mean Ocean Water); the values in the vicinity of the delta are between -5% and $+2\%$. As the Chari water spreads out and the lighter ^{16}O is lost preferentially by evaporation its δ^{18}O ratio increases still more to between 10 and 16‰.

Evaporation from the lake surface results in an increase in the

68

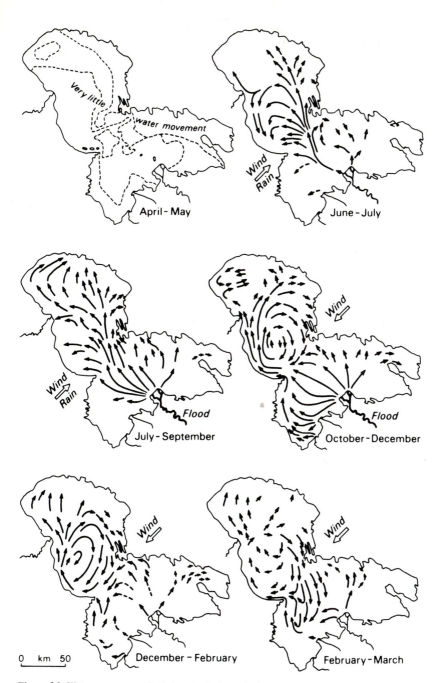

Figure 36. Water movement in Lake Chad through the year. The movements have been traced from the changing values of electrical conductivity and ^{18}O (after Roche 1981 and Carmouze 1976).

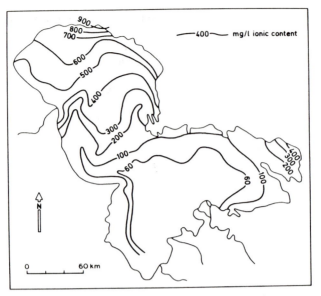

Figure 37. Mean pattern of ionic content of the lake when water moves freely from the southern into the northern basin (Roche 1975).

concentration of ions and silica in the water of the lake which is portrayed by the pattern of electrical conductivity (Figure 37). Tracing the changes in the distribution of conductivity values from month to month through the year shows the Chari floodwater becoming more saline as it spreads northwards, reaching the Great Barrier in September and swirling clockwise around the northern basin in April and May. The highest values, about 1500 μmhos are registered at the northern extremities of the lake and in the innermost bays of the archipelago about June; they then diminish quite quickly with the arrival of water that fell as rain in the previous year in the headwaters of the Chari.

As the residence time of water in the lake increases so the proportion of the different ions changes and the concentration of silica diminishes. The pattern of the water quality varies from month to month and differs from year to year according to the volume and shape of the lake. The western corner of the southern basin is affected by the spread of Chari water in October and November; otherwise it is supplied by the El Beid, the waters of which have been modified by residence on the floodplain and in consequence have a higher sodium content than Chari water. In the early rains, the saline material that had accumulated in the dry season in pools on the floor of the El Beid channel and in depressions on the yaérés is redissolved and carried into Chad. A few weeks later El Beid has an increased level of potassium, probably derived from the ash of burned grasses and dung. After November sodium is the main cation brought into

70

the lake by the El Beid, other cations being taken up preferentially by the clays and organic matter of the floodplain soils. The El Beid's discharge is only about 4% of the Chari's discharge into Chad, but its quality deserves special mention because the waters of the flood plain river are now being used for irrgating the clay plains of Borno.

The changes in the proportions of the dissolved substances in the lake waters as they move away from the Chari mouth are the result of several processes of which the most important are evaporation, clay synthesis and the incorporation of nutrients into animals and plants.

3.3.3 *Clay synthesis in the lake*

It has already been noted that kaolinite constitutes about 40% of the particulate load carried into Chad by the lower Chari, yet the predominant clay minerals on the floor of the lake are blue-gray smectites such as montmorillonite and related microcrystalline materials (Carmouze 1979). In the south near the Chari delta, the sediments over an area of 3000–4000 km^2 on the lake floor consist of granules the size of dune sand (pseudo-sands they are often called) between 125 and 500 microns in diameter (Figure 38). They seem to have formed as a result of goethite being converted into nontronite, a reaction which involves silica, SiO_4H_4, being removed from the water plus calcium and magnesium; at the same time carbon dioxide, CO_2, is liberated reducing the pH of the water. In the central part of the lake, smectite in the sediments is in the form of a ferriferous beidellite built of iron and aluminium hydroxides plus silica, calcium and magnesium; again CO_2 is liberated by the synthetic process. In the north, large amounts of magnesium are taken from the lake waters in the formation of magnesous montmorillonites; in

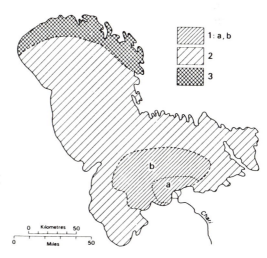

Figure 38. Sediment types on the floor of Lake Chad. 1a: Black and yellow grains of Nontronite; 1b: Yellow grains of Nontronite; 2: Alumino-iron montmorillonite; 3: Magnesian + calcite montmorillonite (Carmouze 1979).

71

addition calcium is precipitated. All these processes take up cations from the water and by liberating carbon dioxide, help to maintain conditions in the lake slightly on the acid side of neutral.

Where it happens that kaolinitic clays have been filtered out of the water reaching any part of the lake, stevensite or calcite are precipitated, the pH of the water increases and so does the concentration of silica increase. This may lead to the precipitation of amorphous silica or provide conditions under which massive diatomites accumulate (Gac 1981).

3.3.4 *Biological processes at work*

The shallow waters of Lake Chad are very favourable for mollusca which are present in great numbers. *Melania tuberculata* predominate in the northern basin, *Cleopatra bulimoides* in the eastern archipelago, but overall, the most important species volumetrically is *Bellamya unicolor*. The annual production of organic matter by benthic molluscs in the lake in 1969–70 was estimated to amount to 279,000 tonnes (dry weight) plus nearly 2 million tonnes of shell material (Lévêque 1979). On many parts of the lake floor the shells are rapidly dissolved and the aragonite of which they are composed is returned to the lake for recycling. On balance, a large amount of $CaCO_3$ is permanently removed from the lake waters as a result of the growth and preservation of molluscan shells. Similarly diatoms, mainly *Melosira granulata* and *Surirella muelleri*, take up ions and silica from the lake water and help to regulate its quality.

The abundance and rate of growth of reeds and other plants in an around the lake depends a great deal on its extent. *Phragmites australis* grows widely in shallow water, *Vossia cuspidata* is common in the vicinity of the delta, *Cyperus papyrus* in the southern basin, *Typha australis* (perversely) has a more northerly distribution, and the natron-tolerant *Cyperus laevigatus* appears in the pools in the extreme north. The above-ground plant biomass was estimated by Carmouze et al. (1978) at 7.2 million tonnes for the whole lake and the total biomass of roots at 13 million tonnes (dry weight). The annual removal of silica from the lake water by plants may well be of the order of 10^5–10^6 tonnes and of potassium 10^5 tonnes, plus lesser amounts of calcium, magnesium and possibly sodium. A large part of these substances must be returned to the lake when the plants decay; however a considerable quantity is burned and the ash blown away by the wind and in addition a significant amount is fixed, at least semi-permanently, in lake floor muds and peats.

3.3.5 *'Cationic chromatography'*

The outcome of the selective absorption of the substances dissolved in the lake as its waters move from the Chari towards the northern shores has been described by Roche (1975) as cationic chromatography. It is generally supposed that the loss of sodium from the water is negligible and the amounts of the other cations removed is calculated on this

Table 5. Chemical budget of Lake Chad for period 1964-69 (Roche 1977).

	Ca^{2+}	Mg^{2+}	Na^+	K^+	Total cations	SiO_2 (mg/l)
Dissolved in river (meq/l)	0.200	0.141	0.131	0.043	0.515	25
Dissolved in lake (meq/l)	1.03	0.96	1.60	0.41	3.95	53
Residence time (years)	7	9	16	12	10	3
Removal by sedimentation (%)	58	45	0	23	37	13

assumption. It would seem, then, that 58% of the annual input of Ca^{++}, 45% of the Mg^{++} and 23% of K^+ are 'sedimented'; of the silica, 83% is removed. The mean proportion of cations in the lake in its 'normal' condition is then as in Table 5.

In the SW corner of the lake, as noted earlier, Na^+ is the most prevalent cation. In the SE, the ratio of Ca^{++}/Mg^{++} increases. In the northern basin the proportion of Ca^{++} diminishes and Na^{++} increases, so that the order of prevalence of cations in the extreme north is Na^+, Mg^{++}, K^+, Ca^{++} throughout the year.

When Lake Chad stands at its mean level, between 92 and 96% of the water entering the lake in an average year is lost by evaporation. The remainder is believed to percolate through its sandy shores where the water-table declines gently away from the lake, especially at the north and north-east corner. The solutes in the percolating water are believed to account for less than 17% of the silica entering the lake but for up to 63% of the ionic input. As the subsurface water moves away from the lake, some of the salts are precipitated and there is some dilution by storms of rain falling on the sandy surface and percolating downwards. Eventually this seepage water emerges in basins at a distance from the lake and evaporites are deposited which consist of sodium carbonate and other much more complicated crystalline substances (Maglione 1974).

3.3.6 *Effects of rising and falling level*

Information about the changes in the water characteristics of the lake as its level rises is scarce because a prolonged rise last occurred before 1963. It would appear that dilution when the lake expands is not as great as might be expected because salts precipitated in marginal depressions in earlier years go into solution again. As the water deepens, allowing freer movement of from the southern basin over the Great Barrier, salinities in the northern basin are reduced. Water flows down the Bahr-el-Ghazal when the lake reaches 283 m and this leads to a freshening of the water in the eastern part of the southern basin. With precipitation 400 mm above the twentieth century mean, water would flow along the Bahr-el-Ghazal and reach the Bodélé depression taking about 150 years to fill it; such a lake would remain fresh for over 100,000 years (Gac 1981).

When the volume of Lake Chad was diminishing in the years around 1970 it was noticed that the density of phytoplankton increased in the northern basin. At about the same time, between 1968 and 1970, the mass of mollusca on the lake floor increased from about half a million to three-quarters of a million tonnes; then, as the lake volume continued to diminish, ecological conditions became less favourable for mollusca and more Ca^{++} was released into the lake waters by shells dissolving than was taken up by living mollusca. Eventually, in 1972-73, the Great Barrier emerged and the northern basin dried up almost entirely. Its floor was colonised quite widely by a blue-green algae *Oscillatoria platensis*. Vegetation died and wide areas were left as bare, cracking mud. The salinity of the main pool remaining in the southern basin was still not much greater than is usually the case in that part of the lake. Salts were precipitated in hollows between the dune islands and pools remaining were in some cases enriched by potassium and magnesium from rotting vegetation. In 1974 the lake reached its lowest level this century and discharge of the Chari remained rather low into the 1980s. Vast areas of reeds spread over the margins of the southern basin and the woody cover of the Great Barrier increased (Gac 1981).

Since 1974 Lake Chad has effectively consisted only of the pool in the southern basin. The reduction of the surface area reduces total evaporation losses, and inputs of dissolved substances have probably been reduced in proportion to the discharge of the Chari. The direction in which the characteristics of the water develops under these conditions presumably depends on the effectiveness of infiltration, notably through the Great Barrier. The floor of the northern basin in 1980 was 4 m below the level of the southern pool, and some waterways continued to discharge through the Great Barrier into the northern pool. Confined to the southern basin and with an area of only 8500 km^2, the lake is a much more homogenous body of water than it was at the medium state. The escaping water is not necessarily the most saline, and the lake itself is likely to become more salty over time. However, unless the climate of the southern part of the basin has entered a prolonged period of aridity, two or three years of above average discharge are likely to restore the lake to something approaching its normal condition.

3.4 THE CLOSED BASIN ENVIRONMENT

The freshness of the lake at the present day and the lack of evaporites in its basin must largely be attributed to the scarcity of limestones in the catchment areas of the rivers and their distance from the sea. The inputs of limey and salty materials has been much less than is the case in most other terminal lakes, in the Kalahari for instance.

In consequence of the freshness of its waters, Lake Chad is a very valuable resource for irrigation and pastoralism in a region chronically short of surface water in the first half of the year and it also supports a

74

thriving fishing industry. However, its violent fluctuations in extent over periods of a few years present hazards to people depending on it. Pastoralists have been able to adapt to the mobility of its shores without too much difficulty. Fishermen around the northern basin face greater problems. Modern irrigation systems employing large pumping stations, find it particularly difficult and costly to adjust.

Lake Chad does not contribute to the underground water of the region to any great extent at its present level. Even quite close to the lake the main feed to groundwater is percolation, through the beds of rivers, and rain infiltrating former dune sands. Both rain and lake water dissolve ancient salt deposits as they move downwards. When the lake was more extensive, standing at the 286-8 m level from 3000 to 1800 BP, the feed to groundwater through the dunes on the north and east must have been greater; supplies to sub-surface aquifers by Megachad in the Early Holocene and again between 30,000 and 20,000 BP were probably very large indeed.

3.5 REFERENCES

Carmouze, J.P. 1976. La régulation hydrogéochimique du lac Tchad. Contribution à l'analyse biodynamique d'un système endoréique en milieu continental. *Travaux et documents ORSTOM* 58.

Carmouze, J.P. 1979. The hydrochemical regulation of the Lake Chad. *ORSTOM for Réunion Trav. Limnol. afr. Nairobi.*

Carmouze, J.P. & G. Pedro 1977. Influence du climat sur le type de régulation saline du Lac Tchad: relations avec les modes de sedimentation lacustre. *Strasbourg Sci. Géol. Bull.* 30: 33-49.

Carmouze, J.P., G. Fotius & C. Lévêque 1978. Influence qualitative des macrophytes sur la régulation hydrochimique du lac Tchad. *Cah. ORSTOM, Sér. Hydrobiol.* 12 65-69.

Carmouze, J.P., G. Pedro. & J. Berrier 1977. Sur la nature des smectites de néoformation du lac Tchad et leur distribution spatiale en fonction des conditions hydrochimiques. *C.R. Acad. Sc. Paris* 284: 615-618.

Carmouze, J.P., J.R. Durand & C.L. Lévêque (eds.) 1983. Lake Chad: Ecology and productivity of a shallow tropical ecosystem. *Monographiae Biologicae* 53. The Hague: Junk.

Chouret, A. 1977. *La persistance des effets de la sécheresse sur le lac Tchad. Contribution à la connaissance du bassin tchadien.* Centre de N'djamena: ORSTOM.

Gac, J.Y. 1981. Géochimie du bassin du lac Tchad: bilan de l'alteration de l'erosion et de la sedimentation. *Travaux et documents ORSTOM* 123.

Grove, A.T. 1978. Geographical introduction to the Sahel. *Geogr. J.* 144: 407-415.

Grove, A.T. & A. Warren 1968. Quaternary landforms and climate on the south side of the Sahara, *Geogr. J.* 127: 187-204.

L'évêque, C. 1979. Biological productivity of Lake Chad. *Réunion Trav. Limnol. afr. Nairobi.*

Maglione, G. 1974. Géochimie des évaporites et silicates néoformes en milieu continental confiné. Les depressions interdunaires du Tchad, Afrique. Thèse doct ès-sc. Paris: ORSTOM.

Pedro, G., J.P. Carmouze & B. Vetde 1978. Peloidal nontronite formation in recent sediments of the lake Chad. *Chemical Geology* 23: 139-149.

Roche, M.A. 1975. Geochemistry and the natural ionic and isotopic tracing; two complementary ways to study the natural salinity regime of the hydrological system of Lake Chad. *Journ. of Hydrology* 26: 153-172.

Roche, M.A. 1977. Lake Chad: a subdesertic terminal basin with fresh waters, In D.C.

Greer (ed.) *Desertic terminal lakes, Logan.* Utah State University.

Roche, M.A. 1980. Tracage natural salin et isotopique des eaux du système hydrologique du lac Tchad. Thèse Doctorat, Université de Paris VI. *Travaux et documents ORSTOM* 117.

Touchebeuf, P. 1969. *Monographie hydrologique du lac Tchad* ORSTOM (Vol. 3).

76

J.RZÓSKA†
†*Deceased 31st December 1984*

The water quality and hydrobiology of the Niger

4.1 WATER CHARACTERISTICS

4.1.1 *Introduction and sources of information*

Along its course of 4200 km the chemistry of Niger water bears the stamp of the physical characteristics of the regions from which it is derived. In the source areas of the Guinean hills rainfall is seasonally abundant, soils are lateritic and strongly leached, and erosion is dominant though slow; further downstream on the Sahelian plains are sedimentary basins where evaporation of the floodwaters diminishes discharge; on the Niger's course south two floods, one of local and the other of distant origin, carry different types of water.

Studies of water quality have mainly been confined to two areas, the Middle Niger and the vicinity of the Kainji Dam in Nigeria. In the former area, investigations were made by French scientists in the 1930s at a biological station first located at Diafarabé and later transferred to Mopti. Measurements in the Kainji area began much later, in 1965, when the construction of the Kainji Dam had already begun. The main features of the transition from river to lake are described in a collection of papers (Imevbore & Adegoke 1975) presented at a symposium held at the University of Ife in June 1970. The only longitudinal study of the river, a rapid one, was made by Grove (1970, 1972; Figure 39) over a distance of 2700 km in the course of the British Hovercraft Expedition of 1969–70. The various sources of information are listed below by region and with the date of sampling, which is of greater significance than the year of publication of the results (Table 6).

4.1.2 *Water movement*

Even in standing water the medium does not remain still; it moves under the influence of winds, density differences and on riverine plains as a result of flooding. In rivers the current, the rate of flow, is a most important factor, dominating water temperatures, the dissolved and solid load as

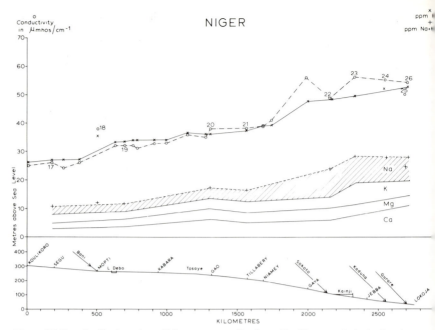

Figure 39. Longitudinal section of Niger water quality from Koulikoro to Lokoja showing the downstream increase in concentration of dissolved load.

well as biological features. Yet limnologists commonly neglect even to mention the strength of this current. Values do, however, appear in hydrological records, for hydrologists calculate discharges by measuring a river's cross-sectional area and velocity and multiplying the two together. An additional source of information is provided by the distinctive colour of particular water masses. A well-known example is that of the annual brown floodwaters of the Blue Nile. In 1967, for instance, this water coming from the Ethiopian plateau reached Khartoum on 15 June, joined the White Nile, and arrived on 27th June at Wadi Haifa, 1500 km downstream. This gives an average velocity of 2m sec^{-1}, the mid-stream velocity being somewhat greater than near the bed and banks.

The advance of the Black Flood of the Niger is also informative. It originates in the Guinean highlands in May to September and runs down to the Internal Delta where it subdivides, spreads over flood plains and fills shallow lakes (Figure 40). It spills over the sill at Tossaye near Bourem in October and reaches Kainji from November onwards, having covered 2000 km in 6 or 7 months, about 10 km per day on average or 0.1 m sec^{-1}. The White Flood is fed by rains falling on the eastern part of the Niger basin contributing to the south-flowing river. In the flood period water velocities are about 1 to 2 m sec^{-1}, around Gao, but vary considerably with the gradient and width of the channel as well as according to the

78

Table 6. Limnological studies in the Niger system according to regions and timing of the work.

1. Upper Middle Niger from Ségou, Mopti, Diafarabé to 'boucle' or great bend

1938	11 April to 31 December (Enikeff 1939); dissolved load, conductivity, flood influence
1952	Water temperatures, some chemical components, morphology of river valley, a full year; biological environment (Daget 1954, Blanc et al. 1955, and others)
1969	Water monitoring by FAO team for rice irrigation. October data compared by Grove (1972) with his own

2a. Lower Niger: Pre-impoundment investigations at Kainji

1965	July to September (39 days); team work on most aspects of Niger, based at Shagunu station (White 1965)
1965-66	Monthly sampling at same sites as above (Imevbore 1970c); limnochemistry of Niger, some tributaries and adjacent waters
1965-67	Number of studies on chemistry, microbiology, some botanical and zoological remarks (Visser 1970)
1966-68	Pre-impoundment studies on chemical and microbiological vertical features, sediment particle-size, swamp soils (Imevbore & Bakare 1974)
1966	Stratification of microbial organisms and their functions; also chemical effects (Imevbore & Visser 1969)
1966	Chemical and microbial effects of leaf decomposition (Visser & Imevbore 1969)

2b. Lower Niger: Post-impoundment investigations at Kainji

1969-71	Mainly fish fauna, but also influence of flood regime (Lelek 1973)
1970-71	Thermal stratification, transparency oxygen, pH at the two ends of the Kainji lake, and annual succession of rotifers (Donner & Adeniji 1977)
1971-72	Primary production, seasonal changes in temperature and oxygen stratification (Karlman 1973)
1971-72	Transparency, thermics, oxygen from 23 stations at 6-weekly intervals (Adeniji 1975)
1971-72	The role of suspended solids on the chemistry was studied at that time (Imevbore & Adeniji 1977)

Review articles on construction, morphology and prospects of the future or completed Kainji reservoir; e.g. Visser (1973), Imevbore (1969, 1970a), El-Zarka (1973), and other notes

3. Tributaries

| 1954-56 | Sokoto river, hydrology thermics, floodwaters, plankton (Holden & Green 1960) |
| | Other tributaries – Benue, Bani – are treated under Niger studies |

4. Longitudinal survey of some water characteristics

| 1969 | October-November: 26 sites on 2700 kilometer stretch of the Niger, from Ségou to near confluence with the Benue (Grove 1972: Figure 1) |

This is the only study which, though compressed into a few weeks of fieldwork, treats the river as an entity and was not confined by political boundaries. It also includes longitudinal sampling and analysis of the Senegal river and, at the other end, some analyses from the Benue which has its sources in the Cameroun plateau; also comments on the tributaries of Lake Chad that issue from the same plateau but flow east.

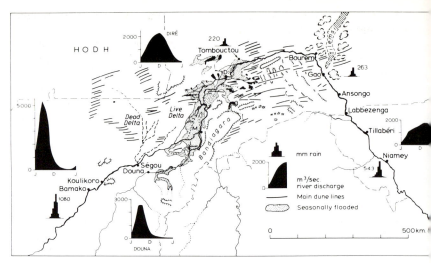

Figure 40. Changing discharge of the Niger as it flows round the great northward loop with the flood peak being retarded in the Central or Inland delta from September at Douna to January at Niamey. J: Jenne; M: Mopti, D: Diré.

discharge. Velocities in the Kainji reservoir are low, the water mass in the reservoir changing only 3 or 4 times in the course of a year. Karlman (1973) was able to trace the advance of a particular water mass with a characteristic turbidity from the head of the reservoir over a distance of 130 km. It took 71 days over the journey, moving with an average speed of 1.83 km day^{-1} or 0.02 m sec^{-1}.

4.1.3 *Water temperature and evaporation*

Water temperatures are influenced by the air with which it is in contact and by evaporation from the surface. In the Diafarabé region of the Middle Niger mid-stream temperatures rise from 20–21°C in December/January to 28–31°C in the hot season. Pre-impoundment temperatures at Kainji ranged from 16 to 32°C. After the reservoir was

Table 7. Water temperatures of Kainji reservoir, 1970 (Donner & Adeniji 1977).

		Temperature (°C)	
	Depth (m)	January	April-May
Northern entry of Niger River	1	23.9	31.2
	10-12	22.0	30.9
Southern part near dam	1	24.7	30.1
	20-30	23.0	28.0

80

filled a series of vertical measurements were made in 1970–71 by Donner & Adeniji (1977) Table 7.

In 1971–72 thermal stratification became apparent in the reservoir (Karlman 1973). Circulation during the months of January and February, under the influence of the Harmattan, was followed by the establishment of a thermocline which gradually deepened vertically, leading to deoxygenation of the hypolimnion.

Annual evaporation from the Kainji Dam has been estimated at about 2000 mm. In the Sahel region losses from water surfaces as high as 2600 mm largely account for the diminution in discharge of the Niger as it floods wide areas in traversing the inland delta.

4.1.4 *Transparency and turbidity*

Daget (1954) and Blanc et al. (1955) give Secchi disc readings for the Middle Niger of 0.6 to 0.9 m; shallow standing waters in the area are less transparent on account of wind stirring up bottom mud. Karlman (1973) gives transparency values in Kainji in 1971–72, which indicate seasonal variation from 0.3 m to 2 m. Generally speaking, water transparency is low in the lake when floodwater raises its level in September and October; by January when the reservoir is at its maximum level, Secchi disc readings reach over 2 m and the water continues to remain clear for several months (Imevbore & Adeniji 1977, Donner & Adeniji 1977).

4.1.5 *Water chemistry*

The flow of the upper Niger is derived largely from an area of about 100,000 km^2 of Guinea and the north-western corner of Ivory Coast. The source areas at about 700 m are mainly on granitised, pre-Cambrian crystalline rocks.

The electrical conductivity of Niger water was measured on various occasions between April and October 1938 at Banankoro, 15 km above Ségou (Enikeff 1939). The discharge of the river that year happened to be close to the median value of 45×10^9 m^3. Other values were obtained at

Table 8. Some chemical components of Niger water at Ségou (Grove 1972).

	pH	Ca^{2+}	Mg^{2+}	Na^+	K^+	Cl^-	HCO_3^-
FAO 15.7.1969	6.9	3.0	0.4	2.8	2.3	0.0	19
(mg/l) 15.8.1969	7.2	3.0	0.5	2.5	1.6	0.0	21
15.9.1969	7.2	2.2	0.6	1.8	1.3	0.0	19
Averages (meq/l)		0.14	0.04	0.10	0.04	–	0.32
Grove 26.10.1969							
mg/l	7.2	2.4	1.0	1.4	1.5	<1	13
meq/l		0.12	0.08	0.06	0.04	<0.03	0.21

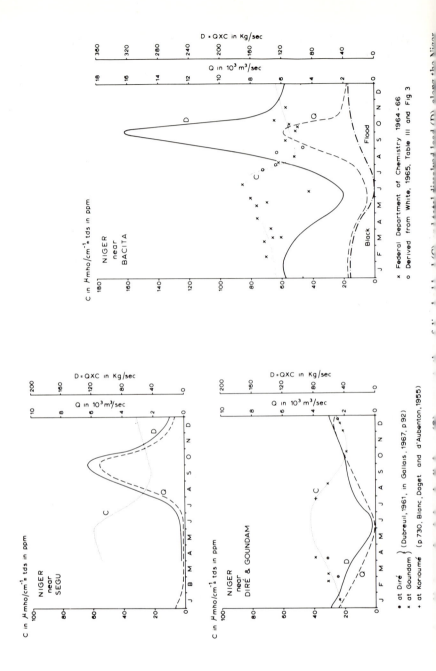

× Federal Department of Chemistry 1964 - 66
o Derived from White, 1965, Table III and Fig 3

• at Diré ⎫
× at Goundam ⎬ (Dubreuil, 1961, in Gallais, 1967, p 92)
+ at Korioumé (p 730, Blanc, Daget and d'Aubenton, 1955)

82

Ségou in 1969 by the FAO and a sample was collected there the same year by Grove (1972) Table 8.

When these values are taken together, the seasonal variation in discharges and dissolved load of the Niger above the inland delta can be plotted as in Figure 41. The mean dissolved load transported past Ségou would appear to be about 35 kg sec^{-1} or a total for the year of 1.2×10^6t.

A short distance downstream of Ségou a barrage at Markala (Sansanding) maintains the river upstream at a height at which it will flow along channels following an old distributary system of the Niger to irrigate cotton and rice. The quality of Niger water at Ségou differs markedly from that of Blue Nile water used for irrigation in the Sudan. Niger water is much more dilute and is likely to leach away soluble plant nutrients, whereas Nile water is an important contributor of nutrients to Gezira soils.

Downstream of Sansanding, between the Macina and the Bani confluence at Mopti, some 40% of the Niger's discharge overflows the left bank. The Bani more than restores the discharge below the Mopti confluence, bringing in water with a slightly higher conductivity and at Lake Debo half the left bank spillage is returned to the mainstream by the Marigot de Diaka (Figure 28).

Below Lake Debo the Niger enters a region of swamps, old dunes and lakes near Niafounké. In its passage through this region the river overflows its banks extensively, and the flood peak is thereby flattened and retarded, reaching Diré in December. Measurements of the conductivity of Niger water at Diré and nearby at Goundam were made on several occasions between August 1959 and April 1960 (Dubreuil 1961). The values have been plotted on Figure 41, plus an additional value from Korioumé for 26th July 1964 (Blanc et al. 1955).

The total mean annual discharge of the river near the lower end of the delta at Diré is about 4×10^{10} m^3 and total dissolved load carried in a year 1.2×10^6t; both figures are very similar to those for Ségou. Effectively, a volume of water about equal to the annual discharge of the Bani, including its dissolved solids, is removed from the Niger each year in its passage through the Inland Delta. Presumably some salts are taken up by vegetation and others are involved in clay synthesis or accumulate on the

Table 9. Bani water at Mopti (Grove 1972).

	pH	Ca^{2+}	Mg^{2+}	Na$^+$	K$^+$	Cl$^-$	HCO$_3^-$
FAO 15 7.1969	7.2	3.4	1.0	1.8	3.0	0 0	23
(mg/l) 15.8.1969	7 1	3.2	1.2	3.2	2.7	0.7	21
15.9 1969	6.9	2.6	0.8	2.5	1.6	0.0	22
Averages (meq/l)		0.15	0.08	0.11	0.06	–	0.36
Grove 29.10.1969							
mg/l	6.7	3.4	1.4	1.6	1.4	<1	17.8
meq/l		0.17	0.11	0.07	0.04	<0.03	0.29

floors of temporary lakes. Some part may be carried away as dust by the wind when the lakes dry out.

Below Diré the Niger tributaries come together and from Kabara, the port of Tombouctou, to the sill at Tossaye the river flows ENE along a straight course in a single channel parallel to linear dunes on either side. The water chemistry scarcely changes along this reach. Below Tillabéry the Makrou, Alibori and Sota enter the Niger on the right bank and the Sokoto draining much of north-west Nigeria enters on the left. Below the Sokoto confluence at Lafiagu the sodium content of the water was 4.9ppm compared with 1.9ppm at Tillabéry in early November 1969. Analyses of Sokoto water in 1956 (Holden & Green 1960) showed the total dissolved solids rising from about 66 ppm on 1st October to 131ppm on 10th December.

Below the Sokoto confluence, 30 km south-east of Yelwa, the Niger enters the Kainji artificial lake. Here the water quality was studied by White et al. (1965), Imevbore & Visser (1969) and Visser (1973) in the period 1965–1967 before the dam was closed in 1968.

Before the construction of the dam at Kainji the river flow was at a minimum and conductivity at a maximum in early June. Local rains then depressed the conductivity in July from about 80 to 50 μmhos and the river discharge increased to reach a maximum of about 6000 m^3 sec^{-1} towards the end of September. By November, when the discharge had diminished to 2000 m^3 sec^{-1}, most of the flow was derived from rain that had fallen in the Guinean highlands far upstream of the Inland Delta and this 'Black Flood' provided most of the river's discharge until May (Figure 42). It had a conductivity exceeding 55 μmhos. The total discharge of dissolved salts through the Kainji-Jebba reach of the Niger was probably and still is of the order of 4$\times$10^{6}t annually.

The Kaduna river draining the Jos Plateau is a highly seasonal river with its mean annual discharge of 25$\times$10^9 m^3 mainly concentrated in July to September. In these three months, before the construction of the Kainji dam, its discharge was similar to that of the Niger at Kainji. According to measurements made at Wuya on the lower Kaduna river in 1963 (Bennett 1967) the conductivity of the floodwaters was between 30 and 40 μmhos. In mid-November 1969, conductivity in the Kaduna just above its confluence with the Niger was 55 μmhos; later into the dry season Bennett obtained values exceeding 70 μmhos. In the course of an average year the Kaduna probably contributes about 1 million tonnes of dissolved solids to the mainstream; other rivers entering the Niger between the Kaduna

Table 10. Niger water at Kainji (pre-impoundment).

	Ca^{2+}	Mg^{2+}	Na$^+$	K$^+$	Cl$^-$	Si
mg/l	6.3	2.68	4.19	5.16	0.3	12
meq/l	0.31	0.22	0.18	0.13	0.01	–

84

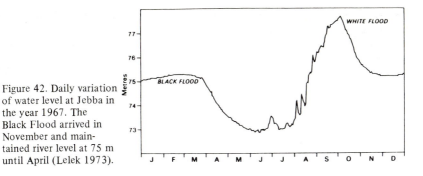

Figure 42. Daily variation of water level at Jebba in the year 1967. The Black Flood arrived in November and maintained river level at 75 m until April (Lelek 1973).

confluence and Lokoja probably bring in a further half million tonnes giving a total of about 5.5×10^6t.

The mean annual discharge of the Benue at Lokoja is about 3200 $m^3 sec^{-1}$ (NEDECO 1959) as compared with the Niger's 3000 $m^3 sec^{-1}$. The main sources of the Benue river lie on the highlands of western Cameroun Republic where there are extensive areas of volcanic lava. Grove (1972) took the mean dissolved load to be about 40ppm giving an annual transport of some 4.5×10^6t, somewhat less than that of the Niger, and a combined carriage in solution past Lokoja of about 10^7t annually.

4.1.6 Oxygen

Running waters seldom exhibit thermal stratification, which in lakes often causes oxygen gradients. Not many observations exist of the oxygen content of Niger water in free-flow but Imevbore (1970c) has given some results of monthly samples at Kainji from December 1965 to December 1966 ranging from 6.2–10.4 mgl^{-1}. Vertical distribution of oxygen on 21 June 1966 was 0.9–1.2 $meql^{-1}$ (7.2–9.6 mgl^{-1}) at a depth of 1 to 6 m (Imevbore & Visser 1969). As turbulence diminishes in quiet stretches of water and particularly behind dams, so temperature stratification becomes more marked and deoxygenation at depth more apparent.

A set of vertical measurements of temperature, oxygen, pH and ionic concentration was given by Donner & Adeniji (1977) for the Kainji reservoir in 1970–71, shortly after it filled. Two stations separated by about 12 km were sampled each month, one at the entry of the Niger into the reservoir-lake, the other at the southern end near the dam. Measurements made down to 10 m in the north and to 33 m near the dam gave ranges of water temperature as in Table 11.

The initial fragmentary observations on oxygen depletion were later confirmed ·and extended by Karlman (1973), an FAO scientist, in his study of 'Pelagic primary production in Kainji Lake' (Figure 43); additional information is given by Henderson (1973) and Adeniji (1975). Total mixing occurs in December-January, under the influence of the

Table 11. Water temperature ranges in Kainji lake.

Kainji lake	North	South
Surface	23.9-31.2°C	24.7-30.1°C
8-10 m	22.0-30.9°C	
30 m		23.0-29.4°C

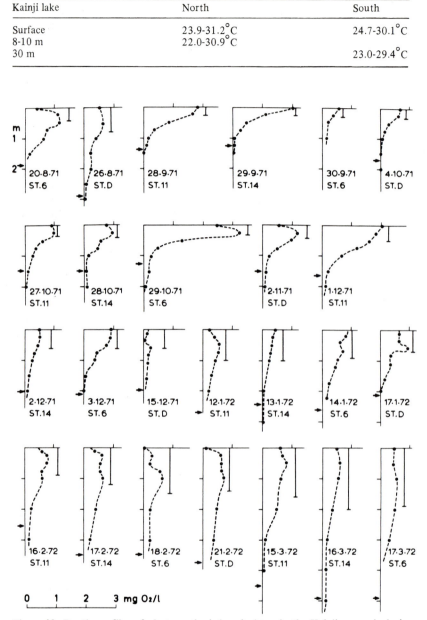

Figure 43. Depth profiles of photosynthesis by plankton in the Kainji reservoir during 1971-72. Also shown are the measurements of light penetration: Secchi disc transparency (⊥) and the depth of 1 % transmission for the most penetrating (green) light (→); from Karlman (1973).

Harmattan, followed by increasing temperatures of the upper waters and the formation of a thermocline between 7 and 10 m. Oxygen below the thermocline is depleted and reaches zero after 5 weeks; hydrogen sulphide is then produced in the bottom water until the arrival of the White Flood.

4.1.7 *Nutrient status*

The Niger and the majority of the other rivers in West Africa are more dilute than the Nile and other rivers in East Africa. The contrast is probably caused by the extensive area of young volcanic rocks in the east and the greater relief and erosion there. In West Africa, soils and weathered layer are ancient and strongly leached and much of the material carried in solution by rivers is probably derived from the rain.

In the river waters, silica is usually abundant but can be depleted by the growth of diatoms. The situation as regards phosphorus is not clear; Imevbore (1970c) comments that the general nutrient poverty at Kainji includes soluble reactive phosphate and nitrate, but his measurements included some very high concentrations and abrupt fluctuations of phosphate values as well as silica.

In the flurry of activity associated with the construction of Kainji, Karlman (1973) three years after the dam closure in 1971–72, found that the development of a thermocline in the months from June to October prevented nutrients incorporated in sinking phytoplankton organisms from being fully recirculated, the hypolimnion acting as a nutrient trap. It is this nutrient-rich water that is drawn through the turbines and discharged downstream. The surface water of Kainji lake has a relatively low nutrient content especially in the latter half of the year and primary production of phytoplankton is low in comparison with most other tropical waters in spite of favourable radiation inputs and warm water.

Some estimates of phytoplankton density, in terms of chlorophyll *a* concentrations of 0.3–0.63 mgl^{-1}, given by Imevbore & Visser (1969) are very high. They may have been miscalculated, for much lower values, less than 0.012 mgl^{-1}, are given by Imevbore (1970c).

4.2 HYDROBIOLOGY

4.2.1 *Sources and approach*

Information about the hydrobiology of the Niger comes mainly from two regions, the Niger bend in Mali and the Kainji region. Daget (1954) and Blanc et al. (1955) have described the various habitats of plants and animals in the Middle Niger and over its enormous flood plains. Notes on the distribution of vegetation and animals, including fishes, are given by Daget and it is clear that the littoral zone, the shore, is the most important centre of biological activity. At Kainji pre-impoundment studies edited by White (1965) and Visser (1970) are collective works, including the shore flora, fishes, algae, zooplankton, fish parasites and vectors of disease. Later contributions have been written by those associated with the Kainji Lake Research Institute. It is strange to note that almost no cross-references exist between the research results of the Middle Niger and the work at Kainji. The studies described here predate Durand & Lévêque (1981); the identification keys in their two volumes will greatly assist future ecological work in this region and, indeed, in much of Africa.

The basis of biological phenomenon in water is primary production by plants, from algae or higher plants, both emergent and in the water. Plants are the primary producers; on them depends the web of animal food chains leading up to fishes and other vertebrates. The pattern of biological production is followed here in outlining the results of various investigations on the Niger.

4.2.2 *Algae*

A study by Couté and Rousselin (1975) is the only substantial taxonomic contribution to the algae of the Niger system. Their collections were made in December–January 1970/71 from a 'pirogue' using a plankton net and following the 'boucle' of the Niger from Ansongo to Mopti. Along this 800 km stretch, the river and its vicinity were sampled with attention being paid to the bottom, shores, floodplains and detrital deposits as well as to the mainstream river water. Their paper contains a long systematic list of species with remarks on the conditions in which they were found. The distribution of species amongst the algal groups is summarised in Table 12.

The significant feature of the algal composition is the dominance of desmids (*Desmidiales*), the presence and abundance of which are shown in Table 13. These remarkable and elaborate cells are illustrated in Figure

Table 12. The numerical distribution of algal taxa amongst the systematic groups.

	Total	%	New taxa	Tropical	African
Cyanophyceae	16	5	–	1	–
Chrysophyceae	4	1.2	–	–	–
Euglenophyceae	14	4.4	–	2	–
Xanthophyceae	7	2.2	1	–	2
Dinophyceae	4	1.2	–	–	–
Rhodophyceae	1	0.3	–	–	–
Chlorophyceae					
Volvocales	1	0.3	–	–	–
Chlorococcales	31	9.8	–	–	–
Chaetophorales	2	0.6	–	1	–
Oedogoniales	8	2.4	1	–	2
Zygnematales	4	1.2	–	–	–
Desmidiales	222	70.7	28	63	39
	314	100	30	67	43

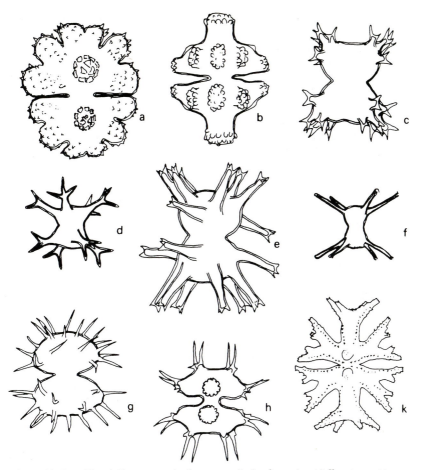

Figure 44. Desmids: a) *Euastrum spinulosum* var. *lindae* fo. *major*; b) *Euastrum attenuatum* var. *splendens*; c) *Staurastrum libeltii* fo. *major*; d) *Staurastrum brachiatum*; e) *Staurastrum tohopekaligense* var. *trifurcatum*; f) *Staurastrum heimii* fo. *minor*; g) *Staurastrum setigerum*; h) *Xanthidium calcarato-aculeatum* var. *sudanese*; k) *Micrasterias mahubuleshwarensis* var. *comperei*.

44. The authors attribute the richness of the water in desmids to its 'acid reaction', mentioning also the presence of iron oxide in the soils. A similar proliferation of desmids, it might be noted, also occurs in Lake Ambadi on the Ghazal tributary of the upper White Nile where Grönblad et al. (1958) and Grönblad (1962) recorded over 200 species and forms as compared with only 24 forms in the Nile elsewhere. The lake is slightly acid with a pH of around 6 and the Ghazal comes from laterite soils of the Congo (Zaire) divide (Rzoska 1974).

The generic analysis in Table 13 shows a preponderance of forms in

Table 13. The numerical strength of algal taxa amongst the systematic groups (from Couté & Rousselin 1975).

	Total	New forms	Tropical	African
Gonatozygon	5	2	1	2
Closterium	23	–	–	–
Pleurotaenium	3	–	2	–
Triplastrum	1	–	1	–
Euastrum	19	3	6	2
Micrasterias	19	2	10	2
Actinotaenium	1	1	–	–
Cosmarium	55	7	11	11
Xanthidium	10	2	4	3
Arthrodesmus	3	–	2	1
Staurodesmus	19	–	3	1
Staurastrum	55	11	21	17
Sphaerozosma	2	–	–	–
Tilingia	1	–	–	–
Desmidium	2	–	–	–
Phymatodocis	1	–	1	–
Hyalotheca	3	–	1	–
	222	28	63	39

Cosmarium and *Staurastrum* (examples in Figure 44) which make up half the 222 recorded forms; 4 other genera are also strongly represented. Over half of all the desmids found are new forms.

J.W. Eaton conducted algal investigations in the team led by White (1965) over a period of 39 days in July–September 1965 before the damming of the river at Kainji. Besides the phytoplankton, the algal assemblages of the various bottom substrata — rocks, sand, mud and epiphyton – were sampled and evaluated. The most significant result was the estimate that mud-surface ('epipelic') algae were at that time 50 times as numerous as algae in the plankton; one should note that many fishes in the Niger are mud-feeders. Counts of phytoplankton can vary markedly according to discharge and degree of dilution. Chlorophyll *a* fluctuated from 11 to below 1 $\mu g l^{-1}$ in the plankton but on bottom substrata 80,000 cells per cm^2 and 1.15 $\mu g cm^{-2}$ were measured. These results show the importance of the algal production of shore and bottom and the small contribution of phytoplankton at least in this particular case to the general framework of organic production.

A post-impoundment study at Kainji by Karlman (1973, 1982) and a much less detailed one by Imevbore & Boszormenyi (1975) deal specifically with production by phytoplankton. Karlman was seconded by the Finnish government to the United Nations (agencies of FAO and UNDP) at the special request of the Nigerian government to assist in the exploration of biological resources of the Niger river. Before starting his biological studies he examined the morphology of the Kainji reservoir as it existed at this time (November 1970–September 1973) presenting a variety of habitats which

Karlman took into account when selecting sites for research. He also made measurements of incident solar radiation, its transmission into the water, transparency, oxygen stratification, distribution and temperature. These were necessary for his method of assessing primary production by means of a series of light and dark bottles, incubated with the existing phytoplankton and held horizontally below the surface for four hours. Photosynthesis was assessed by measuring oxygen production and calculating carbon production. The measurements were repeated at intervals of four to six weeks.

Most important, of course, is the transmission of light through the water delimiting a productive euphotic zone which, according to Karlman, varies in depth through the year. Taking the transmission of 1% as a minimum, he concluded that although photosynthesis may occur as much as 12 m below the surface, 4 m is normally the limit and commonly 2 m.

Estimates of daily (gross) production per unit area ranged from 220 mg O_2 m^{-2} day^{-1} in September 1972 to 4563 mg O_2 m^{-2} day^{-1} in July 1971, and annual production from 745 to 854 g O_2 m^{-2} at his four stations. Expressed in carbon the annual production was 279–320 g C m^{-2}. The average daily production of carbon was 822 mg C m^{-2} day^{-1}. Below 12 m no living phytoplankton was found. The main agents of photosynthesis were blue-green algae, with *Microcystis* as the dominant form. Species of *Melosira* (diatom) and *Peridinium* (dinoflagellate) were also important.

On the basis of this phytoplankton production Karlman estimated the potential fish catch at about 15 kgha^{-1}y^{-1} assuming that 20% of the total production of fish is harvestable and mainly composed of secondary and tertiary consumers. He listed the primary production of a number of tropical water bodies and pointed out that Kainji appears well down towards the bottom. There have been occasions when phytoplankton density has been high but they occurred in the early history of the lake. In the first 18 months of its existence for instance, Imevbore (1971) noted several surface blooms that included species of *Anabaena, Microcystis, Volvox* and *Eudorina*. Later, Adeniji (1973, 1975, 1977) gave instances of cell densities in excess of 10,000 cells ml^{-1}. Some very high estimations of chlorophyll *a* concentration have also been cited but there is some doubt as to whether the calculations were correct.

4.2.3 *Shore and water vegetation*

Along most of its length the floodplains of the Niger have not been greatly modified by man's interference. The river is fringed by a rich vegetation which also spreads over the shores of the floodplain lagoons. On the most extensive floodplain of all, between Mopti and Tombouctou, 20,000 to 30,000 km^2 are flooded annually for a period varying from two to six months whereas in the late dry season only 4000 km^2 are under water. Frolow (1940) studied several of the large lagoons; Daget (1954) and Blanc et al. (1955) have made broader surveys of the ecology of the

Table 14. Aquatic and marsh plants recorded from the Kainji area before impoundment (from Cook 1965). (Identification keys in Durand & Lévêque, 1981).

WATER PLANTS

1. Plants encrusting on rocks periodically inundated by swiftly flowing water
   Tristicha trifara (Bory) Spreng.

2. Plants with vegetative parts completely adapted to a submerged existence; exposure to air even for short periods results in death
   a) Generative organs completely submerged
      Ceratophyllum demersum L.
      Naias affinis Rendle
      Nitella furcata (Rox. ex Bruz.) Ag.em.
   b) Generative organs above the water surface
      Ottelia ulvifolia (Planch.) Walp.
      Utricularia gibba L. subsp. *exoleta* (R.Br.) P.Taylor
      Utricularia inflexa Forsk. var. *stellaris* (L.fil.) P.Taylor

3. Plants with vegetative parts coming into contact with air
   a) Free-floating
      Ceratopteris cornuta (P.Beauv.) Lepr.
      Lemna perpusilla Torr.
      Pistia stratiotes L.
      Salvinia nymphellula Desv.
   b) Bottom rooted
      Ceratopteris cornuta (P.Beau.) Lepr.
      Eichhornia diversifolia (Vahl) Urb.
      Limnophila sp.
      Nymphaea lotus L.
      N.maculata Schum. and Thonn.
      N.micrantha Guill. and Perr.
      N.rufescens Guill. and Perr.

EMERGENT AND REEDSWAMP PLANTS
   Aeschynomene afraspera J.Léonard
   A.nilotica Taub.
   Alloteropsis cf. *paniculata* Stapf.
   Alternanthera nodiflora R.Br.
   Commelina sp. 481
   Cyperus cf. *denudatus* L.
   C.digitatus Roxb.
   C.procerus Rottb.
   Echinochloa pyramidalis Hitchc. & Chase
   Eclipta prostrata (L.) L.
   Eragrostis sp. 380
   Fuirena cf. *umbellata* Rottb.
   Hydrophila sp.
   Ipomoea aquatica Forsk.
   I.ascarifolia (Desr.) Roem. & Schultes
   Ludwigia erecta (L.) Hara
   L.hyssopifolia (Don.) Exell
   L.leptocarpa (Nutt.) Hara
   L.octovalvis (Jacq.) Raven subsp. *brevisepala* (Bren.) Raven
   L.stenorraphe (Bren.) Hara subsp. *stenorraphe*
   L.stolonifera (Guill. & Perr.) Raven
   Marsilea diffusa Lepr. ex A.Br.
   Mimosa pigra L.
   Mitragyna inermis (Willd.) O.Ktze

Table 14 (cont.).

Oldenlandia sp.
Oryza perennis Moench.
Polygonum salicifolium Brouss. ex Willd.
P.senegaleuse Meisn.
Pycreus cf. *odoratus* Urb.
P.tremulus C.B.Cl.
Scirpus sp. 323
Sphenoclea zeylanica Gaertn.
Striga bilabiata (Thunb.) O.Ktze subsp. *rowlandii* (Engl.) Hepper
Striga Forbesii Benth.
Tristemma littorale Benth.

region. The most productive areas biologically occur where emergent shore vegetation mingles with the water plants themselves. Welcomme (1979) underlines the importance of such swamp areas for fisheries in the Niger bend and elsewhere in his book *The fisheries ecology of floodplain rivers.*

Besides providing a rich environment for invertebrates and shoals of fish, the riverine fringe is the scene of great bacterial activity, decomposing dead vegetation recirculating protein deposits and plant debris. This part of the productivity of swampy flats was given special attention in the Kainji region before impoundment of the reservoir. Reid (1967), Visser & Imevbore (1969) and Imevbore & Bakare (1974) contributed greatly to the understanding of the functioning of food chains in the fringe swamps.

The plants constituting the rich vegetation of the Kainji floodplain were listed by Cook (1965) in his contribution to White's pre-impoundment studies (Table 14). A striking absentee from the list is papyrus (*Cyperus papyrus*). This has never been found in West African waters though it is present in Lake Chad and, of course, the Nile, though not in its former headwaters draining the rift valley of southern Ethiopia nor in the Lake Turkana catchment. Absent also at present from Kainji are the free-floating invaders of East African waters *Eichhornia* and *Salvinia* which are such nuisances in the Congo (Zaire) and the Nile.

Conflicts arise between different interests when development of the Niger and other West African rivers is being considered because of the differing perceptions of hydrologists, engineers and ecologists of the value of floodplain and swamp environments. Engineers want to the regulate and straighten river courses. Ecologists are more concerned with preserving the habitat because of its inherent interest and also for the purposes to which the local people traditionally put it. Such controversy arose at Kainji. Before the closure of the dam 40% of the riverine plains were occupied by swamps and sandbanks covered with forest and shrubs. The woodland was partly cleared, unnecessarily as it turned out. After closure of the dam and with the rise and fall of lake level through 10 m

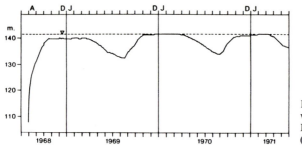

Figure 45. Seasonal variation in the level of Kainji Lake 1968-71 (Lelek 1973).

Table 15. Invertebrate Fauna of Kainji Lake (from Bidwell & Clarke 1977). The commonest species are marked with an asterisk.

ZOOPLANKTON

Protozoa –
Rhizopoda
   Arcella vulgaris Ehrenberg
   Al.vulgaris var. *penardi*
   Difflugia acuminata Ehrenberg
   D.corona Wallich
   Cyclopyxis impressa Daday

Coelenterata –
Hydrozoa
   Limnocnida victoriae Gunther

Platyhelminthes –
Turbellaria
   Rhabdocoelids
Rotifera
   *Brachionus calyciflorus Pallas
   *B.caudatus Barrois and Daday
   B.diversicornis (Daday)
   *B.falcatus Zacharias
   B.quadridentatus Hermann
   B.patulus O.F.Muller
   Dipleuchlanis propatula (Gosse)
   Euchlanis dilitata Ehrenberg
   *Keratella tropica (Apstein)
   *K.cochlearis Gosse
   Platyias quadricornis (Ehrenberg)
   Manfredium eudactylotum Gosse
   Epiphanes macroura Barrois and
      Daday
   Lecane bulla (Gosse)
   L.curvicornis (Murray)
   L.leontina (Turner)
   L.ungulata (Gosse)
   L.papuana Murray
   *Trichocerca similis Wierzejski
   *T.chattoni de Beauchamp
   *T.cylindrica Imhof
   Asplanchna brightwelli Gosse

   A.priodonta Gosse
   *Synchaeta pectinata Ehrenberg
   *Polyarthra dolicoptera (Idelson)
   Monommata sp.
   *Hexarthra mira (Hudson)
   Horaella brehmi Donner
   *Filinia longiseta (Ehrenberg)
   *F.(Tetramastix) opoliensis
      (Zacharias)
   Conochilus unicornis Rousselet
   Conochiloides dossuarius Hudson
   *Collotheca pelagica (Rousselet)
   Rotaria neptunia Ehrenberg

Crustacea –
Cladocera
   *Daphanosoma excisum Sars
   *Ceriodaphnia cornuta Sars
   C.dubia (= affinis) Richard
   *Moina micrura (= dubia) Kurz
   Simocephalus serrulatus (Koch)
   S.latirostris Stingelin
   *Bosmina longirostris (O.F.Muller)
   *B.meridionalis Sars
   *Bosminopsis deitersi Richard
   Macrothrix triserialis Brady
   Ilyocryptus spinifer Herrick
   Alona diaphana (= davidi) King
   A.holdeni Green
   A.eximia Kiser
   A.pulchella King
   A.rectangula Sars
   Biapertura verrucosa (Sars)
   B.karua (King)
   Kurzia longirostris (Daday)
   Euryalona occidentalis Sars
   Camptocercus rectirostris Schodler
   Oxyurella singalensis (Daday)
   Leydigia ciliata Gauthier
   Monospilus dispar Sars

94

Table 15 (cont.).

Conchostraca
 Cyclestheria hislopi (Baird)
Copepoda
 **Tropodiaptomus banforans* Kiefer
 **Mesocyclops leuckarti* (Claus)
 **Thermocyclops neglectus neglectus*
   Kiefer
 **T.emini* (Mrázek)
 Eucyclops serrulatus (Fischer)
 Ectocyclops phaleratus rubescens
   Brady
 Microcyclops pseudo-anceps Green
 Ergasilus kandti van Douwe
 E. sp.
Ostracoda
 Stenocypris malcolmsoni (Brady)
 Acocypris capillata Vávra

Arachnida –
Acari
 Unionicola (S S) *dentifera* Cook
 Neumania sp.

Insecta –
Diptera
 Chaeoborus anomalus Edwards
 C. sp.

BENTHOS AND PERIPHYTES

Protozoa –
 Anthophysa sp.
Porifera
 1 unidentified species

Annelida –
Oligochaeta
 **Aulophorus* spp.
 **Dero* spp.
 **Nais* spp.
 1 unidentified species
Hirudinea
 *Several species, all unidentified

Crustacea –
Cladocera
 Ilyocryptus spinifer Herrick
 Alona spp.
 **Cyclestheria hislopi* Baird
Ostracoda
 *Several species, all unidentified
Decapoda
 **Caridina nilotica*
 Macrobrachium spp.

Arachnida –
Acari
 *Several species, all unidentified

Insecta –
Ephemeroptera
 Centroptilum sp.
 Cloeon perkinsi Barnard
 **C.aeneum* Barnard
 **Baetis bellus* Barnard
 Procloeon smaeleni Lestage
 **Caenis ?cibaria* Eaton
 Afronurus ugandanus Kimmins
 Notonurus njalensis Kimmins
 Eatonica schoutedeni Navas
 **Euthraulus curtus* Kimmins
 **E.bugandensis* Kimmins
 **Povilla adusta* Navas
 Tricorythus varicauda Pictus
Plecoptera
 Neoperla bredoana Navas
Odonata
 **Brachythemis leucosticta*
   Burmeister
 **Brachythemis lacustris* Kirby
 Bradinopyga strachani Kirby
 Acanthagyna manderica Grünberg
 Acanthagyna vesiculata Karsch
 Chalcostephia flavifrons Kirby
 Crocothemis erythaca Brullé
 **Macromia africana* Selys
 Macromia ?pseudafricana Pinhey
 **Pantala flavescens* Fabricius
 **Palpopheura lucia lucia* Drury
 Tholymis fillarga Fabricius
 Trithemis annulata Palisot de Beauvois
 Sympetrum navasi Lacroix
 Urothemis edwardsi Selys
 Agriocnemis ?gerafica LeRoi (= *A.*
   ebnesi LeRoi)
 Agriocnemis exilis Selys
 Ceragrion sp.
 **Metacnemis robusta* Selys
 **Pseudagrion nubicum* Selys
 Pseudagrion sp.
Hemiptera
 Hydrometra spp.
 Mesovelia vittigera Horvath
 Mesovelia sp.
 Microvelia sp.
 **Limnogonus (Limnogonus)* sp.
 **Naboandelus* sp.
Corixidae
 **Micronecta* spp.
 **Anisops* spp.
 Enithares sp.
 Sigara sp.
Nepidae
 **Diplonychus* sp.

95

Table 15 (cont.).

Hydrocyrius sp.
Laccotrephes sp.
Lethocerus corfanus Mayr
Ranatra sp.
Trichoptera
  Hemileptocerus gregarius Ulmer
  Oecetis maculipennis Ulmer
  Parasetodes sudanensis Ulmer
  Pseudoleptocerus schoutedeni Navas
  Ecnomus dispar Kimmins
  Dipseudopsis capensis Walker
  Orthotrichia straelini Jacquemart
Hydropsychidae
  Aethaloptera dispar Brauer
  Cheumatopsyche copiosa Kimmins
  C.digitata Mosely
  Macronema capense var. *inscriptum*
    Walker
  Polymorphanisus sp.
  1 unidentified species
Lepidoptera
  *Schoenobiinae sp. (found in stems of
    aquatic plants)
Coleoptera
  Aulonogyrus sp.
  Dineutus africanus Ol.
  Bidessus spp.
  Cercyon spp.
  Noterus spp.
  Limnichus sp.
Dytiscidae
  Cybister sp.
  Eretes sticticus Linnaeus
  Eretes sp.
  Hyphydrus scriptus Fr.
  Hyphydrus spp.
  Hydracticus spp.
  Hydrocanthus spp.
  Hydroctopus spp.
  Hydrovatus sp.
  Laccophilus sp.
  Renotus deyrollei Sharp
  Renotus spp.
  Rhantus spp.
  Rhantacticus sp.
  Synchortus spp.
Diptera
Tipulidae
  Conosia irrorata Wiedemann
  Conosia angustissima Alexander
  Conosia minusculoides Alexander
  Clydonodozus fumicostatus Alexander
  Limonia spp.
  Toxorhina (Ceratocheilus) sp.
  Trentepohlia (Trentepohlia) spp.

Styringomyia sp.
Psychodidae
  1 unidentified species
Culicidae
  Chaoborus (Sayomyia) ceratopogones
    Theobald
  C.(Neochaoborus) anomalus Edwards
  Chaoborus sp.
Dixidae
  2 unidentified species
Simulidae
  Simulium damnosum
  Simulium spp.
Ceratopogonidae
  ?Artichopogon sp.
Chironomidae
  Ablabesmyia melaleuca Goetghebuer
  Ablabesmyia appendiculata Kieffer
  Clinotanypus maculatus Freeman
  Procladius maculosus Freeman
  Procladius sp. indet.
  Cricotopus sudanicus Freeman
  Cricotopus tricinctellus Goetghebuer
  Chironomus caffrarius Kieffer
  Chironomus calipterus Kieffer
  Chironomus formosipennis Kieffer
  Chironomus imicola Kieffer
  Dicrotendipes sudanicus Freeman
  Dicrotendipes sp.nov. near kribiicola
    Kieffer
  Dicrotendipes sp.nov. near ealae
    Freeman
  Dicrotendipes schoutedeni Goetghebuer
  Dicrotendipes sp. indet.
  Kiefferulus chloronotus Kieffer
  Nilodorum brevibucca Kieffer
  Nilodorum brevipalpis Kieffer
  Nilodorum rugosum Freen
  Cryptochironomus niligenus Kieffer
  Cryptochironomus nigrocorporis
    Freeman
  Cryptochironomus lindneri Freeman
  Cryptochironomus diceras Kieffer
  Gillotia trifida Freeman (=
    Chironomus (Cryptochironomus)
    trifidus Freeman)
  Microchironomus stilifer Freeman (=
    Cryptochironomus stilifer
    Freeman)
  Parachironomus dewulfianus
    Goetghebuer
  Parachironomus unicalcar Freeman
  Parachironomus sp.nov. near
    dewulfianus Goetghebuer
  ?Harnischia acutus Goetghebuer

Table 15 (cont.).

Harnischia curtilamellata Malloch (= *Chironomus (Cryptochironomus) nudiforceps* Kieffer)	Tabanidae
	2 unidentified species
Genus uncertain (near *Harnischia*) sp. nov.	Syrphidae
	Tubifera sp.

Harnischia curtilamellata Malloch (=
  Chironomus (Cryptochironomus)
  nudiforceps Kieffer)
Genus uncertain (near *Harnischia*) sp.
  nov.
Nilodosis fusca Kieffer
Stenochironomus spatuliger Kieffer
Polypedilum deletum Goetghebuer
Polypedilum fuscum Freeman
Polypedilum ?incoloripenne
  Goetghebuer
Polypedilum abyssiniae Kieffer
Polypedilum longicrus Kieffer
Polypedilum tridens Freeman
Polypedilum griseoguttatum Kieffer
Polypedilum fuscipenne Kieffer
Polypedilum declivis Kieffer
Polypedilum bifalcatum Kieffer
Polypedilum ?laterale Goetghebuer
Polypedilum kibatiense Goetghebuer
Polypedilum annulatum Freeman
Polypedilum bipustulatum Freeman
Polypedilum sp. indet.
Polypedilum sp.nov.
Pentapedilum vittatum Freeman
Pentapedilum wittei Freeman
Stictochironomus festivus festivus
  Kieffer
Stictochironomus puripennis Kieffer
Tanytarsus spadiceonotatus Freeman
Tanytarsus horni Goetghebuer (=
  Tanytarsus (Tanytarsus) nigrocinc-
  tus Freeman)
Cladotanytarsus pseudomancus
  Goetghebuer

Tabanidae
  2 unidentified species
Syrphidae
  Tubifera sp.

Mollusca —
Gastropoda
  Biomphalaria pfefferi Kraus
  Planorbis spp.
  Ancylus sp.
  Bulinus (Bulinus) truncatus rohlfsi
    Clessin
  Bulinus (Physopsis) globosus Morelet
  Bulinus sp.
  Cleopatra senegalensis
  Cleopatra bulimoides Oliver
  Gabbia sp.
  Lanistes ovum
  Viviparus (Bellamya) mweruensis
    Smith
  Viviparus (Bellamya) unicolor Oliver
Bivalvia
  Caelatura aegyptiaca Cailliaud
  Caelatura ?stanleyvillensis Pilsbury and
    Bequaert
  Caelatura ?mesafricana Pilsbury and
    Bequaert
  Caelatura sp.indet.
  Corbicula (Corbicula) radiata Philippi
  Etheria elliptica var. *tubifera* Sowerby
  Etheria sp.indet.
  Mutella dubia Gremlin
Ectoprocta
  1 unidentified species

(Figure 45) necessarily resulting from maintaining so far as possible a constant discharge through the turbines, both the ecology and usage of the lake margins have been greatly modified (Bidwell 1976; Imevbore 1971; Hall 1975). The spread of the grass *Echinochloa* is viewed with some alarm by Chachu (1979) though between Gao and Niamey the same grass is harvested for fodder and building material and is regarded as a useful asset by the local population (Bacalbasa 1971).

Downstream of Kainji, floodplains formerly watered annually by the rise in the river and capable of growing rice are now deprived of this natural irrigation except at the lowest levels. Although the dam traps sediment that was formerly carried down to the delta it is unlikely that problems will arise comparable with those that have afflicted the coastal margins of the Nile Delta, for the natural transport of sediment by the

Niger is much less than that which the steep slopes of western Ethiopia supply to the Blue Nile. And in any case the Benue, not the Niger above Kainji, has long been the chief source of sediment supply to the Niger Delta.

4.3 REFERENCES

Adeniji, H.A. 1973. Preliminary investigation into the composition and seasonal variation of the plankton in Kainji Lake, Nigeria, *Geophys. Monogr. Ser. (Am. Geophys. Union)* 17: 617–619.

Adeniji, H.A. 1975. Some aspects of the limnology and the fishery development of Kainji Lake, Nigeria. *Arch. Hydrobiol.* 75: 253–262.

Adeniji, H.A. 1977. Preliminary study of the silica content and diatom abundance in Kainji Lake, Nigeria. In H.L. Golterman (ed.), *Interactions between sediments and fresh water*. The Hague: Junk & Pudoc.

Bacalbasa-Dobrovici, N. 1971. The economic importance of the Burgu (*Echinochloa stagnina* P. Beauv) on the Middle Niger in the Niger Republic. *Hydrobiologia (Bucarest)* 12: 41–93.

Bennett, A.J. 1967. *A survey of river quality in Northern Nigeria, with particular reference to irrigation agriculture*. Samaru Miscellaneous Paper 17, Ahmadu Bello University, Zaria, Nigeria.

Bidwell, A. 1976. The effect of water level fluctuations on the biology of Lake Kainji, Nigeria. *Niger. Fld.* 41: 156–165.

Bidwell, A. & N.V. Clarke 1977. The invertebrate fauna of Lake Kainji Nigeria. *Niger. Fld.* 42: 104–110.

Blanc, M., J. Daget & F. d'Aubenton 1955. Recherches hydrobiologiques dans le bassin du Moyen Niger. *Bull. Inst. Francais d'Afr. Noire* (A) 17: 680–746.

Chachu, R.E.O. 1979. The vascular flora of Lake Kainji. In *Kainji Lake Research Institute*.

Cook, C.D.K. 1965. The aquatic and marsh plant communities of the reservoir site. In E. White (ed.), *The first scientific report of the Kainji Biological Research Team*. Univ. Liverpool.

Couté, A. & Rousselin 1975. Contribution à l'étude des algues d'eau douce du Moyen–Niger (Mali). *Bull. Mus. Nat. Hist. Nat. Paris, Ser. 3* 277: 73–175.

Daget, J. 1954. Les poissons du Niger supérieur. *Mém. Inst. Francais d'Afr. Noire* 36.

Donner, J. & H.A. Adeniji 1977. Eine Jahressukzession von Rotatorien aus dem Plankton des Kainji-Sees in Nigeria. *Int. Revue ges. Hydrobiol. Hydrogr.* 62: 109–132.

Dubreuil, P. 1961. Aménagement des lacs Télé et Faguibine. Etude hydroclimatique. *Sér. Hydro. ORSTOM*.

Durand, J.R. & C. Lévêque (eds.) 1981. *Flora et Fauna aquatique de l'Afrique Sahelo-Soudanienne* (2 vols.). Paris: ORSTOM.

El-Zarka, S.E.-D. 1973. Kainji Lake, Nigeria. *Geophys. Monogr. Ser. (Am. Geophys. Union)* 17: 197–219.

Enikeff, M.G. 1939. Le transport de sels dissous par le Niger en 1938. *C. Rend. Acad. Sci. (Paris)* 209: 229–321.

Frolow, W. 1940. Les lacs du Niger: Horo, Fati, Faguibine. *Bull. Ass. Géogr.* (128–129): 32–33.

Gallais, J. 1967. Le delta intérieur du Niger et ses bourdures. *Mém. et Documents, Centre de Recherches et Documentation Cartographiques et Géographiques, C.N.R.S.* Paris (Vol. 3).

Grönblad, R. 1962. Sudanese Desmids II. *Acta Bot. Fenn.* 63: 3–19.

Grönblad, R., G.A. Prowse, & A.M. Scott, 1958. Sudanese Desmids. *Acta Bot. Fenn.* 58.

Grove, A.T. 1970. Two rivers: the Senegal and the Niger. *Geogr. Mag.* 42: 362–367.

Grove, A.T. 1972. The dissolved and solid load carried by some West African rivers: Senegal, Niger, Benue and Shari. *J. Hydrol.* 16: 277–300.

Hall, J.B. 1975. The vascular flora of Lake Kainji and its shores. In A.M.A. Imevbore & O.S. Adegoke (eds.), *The Ecology of Lake Kainji*. Univ. Ife Press.

Henderson, F. 1973. Stratification and circulation in Lake Kainji *Geophys. Monogr. Ser. (Amer. Geophy. Union)* 17: 489–494.

Holden, M.J. & J. Green, 1960. The hydrology and plankton of the River Sokoto. *J. Anim. Ecol.* 29: 65–84.

Imevbore, A.M.A. 1969. Biological research at the Kainji Lake Basin, Nigeria. July 1965–Sept. 1966. In L.E. Obeng (ed.), *Man-made lakes: the Accra Symposium*. Ghana Univ. Press.

Imevbore, A.M.A. 1970a. Some general features of the Kainji Reservoir basin. In Visser, S.A. (ed.), *Kainji Lake studies; Ecology* (Vol. 1). Ibadan Univ. Press.

Imevbore, A.M.A. 1970b. The chemistry of the River Niger in the Kainji Reservoir Area. *Arch. Hydrobiol.* 67: 412–31.

Imevbore, A.M.A. 1971. Floating vegetation of Lake Kainji, Nigeria. *Nature. Lond.* 230: 599–600.

Imevbore, A.M.A. & O.S. Adegoke (eds.) 1975. *The Ecology of Lake Kainji*. Univ. Ife Press.

Imevbore, A.M.A. & F. Adeniji, 1977. Contribution on the role of suspended solids to the chemistry of Lake Kainji. In H.L. Golterman (ed.) *Interactions between sediments and fresh water. The Hague: Junk & Pudoc.*

Imevbore, A.M.A. & O. Bakare, 1974. A pre-impoundment study of swamps in the Kainji Lake basin. *Afr. J. trop. Hydrobiol. Fish.* 3: 79–93.

Imevbore, A.M.A. & Z. Boszormenyi, 1975. Preliminary measurements of photosynthetic productivity in Lake Kainji. In A.M.A. Imevbore & O.S. Adegoke (eds.), *The Ecology of Lake Kainji*. Univ. of Ife Press.

Imevbore, A.M.A. & S.A. Visser, 1969. A study of microbiological and chemical stratification of the Niger River within the future Kainji Lake area. In L.E. Obeng (ed.), *Man-made Lakes, The Accra Symposium*. Ghana Univ. Press., Accra.

Karlman, S.G. 1973. *Kainji Lake Research Project, Nigeria. Pelagic primary production in Kainji Lake*. F.A.O. Rome FL: DP/NIR/24 Tech. Rep. 3.

Karlman, S.G. 1982. The annual flood regime as a regulatory mechanism for phytoplankton production in Kainji Lake, Nigeria. *Hydrobiologia* 86: 93–97.

Lelek, A. 1973. Sequence of changes in fish populations of the new tropical man-made lake, Kainji, Nigeria, West Africa. *Arch. Hydrobiol.* 71: 381–420.

Livingstone, D.A. 1963. Chemical composition of lakes and rivers. *Data of Geochemistry* (Sixth Edition), U.S.G.S. Prof. Paper 440–G.

NEDECO 1959. *River studies and recommendations on improvement of Niger and Benue.* Amsterdam: North Holland Publ. Co.

Reid, W. 1967. *Fish and fisheries of Northern Nigeria*. N. Nigeria: Min. Agric.

Rzóska, J. 1974. The Upper Nile swamps, a tropical wetland study. *Freshwat. Biol.* 4: 1–30.

Visser, S.A. (ed.) 1970. *Kainji Lake studies; Ecology* (Vol 1.). Ibadan Univ. Press.

Visser, S.A. 1973. Pre-impoundment features of the Kainji area, and their possible influence on the ecology of the newly formed lake. *Geophys. Monogr. Ser. (Amer. Geophys. Union)* 17: 590-595.

Visser, S.A. & A.M.A. Imevbore 1969. Physical and chemical changes observed in mixture of dried or burnt *Detarium microcarpum* leaves decomposing in the presence of clay or sand and under different water régimes. In L.E. Obeng (ed.), *Man-made Lakes, the Accra Symposium*. Accra: Ghana Univ. Press.

Welcomme, R.L. 1979. *Fisheries ecology of floodplain rivers*. London: Longman.

White, E. (ed.) 1965. *The first scientific report of the Kainji Biological Research Team.* Univ. Liverpool.

R.H.LOWE-McCONNELL
Streatwick, Streat near Hassocks, Sussex

The biology of the river systems with particular reference to the fishes

5.1 INTRODUCTION AND SOURCES OF INFORMATION

The Niger River system lies in the 'sudanian' fish fauna province which stretches right across Africa south of the Sahara from the Atlantic to the Red Sea (Figure 46). As we have already seen (Chapter 2) the present Niger is made up of two rivers, differing both historically and in physical characteristics. It has been suspected that tributaries of the Upper Niger formed part of the Senegal system in Pliocene and Early Pleistocene times but it is not easy to prove this from the geological evidence and it seems unlikely that dunes formed as late as the arid period of Late Pleistocene would have been responsible for diverting the river eastward into the basin south of Tombouctou. In fact the Upper Niger has probably followed a course comparable to that of the present day for much of the Pleistocene, though its flow was interrupted during dry periods, notably in the last hyper-arid period between 20000 and 12000 years ago. The Upper Niger, originating in hilly country has a rapidly flowing section, then spreads out over the immense Middle Niger floodplain at high water, shrinking into a narrow (6 m wide) river at low water, leaving shallow lakes, pools and swamps isolated on the floodplain at the height of the dry season. Below this central 'Inland Delta' the Lower Niger flows between well-defined banks. It receives several large tributaries, such as the Sokoto River from the northeast, entering the Niger c. 1200 km downriver from Tombouctou, and the Benue River entering another c. 600 km further downstream. Between these two tributaries the hydroelectric barrage at Kainji, closed in 1968, has led to the formation of a 1280 km^2 lake, lying from 9° 50′ to 10° 57′ N, in northern Nigeria.

The close proximity and possibly former drainage of the Upper Niger basin to the Senegal River accounts for the similarity of their fish faunas. The Benue River, which drains country far to the east of the Main Niger, is at times of highwater in contact with the Mayo Kebbi and is then connected with the Lake Chad drainage, which also has many of the same fish species. As we have already seen (Chapter 2) the Megachad of Late Quaternary times was immense, and there were at some time, it is not

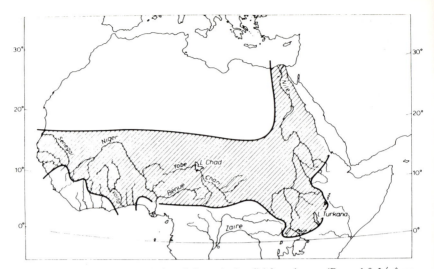

Figure 46. The geographical limits of the sudanian fishfaunal zone (Durand & Lévêque 1981).

clear just when but probably between 12000 and 5000 years ago, channels linking the Nile and Chad systems. It is therefore not surprising to find so many fish species distributed right across Africa from the Atlantic to the Nile, forming this vast 'sudanian' ichthyological province. The term was used by Daget & Durand (1981) in its French form soudanienne, and anglicized by Beadle (1974) and Lowe-McConnell (1975) as soudanian; it is referred to as the 'Nilo-Sudan Province' by Roberts (1975) and the 'Occidental Province' by Poll (1973) and Greenwood (1976).

Of the 190 species now listed from the Niger-Chad system (Table 16) c. 70 species (37%) also occur in the Nile, and most of these also occur in other major West African rivers (the Volta, Senegal, Gambia). It may be noted that the Black Volta may once have been a tributary of the Niger between Gao and Niamey. Some of these species are considered to be subspecifically distinct, but the view is taken here that it is premature to consider subspecific distinctions. The Niger does have some endemic species (at least 24), but their closest relatives are in the Nile, suggesting derivation from a common ancestor (Greenwood 1976). Much of this fish fauna seems to be a persistent segment of an ancient African fish fauna once more widely distributed north of latitude 10°S. Most of these savanna-river fishes move up and down river for long distances and out onto the floodplain at highwater, behaviour which helps to explain their wide distribution, particularly when the geomorphological changes and climatic history of the region are considered. The lakes of the region are shallow with swampy margins, populated with riverine fishes and, unlike the Great Lakes of East Africa, with few endemic species.

In these vast West African river systems, with their complex biotas,

102

faunal diversity appears to reflect the available biotopes, rather than increasing from source to mouth of the river. For the smaller neighbouring rivers, Mérona (1981) and Sydenham (1977) have looked at the longitudinal zonation of the biota and fish species in the Bandama river of the Ivory Coast and Ogun River in Nigeria respectively.

We know more about the flora and fauna of the Niger system, and the ecology of the fishes, than for any other African river. The foundations were laid by Daget in his numerous studies of the fishes and their ecology in the Upper Niger and the Middle Niger Inland Delta (Daget 1950, 1952, 1954, 1957a, b, 1959, 1962, 1964, 1967, 1975 and other papers). Identification keys to the fishes of the Sahelo-Sudanian region are given by Daget & Durand (1981); earlier publications with useful keys include Daget (1954) on the fishes of the Upper Niger and Blache et al. (1964) on the fishes of the Lake Chad and adjacent Mayo Kebbi basins. In Nigeria, Holden (1963) studied the fish populations in the dry season pools of the Sokoto tributary river. The building of the hydroelectric barrage at Kainji stimulated pre- and post-impoundment studies in this area (see references given below, p. 115). Kainji Lake has much the same flora and fauna as the Volta Lake in Ghana, formed by the closure of the Volta Dam in 1964, and the information on how the Volta riverine communities changed to lacustrine ones (notably papers by Petr and Reynolds) was very relevant for the development of the lacustrine fish communities at Lake Kainji.

Below the Kainji barrage, its effects on the river fisheries have been studied by Otobo (1978) and Sagua (1978). Scoopnet fisheries along the lower river were looked at by Awachie & Walson (1978). Boeseman (1963) had made an annotated checklist of Niger Delta fishes, and Pillay (1967) reported on the estuarine fisheries of West Africa generally; marine fish families were prominent in the delta and estuaries. The Benue River fish and fisheries had been studied by Daget & Stauch (1963), Stauch (1966), Daget (1966), who figured the fishing gear, and later Reid & Syndenham (1979) prepared an annotated list of fishes in the Lower Benue in Nigeria.

In wet periods, the Benue is linked to the Lake Chad basin via the Mayo Kebbi. Fisheries from these basins were described by Blache & Miton (1962), the fishes by Blache et al. (1964). In the northern, more lacustrine basin of Chad in Nigeria, A.J. Hopson (1972a) and J. Hopson (1972b) studied some species, while fishes migrating up the Chari and Logone Rivers from the southern basin of Lake Chad were investigated by Durand and other French scientists. The establishment of the ORSTOM laboratory in 1964 for intensive limnological studies on Lake Chad, (see p. 125) as the French contribution to the International Biological Programme, led to an outpouring of ecological information from this area (see papers listed on pages 125–126).

The severe drought in the Sahelian region in 1972–74 stimulated a special meeting convened by the Food and Agricultural Organisation of the United Nations (FAO) at Bamako, Mali, to study its consequences (FAO 1975). The drought also stimulated the production of two volumes

Table 16. Families of fishes represented in the Niger system. These families or their closest relatives also occur, as indicated, in the sea (M), Neotropical (N) or Oriental (O) regions, or are endemic to Africa (E).

Family	Also occur	Approximate number in Niger system Genera	Species	Principal genera mentioned in text
Dasyatidae	M	1	1	*Dasyatis,* stringray, Benue
Lepidosirenidae	N	1	1 or 2	*Protopterus,* lungfish
Polypteridae	E	2	4	*Polypterus*
Clupeidae	M	4	4	*Pellonula, Cynothrissa,* sardines
Osteoglossidae	N, O	1	1	*Heterotis*
Pantodontidae	E	1	1	*Pantodon,* aquarium fish
Notopteridae	O	2	2	*Notopterus, Xenomystus*
Mormyridae	E	10	24	Numerous; electric organs
Gymnarchidae	E	1	1	*Gymnarchus*
Ostariophysi				
Kneriidae	E	1	1	*Cromeria,* small species
Phractolaemidae	E	1	1	*Phractolaemus,* small, swamps
Cyprinidae	O	6	39	*Barbus, Labeo*
Hepsetidae	E	1	1	*Hepsetus*
Characidae	N	4	16	*Alestes, Brycinus, Hydrocynus*
Citharinidae	E	2	4	*Citharinus*
Distichodontidae	E	6	10	*Distichodus*
Catfishes				
Bagridae	O	4	11	*Bagrus, Chrysichthys, Auchenoglanis*
Clariidae	O	2	6-7	*Clarias, Heterobranchus*
Schilbeidae	O	4	5	*Schilbe, Eutropius, Physalia*
Mochokidae	E	5	20	*Synodontis*
Malapteruridae	E	1	1	*Malapterurus,* electric catfish
Ariidae	M	1	1	*Arius*
Cyprinodontidae	N, O	5	11	Small toothed carps, 'mosquito fish'
Syngnathidae	M	1	?	Pipefish, coastal
Perciform fishes				
Centropomidae	M	1	1	*Lates,* Nile or Niger perch
Nandidae	O, N	1	1	Small species
Cichlidae	N, O	8	13	*Tilapia, Sarotherodon, Oreochromis*
Gobiidae	M	1	2	Small, estuarine
Channidae	O	1	1	*Channa (Ophiocephalus)*
Anabantidae	O	1	1	*Ctenopoma,* small species
Mastacembelidae	O	1	1	*Mastacembelus*
Synbranchidae	M	1	1	Small, swamps
Soleidae	M	1	1	*Dagetichthys,* Benue
Tetraodontidae	M	1	1	*Tetraodon,* puffer fish, small

dealing with the aquatic flora and fauna of the Sahelo-Sudanienne region by French scientists (Durand & Lévêque 1981). Chapters by various specialists give identification keys to the plants, algae, the numerous groups of aquatic invertebrates (including suborders or families of the larvae and nymphs of many aquatic insect groups), fishes, amphibia, reptiles, aquatic birds and floodplain mammals, thus providing invaluable assistance for further ecological work in the sudanian zone, and indeed for much of Africa.

5.2 THE COMPOSITION OF THE FISH FAUNAS

The Niger system has a rich fish fauna made up of over 190 species representing 34 families of fishes (Table 16, Figure 47). These include (1) relict species of archaic groups with a wide distribution outside Africa, such as lungfish and other species which are also found in South America and Australia, and osteoglossids in South America and Southeast Asia; (2) species of families found only in the Neotropical region outside Africa, indicating that they have descended from stock present in Gondwanaland before Africa and South America drifted apart (though no genera occur in both continents); (3) species of families found in tropical Asia (Oriental region) as well as Africa; about eight genera occur in both these regions, indicating that these faunal exchanges have been relatively recent (presumably through the Middle East to the Nile, as discussed by Banister & Clarke (1977); (4) endemic families of fishes that have evolved within the African landmass; these are mostly rather primitive, archaic families, many with accessory respiratory organs enabling them to breathe atmospheric air, devices which have great survival value when waters dry up and become deoxygenated; and (5) immigrants from the sea, members of marine fish families from which freshwater species have evolved, and euryhaline marine fishes moving upriver from the estuarine regions seasonally or sporadically.

In West Africa Daget distinguished between the 'soudanian' fishes living in the waters of the extensive savanna-covered floodplains ('formes soudaniennes'), and species in the forest streams ('formes guinéennes'), where there may be two floods a year and there are less extreme variations in environment between the wet and dry seasons. These guinean species are often small, unlikely to undertake long movements. Ecological replacement species, with representatives in the two zones, are well marked in certain groups (among the clariids, anabantids, cyprinodonts). The changing river patterns and long-term climatic variations, discussed in earlier chapters, have resulted in sudanian and guinean species occupying the same river systems, separated neither by watersheds nor waterfall barriers. Ecological conditions, particularly the presence or absence of forest, appear to account for their coexistence. Guinean species are found in the upper reaches of Niger tributaries and in the higher more dissected country in Guinea, but in the

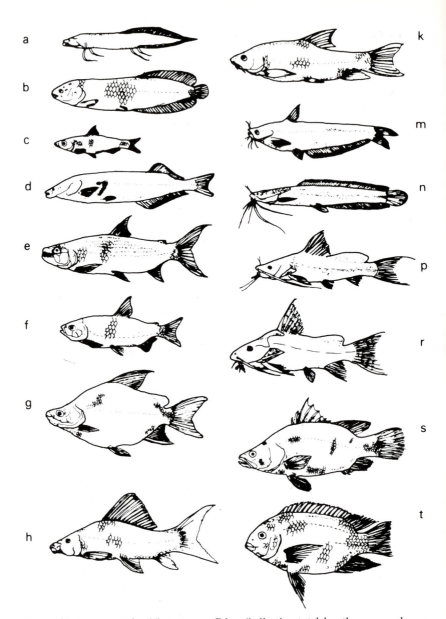

Figure 47. Representative Niger system fishes (indicating total lengths commonly encountered): a) *Protopterus,* lungfish (100 cm, Dipnoi); b) *Heterotis* (50 cm, Osteoglossidae); c) *Pellonula* (14 cm, Clupeidae); d) *Mormyrops* (100 cm, Mormyridae); e) *Hydrocynus* (50 cm, Characidae); f) *Alestes* (30 cm, Characidae); g) *Citharinus* (70 cm, Citharinidae); h) *Labeo* (50 cm, Cyprinidae); k) *Barbus* (50 cm, Cyprinidae); m) *Schilbe* (20 cm, Schilbeidae); n) *Clarias* (50 cm, Clariidae); p) *Bagrus* (100 cm, Bagridae); r) *Synodontis* (50 cm, Mochokidae); s) *Lates*, Nile Perch (100 cm, Centropomidae); t) *Sarotherodon,* tilapia (30 cm, Cichlidae).

106

Ivory Coast the situation is reversed as they occur in the lower reaches of the rivers which are here forested, while the open country to the north carries sudanian species. This suggests that the overriding factor is now shade or food from the forest (though finding refuges in arid periods will have influenced these distributions initially). Ecological differences are being discovered, for example the sudanian species *Alestes nurse* has an annual spawning season in the floods, producing far more eggs than the comparable guinean species *Alestes imberi*, which produces small batches of eggs throughout the year (Paugy, 1979-80a, b). The Dahomey Gap, where a savanna belt comes right to the coast (see Figures 3 and 46), breaks the guinean zone into eastern and western sectors showing some faunal differences.

Table 16 shows clearly that the fish families are very unequally represented. The Niger fauna, like that of most rivers, is dominated by ostariophysan fishes (carps, minnows, catfishes). Over 60% of the Niger fauna is of ostariophysans. These include about 40 cyprinid species, over 30 species of characoid fishes (in the families Hepsetidae, Characidae, Distichodontidae, Citharinidae), and about 47 catfish species (Bagridae, Clariidae, Schilbeidae, Mochokidae, Malapteruridae, Amphiliidae, Ariidae). The cyprinids are mostly small kinds of *Barbus*, omnivorous little fishes living in schools, but two kinds of mud-sucking *Labeo*, *L. senegalensis* in sandy places, *L. coubie* in more open water and rockier areas, are important food fishes. The characoids include the deep-bodied mud-feeding *Citharinus* and the macrophyte-feeding *Distichodus*, and among the characids several large *Alestes* species such as the omnivorous *Alestes baremose* and *A. dentex*, and the highly piscivorous *Hydrocynus* species; all these grow large and are important in the fisheries. The catfishes also include many large species important in commercial catches: *Bagrus, Chrysichthys, Clarias, Heterobranchus, Clarotes, Eutropius* and *Schilbe*, about twenty species of mochokid semi-armoured catfishes of the genus *Synodontis, Arius gigas* – the only catfish with marine affinities. *Malapterurus electricus* has, as its name implies, electric organs used to stun its prey. The amphiliids are small stream-dwelling species.

Next to the ostariophysans, the endemic family Mormyridae is best represented. Mormyrids also have electric organs, but their weak electric signals seem to be used to sense their way around their environment – they are nocturnal fishes – for social communication, and possibly to detect predators and food, rather than for defensive purposes. *Gymnarchus niloticus* is also a mormyroid fish which emits weak electric signals; growing to over a metre long this is a favourite food fish. Several of the mormyrids grow large, and they are important in the river fisheries.

The Cichlidae, so important in the faunas and fisheries of most of the Great Lakes of Africa, are but poorly represented in the Niger (c. 13 species), as in other riverine faunas. Nor are there any endemic species in Lake Chad; in this paucity of cichlids compared with the other Great Lakes the Chad fauna resembles that of Lakes Albert and Turkana

(Rudolf) in East Africa which also have nilotic (sudanian) faunas. Although Lake Chad has been a much deeper lake at times in the past (see p. 33), the drying out in arid periods must have helped mitigate against the evolution of endemic cichlids. But more likely the presence of a fully-differentiated riverine fauna, with numerous large piscivores (fisheaters) has had an even greater role in this.

Two other large-growing important food fishes are the osteoglossid *Heterotis niloticus*, a detritus-eater which lives in shallow waters and does well in ponds, and the large piscivorous centropomid *Lates niloticus* (Nile or Niger perch), the top of the food webs. Unlike fisheries in the Great Lakes of eastern Africa which are based mainly on cichlids (or in the case of Lake Tanganyika on small clupeid sardines and their centropomid *Lates* predators), these sudanian river and Niger floodplain fisheries take over fifty different types of fish in their catches, fishes of all sizes and shapes, which complicates net legislation.

Many of the ostariophysan fishes, and some of the others migrate up rivers to spawn and disperse over the floodplains to feed at highwater. River fishing tends to be much more seasonal than lake fishing. The main catches are often of migrating fishes, and many young-of-the-year are caught as these return to the rivers from the floodplain when the waters subside.

5.3 ECOLOGICAL STUDIES

5.3.1 *The seasonal cycle in floodplain rivers*

In this sudanian subtropical zone, with its short wet season, flooding is very seasonal, inundating vast stretches of country – an estimated 90,000 km^2 south of Lake Chad and 30,000 km^2 in the Inland Niger Delta and its affluents in wet years – and the whole biology of the fishes and other organisms is geared to changes in the water level.

The seasonal cycle of events is summarized in Figure 48. As the rains follow the overhead sun, they occur in the summer months when days are long and temperatures high. But in most rivers peak floods occur well after the rains have started – in some cases even several months after the local rains have ceased; the delay depends on the origin of the main floodwater and how long it takes to travel downstream. The River Niger in Nigeria above the Kainji dam has two floods a year, a White Flood due to local rains and a later Black Flood due to water from the Inland Delta moving downstream, having deposited its silt en route. The time of peak flood varies slightly from year to year.

As the floods spread over the savanna the enrichment of the water by nutrient salts from the breakdown of organic matter, decaying vegetation and the droppings of animals which grazed on the floodplain, leads to an explosive growth of bacteria, algae and zooplankton. This in turn supports a rich fauna of aquatic insects and other invertebrates. Aquatic

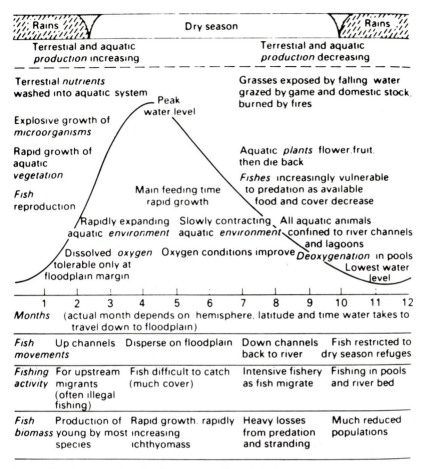

Figure 48. The seasonal cycle of events in a floodplain river.

vegetation grows rapidly, flowering and fruiting when the water is high, dying back as the water recedes and the plain dries out. Terrestrial insects are also more abundant in the rainy season, and many are blown onto the water surface, forming another source of fish food.

There is thus an extremely rapid increase in the production and biomass of all kinds of fish foods of both plant and animal origin, and the fishes grow very fast and lay down fat stores at highwater time. The abundant aquatic vegetation also provides cover for the young fish from the many piscivores. As the water rises, the rapid decomposition leads to temporarily deoxygenated conditions except at the margins of the floodplain. But these shallow waters soon become oxygenated, and the fishes disperse to cover the whole floodplain.

In the dry season fishes are confined either to the bed of the river, where

109

the flow may be broken into pools, or trapped in small lakes, ponds and swamps isolated on the floodplain. These waters often become deoxygenated, and only fishes which can withstand such conditions can survive through the dry season. Many have some form of aerial respiration: this occurs in the lungfish, *Protopterus*, the polypterids, *Heterotis*, the notopterids and *Gymnarchus*, all rather primitive fishes (Table 16), and in the ostariophysan clariid catfishes (which have an arborescent organ above the gills), also in the anabantids, probably in the African *Mastacembelus* (as in the Asian ones), and the synbranchid. Many waters dry up, and adaptations to cope with this include aestivation in a mucous cocoon in the lungfish *Protopterus*, burrowing in damp mud in *Clarias* (which can also wriggle from pool to pool through damp vegetation), and drought-resistant eggs in certain small cyprinodonts (*Nothobranchius*).

Many species make longitudinal migrations up and down river and lateral movements out onto the flooded plain as the water rises. Some species move upriver as the waters recede, presumably to find dry season habitats. Many kinds of ostariophysan fishes and mormyrids make long movements. The majority of these ostariophysans are 'total spawners', in which all the eggs ripen at one time of year. These spawn early in the flood season, either in the main river (as between the coffer dams at Kainji, see below) or in the channels as the fish move out onto the floodplain, or on the floodplain. Related species may behave differently in this respect, for example *Hydrocynus brevis* spawns on the Niger floodplain, *H. forskahlii* in the river channels (Dansoko et al. 1976). In the small forest streams some small species spawn early in the rains, as reported for *Barbus liberiensis* (Payne 1975), while other *Barbus* have dry season spawning peaks (Lowe-McConnell 1979), as do small clupeids which have planktonic larvae (Reynolds 1974).

The eggs generally hatch fast (most within about two days). The juvenile fishes are thus born at a time when food is plentiful and plant cover protects them from predators. Species which guard their young (cichlids and some catfishes) produce small batches of young at frequent intervals, and often have their first batch before the floods, or at the start of the rising water. Certain zooplankton-feeders (such as the small clupeids and cyprinids) are unusual in spawning at low water; zooplankton develops best in stillwater pools as the water is subsiding.

The highwater season is the main feeding, growing and fattening season for nearly all the floodplain fishes. The abundance of food is then greatest, though young fishes are more readily available to piscivores as the floods subside and the fish are concentrated into channels to run back to the rivers, and as the habitats shrink. A wider spectrum of foods is available at high water; aquatic insects, crustaceans, molluscs, fruits and seeds of aquatic and terrestrial plants, also terrestrial insects blown onto the water surface. Fish growth is very rapid and fat stores are laid down which last the fish through the ensuing dry season, when feeding levels are reduced.

110

As nutrients are depleted and the aquatic environment shrinks, the vegetation dies back and fishes move back to the main river. The large piscivores move down first and lurk around the mouths of the channels down which the very abundant young-of-the-year pass to the main river. This is also the main fishing season for other piscivores, such as birds (which also produce their young mainly in the rains) and man. Many fishes remain stranded in the rapidly diminishing pools and fish mortality is particularly high at this time. Mortality must also be very high in the dry season refuges, where there are few types of food and cover available. Many floodplain fishes feed on different items at high and low water; *Alestes* for example feed on insects and seeds at highwater, but have to survive, losing weight, on plankton at low water (Daget 1952).

Changes in growth rates, particularly growth checks at low water, which is also the cooler season, are recorded on skeletal structures (scales and bones). This enables ages and growth rates to be determined for most floodplain species. Many floodplain fishes mature by the next flood season or the one after that, in contrast with fish in large lakes which may take three or more years to mature (and much longer in temperate regions).

Fishes in seasonal rivers may make very long migrations between feeding and spawning grounds. Few tagging experiments have been carried out in Africa, but in Nigeria a tagged *Alestes baremose* was recaptured 80 km up the Yobe River from where it was marked near Lake Chad (Hopson, personal communication). Daget (1952) concluded that *Brycinus leuciscus* (*Alestes leuciscus*) in the Middle Niger move 50 km to the edge of the floodplain, and may move 125-400 km upriver to the Markala barrage as the delta waters subside; they are followed by piscivorous fishes as they move upstream. The various species move up or downstream in a definite order, often moving only at a certain time of day, or at a particular water level, or, in some species, only at particular phases of the moon, as for example *Brycinus leuciscus* do when arriving in successive shoals at Markala barrage, but *Brycinus nurse* does not show such lunar-related movements; such differences in behaviour must help to keep species distinct.

Lakes form when rivers are dammed, either by natural causes or by man for hydroelectric power or irrigation. In contrast with the Rift Valley lakes of eastern Africa, Tanganyika and Malawi, the lakes of West Africa are shallow and recent geologically, having come into existence as a result of increased river discharges after the Late Pleistocene arid period or as a result of damming. The creation of large man-made lakes in West Africa – among them Kainji on the Niger, following that of the much larger (8800 km^2) Volta Lake on the Volta River in Ghana in 1964, and also by Lake Kossou on the Bandama river in the Ivory Coast – has stimulated much research on the ecology of the riverine fishes and how riverine communities change into lacustrine ones. In general lacustrine conditions present opportunities for plankton-feeding fishes to thrive, but difficulties to the many bottom-feeding riverine fishes which cannot change their

111

feeding habits, because the bottom waters of the new lakes become deoxygenated from the decomposition of the flooded vegetation. For the many riverine species which migrate upstream to spawn, lacustrine conditions may interfere with breeding, leading to a decline in populations of fish which cannot adapt. The effects of such changes are discussed further below.

5.3.2 Biotopes of the Upper and Middle Niger

Daget laid the foundations of our knowledge of Niger fishes by his many studies in the Upper Niger, with its mountain streams, and in the Middle Niger with its Inland Delta, a huge floodplain inundated seasonally. By October this country is a vast sheet of water; before the Sahelian drought it was estimated to cover 17,000–30,000 km^2 including land flooded along affluent rivers; by May the main river was reduced to 6 m wide. Fish traps in the Markala barrage above the Inland Delta, completed in 1946 for controlling irrigation for rice and grain crops, provided information about fish movements.

In the Inland Delta the water cools to a mean minimum surface temperature of 20°C in January, compared with 28.5–29.2°C in May–October, which affects fish growth; surface temperatures show over 2°C diurnal fluctuation (Daget 1954). Chemically the Middle Niger water (pH 6–7) is not very rich in nutrients and throughout the area the inundation zones are the main feeding grounds for the fishes. At Mopti on the Inland Delta Daget (1957a) divided the biological year into low water of 111 days (25 March to 13 July), rising water 41 days (14 July to 23 August), highwater 150 days (24 August to 20 January), and subsiding waters 64 days (21 January to 24 March).

The numerous biotopes in the Upper and Middle Niger have been described by Daget (1954, 1957), comparable ones from the Chad basin by Blache et al. (1964). The riverine faunas vary with the type of bottom and speed of flow. Rocky stretches with rapids and falls occur mainly in the upper reaches. In the Niger tributaries these shelter a specialized fauna, species such as the cyprinid *Garra waterloti* which has an adhesive buccal disc, and the elongated cichlid *Gobiocichla wonderi*, the only endemic cichlid in the Niger. In the lower stretches sandy bottoms are most frequent. Moving sands are rather barren, though frequented by small cyprinids (*Barbus*). Where the sand is hard it is colonized with filamentous algae and has a rich fauna of aquatic insects, particularly Odonata, Hemiptera and Coleoptera. Such places are the habitats of the rather omnivorous *Alestes* and *Brycinus* species and the predatory *Hydrocynus*, also of *Barbus, Labeo senegalensis* and tilapia (especially *Sarotherodon galilaeus*) which take algae off the sand surface. Where the bottom is muddy, with aquatic plants growing in the shallows, live many kinds of mormyrids and *Synodontis* catfishes, the tilapias *Oreochromis niloticus* and *Tilapia zillii* and the osteoglossid *Heterotis* where there is detritus, with large nocturnal catfishes *Auchenoglanis* and *Heterobranchus*.

112

The residual pools, depressions where the water is deeper than over the most of the flood plain, have clay or mud bottoms. The turbidity varies very much from pool to pool, being affected by the fishes present – *Clarias* stir up the bottom water. Many pools lack vegetation, others have *Nymphaea* (water lilies) and *Utricularia* (bladderwort) and many other kinds of widely distributed aquatic plants. Fish faunas vary very much from pool to pool; pools tend to keep the same types from year to year, but conditions change as pools silt up, and new pools are formed as the rivers change course. As the water level falls, the fish populations from a wide area become concentrated in these pools and spectacular catches can be made from them. (In the Lake Chad basin Blache et al. (1964) quote 8 tonnes from a 0.2 ha pool.) In Dahomey special trenches ('whedos') are dug on the floodplains to retain water and fishes well into, or through, the dry season.

The channels open to the sun do not carry any special fish faunas; these merely provide seasonal passageways to and from the floodplain. Streams shaded by gallery forest do have a specialized fauna of small (guinean) species living in them (*Barbus*, small *Alestes* and mormyrid species, cyprinodonts, *Amphilius* catfish). Leaves falling into the water make the waters rather acid and provide foods for the many higher crustaceans living here (*Caridina* and *Palaemon* prawns and *Potamon* crabs); molluscs are rare in the acid waters.

The large lakes associated with the floodplain receive their water and fishes from the river or its tributaries in the flood season. Welcomme (1979) figures 24 lakes (18 with a combined low-water area of 2400 km^2) which form part of the general floodplain of the Internal Delta at high water. The vegetation includes beds of *Echinochloa, Oryza, Vossia, Paspalidium.* Fishes are said to be very abundant in these lakes, restocked from the rivers and acting like huge fishtraps, but they have been little studied.

More recent studies in the Inland Delta include those by Dansoko et al. (1976) on the effects of the drought on *Hydrocynus* growth and that by Matthes (1978) on the problems of rice-eating fishes in the irrigated areas, discussed on p. 134.

In the Sokoto tributary, entering the Niger some way downriver from the Inland Delta, tagging experiments by Holden (1963) on 14 of the 27 species common in residual pools showed that some individual *Hydrocynus vittatus* and *Lates niloticus* were found in a particular pool from one year to the next, but other species (*Distichodus, Alestes, Hepsetus, Channa*) were only caught in particular pools in certain years. Good year classes appeared to be related to an early rise in river level. These pools (of 0.07–4.7 ha) were cut off from the river for about four months each year. Pools with a sandy or sandy-mud bottom had a higher biomass of fish (585–1440 kg ha^{-1}) than mud bottomed pools (196–270 kg ha^{-1}); the latter appeared to be used as nursery pools and had few large fish. There was a direct relationship between fish size and pool size. The ichthyomass in a particular pool depended both on species present and the area drained by the pool (not on primary production within the pool), and varied considerably from year to year. Some species were represented in pools by only one or two year classes. The mean biomass was 415kg ha^{-1} for the dry season area of the pools, but as these represented only about 3–4% of the floodplain, this crop was estimated to represent only about 12–17 kg ha^{-1} from the floodplain as a whole.

5.3.3 *Pre- and post-impoundment studies in the Kainji area*

A unique opportunity to census the fishes in a stretch of the R. Niger was provided during the construction of the Kainji hydroelectric dam (Motwani & Kanwai 1970). Half the river, here divided by an island, was enclosed between two coffer dams in mid-May 1966. The enclosed area formed a lake 1.7 km long, 18 ha in area, with steep rocky walls over a rocky bottom with coarse sand, a channel which lacked aquatic vegetation. When the water was pumped out in July–August 1966, over 73 species of fish were collected of which 50 species had mature or ripe gonads or had just spawned (Table 17). That spawning had already commenced in the enclosed area, was evident from the gonad states of the fish and from the many fry and young stages collected from the delivery end of the pumps. This channel would appear to be an inhospitable home for the fish; it was probably used as a low-water refuge, but some fishes may have been moving up or downriver when they were trapped between the coffer dams. The water level here normally starts to rise in August, but the local rains at Kainji start in April/May and are at a maximum in July.

The fish communities of Lake Kainji, a 1280 km^2 lake which formed behind the Kainji hydroelectric dam closed in August 1968, have been much studied. The 60 m deep lake has a 10 m drawdown which results in

Table 17. The relative abundance of fish species caught in the 18 ha coffer-dammed lake in the Niger River at Kainji, August 1966 (data from Motwani & Kanwai 1970).

Family	No. of species	No. of individuals	% of individuals	Total weight (kg)	% weight	Species ripe or spawned
Mormyridae	19	1198	20.7	219	19.5	13
Characidae	8	2103	36.3	136	12.1	6
Citharinidae	3	288	5.0	94	8.8	3
Distichodontidae	2	66	1.1	118	11.0	2
Cyprinidae	5+	192	3.3	48	4.3	2
Bagridae	7	422	7.2	204	18.2	7
Schilbeidae	3	463	8.0	40	3.6	2
Mochokidae	18	1064	18.0	209	18.7	11
*Total catch	65	5796		1068		46

* Plus some specimens of *Polypterus, Heterotis, Microthrissa, Gymnarchus, Malapterurus, Lates, Oreochromis, Tilapia, Tetraodon*, representing another eight families (four of them breeding).

114

20% of the lake floor being exposed during the rainy season each year (Figure 45). The lake has a storage: outflow ratio of 1:4 (i.e. a much greater throughflow of water than has the 8800 km² Volta Lake, where the storage: outflow ratio is 4:1). Pre-impoundment studies were made by Daget (unpublished) and Banks et al. (1966). The numerous post-impoundment studies on the fishes include those of Imevbore & Bakare (1970), Imevbore & Okpo (1975), Lelek (1973), Lelek & El Zarka (1973), Lewis (1974a, b, c), Otobo (1974, 1977), Olatunde (1977, 1978), Blake (1977a, b, c), Ita (1978), Sagua (1978) and Willoughby (1974).

About ninety species of fish occur in the lake (the majority of them the same species as in Volta Lake), representing about 24 fish families. Immediately after impoundment catches rose far above the estimated 10,000 ty⁻¹, to a maximum of 28,000 t in 1970 and 1971, but the boom was short-lived. Commercial catches declined rapidly; Blake (1977c) considered they had stabilized by 1974–75. Ita (ms quoted by Welcomme) gives the stabilized figure as 4500 t in 1978. This represents a catch of 35 kg ha⁻¹, very similar to that from the floodplains. The composition of the fish fauna started to change as soon as the dam was closed (see Figure 49). Mormyrid fishes, very abundant in the river, almost disappeared from the shallow lentic parts of the lake (as they did in Volta Lake, Petr (1967, 1968a, b)).

Cichlid fishes, though fairly numerous along the edges of the river, and expected to increase in the lake, surprisingly did not become a commercial species right away (as tilapias did in Kariba and Volta lakes). The delay in build-up of their populations in Kainji lake was perhaps related to the inhibiting effects of water level fluctuations in the littoral zone where they make their nests. *Sarotherodon galilaeus* populations did, however, build up in the flooded bush, where they could not be fished, and by 1972 were an important element of the inshore fauna, caught in castnets though not common in the experimental gillnets, together with *Tilapia zillii*. In the preimpoundment gillnet samples *O. niloticus* had been commoner than *S. galilaeus* (Banks et al. 1966), leading to the prediction that this would become the dominant tilapia in the lake. However, preimpoundment castnet catches in the open river over sand banks took mainly *S. galilaeus*. The increased tilapia populations can be cropped by seines pulled onto cleared beaches; clearing the beaches is relatively easy in this lake at the height of the drawdown when so much of the lakefloor is exposed (Otobo 1977).

In the first year of filling the deep-bodied *Citharinus citharus* became the most important commercial fish, probably because of successful spawning as the lake filled. This species declined rapidly in 1971–72; there was a slight increase in 1975, but more so of another large characoid, the macrophyte-feeding *Distichodus rostratus*.

Of the smaller species, many too small to be caught in gillnets, the openwater living catfishes increased in abundance (Olatunde 1977), as they did in Volta Lake (Reynolds 1970); these school with, and feed on, the small zooplankton-feeding sardine clupeids, which also increased here rapidly (Otobo 1974) as they did in Volta Lake. Of the five schilbeid catfish species in Kainji, Olatunde (1977) found that *Eutropius niloticus* was most abundant and increasing, living in the openwater with *Physailia pellucida*, also increasing in numbers (as in Volta Lake). *Schilbe mystus* was less common, decreasing and found mainly in riverine areas. *S. uranoscopus*, the common *Schilbe* in Lake Chad, is here very rare, as is *Siluranodon auritus*. Of the two species of clupeid in Kainji, the smaller *Sierrathrissa leonensis* (maximum size 34 cm SL) was more numerous in the shallows, the larger *Pellonula afzeliusi* (growing to 75 mm SL) in the openwaters where it feeds on zooplankton (especially the dominant plankter *Bosminopsis dietersi*). These clupeids can be caught in 'atalla' lift nets, and by a midwater trawl dragged between two boats. Towing at 2.8 $kmhr^{-1}$, catches averaged c. 125 $kghr^{-1}$ (Otobo 1974, 1977).

There was a boom in the predatory *Hydrocynus* and *Lates*. In Kainji *H. forskahlii* feeds almost exclusively on the clupeids, *H. brevis* on tilapia and by biting pieces from larger fishes such as *Citharinus* (Lewis 1974a). The predatory *Bagrus docmac* in Kainji takes mainly bottom-living fish, particularly the bagrid *Chrysichthys auratus* (Blake 1977c). The two species of *Chrysichthys*, both omnivores, live in different habitats: *C. auratus* in inshore waters (with an estimated biomass of 9.5 $kghr^{-1}$) where it feeds on insect larvae, crustacea, fish and plants, and *C. nigrodigitatus* on the bottom in deep water, where it takes bivalves, detritus, chironimids, trichoptera larvae, pupae etc. (Ita 1978).

The changes in percentage composition of the numbers of fish in the main fish families caught in pre- and post-impoundment gillnet samples are shown in Figure 49 (pre-impoundment data from Banks et al. 1966, post-impoundment data from Lelek (1973), Lewis (1974b), Blake (1977c), Ita (1978), Sagua (1978); the percentage numbers from the coffer-dammed channel (Motwani & Kanwai 1970) are also shown. In the river, pre-impoundment gillnet catches were mainly of mormyrids (14 species making up 40% of the total numbers of fish caught) and mochokid catfishes (11 species, 25% of the total numbers), though the rocky channel of the main river bed when drained produced more characids (8 species making up 36% of the fish caught), with mormyrids (19 species, 21% of the catch) and mochokid catfishes (18 species, 18% of the catch). In the lake, gillnet catches indicated an immediate drop in percentage of mormyrids (to 1%), and a dramatic increase in citharinids (due mainly to one species *Citharinus citharus*). Catches of the predatory centropomid *Lates niloticus* also increased, following the increase in small clupeid prey, fish too small to be taken in the gillnets. Schilbeid catfishes also increased and have remained important in the catches (as in the Volta Lake). By 1976 tilapias had become the main component in inshore water less than 7 m deep, with a standing crop of 104.7 $kgha^{-1}$ (Ita 1978). *Sarotherodon galilaeus*: *Oreochromis niloticus*: *Tilapia zillii* were then caught in a ratio of 16:5:1. In the lake *S. galilaeus* is an algae and detritus feeder, *O. niloticus* takes some worms and insects along with algae, and *T. zillii* is a macrophyte-feeder.

116

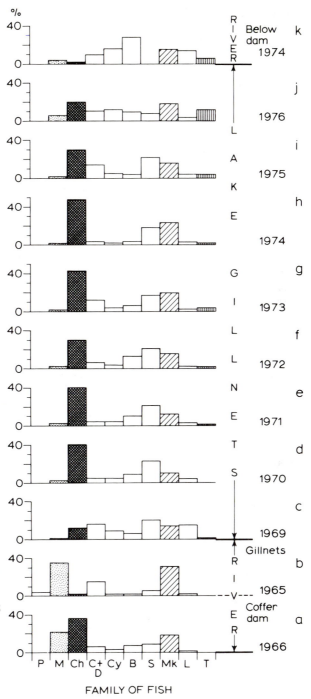

Figure 49. Changes in faunal composition after lake formation at Kainji: P: Polypteridae; M: Mormyridae; Ch: Characidae; C+D: Citharinidae and Distichodontidae; Cy: Cyprinidae; B: Bagridae; S: Schilbeidae; Mk: Mochokidae; L: Lates; T: Tilapia.

117

The species composition of the mormyrid and mochokid families which dominated riverine catches underwent substantial changes under the new lacustrine conditions. Only three mormyrid species (*Marcusenius senegalensis, Hyperopisus bebe* and *Hippopotamyrus pictus*) were of some secondary economic importance in the new lake (Ita 1978). *H. pictus* is the dominant mormyrid in openwater gillnets, its young stages caught in smaller-mesh nets inshore. The larger species *Mormyrops deliciosus, Mormyrus rume* and *M. macrophthalmus*, were still present in small numbers. But the marsh-loving *Brienomyrus niger*, found elsewhere in muddy pools, vanished, as did the rock-loving *Campylomormyrus tamandua* (which feeds by probing into rock and other crevices). The small species *Petrocephalus bovei* and *Pollimyrus isidori* were the main mormyrid species in small mesh gillnets set inshore, where they feed on *Povilla* ephemeropteran nymphs and chironomid larvae.

The Kainji mormyrids fall into three trophic groups (Blake 1977b): (1) *Mormyrops deliciosus*, piscivorous when adult; (2) *Hyperopisus bebe* taking plant material (mainly seeds) and molluscs, and (3) the other species in which insect nymphs and larvae are the main food, though some specialize on particular items: *Marcusenius* utilizes more conchostracans and ostracods, *Mormyrus macrophthalmus* small ephemeropteran nymphs other than *Povilla*, while *H. pictus* relies heavily on *Povilla* nymphs for much of the year. These *Povilla* nymphs, which bore into wood or reed stems, emerge from their crevices to feed at night, when they are vulnerable to the mormyrids as these feed nocturnally; in Volta Lake *Povilla* were found to form a most important food source for the many species of fishes which feed on bottom-dwelling invertebrates in rivers but lost this food source in the new lake as the bottom waters were deoxygenated. These *Povilla* became very abundant in the trees drowned by the rising waters of these man-made lakes.

Thus many of the mormyrid species at Kainji utilized the same prey organisms as Corbet (1961) had found amongst the mormyrids in Lake Victoria, East Africa). The paucity of benthos in the new lake was reflected by the very limited range of prey organisms in stomachs. Unlike Lake Victoria, there was no evidence of lunar cycles of insect emergence which might affect food availability. Blake (1977d) looked at the feeding of lake mormyrids whose populations had declined and concluded that the declines were unlikely to be the result of feeding limitations alone, even though the draw-down adversely affected the populations of benthic invertebrates, as submerged trees still offered extensive feeding grounds when the lake was at its lowest level. Within the lake mormyrids appeared to be restricted to sheltered shallow water, especially where there were extensive reed beds. The need for riverine conditions for reproduction may have been an important factor in the mormyrid declines. We know very little yet about where the mormyrids spawn. Some species are probably potamadromous, moving up inflowing streams and rivers (as Okedi (1969) found them to do from Lake Victoria). *H. pictus* was the most often found ripe in Kainji Lake, but this too may be potamadromous. Breeding here when 16-19 cm SL (probably two years old) the three ova sizes found in the ovaries suggested an extended or double spawning season (mainly between July-September, but some were ripe in December). The eggs are adhesive, so unlikely to be pelagic.

The species composition of the mochokid catfish fauna also changed as riverine conditions gave way to lacustrine ones. Willoughby's (1974) studies have shown that such changes tied up very well with changes in the available foods. There is as yet virtually no information on the breeding places and habits of these fishes. Distribution may also be affected by oxygenation of the water; Green (1977) found oxygen tolerances to vary greatly from species to species; the blood haemoglobin content appeared to be related to their normal habitat, and the most tolerant species (*Synodontis schall*) had the widest distribution.

Mochokid catfishes fall into two main trophic groups; (1) pelagic feeders, taking zooplankton and surface insects, often living inverted and with reversed countershading (*Hemisynodontis membranaceous, Synodontis resupinatus*, with *Brachysynodontis batensoda* living like this part of the time) (2) benthic feeders eating mainly invertebrates (particularly juvenile insects and molluscs).

Among the thirteen synodontid species caught in the rocky cofferdammed channel of the river, *Synodontis gobroni* predominated (37%) with *S. gambiensis* (14% – an invertebrate feeder greatly resembling *S. schall*), *S. budgetti* (12% – a robust species taking mud and humus with insect larvae), and the zooplankton-feeding *H. membranaceous* (11%), along with nine other *Synodontis* species. The castnets in the main river over sandy shallows took three species, all surface-feeders: *H. membranaceous*, with *B. batensoda* and *S. resupinatus*. Gillnets along the river margins in channels and flooded areas took *S. gambiensis* (27%), *S. nigrita* (26% – a small species feeding on bottom deposits and the main species caught in traps set in grassy channels), *S. budgetti* (21%), *S. clarias* (17% – a feeder on benthic insects and molluscs). The traps also took *S. ocellifer*, another small species and the most omnivorous one, eating plant material and insect larvae.

In the open lake the standard gillnet fleet took mainly *B. batensoda* (43%) *S. nigrita* (26%) and *S. schall* (9%); smaller nets inshore took juveniles of *S. nigrita, B. batensoda, S. schall* and *S. filamentosus* (a chironomid feeder) (Blake 1977c). Of the seventeen species in the lake studied by Willoughby, the rare species preferred shallow and more sheltered regions. The three plankton-feeders had different habitat preferences: *H. membranaceous* in midlake, *S. resupinatus* close to shore where there was deep water, *B. batensoda* more evenly distributed at the surface and bottom in deep water. *S. filamentosus*, which feeds mainly on chironomids, all came from inshore. In the river below the dam Sagua (1978) found *H. membranaceous* (32%) *S. gambiensis* (18%), *S. budgetti* (17%) and *S. violaceous* (15% – a species rare in pre-impoundment samples from the river and not seen in the lake).

Thus under lacustrine conditions the main increase was of the plankton-feeding *B. batensoda* and the bottom feeding *S. schall* (instead of the very similar *S. gambiensis* commoner in the river). *S. filamentosus* and *S. nigrita* continued to be caught (mainly in inshore waters), while *S. violaceous* and *S. clarias* (a benthic mollusc and insect feeder) were lost from samples.

Willoughby suggested that the lack of molluscs on Kainji Lake floor forced some synodontids into competition with the insectivorous synodontid species in the lake. He attributed the success of these catfishes to the stout dorsal and pectoral spines. When locked into erect position these reduce the size of fish that a predator can swallow (as Hopson (1972a) demonstrated for *Synodontis* from *Lates* stomachs in Lake Chad). It is interesting that the mormyrids, the other group with so many species in the sudanian fauna, also have a special device (the electrical system) which may help them to avoid the intense predation, and that both these groups are nocturnal.

5.3.4 *The Niger system below the Kainji barrage*

The Kainji barrage has greatly affected fishing in the river below the dam. The floodplains have diminished and together with this so have the fish stocks. The barrage is an effective barrier to upstream movement, but many kinds of fish congregate just below the dam; Sagua (1978) reported catches of c. 21 tyr^{-1} here. *Lates* have increased in numbers here, but catches are very seasonal, greatest when the outflow is highest (January peak, scarce May-June). *Lates* appear to do better in the river than in the lake. The proportions of predatory fishes generally has risen here; of the characids, *Hydrocynus brevis* is common, but few *H. forskahlii* are caught. *Malapterurus electricus* has become important below the dam since it was closed; this species is also seasonally abundant (April-July) (Sagua 1979). Of the eight bagrid species, *B. bayad* and *Clarotes laticeps* have superceded *B. docmac* and *Chrysichthys auratus* which were the commoner species in the coffer-dammed area. *Distichodus* is much commoner than *Citharinus citharus* here, and of the cyprinids *Labeo coubie* compared with *L. senegalensis*. Five species of mormyrid make up less than 5% of the numbers of fish caught below the dam, *M. deliciosus* and *M. rume* are the main species here (with *M. oudoti*, *H. bebe* and *C. tamandua* rarely seen). Of clariid catfish *Heterobranchus bidorsalis*, and of the cichlids *S. galilaeus*, are the species most common here.

In the Lower Niger down to the delta, and in the Benue tributary liftnets known as *atalla* are used from canoes along the river during the six month highwater season. Five hundred such units were found to land 600 t fresh fish during the six month season (Awachie & Walson 1978). Catches included 38 species of 13 families, small fishes dominated by clupeids, schilbeids and characids, mostly small species with fry and fingerlings of large species (*Alestes, Hydrocynus, Citharinus,* bagrids, mormyrids) making up less than 20% of the catch. These small fishes present an important source of cheap protein for riverside dwellers.

120

In the Niger delta, an estimated 8800 km^2 of which over 80% consists of mangrove swamps, salinities are very variable; freshwater reaches almost to the river mouths at heavy floods. Despite the low salinities, marine species predominate in catches throughout the year (Boeseman 1963; Pillay 1967); Pillay lists 128 fish species from these estuarine stretches. Castnets here take the clupeid West African shad *Ethmalosa dorsalis*, other clupeids and grey mullets (*Mugil* spp.). Set nets and long lines catch barracuda (*Sphyraena*), snappers (*Lutjanus*), croakers (*Otolithus* and *Sciaena*), and grunts (*Pomadasys*). Many types of trap take prawns and small fishes, also tilapia species that can withstand brackish water, and catfishes. Mangrove oysters (*Ostrea tulipa*), other molluscs (periwinkles) and crabs are cropped from the mangrove swamps. These estuarine regions present great possibilities for fish culture.

In an annotated checklist of the Lower Benue tributary fishes Reid & Sydenham (1979) comment on the endemic stingray (*Dasyatis garouaensis*) and the flatfish sole (*Dagetichthys senegalensis*) found here, the only representatives of these families known from African freshwaters. Once considered to be relics from ancient seas, these are more likely to be recent immigrants from the sea. The fish communities in Upper Benue and Cameroun were studied by Daget & Stauch (1963) who figured the fishing gear used there.

5.3.5 *The Volta Lake*

Studies on the neighbouring Volta Lake, formed a few years earlier than the Kainji lake, by closing the hydroelectric barrage across the Volta River in Ghana in May 1964, were very relevant to those at Kainji, as the two lakes share the sudanian fauna and the majority of the species are the same. The numerous pre- and post-impoundment Volta studies include those reported by Attionu (1976), Biswas (1977, 1978), Evans & Vanderpuye (1973), Ewer (1966), Lawson et al. (1969), Obeng (1968), Petr (1967, 1968a, b, 1970a, b, 1971, 1975, 1978), Reynolds (1970, 1972, 1974), Viner (1970) and others, touching on many aspects: physical and chemical, as well as floral and faunal changes as the riverine conditions were converted to lacustrine ones. Over thirty times larger than Kainji lake, the Volta lake is not much deeper (70 m mean depth), with a smaller (3 m) annual drawdown. It lies nearer to the equator (6–9° N) than Kainji, with a rainy season starting in May, followed by floods in October; the outflow is only about a quarter of the stored volume. Thus the Volta Lake presents more truly lacustrine conditions than Kainji.

As relatively little of the riverine forest and bush was cleared (owing to the expense of clearing it) rapid deoxygenation at Volta dam closure led to fish deaths. In the more open waters oxygen extended deeper, to about 20 m where there was an abrupt discontinuity, and in the deeper waters there was virtually no oxygen (Lawson et al. 1969). As the lake filled, which it did very gradually until c. 1971, there was more extensive mixing of the water, so oxygen became available in deeper water. The duration of periods of deoxygenation when the lake was stratified in the dry season diminished, and the lake became an increasingly attractive environment for the fishes. The Volta River flows in at the northern end, where conditions remained more riverine than in the south where the lake is wider and deeper.

The Volta Lake is low in nutrients, with a low standing crop of plankton. The aufwuchs on the drowned trees formed the main basis of the food webs, supporting surprisingly high catches of fishes in the early years after impoundment. The fishes comprised both potamadromous (migratory) species (*Alestes, Citharinus, Distichodus, Labeo*), especially at the north end of the lake from where they moved into inflowing rivers in the wet season, and species which spawned within the basin, either annually (as in *Lates niloticus*) or throughout the year (tilapia species). The potamadromous species relied heavily on the floodplains as feeding areas during the rainy season.

The new lake produced up to 40,000 t of fish per year. Initial stock assessment sampling with gillnets and rotenone (completed in 1971) showed that many small species were being underutilized. This stimulated the development of a scoop net fishery, using attractent lights at night, for the abundant clupeids, also the use of monofilament gillnets, and the supply of better boats to encourage fishing in offshore deeper waters (Vanderpuye 1972). Rotenone sampling of 150 m^2 areas in the littoral zone (less than 2 m deep) took sixty species averaging c. 170 kgha^{-1} biomass ranging from 1.2 kgha^{-1} to 651 kgha^{-1}), 30% of this of cichlids, especially the tilapias *S. galilaeus* (14%) and *O. niloticus* (7%). The rest was mainly of catfishes *Chrysichthys auratus, C. velifer* and *Synodontis nigrita*, with *Polypterus senegalus*. The commercial gillnets caught tilapia, *Alestes, Lates, Labeo, Citharinus, Distichodus* and *Hydrocynus*, the species composition changing as the lake stabilised. The seasonal rise and fall was so gradual that it did not appear to disrupt cichlid spawning here as it did in Kainji lake.

Apart from a sudden fish kill attributed to deoxygenation just after dam closure, most of the Volta River fish throve initially in the new lacustrine conditions (Petr 1967–71). Exceptions were the mormyrids, which almost completely disappeared from the south end of the lake. The mormyrids, which are bottom-feeders, may have vanished because their benthic insect food supply was submerged by deoxygenated water. Cichlids became very common in the south. The predominance of insectivorous fishes in the Volta River gave way to predominantly herbivorous and plankton-feeding fish in the new lake. After the first two years characid and cyprinid fishes (such as *Alestes* – except for one species – and *Labeo*) also disappeared from the south. These may have migrated up rivers to spawn and failed to return, or died out if they could not find suitable spawning grounds. Species common in Black Volta River samples became limited to the northern arm where the Black and White Volta rivers flow into the lake.

Tilapia, on the other hand, flourished and fairly rapidly became the

122

dominant fishes in most of the lake. Of the three species present, *Sarotherodon galilaeus* fed mainly on phytoplankton, *Oreochromis niloticus* took mainly periphytic algae, and *Tilapia zillii* fed mainly on submerged grass and detritus.

The bark of the flooded trees developed a rich growth of periphyton and the burrowing nymphs of the ephemeropteran *Povilla adusta* became exceedingly common in the dead trees (Petr 1970a). These provided a food source for fishes which had been benthic feeders in the river, such as *Schilbe mystus* and *Eutropius niloticus*, good examples of generalized feeders in the river taking to a more specialized food in the new environment. However, these same schilbeids also fed on the freshwater clupeid *Pellonula afzeliusi* which had become very numerous in the open waters of the new lake and formed the major food item of both the Nile Perch *Lates niloticus* and the smaller common predatory cichlid *Hemichromis fasciatus*.

In the Volta Lake the flooded trees with their flora of periphyton and *Povilla* were a major element in the unexpectedly high production of fish, for this new lake produced about ten times the weight of fish produced by Lake Kariba (on the Zambezi) in the early years after impoundment. The trophic relationships between the most important organisms in Volta Lake in its first six years were summarized by Petr (1971) as follows:

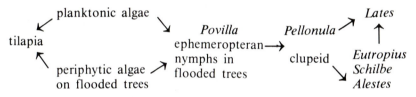

The ecological studies of clupeid populations in Volta Lake (Reynolds 1970-74) were the first to be made on how pelagic fishes adapt to life in a new tropical lake. The pelagic zone is much enlarged as the lake forms, offering special opportunities for plankton feeders. Of the five small pelagic species, all fractional spawners, which have colonized Volta Lake, the two clupeid species and the cyprinid (*Leptocypris niloticus*) were dry-season spawners in rivers, and two schilbeid catfishes (*Physalia* and *Siluranodon*) wet-season spawners. One clupeid, *Pellonula afzeliusi*, extended its breeding season to spawn throughout the year in the new lake, where high water no longer presented a danger to its planktonic larvae (the other, larger clupeid *Cynothrissa mento*, probably migrated to rivers to spawn). The wet-season spawning schilbeids both extended their breeding seasons, throughout the year in *Physailia pellucida* and into the early dry season in *Siluranodon auritus*; for these species, lacustrine conditions provided a continued high water season. The species which extended their breeding seasons rapidly became abundant in the lake (Reynolds 1974).

Both clupeid species make diel vertical migrations, appearing at the lake surface c.1730 hr. Individuals then disperse in surface waters where they feed on emerging insects. They stay close to the surface in bright moonlight and are attracted to a light source. These feeding associations in Volta Lake often contain other fish species, such as the transparent schilbeid catfish *Physailia pellucida* (up to 40% of the feeding school), *Barbus macrops* (up to 10%), the cyprinid *Leptocypris niloticus*, and the three predators *Eutropius niloticus, Schilbe mystus* and *Cynothrissa mento*. In shallow areas, two other predators, the cichlid *Hemichromis fasciatus* and the characid *Hepsetus odoe* also join them. At dawn the clupeids reform schools and vanish from the surface. *Pellonula* is, however, essentially a riverine fish, which can inhabit fast-flowing or calm muddy habitats; it is not known whether it carries out similar diel vertical migrations in rivers when conditions permit.

Pellonula is a facultative feeder, taking mainly aquatic and terrestrial insects (these being eaten soon after their emergence) also small Crustacea (Ostracoda, Cladocera and Copepoda). *Pellonula* is in turn preyed on by a variety of fish: *Clarias, Hepsetus, Hydrocynus, Schilbe, Alestes, Synodontis, Eutropius. Pellonula* ova are relatively large and may be anchored to a substratum in the lake, but the larvae are pelagic. Both clupeid species mature within one year. Reynolds commented that for these largely annual forms predation probably outweighs all other factors in determining population size each year, but the flexible and extended breeding season in *Pellonula* (also in *Physailia*) has had a major role in allowing rapid population growth and the effective exploitation of the changed environment.

5.3.6 *Lake Chad studies*

Lake Chad normally has two basins; a southern one greatly influenced by the seasonal inflow of the large rivers of the Chari-Logone system draining wetter regions far to the south, and a northern more lacustrine one. During studies made between 1965–72 the open water of the north basin was c 4000 km^2 in area, 4–7 m deep, while the southern one was shallower, (2–4 m). During this period the lake level fell by over 2 m. The Sahelian drought began in 1968 and after the rivers failed to flow in 1973 the northern basin dried out completely. The 20,000 km^2 lake in 1968 was reduced to 6000 km^2 in 1975 (see Carmouze *et al.* 1983).

The ecology of Chad fishes has been investigated since 1963 in considerable detail by ORSTOM scientists as part of the comprehensive International Biological Programme limnological study of this lake. Carmouze et al. (1972) have described the main ecological zones of the lake, and Lauzanne (1976) the trophic relationships of the fishes. Information on fish growth here and elsewhere in Africa was collated by Merona & Ecoutin (1979), and on fish fecundities by Albaret (1979). Durand (1979–80) and Stauch (1978) studied the Chad fisheries. Quensière (1978) examined the influence of the drought on the Chari-Logone delta fisheries, and Chouret (1978) the continuing influence of the drought. FAO convened a special meeting to assess effects of the drought

(FAO 1975). The many autecological studies on the main food fishes and key species include those by Benech (1974) on *Citharinus*, Benech (1975) on *Brachysynodontis batensoda*, Durand (1978) on *Alestes baremose* (and see also Paugy (1978) for comparative data on this species in the Ivory Coast and other rivers), Lauzanne (1978) on *Sarotherodon galilaeus*, Lek & Lek (1977) on the little, short-lived, but very abundant *Micralestes acutidens*, Lek & Lek (1978) on the small species of Mormyridae, Lek & Lek (1978a, b) on *Ichthyoborus besse*, Loubens (1974) on *Lates niloticus*, Mok (1974) on the two *Schilbe* species in the lake. Previously Blache et al. (1964) had collated the information then available on the biology of the Chad fishes, and given identification keys for the species. Certain species (*Lates* and *Alestes* in particular) had been studied in the northern basin in Nigerian waters by Hopson (1972a) and Hopson (1972b) while Tobor (1972) examined the food of the commercial fish.

At 'normal' levels (Figure 16) the lake had three main ecological zones (1) openwater; (2) the archipelago of islands, mainly along the east and southeast coasts; (3) the south coast with its deltas which receives the inflowing Chari and Logone rivers. Many of the lake fishes migrate long distances (several hundred kilometers) up these rivers to spawn, the resulting juveniles feeding in the inundation zones and returning to the lake down the El Beid (Figure 50). Evaporation from the lake is very high and conductivity increased very much towards the north, from where it appeared to limit certain elements of the fauna, as oligochaetes, benthic snails and mormyrid fishes were not found in the northern basin. The fish fauna has many more species in the southeastern archipelago than in the northern basin (a trend which became further exaggerated during and since the drought).

Lake Chad is far enough north for a winter fall in temperature (to 18° C) to affect fish growth, particularly in the northern basin; in the south the biology of the fishes is governed mainly by the seasonal inflow of the great rivers. Daget (1967) regarded Chad as an extension of these river systems in which fluviatile species had decreased in importance while lacustrine species flourished; this appeared particularly true in the southern basin.

5.3.6.1 *Trophic interrelationships of Lake Chad fishes.* Intensive studies of the diets of the most abundant fishes (a) in the southeastern archipelago, and (b) in the openwaters of the southern basin, comparing foods used at high and low water levels (Lauzanne 1972, 1976) led to the conclusions that: (1) fish diets of the archipelago are much more varied than in openwaters, which lack many food sources such as prawns, aquatic insects, plants and many small species of fish (*Barbus, Haplochromis*); (2) seasonal variations in foods eaten were most marked in terminal predators, which at low water feed on small species of fish (e.g. *Barbus, Haplochromis, Brycinus dageti*), but utilize the fry and young stages of the larger species at high water; terrestrial insects blown onto the water surface were also an important food source at highwater. Prawns were a

125

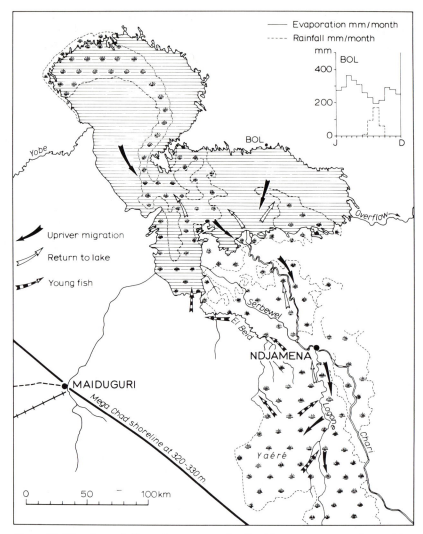

Figure 50. Migrations of *Alestes baremose* up the Chari-Logone to spawn, the resulting juveniles (dashed arrows) travelling through the inundation zone and down the El Beid to Lake Chad (Daget & Durand 1981).

very important food within the archipelago at low water; (3) consumers belong to three trophic levels; within the archipelago, zooplankton-feeders were most abundant. In the open-water terminal carnivores were the most abundant.

Primary consumers: in the archipelago included the detritus-feeding *Citharinus citharus* and *Labeo senegalensis*, the phytoplankton-feeding

126

tilapia *Sarotherodon galilaeus*, and *Brycinus macrophthalmus* which includes some macrophytes in its diet (together with terrestrial insects). In openwater the primary consumers were all detritivores: *Citharinus citharus* and *C. distichodoides*, *Labeo senegalensis* and *L. coubie*, *Distichodus rostratus*.

Secondary consumers fell into two groups, zooplankton-feeders and benthic invertebrate-feeders. In the archipelago, *Alestes baremose*, *Hemisynodontis membranaceous* were strict zooplankton-feeders, while *Brychysynodontis batensoda* fed mainly on zooplankton and *Alestes dentex* took it together with other food items. The benthic invertebrate-feeders included *Synodontis schall*, the mormyrid *Hyperopisus bebe* (which also took some macrophytes) and the osteoglossid *Heterotis niloticus*, which also took macrophytes, prawns and zooplankton. In the openwaters, *A. baremose*, *H. membranaceous* and *B. batensoda* were all strict zooplankton-feeders. Benthic invertebrates included molluscs fed on by *H. bebe*, *Syndontis schall* and *S. clarias*.

Terminal consumers: in the archipelago, where food webs were very complex, these included the piscivorous fishes *Lates niloticus*, taking mainly detritivous fishes, and *Hydrocynus*, *H. brevis* feeding mainly on zooplankton-feeders and some tilapia (*S. galilaeus*), which *H. forskahlii* included some prawns in its diet as well as fish of many kinds. The less strictly piscivorous *Bagrus bayad*, *Schilbe uranoscopus* and *Eutropius niloticus* all included prawns in the diet, and *E. niloticus* took many terrestrial insects. In openwater, where food chains were simpler, zooplankton-feeding fishes were the main source of food, and terrestrial insects were important in the highwater season; few benthic detritivores were eaten. *E. niloticus* was itself preyed on by larger piscivores.

During the International Biological Programme studies of production it had been hoped to be able to quantify the transfer of energy from one trophic level to the next in various environments. This Lake Chad work showed some of the difficulties of trying to do so. Figure 51 indicates the complexity of interrelationships among the top consumers in openwater (where food webs were simpler than in the archipelago). Some fishes took foods from their own trophic level (for example *Lates* feeding on *Eutropius*), or from several levels. Calculations indicated that starting with 100 calories provided by the algae, the top piscivore *Lates niloticus* accumulates 5.2 cals when feeding on the algivorous tilapia (*S. galilaeus*), but only 1.7 cals if it crops the zooplankton-feeding *Alestes baremose* (Lévêque 1979). Moreover, Hopson's (1972a) study of *Lates*, mentioned below, had indicated how much the food eaten varies with the size of fish, biotope and time of year. Juveniles of many species start as zooplankton-feeders before turning to other foods, be these algae, benthos or fish.

The quantitative studies did, however, bring out that the main weight of fishes (44% of the ichthyomass) cropped from the archipelago waters was of zooplankton-feeders, kept going by the high and stable plankton biomass here throughout the year. In the openwaters the top consumers which formed the main weight (64% of the ichthyomass) were kept going

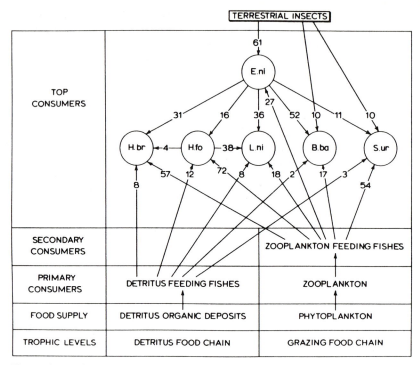

Figure 51. The food webs of terminal consumers in the open waters of Lake Chad, indicating the percentage composition of their diets (after Lauzanne 1976). H.br.: *Hydrocynus brevis*; H.fo.: *Hydrocynus forskahlii*; L.ni: *Lates niloticus*; B.ba: *Bagrus bayad*; S.ur: *Schilbe uranoscopus*; E.ni: *Eutropius niloticus*.

by the great biomass of terrestrial insects blown onto the water surface and the abundance of small zooplankton-feeding fishes (such as *Micralestes acutidens* and *Pollymyrus isidori*) whose production is high.

Lévêque (1979) commented that because of its shallow depth and well-oxygenated water Chad is comparable to a vast littoral zone. Macrophytes are very abundant, and may be underutilized by the fish. The benthic fauna, averaging 37 kgha^{-1} (dry weight) is one of the richest known (compare with 7.4 kgha^{-1} from the equatorial Lake George in Uganda, another IBP study site). Molluscs dominate the benthic fauna in Chad, as in other lakes in the sudanian zone. Despite this rich fauna, the biomass of benthos-feeding fishes is not very high, nor are these much used by top consumers. In Chad the mean zooplankton biomass, 8.1 kgha^{-1} dry weight, was very close to that of Lake George (8.3 kgha^{-1} DW); this varies little throughout the year. In Chad zooplankton production corresponded to about 6% of the gross phytoplankton production, or about 0.14% of the incident radiation (2308 joules cm^{-2} day^{-1}) on the lake. It was not possible to determine the mean biomass of fish in the lake, but the fisheries yield was estimated to be 70 kgha^{-1} yr^{-1} (fresh weight), indicating that the biomass must be at least 2–3 times higher than this (Lévêque 1979).

The numerous autecological studies on fish species in Chad brought out many interesting points. *Lates niloticus* is well adapted for lacustrine existence here as it spawns in the lake and has pelagic eggs and larvae (Hopson 1972). Winter checks in growth enabled ages and growth rates to be determined; this showed that growth speeded up when fish are about 75 cm long (6–7 years old), the size at which *Lates* turned to a diet of larger fishes (especially *Hydrocynus*). Juvenile *Lates* include prawns and other invertebrates in their diet. In Chad *Lates* males mature at about 50 cm long, females at 60 cm (3–4 years old); they grow to 140 cm SL. Durand's (1978) very thorough studies of the population dynamics of *Alestes baremose* supported earlier suggestions that the lake has distinct populations of this species, one of which may spawn in the lake. Durand's analyses provide a model for work needed on other commercial species. Benech (1974) found the first year growth of *Citharinus citharus* to be very variable in the Chari-Logone; growth stops November-March when the water temperature falls below 25°C. Benech's (1975) study of *Brachysynodontis batensoda* showed the direct effects of the drought years on growth.

Dealing with the smaller species, Lek & Lek (1978c) found that during the drying up period (1970–77) the small mormyrids *Petrocephalus bane* and *Pollimyrus isidori* disappeared from the southeast archipelago, which turned progressively into a swamp. They were later replaced here by *Brienomyrus niger*, but *P. bane* and *P. isidori* became abundant in openwater when lacustrine conditions returned. The eighteen species of mormyrids known in the Chad basin are widely distributed, and some are present in most biotopes. Lek & Lek (1977) also looked at the biology of the small characid *Micralestes acutidens*, a surface living species in the openwater, where it feeds on Cladocera and terrestrial insects, and is itself an important prey of *Lates* and *Hydrocynus*. These *Micralestes* spawn with the Chari floods when about five months old; they only live about a year and die after spawning when 30–40 mm long.

In addition to these species studied intensively, there were many other species present. Zooplankton was also utilized by the endemic little *Brycinus dageti*, while the mormyrid *Pollimyrus isidori* ingests some as well as insects. In the openwater, *H. forskahlii*'s main prey were *Micralestes* and *Pollimyrus*. Phytoplankton was used mainly by juvenile fishes of numerous species, also taken from the bottom by the numerous detritus-feeders. Oligochaete worms were scarcely cropped. Molluscs only appeared to be essential food in the openwaters of the southeast where five species (*H. bebe, S. schall, S. frontosus, S. clarias* and the little puffer fish *Tetraodon fahaka*) feed on them.

Aquatic insects were found to be less important as food in the openwater, where however they were more important foods for the little mormyrids than in the southeastern archipelago. Here they were found in stomachs of numerous species, but never formed the exclusive food of any one species.

The conclusion was reached by the ORSTOM team that in Lake Chad the search for food does not seem to be a determining factor in the distribution of the fishes; there is a great variety of available foods, and the feeding regimes of most of the predatory species shows great plasticity. But where there are large concentrations of predatory fishes they may limit the density of prey organisms, such as of certain benthic invertebrates.

5.4 UTILIZATION OF THE FISH STOCKS

5.4.1 *Fishing gear*

The traditional types of gear used in the rivers and floodplains of the Chad basin have been illustrated by Blache & Miton (1962), much of it passive gear, designed to catch actively moving fishes. The gear includes shore seines with poles, floating drift nets, gillnets, many forms of scoop nets and hand nets, beautifully made basket traps of great intricacy, long lines of hooks, traps set in fish weirs across the river channels, harpoons. Fish poisons, derived from some sixteen different plant species, were used on the Benue (Stauch 1966, Welcomme 1979a). Elsewhere in the Niger system gillnets of various mesh, set anchored along river margins or drifted downriver, and castnets used in openwater take most of the commercial catch. Traps set amongst vegetation and in channels, hooks and lines are used by subsistence fishermen. Traditional methods are being replaced by gillnets, castnets and seines of manufactured twine. Experimental fishing methods tried included trials of an electrified trawl in Lake Chad (Benech et al. 1978). Very large commercial seines are now being used in the Middle Niger. The fishery follows a seasonal pattern according to the accessibility of the fish, minimal at highwater, maximal as the water drains from the plains to the rivers and through the dry season. Floodplain retention dams have been built in some places to hold back the water and fish through the dry season (as shown in an aerial photograph taken of the Benue/Niger confluence, Welcomme 1979a, figure 4.5). Welcomme also describes 'whedos', drain-in channels and ponds dug to retain water and fish on the Ouémé floodplains, a system which could be extended to many of the Niger floodplains.

5.4.2 *Numbers of fishermen*

In addition to fulltime professional fishermen, many people fish locally on a part-time, occasional or subsistence basis. The fulltime fishermen often have to move from place to place following the fish, for example they moved northwards to Lake Chad when the floods failed in the rivers, their usual fishing grounds. Data from FAO/UN surveys, collated by Welcomme (1979a) indicate that there were over 50,000 fishermen in the Inland Delta, some 1,300 on the Niger River in Niger, plus 4,600 in Nigeria, another 5,000 on the Benue tributary in Nigeria. Their catches totalled c. 120,000 tyr^{-1}, most of it (90,000 t) from the Inland Delta of the Niger (Table 18).

5.4.3 *Fish landings*

River gillnets and castnets take over fifty species. In the Inland Delta the nine most important species were: *Alestes dentex, Brachysynodontis batensoda, Hydrocynus forskahlii, Oreochromis niloticus, Labeo senegalensis, Lates niloticus, Bagrus bayad, Mormyrus rume, Citharinus latus*. Other species commonly taken included *Auchenoglanis occidentalis, Clarias anguillaris*, and the small *Brycinus leuciscus* which forms the basis of a specialized fishery for fish-oil production.

In the Chari-Logone delta region of Lake Chad *Alestes baremose* and *A. dentex* were the mainstay of the fishery before the drought. In 1972–73 catches included forty four species, but 95% of the catch was of the ten species: the characids *Alestes baremose* (28%), *A. dentex* (13%), *Hydrocynus forskahlii* (2%), the mormyrids *Marcusenius cyprinoides* (9%) and *Hyperopisus bebe* (4%), the catfishes *Brachysynodontis batensoda* (16%), *Hemisynodontis membranaceous* (15%), *Synodontis schall* (1.8%), *Schilbe* spp. (4%) and *Eutropius niloticus* (2%).

Overall, the Niger gillnet catches averaged 9.3 kg 100 m^{-2} of net per day, which is in line with catches from other African rivers (10.4 kg from the Ouémé, 10 kg from the Kafue), and the Niger castnets averaged 7.9 kg per net per day (Welcomme, 1979a). The landings from the various areas are shown in Table 18. In addition to these catches recorded in market statistics, perhaps nearly half as many again would be consumed by subsistence fishermen. The numbers of fishermen may vary from year to year. Furthermore catches vary very much with the extent of the flooding, which varies greatly from year to year, so such estimates can only be approximations.

The effects of the 1972-73 drought on catches were demonstrated by an abrupt decline of fresh and smoked fish landings at Mopti (Daget

Table 18. Utilization of Niger system fishes (data collated by Welcomme 1979a from FAO/UN sources).

River	Estimated number fishermen	Catch (t/yr)	Estimated area fished (km^2)	kg/ha	Catch per fisherman	Density of fishermen per km^2
Inland Delta	54,112	90,000	20,000	45.0	1.66	2.71
Niger in Niger	1,314	4,700	907	51.8	3.58	1.45
Niger in Dahomey	?	1,200	274	43.7	–	–
Niger in Nigeria	4,600	14,350	4,800	29.9	3.12	0.96
Benue in Nigeria	5,140	9,570	3,100	30.9	1.86	1.66
Delta in Nigeria	–	60,000	15,000	40	–	–

Table 19. Annual fluctuations in fish landings from the Inland Delta (Mopti-smoked fish) and Senegal River, showing drop following the 1972-73 drought and subsequent recovery (data collated by Welcomme 1979a, from FAO/UN sources).

| | Landings (tonnes × 1000) | | | | | | | | |
	1967	1968	1969	1970	1971	1972	1973	1974	1975
Mopti (smoked fish)	9.5	10.8	11.1	11.2	8.8	7.8	4.2	3.6	7.6
Senegal River	30	25	20	18	18	15	12	21	25

1975; and Welcomme's figures for smoked fish in Table 19). A comparable drop, and subsequent recovery when the floods returned, also occurred in the Senegal river landings (Table 19). The responses to environmental events are very rapid in these fishes which grow fast and mature at an early age. The recoveries at these places suggested that stocks here were not being over-fished at normal rainfall regimes, and demonstrated the resilience of these riverine fish populations which recover rapidly where catches are very largely young-of-the-year.

In the Chari-Logone Chad system Durand (1979-80) found that catches increased steadily from 30,000-40,000 tyr^{-1} between 1962-70, to 75,000-80,000 tyr^{-1}. During this period the fishermen moved progressively northward along the Logone and Chari rivers towards the delta and the lake, and the total fishing effort was multiplied about thirty times. During the 1971-74 drought fisheries became entirely lacustrine and catches increased even faster as fish became easier to catch in the diminished lake area. The maximum total, 220,000t, was landed in 1974 the year of maximum drought in Lake Chad when fish stocks were concentrated in the very reduced area of water. This catch made severe inroads into fish stocks; catches declined the very next year, and have stayed around 100,000 tyr^{-1} since 1975. Based on the reduced area of Lake Chad (8 to 10,000 km²) this represents a yield of 100-120 kgha^{-1}.

Despite an important flood in 1976, the effects of the drought on Lake Chad have had a long-lasting effect on the northern basin of the lake (Chouret 1978; Stauch 1978). The Great Barrier which divides the two basins was colonized by plants (including an ambatch forest) during the drought (see p. 74), which impeded water from flowing into the northern basin when rivers flooded from the south. Only fishes such as *Tilapia zillii* and *Clarias*, which can withstand the increased salinity and deoxygenated swampy conditions in the northern basin, were then caught there. In the southern basin, too, fish stocks declined; many of the large species vanished. Meanwhile the numbers of fishermen increased, putting extra pressure on the diminished fish stocks. In the past, traditions and respected customs ruled fishing activities, but exploitation patterns became ruthless (Stauch 1978). Steps are needed to control overfishing and also to eliminate wastage: the c. 100,000 tyr fresh fish landed are reduced to c. 50,000t by drying, breakages in transport, insect pests etc.

Although Welcomme (1979a,b) had demonstrated a linear relationship between Inland Delta and other floodplain fish landings and an index of flood intensity, attempts to use such an index to forecast catches in subsequent years were not very successful in our present state of knowledge. Some floodplain fish populations may be more affected by the height and duration of the high water, others by the height of water remaining in dry season refuges. The various effects may vary from year to year with different predation pressure etc., the whole forming a kaleidoscope of interacting factors about which much more information is needed.

Quensière (1978) studied how the drought affected Chari delta fisheries in 1971-73, mainly gillnetting with drift nets. Catches here fell as the lack of floods interfered with spawning migrations, nor were there flooded zones in which the juvenile fishes could feed. The professional fishermen left the delta. In experimental fleets of gillnets, the species composition changed: large species such as *Citharinus, Distichodus* and large *Alestes* vanished. *Alestes baremose* and *A. dentex* formerly the mainstays of the river fisheries, were replaced by a higher diversity of smaller species, mainly mochokid catfishes. In Lake Chad, Benech et al. (1978) found that mortalities during the drought were mainly due to anoxic conditions caused by decomposition of macrophytes; some large-scale fish kills resulted from local 'tornados' stirring up the bottom mud, and in the longer term recruitment was depleted as spawning migrations up affluent rivers were curtailed. Experimental studies of oxygen requirements of the various species supported these conclusions (Benech & Lek 1981).

5.4.4 *Management of river fisheries*

A characteristic of floodplain fisheries is that they exploit the juvenile young-of-the-year, moving to dry season habitats from the floodplain as the waters subside. Durand (1970) estimated that up to 90% of the numbers and weights of Ebeji (El Beid) river catches were made up of juvenile fishes moving from the flooded yaérés floodplains down to Lake Chad (Fig. 50). The atalla scoopnet fishery in the lower Niger (Awachie & Walson 1978) also takes many juvenile fishes. As these floodplain fishes are typical 'r'-strategists, i.e. geared for very rapid population increases, able to colonize new habitats and to cope with the fluctuations in environmental conditions that they encounter in floodplain rivers (see discussions in Lowe-McConnell 1975, 1979), removing juveniles does not have the drastic effects that it would have if comparable large numbers were taken from the more stable, 'K' strategist, populations found in the deep African lakes. However, overfishing ripe fish on their upstream spawning migrations can cause the collapse of the fishery, as it has for *Labeo* fisheries in various parts of Africa, notably of the Mweru/Luapula fishery in Zambia.

Floodplain fisheries have a built-in close season, as the fishes are too dispersed, and many of them too small, to be caught at highwater. Mesh regulations are difficult to formulate where so many different kinds of fish, of such varied shapes and sizes, make up the fishery. The catch by individual fishermen is bound to drop as the numbers of people fishing rises. For tropical floodplains Welcomme (1979a) suggested that the total catch often increases up to a density of about 10 fishermen per km^2. But here the distances are so great that there will be concentrations of fishermen near to the markets, rather than dispersed over the whole floodplain. Welcomme's figures indicate that the yield from the Niger floodplains is of the order of 38 kgha^{-1}, in line with the 40–60 kgha^{-1} from most floodplains in Africa.

5.4.5 *Impacts of other floodplain uses on the fishes*

It has been estimated that some 200,000 head of cattle feed on the Inland Niger delta floodplain during the dry season. In general, herding cattle and fishing are very good complementary uses of the floodplain. The cattle dung helps to fertilize the waters. The development of large irrigation schemes for crops such as rice may not, however, be so beneficial. Rice culture requires complete control over the hydrological regime, and modifications of the environment associated with rice may be detrimental to the fish. Furthermore, the need to control insect pests in the crops may lead to pollution of the waters downstream of the rice fields. An inland drainage basin, such as Lake Chad, which receives waters from many countries, will have to be guarded carefully against the effects of pollution.

Conversely, some fish may be detrimental to the rice. Matthes (1978) lists *Alestes baremose, Distichodus brevipinnis* and *Tilapia zillii* as the species which will feed on rice plants in rice fields; *Alestes nurse* bites at the leaves of young plants, *Oreochromis niloticus* nibbles epiphytic algae off their stems and may tear their stalks. *Heterotis* and *Gymnarchus* may construct nests of rice stems; *Clarias, Heterobranchus* and *Protopterus* uproot small plants when probing in the mud for benthic food.

Engineering works which lead to a loss of floodplain area for fish feeding and breeding have serious effects on fish populations. The reaction of fish communities to flood failures during the Sahelian drought demonstrated the effects of suppressing floods. Changes in time of flood, and irregular floods as the water level is artificially controlled below hydroelectric barrages, also affect the breeding and feeding regimes below the dams; in the Niger below Kainji, catches fell about 50% in three years, and the species composition changed (Sagua 1978). The Kainji dam has no fish pass. Very few rivers in Africa have. Fish ladders which were installed at the Markala barrage above the Inland Delta did not prove very satisfactory. This was largely because upstream fish movements here turned out to be dispersal movements rather than highly motivated spawning migrations (Daget 1950, 1959a). Large numbers of fish congregate below this barrage at low water; but fisheries above the dam declined considerably.

The floodplains are the main producers of fish protein in the subtropical savanna zones. As floodplains become modified for other uses, traditional fisheries will be affected, and other methods will have to be sought whereby such areas can continue to produce the fish. Fish protein is more than ever needed now the human populations of West Africa are rising so rapidly.

5.5. REFERENCES

Albaret, A.A. 1979. *Revue des recherches enterprises sur la fécondité des poissons d'eau douces africians.* ORSTOM for Réunion Trav. Limnol. afr., Nairobi.

Arawomo, G.A.O. 1976. Food and feeding in *Citharinus* species in L. Kainji, Nigeria. *J. Fish Biol.* 9:3–10.

Attionu, R.H. 1976. Some effects of water lettuce (*Pistia stratiotes,* L.) on its habitat. *Hydrobiologia* 50: 245–254.

Awachie, J.B.E. 1979. On fishing and fisheries management in large tropical African rivers with particular reference to Nigeria. In R.L. Welcomme (ed.), *Fishery management in large rivers.* FAO Fish. Tech. Pap. 194: 37–47.

Awachie, J.B.E. & E.C. Walson 1978. The atalla fishery of the Lower Niger, Nigeria. In R.L. Welcomme (ed.), *FAO, Rome CIFA Tech. Pap.* 5: 296–311.

Banister, K.E. & M.A. Clarke 1977. The freshwater fishes of the Arabian Peninsular. In *The Scientific Results of the Oman Flora and Fauna Survey 1975.* J. Oman Studies, Special Report, Min. Information & Culture, Oman.

Banks, J.W., M.J. Holden & R.H. McConnell 1966. Fishery Report. In E. White (ed.), *The first scientific report of the Kainji Biological Research Team.* Liverpool University.

Beadle, L.C. 1974. *The inland waters of tropical Africa: and introduction to tropical limnology.* London: Longman (second edn. 1981).

Benech, V. 1974. Données sur la croissance de *Citharinus citharus* (Poissons, Characiformes) dans le bassin Tchadien. *Cah. Off. Rech. Sci. Tech. Outre-Mer, sér. Hydrobiol.* 8: 23–33.

Benech, V. 1975. Croissance, mortalité et production de *Brachysynodontis batensoda* (Pisces, Mochokidae) dans l'archipel sud-est du lac Tchad. *Cah. Off. Rech. Sci.Tech. Outre-Mer, sér. Hydrobiol.* 9: 91–103.

Benech, V., J. Franc & P. Matelet. 1978. Utilisation du chalut électrifié pour l'échantillonnage des poissons en milieu tropical (T'chad). *Cah. Off. Rech. Sci. Tech. Outre-Mer., sér. Hydrobiol.* 12: 197–224.

Benech, V. & S. Lek. 1981. Résistance à l'hypoxie et observations écologiques pour seize espèces de poissons du Tchad. *Rev. Hydrobiol. trop.* 14: 153–168.

Benech, V., J. Lemoalle & J. Quensière. 1978. Mortalités de poissons et conditions de milieu dans le lac Tchad au cours d'une période de secheresse. In R.L. Welcomme (ed.), *CIFA Tech. Pap.* 5: 123–134.

Biswas, S. 1977. Thermal stability and phytoplankton in Volta Lake, Ghana. *Hydrobiologia* 56: 195–198.

Biswas, S. 1978. Observations on phytoplankton and primary productivity in Volta Lake, Ghana. *Verh. int. Verein, theor. angew. Limnol.* 20: 1672–1676.

Blache, J. & F. Miton. 1962. *Première contribution à la connaissance de la pêche dans le bassin hydrographique Logone-Chari-lac Tchad.* Paris: ORSTOM.

Blache, J., F. Miton, A. Stauch, A. Iltis & G. Loubens. 1964. *Les poissons du bassin du Tchad et du bassin adjacent du Mayo Kebbi.* Mém. Off. Rech. Scient. Tech. Outre-Mer, Paris.

Blake, B.F. 1977a. Aspects of the reproductive biology of *Hippopotamyrus pictus* in Lake Kainji, with notes on four other mormyrid species. *J. Fish Biol.* 11: 437–445.

Blake, B.F. 1977b. Food and feeding of the mormyrid fishes of Lake Kainji, Nigeria, with special reference to seasonal variation and interspecific differences. *J. Fish. Biol.* 11: 315–328.

Blake, B.F. 1977c. Lake Kainji, Nigeria, a summary of the changes within the fish population since the impoundment of the Niger in 1968. *Hydrobiologia* 53: 131–137.

Blake, B.F. 1977d. The effect of the impoundment of Lake Kainji, Nigeria, on the indigenous species of mormyrid fishes. *Freshwater Biol.* 7: 37–42.

Blake, C. & B.F. Blake. 1978. The use of opercular bones in the study of age and growth of *Labeo senegalensis* from L. Kainji, Nigeria. *J. Fish. Biol.* 13: 287–295.

Boeseman, M. 1963. An annotated list of fishes from the Niger Delta. *Zool. Verh. Leiden* 61: 1–48.

Carmouze, J.P., J.R. Durand & C. Lévêque (eds.) 1983. Lake Chad: Ecology and productivity of a shallow tropical ecosystem. *Monographiae Biologicae* 53. The Hague: Junk.

Carmouze, J.P., C. Dejoux, J-R Durand, R. Gras, A. Iltis, L. Lauzanne, J. Lemoalle, C. Lévêque, G. Loubens & L. Saint-Jean. 1972. Contribution à la connaissance du bassin Tchadien. Grandes zones écologiques du lac Tchad. *Cah. Off. Rech. Sci. Tech. Outre-Mer., sér. Hydrobiol.* 6: 103–169.

Chouret, A. 1978. La persistance des effets de la secheresse sur le lac Tchad. In R.L. Welcomme (ed.), *CIFA Tech. Pap.* 5: 74–91.

Corbet, P.S. 1961. The food of non-cichlid fishes in the L. Victoria basin, with remarks on their evolution and adaptation to lacustrine conditions. *Proc. zool. Soc. Lond.* 136: 1–101.

Daget, J. 1950. La passe à poissons de Markala. *Bull. Inst. fr. Afr. noire* 12: 1166–1167.

Daget, J. 1952. Mémoire sur la biologie des poissons du Niger Moyen. 1. Biologie et croissance des éspèces du genre *Alestes*. *Bull. Inst. fr. Afr. noire* 14: 191–225.

Daget, J. 1954. Les poissons du Niger Superieur. *Mém. Inst. fr. Afr. noire* 36: 1–391.

Daget, J. 1957a. Données recentes sur la biologie des poissons dans le delta central du Niger. *Hydrobiologia* 9: 321–347.

Daget, J. 1957b. Reproduction et croissance d'*Heterotis niloticus* Ehrenberg. *Bull. Inst. fr. Afr. noire 19, Sér. A.* 1: 295–323.

Daget, J. 1958. Sur trois éspèces de *Ctenopoma* (Poissons Anabantidae) de l'Ouest african. *Bull. Inst. fr. Afr. noire 20, Sér. A.* 2: 539–561.

Daget, J. 1959a. Effets du barrage de Markala sur les migrations de poissons dans le Moyen-Niger. *C.R. Réunion Tech. d'Athènes de l'UCIN* 4: 352–356.

Daget, J. 1959b. Les poissons du Niger superieure (1re note complémentaire). *Bull. Inst. fr. Afr. noire 21, Sér. A.* 2: 664–688.

Daget, J. 1962. Le genre *Citharinus*. *Revue Zool. Bot. afr.* 66: 81–106.

Daget, J. 1964. Note sur les *Lates niloticus* (Poissans, Centropomidae) immatures de la region de Mopti. *Bull. Inst. fr. Afr. noire 26, Sér. A.* 2: 1320–1339.

Daget, J. 1966. Abondance relative des poissons dans les plaines inondées par la Béonoué à hauteur de Garoua (Cameroun). *Bull. Inst. fr. Afr. noire 28, Sér. A.* 1: 247–258.

Daget, J. 1967. Introduction a l'étude hydrobiologique du lac Tchad. *C.R. Soc. Biogeogr.* 380: 6–10.

Daget, J. 1975. Biology of the Sahelian fisheries. *Annex 6, FAO, Rome, CIFA/OP* 4: 18–22.

Daget, J., N. Planquette & P. Planquette. 1973. Premières données sur la dynamique des peuplements de poissons du Bandama (Côte d'Ivoire). *Bull. Mus. natn. Nat. Hist. (Paris), 3e Ser., 151, Écol. gén.* 7: 129–142.

Daget, J. & J-R Durand. 1981. Poissons. In J.-R. Durand & C. Lévêque (eds.), *Flore et faune aquatiques de l'Afrique Sahelo-Soudanienne* (vol. 2). Paris: ORSTOM.

Daget, J. & A. Stauch. 1963. Poissons de la partié camerounaise du bassin de la Benoué. *Mélang. Ichthyol., Mém. Inst. fr. Afr. noire, IFAN – Dakar* 68: 85–107.

Dansoko, D., H. Breman & J. Daget. 1976. Influence de la sécheresse sur les populations d'*Hydrocynus* dans le Delta Central du Niger. *Cah. Off. Rech. Sci. Tech. Outre-Mer, Sér Hydrobiol.* 10: 71–76.

Durand, J-R. 1970. Les peuplements ichthyologiques de l'El Beid. *Cah. Off. Rech. Sci. Tech. Outre-Mer, Sér. Hydrobiol.* 4: 1–26.

Durand, J-R. 1973. Note sur l'évolution des prises par unite d'effort dans le lac Tchad. *Cah.*

Off. Rech. Sci. Tech. Outre-Mer, Ser. Hydrobiol. 7: 195–207.

Durand, J.-R.1978. Biologie et dynamique des populations *d'Alestes baremose* (Pisces, Characidae) du bassin Tchadien. *Trav. Doc. Off. Rech. Sci. Tech. Outre-Mer.* 98: 1–332.

Durand, J-R. 1979–80. Évolution des captures totales (1962–1977) et devenir des pêcheries de la région du lac Tchad. *Cah. Off. Rech. Sci. Tech. Outre-Mer, Sér. Hydrobiol.* 13: 93–111.

Durand, J-R. & C. Lévêque (eds.) 1981. *Flore et faune aquatiques de l'Afrique Sahelo-Soundanienne* (2 vols). Paris: ORSTOM.

Evans, W.A. & J. Vanderpuye. 1973. Early development of the fish populations and fisheries of Volta Lake. In W.C. Ackermann, G.F. White & E.B. Worthington (eds.), *Man-made lakes; their problems and environmental effects.* Am. Geophys. Union.

Ewer, D.W. 1966. Biological investigation on the Volta Lake, May 1964 to May 1965. In R.H. Lowe-McConnell (ed.), *Man-made Lakes.* London: Academic Press.

FAO 1975. Report of the consultation on fisheries problems in the Sahelian zone, Bomoko, Mali, November 1974. *FAO Rome CIFA/Occ. Pap.* 4.

FAO 1978. (see Welcomme, ed.).

Green, J. 1977. Haematology and habits in catfish of the genus *Synodontis. J. Zool., Lond.* 182: 39–50.

Greenwood, P.H. 1976. Fish fauna of the Nile, pp. 127–141. In J. Rzoska (ed.), *The Nile, biology of an ancient river.* The Hague: Junk.

Hall, J.B. & D.V.V. Okali 1974. Phenology and productivity of *Pistia stratiotes* on the Volta Lake, Ghana. *J. appl. Ecol.* 11: 709–725.

Holden, M.J. 1963. The populations of fish in dry season pools of the R. Sokoto. *Fishery Publs. Colon. Off.* 19: 1–58.

Holden, M.J. & W. Reed. 1972. *West African freshwater fish.* West African Nature Handbooks. Longman.

Hopson, A.J. 1972a. A study of the Nile Perch in Lake Chad. *Overseas. Res. Publ.* 19. London: HMSO.

Hopson, Jane. 1972b. Breeding and growth in two populations of *Alestes baremose* from the northern basin of L. Chad. *Overseas Res. Publ.* 20. London: HMSO.

Imevbore, A.M.A. & O. Bakare, 1970. The food and feeding habits of non-cichlid fishes in the River Niger in the Kainji reservoir area, pp. 49–64. In S.A. Visser (ed.), *Kainji, a Nigerian man-made lake.* Kainji Lake Studies (vol. Ecology), Nigerian Inst. Social Economic Research, Ibadan.

Imevbore, A.M.A. & W.S. Okpo 1975. Aspects of the biology of Kainji Lake fishes. In A.M.A. Imevbore & O.S. Adegoke (eds.), *The ecology of Lake Kainji : The transition from river to lake.* Ile-Ife: University of Ife Press.

Ita, E.O. 1973. Approaches to the evaluation and management of the fish stocks in Kainji Lake, Nigeria. *Afr. J. trop. Hydrobiol Fish.* (Special Issue) 1: 35–52.

Ita. E.O. 1978. Analysis of fish distribution in Kainji Lake. Nigeria. *Hydrobiologia* 58: 233–244.

Lauzanne, L. 1972. Régimes alimentaires principles especes de poissons de l'archipel oriental du Lac Tchad. *Verh. int. Verein. Limnol.* 18: 636–646.

Lauzanne, L. 1975. Régimes alimentaires *d'Hydrocynus forskalii* (Pisces, Characidae) dans le lac Tchad et ses tributaires. *Cah. Off. Rech. Sci. Tech. Outre-Mer, Sér. Hydrobiol* 9: 105–121.

Lauzanne, L. 1976. Régimes alimentaires et relations trophiques des poissons du lac Tchad. *Cah. Off. Rech. Sci. Tech. Outre-Mer, Sèr. Hydrobiol.* 10: 267–310.

Lauzanne, L. 1978, Croissance de *Sarotherodon galilaeus* (Pisces, Cichlidae) dans le lac Tchad. *Cybium, 3ᵉ Sér.* 3: 5–14.

Lawson, G.W., T. Petr, S. Biswas, E.R. Biswas & J. Reynolds 1969. Hydrobiological work of the Volta Basin Research Project. *Bull. Inst. fr. Afr. noire., Sér. A.* 31: 965–1005.

Lawson, G.W. 1970. Lessons of the Volta – a new man-made lake in tropical Africa. *Biol. Conserv.* 2: 90–96.

Lek, S. & S. Lek 1977. Écologie et biologie de *Micralestes acutidens* (Peters, 1852) (Pisces, Characidae) du bassin du lac Tchad. *Cah. Off. Rech. Sci. Tech. Outre-Mer, Sér. Hydrobiol.* 11: 255–268.

Lek, S. & S. Lek 1978a. Diet of *Ichthyborus besse besse* (Pisces, Citharinidae) from the basin of L. Chad, Africa. *Cybium, 3ᵉ Sér.* 3: 59–75.

Lek, S. & S. Lek 1978b. Ecology and biology of *Ichthyborus besse besse* (Pisces, Citharinidae) from the L. Chad basin, Africa. *Cybium, 3ᵉ Sér.* 74: 65–86.

Lek, S. & S. Lek 1978c. Études de quelques éspèces de petits Mormyridae du bassin du lac Tchad. I. Observations sur la repartition et l'écologié. *Cah. Off. Rech. Sci. Tech. Outre-Mer, Sér. Hydrobiol.* 12: 225–236.

Lelek, A. 1973. Sequence of changes in fish populations of the new tropical man made lake, Kainji, Nigeria, West Africa. *Arch. Hydrobiol.* 71: 381–420.

Lelek, A. & S. El-Zarka. 1973. Ecological comparison of the preimpoundment and post-impoundment fish faunas of the R. Niger and Kainji Lake, Nigeria. In Ackermann, White & Worthington (eds.), *Man-made lakes: their problems and environmental effects.* Geophysical Monogr. (Am. Geophysis. Union) 17.

Lévêque, C. 1979. Biological productivity of Lake Chad. *ORSTOM for Réunion Trav. Limnol. Afr. Nairobi* (Dec. 1979): 1–30.

Lévêque, C. & P. Herbinet 1979–80. Caracteres meristiques et biologie de *Schilbe mystus* (Pisces, Schilbeidae) in Côte d'Ivoire. *Cah. Off. Rech. Sci. Tech. Outre-Mer., Sér. Hydrobiol.* 13: 161–170.

Lewis, D.S.C. 1974a. *An illustrated key to the fishes of Lake Kainji.* London: Overseas Development Administration.

Lewis, D.S.C. 1974b. The effects of the formation of Lake Kainji (Nigeria) upon the indigenous fish population. *Hydrobiologia* 45: 281–301.

Lewis, D.S.C. 1974c. The food and feeding habits of *Hydrocynus forskahlii* Cuv. and *H. brevis* Günther in L. Kainji, Nigeria. *J. Fish Biol.* 6: 349–363.

Loubens, G. 1974. Quelques aspects de la biologie des *Lates niloticus* du Tchad. *Cah. Off. Rech. Sci. Tech. Outre-Mer, Ser. Hydrobiol.* 8: 3–21.

Lowe-McConnell, R.H. & A.A. Wuddah 1972. *Freshwater fishes of the Volta and Kainji lakes.* Accra: Ghana Univ. Press.

Lowe-McConnell, R.H. 1975. *Fish communities in tropical freshwaters.* London: Longman.

Lowe-McConnell, R.H. 1979. Ecological aspects of seasonality in fishes of tropical waters, pp. 219–241. In P.J. Miller (ed.), *Fish Phenology: anabolic adaptiveness in teleosts.* Symp. Zool. Soc. Lond. 44.

Matthes, H. 1978. The problem of rice-eating fish in the Central Niger delta, Mali. In R.L. Welcomme (ed.), *FAO Rome, CIFA. Tech. Pap.* 5: 225–252.

Merona, B. De. 1979–80. Écologie et biologie de *Petrocephalus bovei* (Pisces, Mormyridae) dans les rivieres de Côte d'Ivoire. *Cah. Off. Rech. Sci. Tech, Outre-Mer, Sér. Hydrobiol.* 13: 117–127.

Merona, B. de. 1981. Zonation ichtyologie du bassin du Bandama (Côte d'Ivoire) *Rev. Hydrobiol. trop.* 14: 63–75.

Merona B. de & J.M. Ecoutin 1979. La croissance des poissons d'eau douce africains: revue bibliographique et assai de généralisation. *ORSTOM for Réunion Trav. Limnol. afr. Nairobi* (Dec. 1979).

Mok, M. 1974. Biométrie et biologie des *Schilbe* (Pisces, Siluriformes) du bassin Tchadien. IIe Partie Biologie comparée des deux éspèces. *Cah. Off. Rech. Sci. Tech., Outre-Mer, Sér. Hydrobiol.* 9: 33–60.

Motwani, M.P. & Y. Kanwai 1970. Fish and fisheries of the coffer-dammed right channel of the R. Niger at Kainji. In S.A. Visser (ed.), *Kainji Lake studies*; Ecology (vol. 1). Nigerian Inst. Soc. Econ. Res., Ibadan University.

Obeng, L.E. (ed.) 1968. *Man-made lakes: the Accra symposium.* Ghana: University Press.

Obeng-Asamoa, E.K., D.M. John & H.N. Appler 1981. Periphyton in the Volta Lake. I. Seasonal changes on the trunks of flooded trees. *Hydrobiologia* 76: 191–200.

Okali, D.U.U. & J.B. Hall 1974. Die-back of *Pistia stratiotes* on Volta Lake, Ghana. *Nature, Lond.* 248 (5447): 452.

Okedi, J. 1969. Observations on the breeding and growth of certain mormyrid fishes of the Lake Victoria basin. *Revue Zool. Bot. afr.* 79: 34–64.

Olatunde, A.A. 1977. The distribution, abundance and trends in the establishment of the family *Schilbeidae* (Osteichthyes, Siluriformes) in L. Kainji, Nigeria. *Hydrobiologia* 56: 69–80.

Olatunde, A.A. 1978. The food and feeding habits of *Eutropius niloticus* (Ruppell) family Schilbeidae (Osteichthyes : Siluriformes) in L. Kainji, Nigeria. *Hydrobiologia* 57: 197–207.

Olatunde, A.A. & O.A. Ogunbiyi 1977. Digestive enzymes in the alimentary tracts of three tropical catfish. *Hydrobiologia* 56: 21–24.

Otobo, F.O. 1974. The potential for clupeid fishery in L. Kainji, Nigeria. *Afr. J. Trop. Hydrobiol. Fish.* 3: 123–134.

Otobo, F.O. 1977. Clupeid and cichlid fishing in Lake Kainji. *Nigerian Field* 42: 98–103.

Otobo, F.O. 1978. The commercial fishery of the Middle Niger River, Nigeria. In R.L. Welcomme (ed.), *CIFA Tech. Pap.* 5: 185–208.

Paugy, D. 1978. Ecologie et biologie des *Alestes baremoze* (Pisces, Characidae) des rivieres de Côte d'Ivoire. *Cah. Off. Rech. Sci. Tech. Outre-Mer, Sér. Hydrobiol.* 12: 245–275.

Paugy, D. 1979–80a Ecologie et biologie des *Alestes imberi* (Pisces, Characidae) des rivieres de Côte d'Ivoire comparaison méristique avec *A. nigricauda. Cah. Off. Rech. Sci. Tech. Outre-Mer, Sér. Hydobiol.* 13: 129–141.

Paugy, D. 1979–80b. Ecologie et biologie des *Alestes nurse* (Pisces, Characidae) des rivieres de Côte d'Ivoire. *Cah. Off. Rech. Sci. Tech. Outre-Mer, Sér. Hydrobiol.* 13: 143–160.

Payne, A.I. 1975. The reproductive cycle, condition and feeding in *Barbus liberiensis*, a tropical stream-dwelling cyprinid. *J. Zool. Lond.* 176: 247–269.

Petr, T. 1967. Fish populations changes in the Volta Lake in Ghana during the first sixteen months. *Hydrobiologia* 30: 193–220.

Petr, T. 1968a. Distribution, abundance and food of commercial fish in the Black Volta and Volta man-made lake in Ghana during its first period of filling (1964–1966). I. Mormyridae. *Hydrobiologia* 32: 417–448.

Petr, T. 1968b. The establishment of lacustrine fish population in the Volta Lake in Ghana during 1964–1966. *Bull. Inst. fr. Afr. noire, 30: Sér. A* 1: 257–269.

Petr, T. 1970a. Macroinvertebrates of flooded trees in the man-made Volta Lake (Ghana) with special reference to the burrowing mayfly *Povilla adusta* Navas. *Hydrobiologia* 36: 373–398.

Petr, T. 1970b. The bottom fauna of the rapids of the Black Volta River in Ghana *Hydrobiologia* 36: 399–418.

Petr, T. 1971. Lake Volta – a progress report. *New Scientist* 49: 178–182.

Petr, T. 1975. On some factors associated with the initial high catches in new African man-made lakes. *Archiv. Hydrobiol.* 75: 32–49.

Petr, T. 1978. Tropical man-made lakes – their ecological impact. *Arch Hydrobiol.* 81: 368–385.

Pillay, T.V.R. 1967. Estuarine fishes in West Africa, pp. 639–646. In G. Lauff (ed.), *Estuaries*. Am. Ass. Adv. Sci., Washington, Publ. 83.

Poll, M. 1973. Nombre et distribution géographique des poissons d'eau douce africains. *Bull. Mus. natn Hist. nat., Paris, 3 Sér. 150, Écol. générale* 6: 113–128.

Quensière, J. 1978. Influence de la secheresse sur les pêcheries du delta du Chari (1971–73). In R.L. Welcomme (ed.), *CIFA Tech. Pap.* 5: 107–122.

Reed, W., J. Burchard, A.J. Hopson, J. Jenness & I. Yaro 1967. *Fish and fisheries of Northern Nigeria*. Ministry of Agriculture, Zaria, Northern Nigeria.

Reid, G. Mc & H. Sydenham 1979. A check list of the Lower Benue river fishes and an ichthyological review of the Benue River (West Africa). *J. nat. Hist.* 13: 41–67.

Reynolds, J.D. 1970. Biology of small pelagic fishes in the new Volta Lake in Ghana, Pt. I. The lake and the fish: feeding habits. *Hydrobiologia* 35: 568–603.

Reynolds, J.D. 1972. Pt. II. Schooling and migration. *Hydrobiologia* 38: 568–603.

Reynolds, J.D. 1974. Pt. III. Sex and reproduction. *Hydrobiologia* 45: 489–508.

Roberts, T.R. 1975. Geographical distribution of African freshwater fishes. *Zool. J. Linn. Soc.* 57: 249–319.

Sagua, V.O. 1978. The effect of the Kainji dam, Nigeria, upon fish production in the River Niger below the dam at Faku. In R.L. Welcomme (ed.), *CIFA Tech. Pap.* 5: 210–224.

Sagua, V.O. 1979. Observations on the food and feeding habits of the African electric catfish, *Malapterurus electricus. J. Fish. Biol.* 16: 61–70.

139

Stauch, A. 1966. *Le bassin Camerounais de la Benoué et sa pêche.* Mém. ORSTOM 15.
Stauch, A. 1977. Fish statistics in the Lake Chad during the drought (1969–1976) *Cah. Off. Rech. Sci. Tech. Outre-Mer, Ser. Hydrobiol.* 11: 201–215.
Stauch, A. 1978. The future of the fisheries in the Lake Chad basin. In R.L. Welcomme (ed.), *CIFA Tech. Pap.* 5: 66–73.
Sydenham, D.H.J. 1975. Observations on the fish populations of a Nigerian forest stream. *Rev. Zool. afr.* 89: 257–272.
Sydenham, H. 1977. The qualitative composition and longitudinal zonation of the fish fauna of the River Ogun. *Rev. Zool. Bot. afr.* 91: 974–996.
Tobor, J.G. 1972. The food and feeding habits of some Lake Chad commercial fish. *Bull. Inst. fond. Afr. noire* 34: 179–211.
Vanderpuye, C.J. 1972. Fishery resource assessment and monitoring in the development and control of fisheries in the lake Volta. Symp. Eval. Fish. Res. Devt. Manag. Inland Fish., Fort-Lamy, Chad, 29 Nov.-6 Dec. 1972. *CIFA/72/S.* 11: 1–28.
Viner, A.B. 1970. Hydrobiology of Lake Volta, Ghana. II. Some observations on biological features associated with the morphology and water stratification. *Hydrobiologia* 35: 230–248.
Welcomme, R.L. 1974. The fisheries ecology of African floodplains. Consultation on fisheries problems in the Sahelian zone Bamako, Mali, November 1974. *FAO Rome, FI: FPSZ/74/4:* 1–40.
Welcomme, R.L. 1976. Some general and theoretical considerations on the fish yield of African rivers. *J. Fish. Biol.* 8: 351–364.
Welcomme, R.L. (ed.) 1978. Symposium on river and floodplain fisheries in Africa, Bujumbura, Burundi, November 1977. In R.L. Welcomme, (ed.), *CIFA Tech. Pap.* 5.
Welcomme, R.L. 1979a. *Fisheries ecology of floodplain rivers.* London: Longman.
Welcomme, R.L. (ed.) 1979b. Fishery management in large rivers. *FAO Fish. Tech. Pap.* 194.
White, E. (ed.) 1966. *The first scientific report of the Kainji Biological Research Team.* University of Liverpool.
Willoughby, N.G. 1974. *The ecology of the genus Synodontis (Pisces: Siluroidei) in Lake Kainji, Nigeria.* Ph.D. thesis, University of Southampton.

Part Two
Human use

A.T.GROVE
African Studies Centre, Free School Lane, Cambridge

6

The river people

6.1 ETHNIC DIVERSITY

Nearly all the great language groups of Africa are represented amongst the peoples of the West African river basins, some groups by several different languages. The ethnic diversity is greater alongside the rivers themselves than on the extensive upland plains between them for the rivers make a variety of lifestyles possible; people have always been on the move upstream and downstream to fish and trade, as well as in response to political pressures and warfare. Small language groups are most numerous and the ethnic complexity greatest in escarpment zones and especially in the highland source areas where communities persist that were never absorbed into great states and retain their distinctiveness into the present.

The great states that grew up around long-distance trading centres encompassed peoples belonging to several ethnic groups but over the generations some degree of cultural homogenisation took place. As a result, several millions of people today speak Kanuri, Songhay, Bambara or Malinke. The largest language community of all is that of the Hausa. Living on either side of the Niger-Chad watershed and numbering some 40 millions the Hausa are the largest group in Africa of people speaking one and the same language, apart from the Arab-speakers of the north.

Differences in language in the vicinity of the rivers are allied to differences in economic activities. The Bozo of the Inland Niger Delta, for instance, are primarily fishermen descended, it has been tentatively suggested, from people who lived in the southern Sahara a few thousand years ago and were involved in an 'aqualithic culture' (Sutton 1974). The Sorko of the Niger bend are fishermen who also depend on farming. In addition there are small communities primarily engaged in fishing who belong to larger groups in which the majority of the people are cultivators or pastoralists.

Agriculturalists living close to the rivers depend heavily on seasonal floods for growing rice and other crops. The locations of their settlements and their farms are related to minor variations in elevation and soil conditions which are in turn the outcome of changes in climate and sea-level in the course of the Late Quaternary and more recent shifts in channel positions. Pastoralists, notably the Fulani (or Peul) rely on riverine plains for dry season grazing; in the rains they and their herds diffuse over the semi-arid plains or in more southerly areas ascend to montane grasslands out of reach of tsetse-fly.

When Europeans first penetrated West Africa as traders, missionaries and soldier-administrators, they came into contact first with the peoples living on the coast and along the navigable rivers. When railways were planned late in the last century, the rivers of the interior were often seen as inland termini, but the tracks were aligned away from the valley floors to avoid the construction of bridges and embankments. Administrative centres were removed from the rivers towards the watersheds because of their greater accessibility and healthiness and so riverside peoples were in many cases neglected and little influenced by modernisation.

In recent years hydro-electricity schemes on Guinea savanna stretches of the Niger, Volta and Bandama rivers have thrust riparian peoples into contact with the modern world. Along the rivers of the Sudan and Sahel zones drought, urban expansion and irrigation schemes have modified and locally disrupted economies. In the coastal delta of the Niger, prospecting and oil extraction have brought engineers and machinery to remote creekside villages. New opportunities exist for riverside peoples and new threats are appearing to their established ways of life; they are responding to them according to their cultural backgrounds and associated perceptions of innovation. An attempt is made here to trace some of the strands in the cultural development of the riverside peoples since early times.

6.2 SOURCES OF INFORMATION

River terraces preserve evidence of the earliest human occupation in the form of stone implements in stratified sediments which sometimes allow cultural sequences to be established. Davies (1964, 1967) refers to the archaeological surveys that were made with Ghana government support in connection with the Volta River Project, and his maps of the distributions of Chellean, Sangoan and microlithic finds in Ghana show strong concentrations along the Volta. Breternitz (1975) presents the results of rescue studies made at Kainji. Shaw (1978) regrets more archaeological work was not done before the dam was completed. Connah (1981) shows how his excavations of the Daima tell on the clay plains south of Lake Chad throw light on the changing activities of people living on the plains of Borno. Contributions by Andrew and Susan Smith to Williams & Faure (1980) consider the environmental adaptation of nomads in the Niger bend region as a key to understanding prehistoric pastoralism and the introduction of cattle into West Africa. Ajayi &

144

Crowder (1971) and Swartz & Dumett (1980) bring together a number of regional surveys of West African history and prehistory. Fage (1977) writes about Upper & Lower Guinea before and at the time of the arrival of the Europeans, Rodney (1975) on the Guinea Coast and Levtzion (1975) on the interior. The journals of the early explorers, notably Mungo Park (1799), Denham et al. (1834), Caillié (1968), Barth (1965) and Baikie (1966) provide valuable information about riverine peoples before colonial rule.

Early anthropological studies of West African people were brought together by Forde (1950–60) and by Murdock (1959), Morgan & Pugh (1969) use the Bozo fishing grounds and the homeland of the Songhay as examples of community regions in their geographical study of West Africa. The Niger water folk in their environment have been described by Sundström (1972); Tymowski (1974) traces the development and the regression of Niger bend people in the pre-colonial period.

6.3 RIVERINE PEOPLE IN PREHISTORY

During the millennia from 18000 to 12000 years ago, when desert conditions extended 500 km south of the present Sahara, movement of people between the Mediterranean lands and the equatorial regions must have been very limited. As a result of several thousands of years of isolation from the rest of the world peoples living south of the Sahara may at this time have become more distinct both physically and culturally from those of Euro-Asia.

About 12000 years ago the climate became wetter and, in the interior of West Africa, rivers began to flow again and a great lake filling the Bodélé depression spread far to the south. Then for some centuries about 10000 BP there was a reversion to greater aridity, possibly before the rain forest had spread far from refuge areas lying near the Gulf of Guinea seaward of Cameroon Mountain and in areas further west. Excavations at Iwo-Eleru in south-west Nigeria (Shaw 1978) have revealed the bones of an individual who may have been a member of a community living during that dry interval in what is now the northern margin of the rain forest region. Wetter conditions returned and for much of the next 5000 years annual rainfall may have been some 300–400 mm more than at present over extensive areas.

Implements and weapons found in the vicinity of springs and former lakes and rivers in the southern Sahara make it clear that their users were fishermen as well as hunters. They used harpoons and hooks to catch Nile Perch and other fish in the northern tributaries of great river systems directed towards the Niger, even at the margins of the Tanezrouft in the upper reaches of the Tilemsi (Petit-Maire, et al., 1981). As early as 9000 BP lakeside dwellers were using and presumably making pottery; it was the broad similarity between the styles of pots throughout the southern Sahara, with a typical wavy line decoration, that prompted Sutton (1974)

146

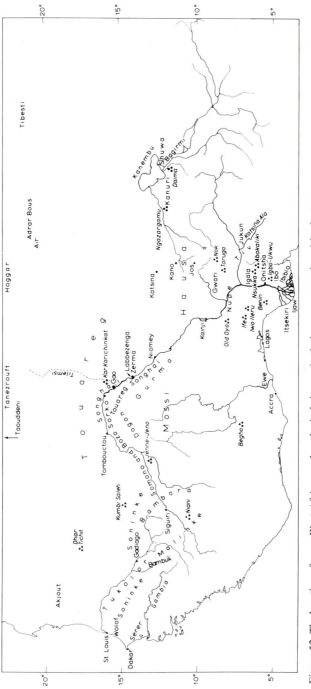

Figure 52. The location of some West African archaeological sites and ethnic groups mentioned in the text.

to refer to an aqualithic culture, implying linkages of some kind between peoples living in a broad latitudinal zone running right across the continent. These peoples or their neighbours engraved and painted pictures of the animals they hunted on near-vertical rock faces by waterholes, under rock shelters, especially in the enneris of Tibesti.

The savanna animals, splendidly portrayed in these barren surroundings, include elephant and rhinoceros, giraffe and buffalo, creatures that require great quantities of herbage and browse, implying that the early Holocene Sahara was a much greener land than it is today.

Following several less humid centuries about 7400 BP, the climate improved for over two millennia. In this final wet phase cattle were being herded in many parts of the Sahara and it is even possible that millet was being cultivated in the vicinity of the Hoggar (Camps 1969). At Adrar Bous, near the foot of a north-eastern extension of the Aïr mountains, the entire skeleton of an ox, a short-horned *Bos brachyseros*, was unearthed which has been dated to 5780±500 BP (Carter & Clark 1976). It is not yet known whether domestic animals were introduced to the Saharan region from the Middle East or the Maghreb. It is at least possible that the indigenous hunters and wild ancestors of the domestic animals in the Sahara, congregating near sources of water in the times of drought, developed symbiotic relationships, the animals providing a convenient source of milk and meat, the men providing some protection against other predators. Such relationships could conceivably have persisted and been developed further when wetter conditions returned (McIntosh & McIntosh 1981).

With the greater aridity after 5000 BP, severe droughts no doubt increased in frequency. Hunters and pastoralists in the course of their seasonal circuits retreated to the margins of the Nile floodplain and shifted down the valleys leading south from the Saharan mountains towards the Niger. Near Karkarichincat at the lower end of the Tilemsi the remains of a pastoral people have been found which indicate they were living in a manner not very different from their predecessors at Adrar Bous (Smith 1980a). For the regions closer to the Gulf of Guinea, information is still sparse but from excavations near Abakaliki and on the Nsukka hills it would seem likely that by four thousand years ago people were living in south-east Nigeria (Hartle 1980).

Domestication of some food crops is believed to have taken place in West Africa, though identification of this process is always difficult. It depends on the discovery and dating of carbonised cereals or the recognition of grain impressions on the surfaces of fragments of clay pots: one envisages the soft clay pots being made and placed on the ground where grain had been dropped and the grains or their impressions being preserved by the subsequent firing of the pots. Evidence of crop domestication from West Africa is summarised in Table 20 from McIntosh & McIntosh (1981).

The most convincing evidence relating to plant domestication in West Africa comes from the Dhar Tichitt villages of southern Mauritania,

Table 20. Evidence of crop domestication from West Africa (McIntosh & McIntosh 1980).

Site	Date	Genus and species	Reference
Amekni	6100-4850 BC	*Pennisetum* sp. (2 pollen grains)	Camps (1969)
Meniet	Mid-4th millendium BC	Cultivated grass (pollen)	Hugot (1968)
Adrar Bous	4000 BC	*Brachiaria* (single pottery impression)	Shaw (1977)
Adrar Bous	2000 BC	*Sorghum* (single pottery impression)	Shaw (1977)
Tichit	1000-900 BC	*Pennisetum* sp.	Munson (1980)
Kintampo (K6)	1400-1250 BC	*Elaeis guineensis*	Smith (1975)
Kintampo (K6)	1400-1250 BC	*Vigna unguiculata*	
Niani	AD 700-900	*Sorghum bicolor*	
Diama	AD 800-900	*Sorghum bicolor*	Connah (1981)

studied by Munson (1980). Implements and rock art show that until 4000 years ago the Dhar Tichitt people were still hunting, fishing and collecting; a lake nearby that had been as much as 30 m deep was drying up. Conditions became somewhat wetter about 1500 BC (as they did in the Chad basin about the same time) and the people took to herding cattle and goats and living in villages. About 1100 BC the Dhar Tichitt lake dried up completely. Pottery made a century or two later carries grain impressions of which the majority are no longer wild *Centhrus biflorus*, 'cram-cram', but domesticated *Pennisetum* millet. Cultivation could have begun with millet seed being scattered on the lake-bed after seasonal rains much as the Egyptians cultivated the Nile floodplain. The cultivators lived in stone-built houses overlooking the lake-bed from the crest of an escarpment; there they remained while the climate deteriorated until the sites were finally abandoned at some time before 400 BC.

Copper implements and ornaments were in use on the south side of the Sahara 3000 years ago and copper ores were mined in southern Mauritania, at Akjout and also in the Aïr mountains. Chariots appear amongst the rock art in the vicinity of the mines and at several other locations scattered across the desert, probably along former routeways. They were evidently light vehicles, comparable to chariots that have been found in Egypt that were drawn by ponies and may have been in use about the time of the Saharan engravings. The purposes for which the chariots were used in the south-west Sahara are uncertain. They were too light for carrying loads; they might have been used for hunting, or by raiding parties, possibly Egyptian or conceivably Carthaginian. Certainly they imply that conditions were less harsh climatically than they are at the present day and that people were crossing the Sahara before camels were used there.

Iron smelting was introduced to West Africa about 500 BC; the earliest furnaces so far discovered are at Taruga only about 150 km north of the confluence of the Niger and Benue (Rustad 1980). They resemble furnaces used by the Carthaginians who were settled at various points along the coast of the Maghreb three centuries earlier. The introduction of iron seems to be associated at many sites with other cultural innovations, particularly clay figurines of the kind first unearthed from alluvial tinfields at Nok and since found at various sites widely distributed over north-central Nigeria from the banks of the lower Katsena Ala to the plains north of the Jos Plateau.

At Jenne, finds of iron dating back to before 50 AD are associated with chaff from West African rice, *Oryza glaberrima*. There can be little doubt that this plant was domesticated in West Africa, most probably in the vicinity of the Inland Niger Delta, conceivably at a time some 3000 years ago when flood levels declined and cultivation of Niger alluvium became possible and attractive on account of increasing aridity on adjacent upland plains. Ancient stone tools are lacking near the surface in such areas of recent alluviation but clay figurines have been found in excavations at Jenne and also at Karkarichincat and far to the east at Daima which was settled originally about 2750 years ago, probably when Lake Chad retreated from its 286 m level.

Evidently special care should be taken when excavations are made in connection with river control works to ensure that archaeologists have the opportunity to study the sections so that terracotta figurines, stone and metal tools and dateable organic material can be recognised and retrieved. The information they yield not only contributes to knowledge of the peopling of the riverine areas, it adds to the story of environmental change and may assist in future project planning.

Whereas *Pennisetum* is the first crop known to have been grown at Dhar Tichitt and rice at Jenne-Jeno, early cultivation at Daima about 600 AD involved sorghum (Connah 1981). *Sorghum bicolor*, the least specialised of the cultivated sorghums probably originated somewhere between Ethiopia and eastern Chad from wild members of the subspecies *arundinaceum*. Various races have been developed by selection from the primitive bicolors to suit different climatic zones and for different uses. In a present-day village, several subspecies and varieties are grown, distributed according to soil texture and water-holding capacity.

A variety of *Sorghum caudatum*, commonly called masakwa is grown today in the firki clay plains near Daima as a dry season crop. The clays, probably lagoonal clays of the 286m lake, are highly impermeable. Low bunds are made along the contour to hold back rain water and encourage it to sink into the ground. Masakwa grown on seed beds during the rains is transplanted in October after the bunds have been broken down to allow surplus water still lying on the surface to drain away. Such intensive cultivation, it has been emphasised by Connah (1981), on plots cropped year after year, would have made it possible for sites such as Daima to be occupied continuously over the centuries. He also points out that a pick-like tool is needed for digging the hard clay and that bund construction may only have begun after iron tools became available.

The introduction of both iron tools and new crops to West Africa about 2500 years ago must have allowed populations to increase considerably. Woodland was now cleared not only for domestic fuel supplies but also to prepare land for cultivation and to make charcoal for iron-smelting and smithing, with resulting increased runoff and erosion. Alluvium washed down from hills overlooking the valley floor at Nok buried the clay figurines several metres deep and it is suspected that gullies near Zaria on the Chad-Niger watershed, originated as a result of accelerated erosion about the same time.

Long-distance trading had begun to develop in West Africa by the beginning of the 'iron-age'. Objects of gold and silver buried alongside great chiefs and excavated from tumuli near the lower Senegal had evidently been brought long distances. Copper ornaments dating to about 400 AD at Jenne-Jeno may have come from Merondet in Aïr where thousands of crucibles have been found that were used for refining copper. The introduction of the camel to the western Sahara about this time allowed parties of Berbers to reach West African rivers in search of trade goods and plunder.

According to oral tradition the Sorko, who had hunted hippo and fished along the Niger in the vicinity of the W, began to settle upstream and about the 6th century AD they reached Kukya near Labbezenga (Tymowski 1974). The Gow, a hunting tribe, called on the Lemta Berbers for assistance against the Sorko and it is possible that descendents of these same Berbers are still pastoralists in the Labbezenga area. The Sorko continued to move upstream, establishing settlements at Gao and Bemba and eventually came into contact with Bozo in the vicinity of Tombouctou.

The Bozo, in their home areas, are recognized by other peoples as the proper intermediaries with the river gods. Their fishing techniques are the most archaic and they are traditional exchange partners of the Dogon, the ancient inhabitants of the Bandiagara plateau. There is a tradition that the Noninke sacrificed a Bozo woman when they founded Jenne. Excavations in a great tumulus at El Oualadji on the banks of the Niger near the confluence of the Bar Issa and the Issa Ber upstream of Tombouctou, have revealed pottery and other remains which suggest it was erected by Bozo about the time of the arrival on the scene of the Sorko. Other tumuli of various ages remain to be studied and may throw more light on the sequence of occupation along the Niger bend (Tymowski 1974).

6.4 EARLY HISTORY OF THE RIVER PEOPLES

Some scraps of information can be derived from Arab writers about the early history of the great river valleys (Hopkins 1981). From these sources and archaeological studies it is known that the Soninke state of Ghana had emerged by 800 AD and that its capital was Kumbi Saleh, well to the north of the Niger and close to the edge of the desert (Figure 52). Its rulers depended on trans-Saharan trade, especially in gold brought from the headwater areas of the Niger and Senegal and from further afield in the vicinity of the Black Volta and probably further south still. Gold has been found at Jenne-Jeno in deposits dating back to 700 AD (McIntosh & McIntosh, personal communication). Already at this stage Saharan trade routes may have extended from the Mediterranean coast to the Niger and the Gulf of Guinea, though it is unlikely that any individual merchants ever attempted to follow such routes from one end to the other. Of the trading stations en route, Jenne, between the Niger and the Bani, was probably the most important. Gold from the south was exchanged for salt extracted far to the north at Taoudenni and Taghaza, slabs of salt being carried south by camel caravan to Tombouctou and shipped upstream to Jenne by canoe. In 1969, slabs of Saharan salt from the same sources could be seen on the quay at Kabara, stacked alongside Cuban sugar and crates of Czecho-Slovakian beer, awaiting shipment up and down the river by stern-wheelers.

The Guinea gold of ancient times purchased weapons, armour, silks and glass beads from the Mediterranean lands. When excavations were made at Igbo-Ukwu, east of the lower Niger not far north of the coastal delta in 1958–60, 165,000 glass beads were unearthed (Shaw 1970). There were dozens of skilfully made bronze and copper vessels and ornaments as well, the most remarkable horde ever discovered south of the Sahara, pointing to a long-established and cultured community in what is now the heart of Iboland. Radio-carbon dates of charcoal and wood fragments associated with the treasure strongly suggest it was buried in the ninth or tenth century. Such a culture cannot have been isolated. Already Oyo may have been founded and the Yoruba culture later to flower at Ife and neighbouring towns beginning to emerge.

Much further to the north, in the Sahel/Sudan, Kanem, a state with its capital north-east of Lake Chad came into existence in the ninth century and the Hausa States were probably founded a century later. Kawkaw, the Sorko settlement on the Niger bend, later to become known as Gao, was capital of a state by 874 AD. Settlements in the vicinity of Jenne, which had itself long been in existence, increased in number from the eighth to the twelfth century. This period, when trade flourished across the Sahara and along the Niger, was indeed a golden age in the interior of West Africa.

In 1076 Ghana submitted to the Almoravids and the most powerful kingdom in the region became Mali. Mali's capital was not on the desert fringes but further south, probably at Niani in the Guinea Republic or possibly further downstream: it is not known with certainty. Jenne continued to thrive through all this period, exporting not only gold and slaves, ivory and ebony, the products of the southlands to Tombouctou, but also supplying its neighbour with rice and other food products of the delta farmlands. Tombouctou was the Sudan town best known to Europe, mainly through the account of Ibn Battuta who had visited the

Figure 53. The tomb of Sonni Ali at Gao as it was in 1955.

more northern city when he travelled in Mali in 1352–3. He also visited Gao and was so impressed by what he saw that he described it as the largest, richest and most beautiful city in the Sudan.

In the course of the fifteenth century, Mali declined and Songhay became the chief state in the western Sudan. At Gao one can still visit the tomb of its greatest ruler, Sonni Ali, a carefully preserved mud pyramid (Figure 53). Suddenly in 1591 the Songhai Empire was shattered by an invasion force armed with guns, sent across the desert by the Sultan of Morocco to establish control over the source of Guinea (Jenne?) gold. Though it succeeded in destroying the armies of Songhai, it failed to secure effective control over the Middle Niger valley let alone the gold fields to the south. The old trading network of the western Sahara was disrupted and commerce shifted east to Katsina and Kano. In Tombouctou the Moors were unable to maintain effective contact with their base in Morocco. They settled down, married local women, and introduced Moorish culture and architectural forms which persist in an attenuated form to the present day.

In the subsequent history of the western Sudan a major part was to be played by the Fulani or Peul, a people about whose origin there is much speculation and uncertainty. It is possible that some of them at least acquired their ethnic distinctiveness in southern Mauritania. In the thirteenth century, conceivably in response to increasing aridity, groups of them crossed the Senegal river with their herds and entered Ferlo. From there they spread into Futa Tora and the headwaters of the Gambia river and moving on eastwards through the Mali Empire, which was in its heyday, reached the Macina area alongside the Inland Delta, north of Jenne (Figure 54).

152

There were and still are two main kinds of Fulani, though the relationships between the two in early times is far from clear. On the one hand there are the pastoralists, typically nomadic or semi-nomadic, not always Muslim. Then there are the members of an aristocracy who made connections with the rulers and urban dwellers of the lands into which they infiltrated and where eventually many of them settled. The chief traders and rulers in the towns were commonly Muslim: the chief of Jenne had been converted to Islam about 1240 AD, though the majority of the people even as late as the mid-fifteenth century were described by Arab travellers as going unclothed and had evidently not been converted.

For a time in the fifteenth century the eastward drift of the Fulani seems to have halted and then in the following century they entered Songhai, Gurma and the Hausa States. Those who remained in Macina at first welcomed the Moroccan invaders of Songhai and relations between them were moderately good for several decades. The Moroccans appointed rulers of Jenne and by degrees reduced western Songhai to a vassal state. An eastern part of the old Empire extending either side of the Niger in the area called Dendi continued to assert its independence. But the main opposition to the Moroccans came from Bambara chiefdoms west of the Inland Delta between Ségou and Jenne in an area which had formerly been a buffer zone between the declining Mali Empire and Songhai.

The Bambara were animists whose clan organisation involved the ton or age-set. The form and function of the ton was extended with the encouragement of the Bambara chiefs to provide them with an authority structure within their expanding state. They established a capital at Ségou and in time gained control of the whole of the Inland Delta, though they never built up a formal imperial administration.

Whenever conditions were disturbed and central power amongst the sedentary peoples was weakened, and especially under pressure of drought, pastoralists from the Saharan margins took advantage of the situation. The Touareg, from the middle of the seventeenth century raided the eastern remnant of Songhai inducing refugees from Dendi to move further still down the Niger. In 1739 the Touareg defeated the Moroccans and for some decades dominated the region around the Niger bend. The Bambara maintained a resistance, on occasions in alliance with Macina Fulani, and about the time of Mungo Park's exploratory voyages down the Niger towards the end of the eighteenth century they expanded north to encompass Tombouctou.

In the Chad region, the empire of Kanem had been disrupted in the fourteenth century when Borno to the west of the lake became autonomous with its capital at Ngazargamu on the Komadugu Yobe near Geidam. To the west lay a sparsely settled zone between Borno and Hausaland. The original seven Hausa States, the bakwai on the Niger-Chad watershed, gained accretions, the banza bakwai or counterfeit states whose rulers adopted Hausa culture though most of their people remained immune. They included Kebbi, Yelwa, Nupe and Ilorin

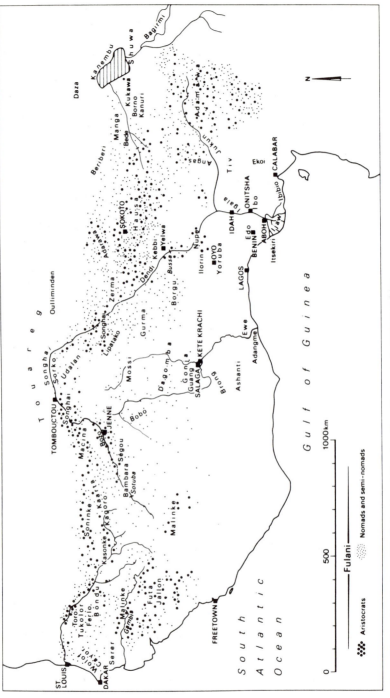

Figure 54. The distribution of the Fulani in relation to other ethnic groups in West Africa.

154

stretching along the Niger, and Kwororofa lying astride the Benue.

Amongst the peoples of the Sahel/Sudan zone in the fourteenth century Islam began to be adopted, especially in the main towns. The Mossi living in the headwater region of the Volta were an important exception (Skinner 1964). Their Kingdom had emerged in the twelfth or thirteenth century and by the time of the Moroccan invasion they were amongst the strongest peoples in the Niger bend region, commonly at war with the Bambara. Fulani were beginning to infiltrate Mossi territory and continued to do so, intermarrying with the cultivators and adopting many of the cultural traits of their hosts.

South of Mossi in the middle of the Volta basin the Kingdom of Dagomba and the state of Gonja date back four or five centuries. Both stand astride routeways between Hausaland and the Akan forests which assumed greater importance when trans-Saharan trade was diverted further to the east after 1591. Gonja was defeated by the Dagomba in 1713 and in 1732 became tributary to a new power in the lower Volta region, Asante (Ashanti) which was expanding north-east along the routes to Hausaland. Thus the lands of the Volta basin were linked by trade to Katsina and Kano to the northeast as well as to Ségou, Jenne and Tombouctou to the north. The routes were mainly overland, kola and other trade goods being carried by donkey. The Volta river was navigable in the dry season only as far upstream as Kete Krachi though for a short time after the rains small boats could reach as far as Daboya. A journey from the coast up the Volta to Salaga, a distance of 500 km by boats carrying salt and dried fish from the coast, involved crossing or bypassing several rapids but normally took less than a month.

On either side of the Volta mouth lived the Adangme and Ewe, people who have come from further east having been disturbed by the southward expansion of the Yoruba some five centuries ago. The Adangme settled on the west side of the Volta mouth; the Ewe split into several groups, some of which settled at Nuatja in Togo about 100 km north-east of the delta where they stayed until the end of the seventeenth century. Then three groups split off, one going north-west to found Kpandu, Kpalime, Leklebi and Wodzeamoy, the second travelling westwards and founding Ho and Adaklucte, and the third, the Anlo, moving south into the Volta delta. By 1682 when the Anlo were already settled there, the delta area was still widely covered by bush and woodland (Grove & Johansen 1968). The Anlo took up farming on the sandbar and fishing in the lagoons and later in the sea, and just as the Ada people made salt in the Songaw lagoon and exported it to the north, so did the Anlo extract salt from the Keta lagoon and trade it up the river.

River traffic has long been active, though information on its early importance is limited (Smith 1970). In the interior, boats were usually smaller and less capacious than near the coast, both because of shortage of large trees and the need for manoeuvreability in narrow channels. On the middle Niger, vessels built with planks were of considerable size and such boats continue to be used today. Fleets of canoes handled by local

Figure 55. A fishing boat on the Niger at Gao with bare dunes on the far side of the river.

fishermen had enable Songhay in the expansive years to bring remote provinces under control and extend upstream beyond the Sotuba rapids and downstream as far as Bussa. The first European travellers described canoes 20 m long and 2 m broad, capable of carrying a hundred men on the creeks and lagoons between Benin and the Bini communities in Lagos. Aboh at the head of the delta and Onitsha were thriving ports by the seventeenth century with boats carrying cows, goats and sheep as well as yams downstream and palm-oil and plantains upstream. The builders of the largest canoes lived here in the forest belt which provided the great tree trunks used as raw material, *Ceiba pentandra*, the silk-cotton tree and *Triplochiton scleroxylon* (Figures 55 and 56).

The Niger delta may have been occupied from very ancient times, the original inhabitants, judging by their oral traditions and the antiquity of their language, being the Ijo or Ijaw (Alagoa 1972). In spite of its uniformly low relief, activities in the delta have always been strongly differentiated according to the physiographic zones. Towards the head of the delta, the land is well above water level in the first half of the year but is usually flooded from the river for a month or two towards the end of the rainy season. Farming is more important than fishing with the production of bananas, plantains, cassava, cocoyam, swamp rice and other crops. The salt water mangrove swamp zone to seaward is flooded at high-tide and is only sparsely peopled, with settlements mainly confined to the higher levées alongside the major distributaries. The majority of the people are fisherfolk who formerly made salt from sea-water, and from the aerial roots of the mangrove, and traded it for foodstuffs with the people inland. The sandy frontal beach-ridge islands rising a metre or two above flood level provided settlement sites for fishing communities and later for commercial centres, (Figure 26).

The expansion of the Benin Empire around the time of arrival of the first Europeans is believed to have had repercussions over a wide area, east of the river in Iboland and as far as Calabar (Connah 1975). The

156

Figure 56. The riverside at Gao.

Itsekiri of the western delta were pressed south and they in turn displaced or infiltrated the Nimbe or Brass Ijo. With the exception of the Igala at Idah there were no large states along the river below Kworarafa on the Benue and Nupe on the Niger, both far upstream. Iboland was fragmented with no paramount chiefs in spite of the antiquity of the Igbo-Ukwu 'culture' and the relative ease of movement through the area by means of the Anambra and Imo rivers and along rolling upland interfluves. However, Ibo towns such as Aboh and Onitsha were in close touch with Benin and had been involved in long-distance trading up and down the river long before European ships steamed up the river about the middle of the nineteenth century.

In Senegambia as in many other riverine areas of West Africa local economies had ceased to be subsistent several centuries ago. The people of the Senegal delta traded salt and dried fish up the river for grain from the upper basin. Riparian farmers exchanged millet from their farms for livestock and milk products from Berber and Fulani herdsmen on the plains to north and south. At Gajaaja (Gadiaga) on the upper river, Soninke Diula (dyoula, jula) operated ancient long-distance trading networks that extended from the southern sources of gold and kola nuts to the Saharan caravan trails, networks that seem to have persisted since the imperial years of Ghana and continued to function through the periods of turmoil that accompanied Fulani expansion and Moorish invasion until the colonial period.

6.5 THE COLONIAL PERIOD

6.5.1 *Senegambia*

European penetration of West Africa first took place where the trading networks and extensive political linkages of the Sahel/Sudan reached the coast. Shortly after their arrival on the coast the Portuguese sailed far up the Gambia river and soon diverted Bambuk gold from the trans-Saharan routes. By the middle of the seventeenth century thousands of slaves were being exported annually as well as skins, beeswax, ivory and gum arabic in exchange for cloth, ironware and weapons. Local craftsmen were unable to complete with European manufactures; inter-regional trading links were weakened; disparities of wealth between nobles and peasants increased.

The Senegal offered a somewhat more difficult way to the interior than the Gambia river. Its mouth was obstructed by a long peninsula and sandbanks and Adanson (1759) notes that pilot-boats of 50 to 60 tonnes, manned by the local Wolof, were used to enter the river. He travelled up and down the Senegal about 1749 and wrote of 'numerous droves of elephants walking on its borders, sea-horses, crocodiles and an infinite multitude of other extraordinary animals'. At Podor 'on the south bank of the River Niger' as the Senegal was still called, the great quantity of wood cut down by the French 'for upwards of ten years they have been settled there has removed the forest further back to the distance of a small half league'.

It was by the lower river, from a base at Dagana, that the French attempted an agricultural colonisation scheme early in the nineteenth century. The Wolof were unwilling to give up their land and in 1827 they systematically broke down the dykes around the fields (Barry 1979). Labour was always in short supply, partly because of the disruption caused by the slave trade, and in 1831 the project failed.

Production of groundnuts, introduced originally by the Portuguese, rapidly increased in the course of the nineteenth century to satisfy European demand for vegetable oil. The areas most suitable for the crop were the sandy plains well to the south of the river. The Senegal valley lost much of its commercial vitality and many of its people, notably Wolof, migrated south into Cayor.

A railway from St. Louis to Dakar was built in the 1880s opening up new areas for groundnuts and about the same time work began on a line from Kayes on the upper Senegal to Bamako on the Niger. Soninke traders on the upper river found it increasingly difficult to compete with the Europeans and both they and the Tukulor from further downstream emigrated to the growing towns of Kaolack and Dakar. Bambara and Malinke from the upper Niger region were now attracted to the groundnut growing areas and as production increased from 50,000 in 1890 to over 250,000 t twenty years later, the Senegal valley to the north became a relatively neglected periphery of colonial Senegal (Figure 57).

Cultivation alongside the Senegal river depends on the annual flood

158

Figure 57. The Senegal at Kayes, 1969.

soaking the soil and allowing crops to be grown in the early dry season as the waters recede. In dry years the extent of land watered is too small; in wet years inundations are excessive; alongside the lowest reaches the land suffers from salting caused by seawater entering the river when the flow of the Senegal is much diminished. Nevertheless the décrue cultivation normally allows riverside dwellers to grow beans, cassava, sweet potatoes and maize to supplement millet and groundnuts from their rainfed farms and in times of drought they suffer less severely than those living on the sandy plains to the south. The people, especially of the middle valley, are tenaciously attached to their way of life and determined to keep control over their land (Adams 1977).

In the course of this century Senegalese townspeople came to rely heavily on imported rice and after the Second World War the colonial authorities, in the form of the Mission d'Aménagement du Senegal (MAS), instituted a project north of the Lac de Guier at Richard Toll which was intended to reduce reliance on rice imports. Control gates were placed across the channel leading from the Senegal river into the lake, allowing floodwaters to enter but excluding salt water in the dry season. Some of the stored water supplies Dakar but a surplus is available for irrigation. By 1960, about 5000 ha were under rice, cultivation being mechanised except for a small area made available to Senegalese settlers. Yields have seldom exceeded about 3 tons per hectare and large subsidies have been required (Figure 58).

Figure 58. Senegal floodwater passing through the control gates at Richard Toll in October 1969 to enter a canal leading into the Lac de Guier.

After independence a new attempt was made to develop the delta by the Société d'Aménagement des Terres du Delta du fleuve Senegal (SAED) which was intended to supervise farmers, provide seed and fertilisers, hire out machinery and market crops. The delta was sparsely settled, mainly by Fulani pastoralists, and so people were brought in and settled in six new villages. Problems were presented by high soil salinity, uneven topography and the costs of the services provided by SAED. Yields were never great and when drought came in 1968 the 8000 hectares under rice yielded only 500 tons and settlers left in increasing numbers.

From 1972 SAED extended its activities up the river where villages already had small irrigated plots called périmètres. Heavy mechanisation was evidently inappropriate and SAED sought to provide seed, fertilizer, fuel and technical supervision and to extend the area under irrigation. Adams (1977) describes how the arrival of SAED officials in a Soninke village was greeted with dismay, for the people had heard of the problems that had arisen in the delta and were anxious to avoid expenditure which might not produce equivalent returns. They did not want to run into debt or to lose control of their own farming concerns. Their opposition was not simply an expression of conservatism but reflected a suspicion that intervention by SAED would benefit the government bureaucracy more than it would themselves. It is the kind of view that is becoming prevalent amongst many rural people in Africa; the peasants feel that they do the work and officials reap the benefits (Hart 1982).

160

6.5.2 *The inland Niger basin*

Towards the end of the eighteenth century, Islamic revolutions gave birth to three Tukolor Muslim states south of the Senegal and about the headwaters of the Niger in Futa Toro, Futa Bondu and Futa Jalon. Shortly afterwards, in Hausaland, Uthman dan Fodio a Fulani scholar and preacher encouraged by the events in The Futas, proclaimed a jihad, a holy war, against unbelievers and by 1809 had established his capital at Sokoto. Fulani 'flag-bearers' commissioned by dan Fodio gained control of Zaria, Kano and Katsina, installing themselves in place of the Hausa rulers and owing allegiance to Sokoto. The jihad was carried south, emirates being created amongst the Nupe on the Niger and in Adamawa across the Benue. Ilorin, to the south of the Niger, was brought within the Sokoto caliphate and a Fulani-Ilorin army sacked Oyo the leading city of Yorubaland (Webster & Boahen 1967).

In the Central Delta region of the Niger, Hamad Bari inspired by the example of Uthman dan Fodio proclaimed a jihad. He defeated the Bambara king of Ségou, captured Jenne and received the submission of Fulani chiefs in Macina. For a time, from 1827 to 1844, the Fulani occupied Tombouctou where they enforced the Islamic code rigorously. Control of the town eventually reverted to the Kenata Arabs and Songhai but Tombouctou continued for many years to pay tribute to Macina.

Thus by a series of civil wars and popular uprisings, much of the western Sudan was brought under the authority of Muslim Fulani in the first half of the nineteenth century. Fulani society, like that of Songhai, was slave-owning; there were entire villages where most of the inhabitants were slaves or serfs working the land for their overlords. People were encouraged to come together into large villages for greater ease of political control. Long distance migratory pastoralism was regulated and rules were laid down for Delta grazing some of which are followed to this day.

The message of social reform and religious renewal that had been preached by Uthman dan Fodio and Hamad Bari was taken up by al-Hajj Umar of Futa Toro. He was much influenced by the militant attitudes of the Tijaniyya, a brotherhood that had originated in Morocco, and in 1848 when he was expelled from Futa Jalon, he carried their teachings amongst the Malinke (Mandinke or Mandingo). Supporters flocked to him and procuring arms from French merchants he formed an army that overran the Bambara states of Bambuk and Kaarta. Faidherbe, governor of the French colonies on the lower Senegal, prevented Umar from extending his empire westwards; on the east Umar's forces swept into the Central Delta and captured Tombouctou.

Umar's Tukolor state lacked the kind of support from the masses of the people that the Sokoto caliphate had enjoyed, at least in its early years, but Umar's son was still ruling in Ségou when the French, in 1880, resumed a forward policy and commenced to extend their communications further up the Senegal. There were revolts against the

French in Cayor; they were crushed. The French made treaties of friendship with Samori, ruler of the Malinke, and in the early 1890s occupied Ségou, Jenne and Macina. The Tukolor empire collapsed but the Tijaniyya remained the dominant Muslim brotherhood of the western Sudan.

The Malinke in the early nineteenth century were mostly animists, living in hundreds of scattered towns and villages without any central political authority. From some Muslim towns Diula traders operated commercial networks extending eastwards amongst the Mossi, north into the Central Delta and reaching to the coast at St Louis and Freetown. About the middle of the century these towns, growing into small states, were brought together under Samori to form an empire that at its height included much of the Upper Niger basin and was comparable in extent with that of Sokoto and El Hajj Umar. Samori, less of a pious scholar than Uthman dan Fodio and Umar, was as intent on reviving the ancient greatness of the Malinke and the power of ancient Mali as on spreading the Muslim faith. He went even further than his predecessors in destroying the position of the old chiefly class and in organising his realm into a centralised hierarchical state, Islamic, but with a strong national spirit (Person 1968). It was not to last.

In 1881 the French began to construct their railway from Kayes and in 1884, before the railway had been completed, an expedition carried a small gunboat, in parts, from Kayes to Bamako and launched it on the Niger. Samori gave up territory north of the river in an effort to gain their friendship but the French, having destroyed Umar's Tukolor empire, were intent on extending their dominion right across the Sudan zone to Lake Chad. In a guerilla conflict that dragged on for seven years, Samori's army was pressed south and east into Ashanti and the Volta basin, laying waste the country as it retired. By the end of the century Malinke resistance had collapsed, Samori had died an exile in Gabon, and the French were in the process of setting up administrations over the western Sahara and Sudan.

The Soudan colony, covering roughly the same area as ancient Mali, had suffered severely from the fighting. Towards the end of the nineteenth century, in common with most of Africa, it was afflicted by the rinderpest epidemic that killed many of the cattle and then came dry years culminating in the great drought of 1913-14. Many people were attracted to the groundnut areas of Senegal. Dryland cotton production in the vicinity of the Central Delta was a failure and after World War 1, pilot irrigation projects were started. By 1931 much larger schemes were being envisaged, involving the irrigation of a million hectares in the western delta. A public enterprise, the Office du Niger, was created to carry out the work and people were transferred, forcibly in some cases, from heavily populated parts of Upper Volta as well as other parts of Soudan to settle on the scheme.

The Office du Niger was never a great success. From its headquarters at Ségou it tried to control constructional works, agricultural operations,

162

crop processing and marketing, and settlement villages 200 km away. After the completion of the Markala barrage in 1945–47 the number of employees mounted to over 5000; other costs were heavy, enormous subsidies were required and yet the settlers found themselves in debt. Rainfall in the 1950s was much higher than usual causing extensive flooding, but irrigation water was available for only a few weeks after the rains had ceased because although the barrage raised the level of the river, it provided very little storage. Problems arose in leading the water to the fields on account of the evenness of the old deltaic terrain; drainage was inadequate and vast areas were never brought under cultivation. Except for the years 1958 to 1960 when an unusually productive area was made available for rice-growing, prospective settlers were rare and shortage of manpower always presented problems.

6.5.3 *The Chad basin*

The old capital of the Kanuri in Borno, at Birni Ngazargamu near the Yobe, was destroyed in wars against the Fulani. El-Kanemi built a new capital further south and nearer the lake at Kukawa which became an important centre on the trade routes from North Africa towards the upper Benue. Natron from the neighbourhood of Lake Chad (Figure 59) was traded to the Hausa states and further afield and in return came kola nuts and slaves; gold and ivory by the nineteenth century were finding their way south to the coast and scarcely figured in exports to Tripoli, and after the death of el-Kanemi in 1837 there was a general decline in the trans-Saharan caravan trade.

In the 1890s the army of Rabeh, a soldier of fortune from the Egyptian Sudan, overran Wadai, conquered the country west towards Lake Chad and in 1893 attacked Kukawa and had the Shehu assassinated. The French were extending their influence eastwards from Zinder and, seeing Rabeh as a threat, they lent their support to one of the refugees from Kukawa, Umar Sanda, and he was installed as Shehu. In 1900 Rabeh was defeated by a French force and killed. Umar Sanda fell out with the French because they demanded he should drive out the Shuwa Arabs, who had been settling in Borno with their flocks and herds; the French wanted them in the territory they were occupying further east. He was deposed for refusing to do so and eventually when the British occupied Borno in 1902–04 his younger brother Abubakar Garbai was appointed Shehu. The Shuwa Arabs remained and now, in Borno, they share the grazing grounds with Kanuri and Fulani.

French military expeditions reached the country near Lake Chad from the west and also from Ubangi to the south. Exploratory journeys were made northwards to Tibesti by Tilho (1910–14). In later years he drew attention to the overflow of floodwaters from the Logone along the Mayo-Kebbi into the Benue and argued that there was a danger of Lake Chad drying up if the process accelerated and the Logone were to be permanently diverted (Tilho 1947). Geological studies made in the years

Figure 59. Natron being collected from the surface of a sebkha, a dry lakebed near Lake Chad.

around 1950 to throw light on the subject showed the risk was negligible and that the Logone was incising its channel rather than spilling westwards more frequently. From these beginnings developed the Office de Recherches Scientifiques et Techniques d'Outre mer, ORSTOM, which has been responsible for so much research into the behaviour of West African rivers.

Agricultural use of the water resources of the Chad basin involved endiking large areas of floodplain near Bongor to control the seasonal flooding and allow large-scale rice cultivation. On the eastern shores of Lake Chad near Bol linear basins between the ancient dune lines were impounded and converted into polders for cultivating cereals and vegetables.

Early British activity in Borno mainly involved digging wells to provide people and livestock with water. After World War Two, the Ngadda river near Maiduguri was used to irrigate the 'Jere bowl' for producing rice, and efforts were made to improve fish marketing and transport. In the years shortly before independence large numbers of boreholes were put down on a rectangular grid with a spacing of roughly 16 km, to tap artesian and sub-artesian water at depths down to about 300 m. In 1960–63, a campaign was mounted under the auspices of USAID to inoculate cattle against rinderpest in the countries bordering the lake; Nigeria, Cameroun, Chad and Niger. These measures accelerated the increase in cattle numbers that had been going on apace over the preceding decade of relatively high rainfall. The new water supplies were

164

welcomed by local pastoralists and sedentary stockowners, but the developments placed more livestock at risk when drought came in the 1970s.

The main value of Lake Chad resides in its fisheries which traditionally have been exploited by the Budduma or, more properly called, the Yedina fisherfolk living on the islands (Sikes 1972). Now there are fishermen from southern Nigeria as well as Hausa, catching, drying and smoking fish on the Nigerian shore. Motor transport and tarmac roads have replaced the camel trails that formerly led towards Maiduguri, and the lake is a great source of protein for the urban centres of northern Nigeria.

In the early 1970s, work began on a scheme to pump water from the El Obeid and the southwest corner of the lake to irrigate large areas of firki clay soils in the vicinity of Marte by canals. This South Chad Irrigation project has had to face many problems, not least those resulting from drought and the shrinkage of the lake.

6.5.4 *The lower Niger and Benue*

While the French in Senegambia were trading 600 km inland by the end of the seventeenth century, Europeans in the Bight of Biafra were confined to the coast for more than a century longer. At numerous points along the Gold Coast castles were built as residences for government agents and for traders from several countries including Denmark and Brandenburg as well as Holland and Great Britain. By the end of the eighteenth century the slave trade was centred further east at Lagos. At the mouths of the Oil Rivers, Europeans living in hulks moored in the creeks remained in ignorance of the interior which first became known from the accounts of trans-Saharan travellers.

The main obstacles to penetration inland were opposition from local African traders, sailing difficulties on the Niger with its strong currents during and after the rains, and hazards presented by rocks and sandbanks at low water. Above all there was the high mortality caused by fevers. The introduction of paddle steamers reduced navigational problems but the disease hazard remained. The British government, responding to pressure from 'abolitionists' who wished to build up legitimate trade, sent out a carefully prepared and expensively equipped expedition under Captain Trotter in 1841 which was intended to establish an experimental farm near the Niger-Benue confluence. It sailed up the river at the right time of year. Samuel Crowther (1970) was gratified by their reception at Aboh and Idah. He did not fully realise that the Ibos were seeking to short-circuit the middlemen of Brass and that the Igala were hopeful of assistance against the Fulani of Bida (Ajayi 1970). The farmland was acquired and seeds brought from Europe were sown; when they failed to thrive local varieties were planted instead. Fever was soon rife amongst the settlers and within a few months the survivors had to be evacuated. Out of the 145 European members of that expedition, over a third died, the majority of malaria.

In 1854 Baikie's expedition steamed up the Benue and demonstrated that regular doses of quinine greatly reduced the incidence and severity of fever. The geographical information about the West African interior that he and other explorers brought back to Europe was made available to the readers of Jules Verne (1870).

By the 1870s five British companies were operating on the Niger. In 1879 four of them amalgamated to form the United Africa Company (Pedler 1974) and began to establish trading stations in the Niger delta. Native towns built on the coastal sand bars and with satellite villages along the delta waterways had operated trading networks extending into the interior for many decades. Now they were bypassed by steamers heading up the river to Onitsha, Lokoja, Yola and Rabba while the delta people were prevented by the white traders from chartering ships and shipping oil direct to Europe. The delta towns were rent by struggles between the ruling families and between the traditional families and newcomers. Only Brass and Lagos traders were able to stand the competition from the United Africa Company. When Goldie acquired a royal charter for his United Africa Company in 1886 and took over the administration and policing of the lower Niger, he eliminated the remaining traders by imposing heavy taxes on them and also by calling on the Royal Navy for assistance at critical moments. The British government revoked Goldie's charter in 1900, but by then the delta ports had lost control of trade on the lower river and it remained in the hands of the Niger Company and its successors for the rest of the colonial period. Deprived of their commercial roles the delta peoples became once more subsistence level cultivators and fishermen, until the scene was transformed by the discovery of oil in the 1950s.

The entrances to the navigable waterways of the Niger delta were dredged in the early years of the century; the Orashi tributary running into Oguta lake was cleared of obstacles; surveys were made of the Anambra and Mamu rivers with a view to using them for transporting coal from the newly-discovered seams in the Udi escarpment; small vessels reached as far upstream as Genole on the Gongola river 1200 km from the sea "the greatest distance of river navigation from a seaport, uninterrupted by rapids in Africa" it was claimed (Ekundare 1973, p. 130). But the new railways soon began to divert traffic from the rivers. By 1909 a line from Lagos had reached Jebba; another line built to link Kaduna on the river of that name with Zunguru (the seat of government in Northern Nigeria) was extended north-east to Kano and south to Baro on the Niger. By 1914 the Niger had been bridged at Jebba, trains were running between Lagos and Kano and river traffic declined from a 1908 peak of 13000 passengers and 21,000 tons of cargo.

After World War One a railway line from Port Harcourt to Enugu was extended northwards to meet the western railway at Kaduna and a road and rail bridge over the Benue was completed in 1932. Road transport was rapidly increasing in importance but towns alongside the Niger and Benue continued to be very dependent on river traffic. Over 20,000 tons of cargo were being unloaded annually at both Onitsha and Baro as late as 1959–60, and at Baro over 40,000 tons were being loaded for movement downstream. The river fleet, operated by UAC and by John Holt & Company, consisted of about forty tugs pulling, or in the case of more up-to-date arrangements, pushing trains of barges. Until the opening of the railway from Douala to Ngaoundéré in 1974, the Benue still provided the cheapest means of transport to northern Cameroun, petroleum and cement moving upstream and cotton downstream. After mid-October the river is too low for shipping and as the cotton harvest comes later it had to be stored for up to seven months before it could be evacuated. Nevertheless, total traffic reached 60,000 tons in the mid-1960s when it was interrupted by the Nigerian Civil War; since then it has failed to recover.

6.6. THE RIVER PEOPLE AT MID-CENTURY

6.6.1 *The slow pace of change*

The pace of development alongside African rivers in the colonial period was relatively slow. Sand bars at the mouths of the Niger creeks were dredged and rocky obstacles were blasted. Modest quays were built with concrete stairways running along the river banks to allow for a seasonal rise and fall of as much as 10 m. But the peaks of water transport for passengers were reached before the First World War, when railways were coming into operation, and for freight after the Second World War when roads were no longer regarded as merely unwelcome competitors to rail and riverboat.

By the middle of the twentieth century, rivers were being looked upon as hindrances to transport, as obstacles that had to be bridged at great expense to obviate delays at ferries entailed by groundings at low water or dangerously strong currents at flood peaks. The attitude is exemplified by the road bridge at Gaya in the extreme north of Benin (formerly Dahomey) which was built so low that only the smallest boats could pass beneath it at high water. The rivers were regarded as potential sources of power; falls and rapids, formerly economic disadvantages, were seen to provide a head of water; the rock bars and narrows were appreciated as ideal sites for dam construction. Bussa rapids, where Mungo Park met his fate, were submerged beneath Kainji lake; locks installed in the dam and downstream to allow shipping to proceed from the lower river to Yelwa and points further upriver are not heavily used.

Opportunities for irrigation clearly existed but they had no great appeal in West Africa. Extensive alluvial plains comparable to those of the Sudan or northern India were confined to the Chad basin and Niger bend, both of them remote, sparsely settled regions. Financial resources for agricultural development were scarce in the first half of a century greatly eaten up by two World Wars, subsequent long periods of recovery and an intervening decade of economic depression. After the Second World War schemes for tractorised rice-growing in Sokoto, at Shemankar in the Benue valley, and near Maiduguri in the Chad basin were scarcely viable on account of the difficulties involved in recovering costs of ploughing and maintaining equipment in good repair. French experience of large-scale canal irrigation on the Inland Niger Delta was much more discouraging, as costly and almost as unrewarding as the rainfed Tanganyika Groundnuts Scheme. By the 1950s it was clear that the colonial episode was nearing its end; attention was mainly directed to the political scene and long-term irrigation schemes were of comparatively limited interest.

Before independence came to the West African countries, the main rivers were little affected by deliberate policies of modernisation. Flood cultivation on riverine plains extended as population pressure increased, but the natural regimes of the rivers were scarcely affected. Small-scale irrigation involved the production of crops for subsistence or at any rate for sale internally, especially to urban dwellers, rather than for export. The quality of river water was scarcely altered; pollution was slight because of slow urban and industrial growth and the limited use of pesticides in agriculture. Alluvial tin-mining on the Jos Plateau and alluvial diamond-mining in Sierra Leone and southern Ghana increased sediment loads in some streams. Some bank erosion accompanied clearing of woodland along river banks, carried out to reduce tsetse-fly infestation. Gully erosion increased as a result of water being led away from roads and villages along drainage channels and footpaths down valleyside slopes. Otherwise, the rivers were still in their natural state.

6.6.2 *The fisherfolk*

The main single intervention on the rivers was the construction of the Markala barrage at the head of the Inland Niger delta; as well as raising the water level it interfered with the movement of fish and in particular hindered the annual migration upstream of *Alestes* 'sardines'. These are particularly important to the Bozo fishermen who dry them and also extract oil from them. As the river level falls at the end of the dry season the *Alestes* leave the floodplain and in June move upstream from the Lake Debo area towards Koulikoro, their movement depending on the phases of the moon. The Bozo follow them, building traps successively further upstream, first at Diafarabé, the next month at Dia and finally at Pikina. The movement of shoals is hindered but not entirely prevented by the barrage.

Greater changes affected the lives of the fisherfolk as a result of greater freedom of movement following the imposition of colonial rule. Both Bozo and Somono now migrated long distances, following the Black Flood of the Niger downstream of Lake Debo into Sorko country as far as Labbezenga, a thousand kilometres from their homes. Ijo from the coastal delta come upstream, fishing in Kainji lake and establishing seasonal camps as far north as Tillabéry.

For the specialist fishermen cereals are a necessity they need to purchase from neighbouring cultivators or grow themselves. Hausa and Sorko, for instance, farm in Kebbi during the rains when fishing is difficult on account of the turbulence in the river and then, towards the end of the dry season, they move upstream to fish the Niger bend and the lakes of the lower delta. Bozo moving downstream appear in the same areas at a similar time, using seine nets rather than constructing fence traps as they do in their home waters.

For the more numerous agriculturalists, Bambara, Malinke, Marka, Senifo and Mossi, fish are a luxury. They fish only at low water, normally having to apply for permission to Bozo and Somono who have the water rights, determine the dates when fishing may start, and commonly require a proportion of the catch. The Songhai of the Niger bend prepare their ricefields in June, harvest the crop in October, and then in March small parties of them range up and down the Niger, fishing often by night and moving camp by day. They sell some of the catch to buy millet, to tide them over the period before the rice is ripe, or exchange it with Fulani for milk and butter that are plentiful in the rainy season and surplus to the pastoralists' own consumption requirements.

A large part of the catch from the Upper Niger, equivalent to some 20,000 tonnes of fresh fish, is smoked and dried and sold in Mopti for export to Ghana and southern Ivory Coast. In return kola from the southern forests are brought downriver via Bamako. Hausa fishermen who arrive in the Niger bend area in large boats weighing 4 to 8 tonnes use both lines and basket traps and smoke their catch in ovens to preserve it for the journey home. If their catch is small they sell some of their boats – the old ones – to the Songhai. Sorkawa fishermen are to be seen in Jebba and Onitsha markets selling fish caught far upstream, or at Aboh arranging to buy a new boat. Amongst the Nupe, whose riverside farms are important for growing root crops and rice, the Kedeare are a specialist fishermen caste who sell their fish not only to the local cultivators but also far away in Yorubaland (Sundstrom 1972).

Fishing and the fish trade have expanded in recent decades in response to urban demand and improved communications. Furthermore, fishing equipment has been modernised. Harpoons and spears are still used in shallow pools; matting fences are erected across distributaries to direct fish into basket traps, but the caste nets of the Somono and the seine nets of the Bozo are now made of nylon, no longer local fibres, and like the lines with 500 or 600 hooks, they are imported from Europe and Japan. Outboard motors, increasingly used where foreign currency allows their purchase, necessitate the use of stronger boats, pegged rather than stitched together. There would seem to be ample opportunities for further technical improvements involving for example, the use of fibre-glass boats. Such innovations carry risks of overfishing and greater economic disparities within and between fishing communities who have so far succeeded in retaining their social structures relatively little distorted.

169

6.6.3 *Floodplain farming*

Farming systems on the floodplains of West African rivers vary according to their location. On the Upper Niger and tributaries such as the Sokoto and Rima rivers, the river flood occurs towards the end of the rainy season, so that crops grown in the floodwater compete for space with those depending mainly on local rains. At the lower end of the Central Delta of the Niger, where the flood is delayed for several weeks after the end of the rains, such competition is much reduced.

The chief flood crop along the Senegal and the Niger and its tributaries and also alongside the Logone near Bongor is rice. It is usually sown early in the rains before the river rises with different varieties being selected according to the micro-relief of the floodplain and the depth of flooding generally expected. On the Sokoto floodplain over 30 varieties of rice have been recorded, the majority of local origin and others evidently introduced in recent years. At the lower levels floating varieties are sown which can grow as long as 5 m; at higher levels shorter varieties of rice are grown and also certain varieties of sorghum that can tolerate waterlogging for a week or two. The risks of crop failure from floods that are either excessive or deficient are great, but the individual farmers have more plots than is usually the case with rainfed cultivation and they are unlikely to lose everything (Figures 60 and 61).

The opportunity to grow a dry season crop on the riverside when the flood has subsided provides an element of security. The décrue culture, comparable to the winter season cropping with barley in ancient Egypt, involves mainly sorghum, millet and a variety of other crops. Harlan & Pasquereau (1968) identify the heart of décrue cultivation in Mali as the region extending from Lake Faguibine through the Circles of Goundam and Diré to Lake Kourarou. On the sandy soils at the higher levels, bull-

Figure 60. Young millet on the banks of the Senegal at high water in October.

Figure 61. Maize and cucurbits being sown on the mud revealed by the receding flood-waters of the Benue near Numan in November.

rush millet which cannot survive flooding for more than about a week is typically grown. *Sorghum* being more tolerant is planted at the lower levels, often on mounds. Land that has been flooded for several months is free of weeds and this reduces labour needs but to make full use of soil moisture before soils dry out crops are usually raised in small beds and then transplanted as the flood recedes, as on the clay plains of Borno.

On the floodplains of the Sokoto river, the lower areas where rice has been grown, are particularly attractive for dry season cultivation because the rice is usually harvested early, freeing the ground for other crops. Onions do particularly well where flooding has been deep. Other crops like sorghum and bullrush millet are found at successively higher levels. On most plots mixtures of two or more crops are grown as an insurance against complete loss and possibly because the combined yields of mixtures are greater than yields of crops grown singly. Such systems of production are prone to damage on account of the natural variability of river discharges. River control projects could improve reliability, but most large schemes are directed towards perennial or at any rate canal irrigation rather than basin flooding, with the consequent risk of communities living far downstream finding the floods no longer water their fields adequately.

Seasonally flooded fadamas, mainly lying on the Niger side of the Chad-Niger watershed in northern Nigeria are cultivated in the dry season in the vicinity of towns and villages, a wide variety of crops being grown on small plots, with shadufs to lift water from pools and shallow wells. Near the cities of Kano and Zaria fruit, vegetables and other perishable crops are important and there is local specialisation in onions, tomatoes, peppers and okra. Rice is grown in the wetter parts of the fadamas, though the lowest areas are left for grazing at the end of the dry season; sugarcane is grown where the soil is moist throughout the year without

171

being deeply flooded. According to Norman (1972) the returns per unit area of fadama are three times greater than from upland fields and in three villages near Zaria where they constituted a tenth of the farm area the fadama fields provided almost a quarter of the net farm income. In addition to cropping and grazing, fadamas provide a variety of plants valued for medicinal purposes and used for weaving baskets and mats, and fish can be caught in pools and streams. Turner (1977) considered there is much scope for the further development of all these activities.

On the firki clay plains south of Lake Chad, falling flood cultivation of masakwa exceeds rainfed cultivation in importance for many villages. According to James (1977) the upland sandy soils are too infertile to support more than four years' cultivation in sixteen, using traditional methods, whereas the clays can be cultivated year after year so long as the rains are heavy enough to flood them. He estimated that in a normal year about 10% of the sand islands and ridges and between 15 and 35% of the clay plain were cultivated in the area around Marte.

6.6.4 *Pastoralism*

Riverside and other wetland grazing plays a part of special importance in the pastoralist economy. In the southern Guinea savannas, woodland bordering streams may still be infested by tsetse flies in the dry season when adjacent areas are fly-free. In the semi-arid Sudan/Sahel, floodplains around the larger rivers provide the best sources of dry season fodder. In fact it is the grazing resources available towards the end of the dry season that commonly determine how many animals can utilise the much more extensive areas available for grazing only during the rains.

Various interchange relationships have developed between the users of the riverside lands; fisherfolk, cultivators and pastoralists. Bozo assist Marka (or Nono) cultivators with their rice in the clay-floored basins of the Inland Niger Delta. Somono fishermen have always been closely attached to Bambara cultivators, from whom they may have been recruited by the Malinke in the thirteenth century as boatmen when the Bozo refused to cooperate. Fulani encroached on some of the rights and privileges of the Bozo and Sorko when they came to dominate the inland Niger basin in the eighteenth century and employed their serfs, the Rimaibe, to exploit river resources.

The Niger floodplains of the Sudan/Sahel are occupied in the dry season by several hundred thousand cattle belonging to Fulani, Touareg and other mobile pastoral groups. They have been studied by Gallais (1984) and his colleagues who have extended their researches into pastoralism throughout the Sahel (Gallais 1981). About June the herds leave for the north to avoid biting flies and other pests in the nieghbourhood of water and take advantage of grazing at the desert margins. When this grazing deteriorates and pools dry up in the latter months of the year, the cattle are brought back to the floodplains; later goats and sheep arrive and camps are occupied on old levée and dune crests alongside borgous, the flooding basins. At first the basins are partly occupied by growing crops, but later in the dry season herds are able to feed on the stubble and other crop residues and on abundant grasses notably *Echinochloa stagina* and *Oryza barthii*. There is always friction between pastoralists and cultivators on account of livestock damaging crops; modern canal and sprinkler irrigation systems are even more at risk from pastoralist herds than is traditional basin cultivation.

In Hausaland, semi-nomadic Fulani move their herds south in the early dry season to graze on stubble and on uncultivated fadamas. As cultivation extends year by year over the fadamas, especially in the vicinity of towns and villages, pastoralists find it increasingly difficult to find sites they can occupy near to markets where they might sell their milk products and buy corn. The felling of trees for fuel alongside the fadamas has reduced the amount of browse on which herds formerly depended heavily in the latter part of the dry season. Life becomes ever more difficult, resources scarcer for man and beast.

The plains of Borno, west and south-west of Lake Chad provide grazing for some two million cattle plus other domestic animals belonging to three quite different ethnic groups. Kanuri, by far the largest group and mainly sedentary cultivators, own about two-thirds of the cattle (James 1977). Shuwa Arabs who also live in villages but move with their herds after the harvest, have most of the rest. In the 1950s and 1960s the Shuwa became more sedentary because of good rains and the installation of boreholes tapping pressure water. Then there are Kwoyam, Kanuri-speakers who are largely dependant on livestock but grow some millet on the sandy areas of the west and move eastwards with their cattle after they harvest onto the clay plains south of Lake Chad. There they are joined by Fulani from the north and west who are rarely cultivators, being more inclined to purchase their grain supplies with receipts from the sales of milk and ghee. In the early dry season all the cattle feed on crop residues and annual grasses growing on the sandy mounds rising a few metres above the level of the clay plains. In January the masakwa growing on the firki is harvested and the stalks not required for house and fence construction are available for cattle feed in addition to browse from *Acacia senegal* and *Acacia raddiana* woodland on the sand mounds. Pure stands of wild sorghum (*Sorghum aethiopicum*), growing up to 2 m tall and constituting the main plant cover on the firki, is of no fodder value, good only for thatching and commonly burned.

Towards the end of the dry season the cattle of the Fulani and many of those of the Shuwa move to the edge of the Lake. The level is falling from December to July, providing pastures, where risks of disease and of animals being stranded in the mud are considerable but grazing is abundant even in years of poor rains. The dry season of 1973 was quite exceptional, according to James (1978), for Kanuri living tens of kilometres from Chad as well as Shuwa took their cattle to the lake edge because of the shortage of grazing in the home areas and lack of feed from the very restricted areas they were able to plant with masakwa.

It should be emphasised that on sandy areas near Lake Chad cultivation and crop residues provide about twice as much fodder as the same area of uncultivated grassland, and on the clay plains, where cattle can otherwise find only some browse on scattered *Acacia nilotica*, dry season masakwa provides an important supply of fodder in the middle of the dry season where there would otherwise be none. Cultivation and grazing are far from being incompatible, rather they are complementary, and irrigation schemes might well allow for both.

6.7 REFERENCES

Adams, A. 1977. The Senegal River Valley: What kind of change? *Review of African Political Economy* 10: 33 57.

Adanson, M. 1759. *A voyage to Senegal, the isle of Goree and the river Gambia.* London: J. Nourse & W. Johnston.

Ajayi, J.F.A. 1970. Introduction to S.A. Crowther, *Journal of an expedition* etc.

Ajayi, J.F.A. & M. Crowder 1971-74. *History of West Africa.* London: Longman.

Alagoa, E.J. 1972. *A history of the Niger delta: an historical interpretation of Ijo oral tradition.* Ibadan: Ibadan University Press.

Baikie, W.B. 1966. *Narrative of an exploratory voyage up the rivers Kwo ra and Binue, commonly known as the Niger and Tsadda, in 1854.* London: Cass.

Barry, B. 1979. The subordination of power and the mercantile economy: the kingdom of Waalo, 1600-1831. In R. Cruise O'Brien (ed.), *The political economy of underdevelopment: dependence in Senegal.* London: Sage.

Barth, H. 1965. *Travels and discoveries in North and Central Africa, being a journal of an expedition undertaken under the auspices of H.B.M's government in the years 1849-55* London: Cass.

Breternitz, D.A. 1975. Rescue archeology in the Kainji reservoir area 1968. *West African J. Archaeol.* 5: 91-151.

Caillié, R. 1968. *Travels through Central Africa to Timbuctoo and across the Great Desert to Morocoo, performed in the years 1824-28.* London: Cass.

Camps, G. 1969. Amekni: Néolithique ancien du Hoggar: *Mémoires du Centre de Recherches anthropologiques Préhistoriques et Ethnographiques* 10.

Carter, P.L. & J.D. Clark 1976. Adrar Bous and African cattle. *Actes du VIIe Congres panafricain de prehist., Addis Ababa* 1971: 487-93.

Colvin, L.G. 1981. *The uprooted of the western Sahel. Migrants quest for cash in Senegambia.* New York: Praeger.

Connah, G. 1975. *The archaeology of Benin.* Oxford: Clarendon Press.

Connah, G. 1981. *Three thousand years in Africa.* Cambridge: Cambridge University Press.

Crowther, S.A. 1970. *Journal of an expedition* up the Niger and Tshadda Rivers undertaken by Macgregor Laird in connection with the British Government in 1854. 2nd ed. London: Cass.

Davies, O. 1964. Archaeological exploration in the Volta basin. *Ghana Geographical Association Bulletin*: 28-33.

Davies, O. 1967. *West Africa before the Europeans.* London: Methuen.

Denham, D., H. Clapperton & W. Oudney 1831. *Travels and discoveries in northern and central Africa in 1822, 1823 and 1824* London: ??

Dickson, K.B. 1969. *A historical geography of Ghana. Cambridge: Cambridge University Press.*

Ekundare, R.O. 1973. *An economic history of Nigeria 1860-1960.* London: Methuen.

Forde, D. (ed.) 1950-60. *Ethnographic Survey of Africa, Parts 1-15, Western Africa.* London: Oxford University Press.

Fage, J.D. 1977. Upper and Lower Guinea. In R. Oliver (ed.), *The Cambridge History of Africa* (vol. 3). Cambridge: Cambridge University Press.

174

Gallais, J. 1981. Histoire et thèmes d'une recherche au Sahel. *Cahiers Géographiques de Rouen* 15: 3-10.

Gallais, J. 1984. *Hommes du Sahel: Le Delta intérieur du Niger 1960-80.* Paris: Flammarion.

Grove, J.M. and A.M. Johansen 1968. The historical geography of the Volta delta, Ghana, during the period of Danish influence. *Bull. Inst. fond. d'Afrique Noire* 30: 1374-1421.

Grove, A.T. 1978. Geographical introduction to the Sahel *Geogr. J.* 144: 409-415.

Harlan, J.R. & J. Pasquerau 1969. Décrue agriculture in Mali. *Economic Botany* 23: 70-74.

Harlan, J.R. & A.B.L. Stemler 1976. The races of sorghum in Africa. In J.R. Harlan, J.M.J. de Wit & A.B.L. Stemler (eds.), *Origins of African plant domestication.* The Hague: Mouton.

Hart, K. 1982. *The political economy of West African agriculture.* Cambridge: Cambridge University Press.

Hartle, D.D. 1980. Archaeology east of the Niger: a review of cultural historical developments. In B.K. Swartz & R.D. Dumett (eds.), *West African Cultural Dynamics.* The Hague: Mouton.

Hopkins, J.F.P. 1981. *Corpus of early Arabic sources for West African history.* Cambridge: Cambridge University Press.

Hopkins, A.G. 1973. *An economic history of West Africa.* London: Longmans.

Ikime, O. 1977. *The fall of Nigeria; the British conquest.* London: Heinemann.

James, A.R. 1977. Livestock movements in north-east Nigeria. Ph.D. thesis. University of Cambridge.

Levtzion, N. 1975. North-west Africa: from the Maghreb to the fringes of the forest. In R. Gray (ed.), *The Cambridge History of Africa* (vol. 4). Cambridge: Cambridge University Press.

McIntosh S.K. & R.J. McIntosh 1980. *Prehistoric investigations in the region of Jenne, Mali.* Cambridge Monographs in African Archaeol. 2. Oxford: British Archaeological Reports.

McIntosh S.K. & R.J. McIntosh 1981. West African Prehistory. *American Scientist* 69: 602-613.

Mauny, R. 1961. Tableau géographique de l'Ouest african au moyen âge, d'après les sources écrites, la tradition et l'archéologie. *Mém. de l'Inst. Francais d'Afrique Noire, Dakar*

Morgan, W.B. & J.C. Pugh 1969. *West Africa.* London: Methuen.

Munson, P.J. 1980. Archaeological data on the origins of cultivation in the south-western Sahara and their implications for West Africa. In B.K. Swartz & R.E. Dumett (eds.), *West African Cultural Dynamics.* The Hague: Mouton.

Murdock, G.P. 1959. *Africa: its peoples and their culture history.* New York: McGraw-Hill.

Nachtigal, G. 1971. *Sahara and Sudan.* London: Hurst.

NEDECO 1959. *River studies and recommendations on improvement of Niger and Benue.* Amsterdam: North Holland Publ.

Park, M. 1799. *Travels in the interior districts of Africa.* London: Bulmer.

Pedler, F. 1974. *The lion and the unicorn in Africa: a history of the origins of the United Africa Company 1787-1831.* London: Heinemann.

Person, Y. 1968. Samori, une revolution dyula. *Mem. de l'Inst. Fundamental d'Afrique Noire* 80 (3 vols.). Dakar.

Petit-Maire, N. & J. Riser 1981. Holocene lake deposits and palaeoenvironments in central Sahara, northeastern Mali. *Palaeogeography, Palaeoclimatology, Palaeoecology* 35: 45-62.

Rodney, W. 1975. The Guinea Coast. In R. Gray (ed.), *The Cambridge History of Africa,* (vol. 4). Cambridge: Cambridge University Press.

Rustad, J.A. 1980. The emergence of iron technology in West Africa. In B.K. Swartz & R.A. Dumett (eds.), *West African Culture Dynamics.* The Hague: Mouton.

Shaw, T. 1970. *Igbo-Ukwu: an account of archaeological discoveries in eastern Nigeria.* London: Faber & Faber.

Shaw, T. 1978. *Nigeria, its archaeology and early history.* London: Macmillan.

Sikes, S.K. 1972. *Lake Chad.* London: Eyre Methuen.

Skinner, E.P. 1964. *The Mossi of the Upper Volta.* Stanford, California: Stanford University Press.

Smith, A.B. 1975. A note on the flora and fauna from the post-palaeolithic sites of Karkarichincat Nord and Sud. *W. Afr. J. Archaeology* 5: 201–4.

Smith, A.B. 1980a. Domesticated cattle in the Sahara and their introduction to West Africa. In M.A.J. Williams & H. Faure (eds.), *The Sahara and the Nile*. Rotterdam: Balkema.

Smith, S.E. 1980b. The environmental adaptation of nomads in the West African Sahel: a key to understanding pastoralists. In M.A.J. Williams & H. Faure (eds.), *The Sahara and the Nile*. Rotterdam: Balkema.

Smith, R. 1970. The canoe in West African history. *J. Afr. Hist.* 11: 515–533.

Stemler, A.B.L. 1980. Origins of plant domestification in the Sahara and the Nile valley. In M.A.J. Williams and H. Faure (eds.), *The Sahara and the Nile*. Rotterdam: Balkema.

Sundstrom, L. 1972. *Ethnology and symbiosis: Niger waterfolk*. Studia Ethnographica Upsaliensa 35. Uppsala.

Sutton, J.E.B. 1974. The aquatic civilization of Middle Africa. *J. Afr. Hist.* 15: 527–546.

Swartz, B.K. & R.E. Dumett. 1980. *West African culture dynamics*. The Hague: Mouton.

Tilho, J.A.M. 1910–14. *Documents scientifiques de la mission* Tilho. 1906–9. *Impr. Nat.* (2 vols.) Paris.

Tilho, J.A.M. 1947. *Le Tchad et la capture du Logone par le Niger*. Paris: Gauthier-Villars.

Turner, B. 1977. The fadama lands of central northern Nigeria: their classification, spatial variation, present and potential use. Ph.D. thesis, University of London.

Tymoski, M. 1974. *Le développement et la régression chez les peuples de la boucle du Niger à l'époque précoloniale*. Warsaw: Uniw. Warszawski, Inst. Historyczny.

Verne, J. 1870. *Five weeks in a balloon*. London.

Webster, J.B. & A.A. Boahen 1967. *The revolutionary years: West Africa since 1800*. London: Longmans.

Wilde, J.C. de 1967. *Agricultural development in tropical Africa* (vol. 2). Baltimore: Johns Hopkins Press.

Zachariah, K.C. & J. Conde 1981. *Migration in West Africa: demographic aspects. A joint World Bank – OECD study*. Oxford: Oxford University Press.

176

W.M.ADAMS
Geography Department, Downing Place, Cambridge

7

River control in West Africa

7.1. INTRODUCTION

Dams are costly, prestigious and controversial structures. On the one hand they can be looked on as central to, and symbolic of, national development. Thus, for example, Nkrumah described the Akosombo Dam as the 'greatest of all our development projects' (Hart 1980), and the Kainji Dam has been similarly eulogised – 'the pillar of Nigeria's economic and social development' (Adeniyi 1976). On the other hand, major dams have their vociferous critics, often because of the severity of geographically remote and unintended side-effects, either ecological, economic or social. Thus Overton (1976) describes what he calls 'the magician's bargain' inherent in hydro-electric development – 'give up your soul and get power in return'. This chapter examines the background to development of some of the larger dams in West Africa, and looks in particular at the environmental and human effects of their development.

7.2 DAMS AND RIVER BASIN DEVELOPMENT IN WEST AFRICA

Scudder (1980) suggests that in the construction of large dams in Africa the opportunity for integrated development of river basins is being lost. Of course, 'integrated river basin development' is a familiar catch-phrase of development planning: Scudder's point is that it is rarely achieved in anything but name. The concept of river basin planning, and the present illusion that it can be embraced successfully, dates back to the success of the Tennessee Valley Authority (TVA) development in the depressed American South of the 1930s and the atmosphere of Roosevelt's New Deal (Lilienthal 1943). The Tennessee River basin covered 208,000 km^2, and in 1933 had a population of 3 m people, of which 77% were rural. The idea of 'a public and integrated development authority' was first suggested in 1914 by the US Corps of Engineers, and developments such as the 1922 Colorado River Compact and the Niagara Frontier Planning Board set some

177

sort of precedent for the creation of the TVA in 1933 (Finer 1944).

The TVA developed a series of 9 multi-purpose high dams on the Tennessee River and concentrated on hydro-electricity, flood control, navigation and shoreline development (Elliot 1973). By 1970 it was estimated that the accumulated benefits of improved navigation amounted to $550 m (twice the investment), of flood control $542 m (investment $190 m) and 100 billion kw hours of hydro-electricity had been generated, plus other development benefits (Elliot 1973).

The implications of the TVA development for other countries have not been lost on observers, including those in West Africa: 'there is no doubt that the Tennessee Valley Authority programmes epitomise the ideal in river basin development, both for the benefit of the six million or so inhabitants directly affected by it and also for that of the entire population of the United States in general' (Faniran 1972). The caveats issued when TVA began have been less avidly remembered: 'the TVA is not transplantable without reservations and qualifications: its characteristics merely help to bring out the problems and suggest alternative solutions' (Finer 1944).

The basic principle of river basin planning is to bring administrative boundaries into line with natural ones. The pragmatic logic of this is great; the practical political problems can be enormous, as the case of Nigeria demonstrates. Nigeria has a Federal System similar to that in the USA, and despite a few earlier approaches to water resource development in coherent units it was not until 1973 that the first two River Basin Development Authorities (RBDAs) were established (the Chad Basin Development Authority and the Sokoto-Rima Basin Development Authority). A full 11 RBDAs were created by Federal Decree in June 1976 and despite some fairly radical boundary changes still featured in the RBDA's Decree of 1979 (Table 21).

It remains to be seen how successfully the RBDAs can relate to the State Governments in bringing about productive development. To a large extent the responsibility of the RBDAs and the State Governments overlap: the breadth of the RBDA's functions is immense (Table 22).

Table 21. River Basin Development Authorities in Nigeria, 1979 (*River Basin Development Authorities Decree* 1979).

1.	The Sokoto-Rima Basin Development Authority
2.	The Hadejia-Jama'are River Basin Development Authority
3.	The Chad Basin Development Authority
4.	The Upper Benue River Basin Development Authority
5.	The Lower Benue River Basin Development Authority
6.	The Cross River Basin Development Authority
7.	The Anambra-Imo River Basin Development Authority
8.	The Niger River Basin Development Authority
9.	The Ogun-Oshun River Basin Development Authority
10.	The Benin-Owena River Basin Development Authority
11.	The Niger Delta Basin Development Authority

Table 22. Functions of the River Basin Development Authorities in Nigeria (*River Basin Development Authorities Decree* 1979).

1. To undertake comprehensive development of both surface and underground water resources for multi-purpose use.
2. To undertake schemes for the control of floods and erosion, and for water-shed management including afforestation.
3. To construct and maintain dams, dykes, polders, wells, boreholes, irrigation and drainage systems and other works necessary for the achievements under this section.
4. To provide water from reservoirs and lakes under the control of the Authority for irrigation purposes to farmers and recognised associations as well as for urban water supply schemes for a fee to be determined by the Authority concerned, with the approval of the Commissioner.
5. The control of pollution in rivers, lakes, lagoons and creeks in the Authority's area in accordance with nationally laid down standards.
6. To resettle persons affected by the works and schemes specified in this section or under special resettlement schemes.
7. To develop fisheries and improve navigation on the rivers, lakes, reservoirs, lagoons and creeks in the Authority's area.
8. To undertake the mechanised clearing and cultivation of land for the production of crops and livestock and for forestry in areas both inside and outside irrigation projects for a fee to be determined by the Authority concerned with the approval of the Commissioner.
9. To undertake the large-scale multiplication of improved seeds, livestock and tree seedlings for distribution to farmers and for afforestation schemes.
10. To process crops, livestock products and fish produced by farmers in the Authority's area in partnership with State agencies and any other person.
11. To assist the State and Local Governments in the implementation of the following rural development work in the Authority's area:
    a) The construction of small dams, wells and boreholes for rural water supply schemes and of feeder roads for the evacuation of farm produce;
    b) The provision of power for rural electrification schemes from suitable irrigation dams and other types of power stations under the control of the Authority concerned;
    c) The establishment of agro-service centres;
    d) The establishment of grazing reserves; and
    e) The training of staff for the running and maintenance of rural development schemes and for general extension work at the village level.

Faniran (1980) comments 'the river basin authorities will of necessity be concerned with virtually all development activities within their area of authority, including agriculture and other forms of rural land use, mining, industrial development and settlement'. Clearly there is a danger of wastage of resources if not more serious difficulties through lack of coordination with other agencies, particularly the State Governments. It is worth noting that the RBDAs were set up during a period of military government, when certainly the financial independence of the States if not their aspirations for regional power were less than they were later.

One commentator writes 'the haphazard manner in which water is being developed in the country as of now certainly doesn't augur well for the nation. Dams are constructed all over places (*sic*) with tremendous speed as if water is an unlimited resource. Reservoir designs are carried out

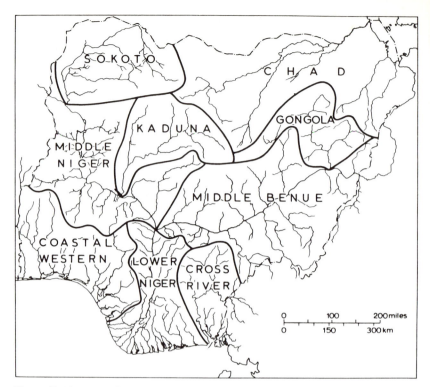

Figure 62. The major river basins of Nigeria.

with insufficient data bases, without coordination between agencies, and without an accepted national formula' (Mustafa 1980). This is hardly a description of integrated development. Elsewhere he laments the poor data base on which big Nigerian dams are being developed: 'unless the situation improves such projects might just turn out to be too expensive and unreliable, and later become uneconomic to operate' (Mustafa 1982).

The lack of coordination within Nigeria between State and para-statal agencies is made worse by the fact that each RBDA tends to include several States within its boundaries, and far from this bringing about a concentration of decision-making and data collection (as Faniran (1972) suggests it should) there is in practice increased bureaucratic diffusion of responsibilities. This is made more acute when, as in the case of the Chad basin and the Upper Benue River Basin Development Authorities, the Authority boundary coincides with the State boundary, between Borno and Bauchi States, and actually runs down the bed of the River Gongola for several kilometres!

It is clear that in Nigeria the River Basin Development Authorities'

180

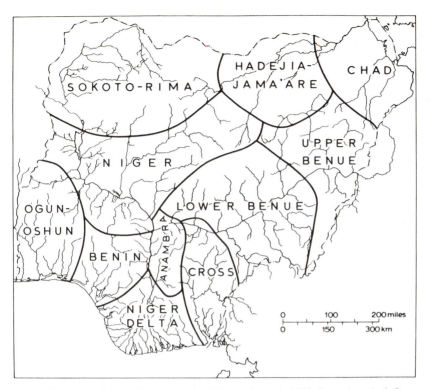

Figure 63. River Basin Development Authorities in Nigeria in 1978 (from Ayoade & Oyebande 1976).

boundaries are in fact influenced as much by politics as topography: Figure 62 shows the major river basins in Nigeria, and Figure 63 the original (1976 Decree) RBDA boundaries. The changes to these in 1979 show the new trend clearly: 9 of the 11 RBDAs are defined entirely in terms of political boundaries; six in terms of State Boundaries alone (Table 23, Figure 64). It is possible that the political function of the RBDAs (in that they tap Federal funds direct and independently of the States' budget allocation) will come to dominate their planning function: the General Manager of the Sokoto-Rima Basin Development Authority agreed in 1981 with a member of the Kaduna State House of Assembly that Kaduna State should have its own RBDA. This kind of development, makes sound contemporary political sense and in 1984 plans for an RBDA in each State were announced, but sadly rivers are no respecters of political boundaries.

International cooperation over water resources in West Africa has also had a chequered history. The Chad Basin and Niger River Commissions have been reasonably successful and despite financing problems the

181

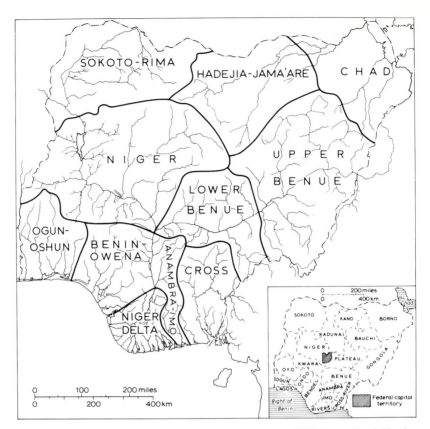

Figure 64. River Basin Development Authorities in Nigeria in 1979 (from Nwa & Martins 1982).

Table 23. Area within which each River Basin Development Authority in Nigeria exercises its functions (*River Basin Development Authorities Decree* 1973). References to actual drainage systems are printed in italics.

1. Sokoto-Rima River Basin Development Authority: The whole of Sokoto State and Katsina Emirate of Kaduna State.
2. Hadejia-Jama'are River Basin Development Authority: The whole of Kano State and those parts of Bauchi State *drained by the Jama'are and Misau River Systems.*
3. Chad Basin Development Authority: The whole of Borno State and those parts of Gongola State *drained by the Yedsaram River System.*
4. Upper Benue River Basin Development Authority: Those parts of Bauchi State *drained by the Gongola River System* and the whole of Gongola State excluding those parts *drained by the Yedsaram River System.*
5. Lower Benue River Basin Development Authority: The whole of Benue and Plateau States.
6. Cross River Basin Development Authority: The whole of Cross River State.
7. Anambra-Imo River Basin Development Authority: The whole of Anambra and Imo States.

182

Table 23 (cont.).

---

8. Niger River Basin Development Authority: The whole of Kwara and Niger States and the Federal Capital Territory and the whole of Kaduna State excluding Katsina Emirate.
9. Ogun-Oshun River Basin Development Authority: The whole of Oyo, Ogun and Lagos States.
10. Benin-Owena River Basin Development Authority: The whole of Bendel and Ondo States.
11. Niger Delta Basin Development Authority: The whole of Rivers State.

---

organisation pour la Mise en Valeur du Fleuve Senegal (OMVS) set up in 1972 by Mali, Senegal and Mauretania to design and promote integrated development of the whole of the Senegal River valley seems to have great potential. On a smaller scale, there has been conflict over the use of water from the small Lamindo/Kalmalo River between Sokoto State of Nigeria and the Republic of Niger and also allegations that a dam under construction in Cameroun will affect seasonal flows in the Benue river further downstream in Nigeria.

7.3 DAMS FOR ELECTRICITY

The 1950s and 1960s saw several of the largest dams in the world being constructed in Africa for the generation of hydro-electric power (HEP). The most notable were the Aswan High Dam on the Nile (begun 1960, finished 1969), the Kariba Dam on the Zambezi, the Akosombo Dam on the River Volta and the Kainji Dam on the Niger. In West Africa, the HEP potential of the major rivers had been recognised for some decades, but development was delayed. The idea of a dam on the Volta to generate power which could be used to smelt Gold Coast bauxite dates from 1915. It was the brainchild of Sir Albert Kitson of the Gold Coast Geological Survey (Moxon 1969), and was expounded by him in a paper in 1924 (Hart 1980). Nonetheless, it was 47 years before the construction of the Akosombo Dam began in 1961. In Nigeria, electrification began in Lagos in 1896, and the first HEP plants were operated on the Jos Plateau by private companies (Akintola 1978). In the 1950s large-scale investigations began into dams on the River Niger and the first phase of major Nigerian HEP development commenced with the construction of the Kainji Dam from 1964. In the Ivory Coast work began on the major dam at Kossou for electricity generation soon afterwards in 1969.

Two factors in particular lay behind this sudden access of enthusiasm for HEP generation. First, abundant power was seen as an essential prerequisite of economic development. The argument ran that abundant cheap energy promoted economic development by stimulating industrial enterprises through forward linkage effects. Thus the chief economist for

Kaiser Engineers International (the Kaiser Corporation designed and supervised construction of the Akosombo Dam, and were the Volta River Authority's main – and privileged – customer for power to process imported alumina) wrote 'Africa must develop her hydro resources at this stage of her economic development to capture the manifold benefits for the next generation' (Smith 1968). Hart (1980) comments 'the rationale behind the VRP (Volta River Project) was that it would provide abundant supplies of electricity. This electricity was seen as a necessary requisite for industrialisation'. Nkrumah himself said 'newer nations such as ours, which are determined by every possible means to catch up in industrial strength, must have electricity in abundance before they can expect any large scale industrial advance' (Hart 1980).

Powerful though the belief was in the efficacy for development of abundant cheap energy, it is interesting to note in passing that the predicted flowering of local industry has tended not to occur. A similar bright industrial future was predicted for Uganda when the Owen Falls Dam was begun in 1948, but there 'the extent of overseas investment has been very small and its contribution to raising the level of living has been marginal if indeed there has been such a contribution at all' (Elkan & Wilson 1968). Very much the same criticism can be levelled at the Volta River Project: because Valco Aluminium absorbs such a proportion of the electricity generated, and that at reduced rates, Hart concludes 'despite the very large amount of electricity made available by the VRP, electricity is still a minor factor in Ghana's energy supply'.

In fact, of course, the political economy of the Volta River Project is such that arguments about the role of its power in national development can have been but a minor factor in the real decision to construct, which was more closely affected by the dictates of international relations and

Table 24. Average % growth of energy consumption per annum (1: Smith 1968, 2: World Bank 1981).

Table 25. Actual energy consumption per annum (World Bank 1981). Units: kg coal equivalent.

	1959-65[1]	1960-74[2]	1974-79[2]	1960	1979
Mauretania	85	21	5	18	185
Togo	37	13	12	23	117
Guinea	36	3	2	67	87
Cote d'Ivoire	27	14	4	75	234
Liberia	23	19	−1	88	488
Nigeria	22	9	1	29	83
Upper Volta	20	8	10	5	29
Benin	20	9	−1	40	68
Niger	18	15	13	6	48
Sierra Leone	15	9	−1	31	89
Mali	9	6	5	15	30
Senegal	9	5	12	110	266
Gambia	8	na	na	na	na

184

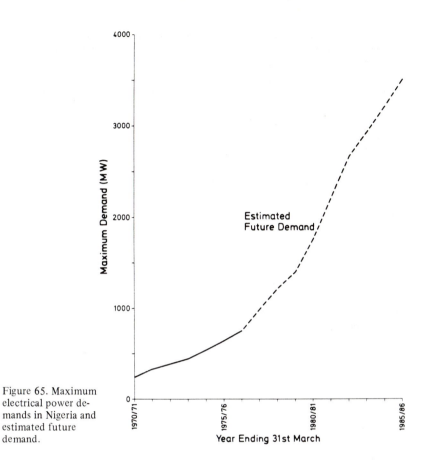

Figure 65. Maximum electrical power demands in Nigeria and estimated future demand.

business profits (Hart 1980 and Lanning & Mueller 1979).

The second factor in the rapid development of HEP generation facilities was simply that demand for power was seen to be rising. Table 24 shows Smith's 1968 estimates of the rate of growth in consumption of electricity in West Africa in the critical years 1959–65. It also shows the World Bank's 1981 figures of the growth in energy consumption in the same countries. From these it is clear that over the longer perspective these apparently very rapid rates of growth have slackened considerably. Of course, percentage figures of this sort are somewhat misleading since they do not include provision for the initial scale of demand. Figures for actual energy consumption per capita do show a considerable increase between 1960 and 1979 (Table 25), even if not of the magnitude perhaps envisaged in the 1960s. (Figure 65).

Smith (1968) comes to the clear conclusion (perhaps unsurprisingly in the light of Kaiser's smelting interests) that HEP was 'the basic and most economic source of electric energy in Africa for the foreseeable future'.

However, the decision to adopt hydro-electric rather than thermal-electric generation is not straightforward. HEP installations have a high capital cost, and hence a higher cost per KW, and only become cheaper than thermo-electric plants over long periods. They generally have to be large to be at all economic, and hence require a large potential market, and because their location is determined largely by topography, costly transmission grids are required to reach a sufficient number of consumers.

Smith (1968) cites a series of factors militating against HEP as an attraction, to potential funding bodies. They are unpopular compared to thermal plants because they are less attractive to foreign equipment suppliers who are, he suggests, a more powerful lobby than dam constructors, because HEP supplants petroleum and hence offends the powerful interests involved in that trade, and because the public ownership generally associated with HEP installations (due to their size) also offends powerful interests. However, given Kaiser's success over the Volta River Project, this tends to sound somewhat disingenuous. Certainly in West Africa the pattern has been for just the pattern of HEP generation and extensive transmission grids that he advocated.

Indeed, so completely did power development in Nigeria come to be associated with HEP that in 1972 the Niger Dam's Authority (established in 1962 to develop the electricity potential of the Niger and Kaduna Rivers) was merged with the Electricity Corporation of Nigeria to form the National Electrical Power Authority (NEPA) (West African Technical Review 1981b). Furthermore, the same advocacy of HEP is still repeated: E.A. Kalitsi of the Volta River Authority told the ECOWAS Symposium on Energy in Sierra Leone in November 1981 that 'hydro is the best low-cost solution to the energy problems in the long run, but admitted that its high capital cost often put it beyond the means of the most of the individuals of the community', such that further international grids were required (West Africa 1981). There has also, however, been criticism of this approach to power supply, particularly because of the high rural population in West Africa which cannot easily be served by grid electricity: it is estimated for example, that no more than 60% of Nigeria will be electrified by grid by the year 2000 despite massive investment in generating installations and power lines (Nolfi 1981).

For whatever reason, the investment decisions have been taken to build dams for hydro-electricity throughout West Africa, and commitment to HEP generation has not waned. The Kainji Dam (completed 1968 costing ₦ 175 m with a capacity of 780 MW), is being followed by the Jebba Dam downstream (560MW, due for completion 1984,) (West African Technical Review 1981b). Although a further project at Lokoja at the Niger/Benue confluence (estimated cost ₦ 2.5 billion) has now, after much opposition, apparently been shelved and a further 4 generators at Kainji will not now be built, investigations are continuing intensively into other sites, including the Mambilla Plateau (Iliasu 1980) and the Shiroro Gorge. The Fourth National Development Plan of Nigeria (1980–85) envisages 4600

MW installed capacity by 1985c. In 1984 1 N or Naira is worth about $1.35 US).

Similarly in Ghana, the Volta River Project was followed in 1977 by a dam downstream at Kpong (160 MW) to supplement the supply from Akosombo (Hart 1980). In the Ivory Coast the Kossou Dam on the Bandama River (completed 1972) is being followed by the Taabo Dam (210 MW) on the same river and the Buyo Dam on the Sassandra River (165 MW) (Bunton 1979). The star of hydro-electric dams seems still to be firmly in the ascendancy in West Africa.

7.4 DAMS FOR IRRIGATION

7.4.1 *Irrigation in relation to climate*

Over a large proportion of savanna West Africa the short seasonal duration and unpredictability of rainfall is a major limitation on crop growth. The climatic pattern is broadly of isohyets running east-west, the timing and duration of the rains determined by the northerly movement of the Inter-tropical Convergence Zone in the first half of the year and its southward movement in the second half. Irrigation which provides the capacity to overcome the limitations imposed by the rains, has a different role in each climatic zone. In the Sahel where rainfall is less than 300 mm, irrigation is essential to settled agriculture. Further south in the Sudan-Sahel zone, with a wet season of less than 160 days, irrigation can serve both to make up the water deficit in dry years and to allow double cropping. Further south in the Sudan and northern Guinea zone irrigation can be used to ensure water supplies throughout the double (bimodal) wet season. The potential for irrigation in West Africa is enormous, but the proportion of land irrigated is still small. In 1965 less than 0.25 m ha, or 0.7% of the annually cropped area, was irrigated (Des Bouvrie & Rydezewski 1977). The area under irrigation is now increasing rapidly (cf. Adams & Grove 1984).

7.4.2 *Traditional water control*

There is a long tradition of small-scale control of water for agriculture in West Africa. West African rice, *Oryza glabberrima*, was domesticated over 2000 years ago, and throughout the region cultivators have recognised the value of floodplain land seasonally inundated by rivers. Various techniques and strategies have been developed to exploit the fertile inundation lands, from the simple adaptation of cropping calendars to bunding and small-scale irrigation by bucket and rope or lifting beam (shadoof).

In the Niger Inland Delta, a complex pattern of crue (rising flood) and décrue (flood recession) agriculture has been developed in association with pastoralism (Gallais 1967, Gallais & Sidikou 1978). Varieties of rice are planted in August or September which are able to keep pace with the

187

Figure 66. Sorghum and rice intercropped on the banks of the River Sokoto, Nigeria.

rising waters in deeply flooded areas, often being harvested as flood waters recede (Scudder 1980). Each village has a set of rice varieties adapted to its own soil conditions, but in general a range of varieties are planted together to guard the loss of the crop through sudden changes in water level or drought. Parallel with this adaptation to unpredictable flooding is a collective rotation of fields in response to perceived cyclical changes in flooding, frequently involving shifts over a wide area (Gallais & Sidikou 1978).

Similar flood-recession farming is carried out on the oualo land of the Senegal valley (Watt 1981), the firki clays of the hydromorphic zone of Lake Chad and the fadama of Northern Nigeria. Cultivation in the Nigeria fadamas is perhaps typical. The area concerned is extensive, possibly 10% of the land of northern Nigeria, 80,000 ha of the Rima valley alone (FAO 1969), but the cultivation is intensive in nature. The complex and variable soil and water resources of the floodplain land systems are matched by selection of suitable crop varieties and appreciation of agroecological conditions. The details of cropping vary widely between the lower wider floodplains where floating rice cultivation may occur and higher reaches of the rivers where the floodplains are more variable topographically and the response of the cultivators correspondingly less uniform (Figure 66).

In the River Sokoto floodplain in the upper reaches of the Sokoto Rima Basin in Nigeria, a series of cropping patterns can be recognised. On unflooded upland soils rainfed crop associations of millet, dryland sorghum and typically beans, groundnuts or cotton are grown, and these are also associated with well-drained raised portions of the floodplain. On land which is inundated seasonally only once or twice, fast-maturing or waterlogging-resistant varieties of sorghum and certain rice varieties are grown in the wet season. In areas likely to be inundated for longer periods, rice is virtually the only wet season crop (Figure 67).

In the fadama associated with each village there will be perhaps a dozen or so varieties of rice and guinea corn for each of which the most suitable growing conditions are known. Although the timing and height of the floods on the Sokoto have always been unpredictable, they have traditionally been certain enough to allow a detailed appreciation of the cropping potential of different parts of the fadama to develop. Field sizes are small (0.2 ha average in one extensive area on the Sokoto developed for formal irrigations), but even within those fields different ecological conditions are recognised and patches of rice as small as 20 m^2 may be planted to make best use of a particularly wet hollow.

Figure 67. The floodplain of the River Sokoto, Nigeria. The floodplain has long supported a dense population and has been intensively cultivated in both wet and dry season.

189

There is also a strong element of risk-avoidance in the juxtaposition of crops in the small floodplain fields which have different water requirements. It is not unusual to see a field of sorghum, millet and beans (a dryland association) together with rice in the lowest areas: if the flood is small the sorghum and beans will yield and the millet do well; if the flood is heavy the millet at least will die, but the sorghum is likely to yield something and the rice will probably do well.

The real significance of the traditional fadama cultivation, however, is in the extension of the rainfed cropping season which it allows. The seasonal flood fills pools and depressions in the floodplain around which relatively high-value vegetable crops (onions, tomatoes, peppers, garden eggs, cucurbits) are grown as the water recedes in dry season gardens (lambu in Hausa). Over wider areas, the water table which has been recharged by the floodwaters is close to the surface and plants such as tobacco or cassava are able to mature long after the rains have ended.

In places field wells (rijia in Hausa) and either a simple bucket lift (guga) or a shadoof beam (kutara or jigo) are constructed and small levelled plots, typically of onions, are laid out in a system of basin micro-irrigation. The water supply and water balance of these gardens is delicate (Ipinmidun 1970) but with the simplest of technology excellent yields are obtained. The improvement of communication in Northern Nigeria is adding an extra impetus to this traditional small-scale irrigation since the dry-season vegetables are valuable cash crops. Shadoof gardens are particularly important in parts of the Kano Close Settled Zone (Farouk 1971), and around Sokoto, but they are by no means recent innovations: in 1924 a shadoof lifting 3–4 m won the grudging admiration of an irrigation engineer in Sokoto Province 'such a high lift shows considerable zeal, and the profit from 'shipki-shipki' (dry season farming) must be considerable to make this worthwhile' (Kaduna National Archives, (KNA SNP 10780 Volume 2).[1]

7.4.3 Early irrigation schemes: The Sokoto Rima Basin, Nigeria

The large-scale control of water by dams and formal irrigation schemes in West Africa are relatively recent developments. The aridity of the Sudan and Sahel zones and the relative abundance of water in the major rivers, however, led to suggestions of irrigation from a fairly early stage after the arrival of colonial government.

Among the first areas to be developed was the Sokoto Rima Basin. As early as 1917 a District Officer assessing part of the Sokoto floodplain saw the potential of increasing and controlling the inundation of seasonally flooded depressions (tapkis) by means of canals, embankments and bunds (KNA SOKPROF 2/10 555/1918). Work costing a total of £227 was begun in time for the 1918 rains, and it was confidently predicted that storage would be increased from 0.75×10^6 m^3 to 21×10^6 m^3 on 1500 ha. In fact, 1918 was a wet year and the works were damaged, while 1919 was dry and the storage disappointing. Nonetheless for a time the possibility of building on this simple water conservation work with full irrigation development was considered with some enthusiasm: 'the native idea of irrigation is primitive and laborious – but here there are considerable areas which can be made available for irrigation by gravity' (KNA SOKPROF 2/10 155/1918).

Although the first small-scale dams fell into disfavour very soon following local opposition, being broken down 'amid great rejoicing' in 1920 (letter Resident Sokoto to Secretary Northern Provinces 18/4/1920), interest was sufficient to bring out an irrigation engineer, Colonel Collins, to report on irrigation possibilities in the Sokoto and Rima Basins (KNA SNP 10708 Vol. 2) in 1923 and 1924. Collins wrote 'perennial irrigation will only be possible on the Sokoto River if reservoirs can be constructed to store water' (KNA SNP 17 10708 Vol. 2), and he pointed to the possibility of storage upstream on basement complex 'for use lower down' (op. cit.). Collins wanted a full topographic survey (refused by the Native Authority on the grounds of cost), complained of the lack of hydrological data (still a problem today), the lack of markets for irrigated crops (such that 'there was not any inducement for the native to grow more than he needs for one season's food and seed, with enough left over to sell immediately to pay his annual tax') and he advocated cooperative mechanisation and control of land tenure on possible schemes. In these and other recommendations Collins accurately presaged the form of later approaches to irrigation in the area, but initially little was done.

Official response to the schemes Collins proposed was cautious, and it was suggested that it might only be possible to 'carry out some small schemes of irrigation by gravity, by way of experiment and object lesson' (letter Secretary Northern Provinces to Lagos 24/12/1923). In practice the only development for a number of years was a small scheme at Kware near Sokoto begun in 1925. The scheme has had a chequered history and on the whole has performed poorly. Palmer Jones (1981) points to the lack of involvement of ordinary farmers, unallayed distrust of government intervention and the lack of assured benefits for farmers as reasons for the poor record. Certainly the scheme did not generate any great interest in irrigation on a larger scale.

The British West African Rice Mission visited Nigeria in 1948 and commented 'in order to improve conditions for the growth of paddy within floodplains, control (or at least partial control) of floods is essential' (Clark & Hutchinson 1948), but made no firm proposals for such control in the Sokoto-Rima Basin for lack of data. Further action waited until the Irrigation Division was established in Northern Region of Nigeria in 1949, and began to develop a number of small schemes (FAO 1966). By the mid-sixties the FAO's long-term agricultural planning study showed how closely irrigation had come to be linked to perceptions of future agricultural development: 'full exploitation of the agricultural potential of Nigeria requires the development of the water resources of the country for irrigation, together with the control of floods to prevent annual inundation of fertile lands along the rivers and in the delta' (FAO 1966). Within a few years the first large-scale schemes were being investigated.

7.4.4 *Large scale irrigation in Nigeria*

The first large-scale irrigation established in Nigeria was the Bacita Sugar Scheme near Ilorin. Now covering 4800 ha (Nwa & Martins 1982) this involves a mixture of sprinkler and surface methods of irrigation and is run by a private company, although when it was begun in 1964 it was a joint venture between the Government and Booker McConnell (Nosworthy 1979). It has now been somewhat overshadowed by a series of large government schemes further north in the Sokoto Rima Basin, Kano River basin and adjacent to Lake Chad.

Interest in the control of the rivers of the Sokoto and Rima basins persisted following the initial burst of activity in the 1920s, albeit not very strongly. A paper by the Ministry of Agriculture in Kaduna entitled 'The Dying River Systems of the Northern Region' (KNA Ministry of Agriculture RR-115, 1959) painted a bleak picture of what would now be called 'desertification' with overcultivation, soil erosion, accelerated sedimentation and eventual blockage of the rivers. Reactions to the report varied. In the view of Harrison Church (1961) the document was very controversial, and he remarks that quite a lot of Government people disagreed with it. Nonetheless it apparently had a considerable effect on administrators in Northern Nigeria (Adams 1983), and was probably a major factor in the successful attempt to obtain United Nations Special Fund finance for a study 'to appraise the soil and water resources of the Sokoto basin and to formulate an agricultural development plan for the area' (FAO 1969).

The executing agency for the Sokoto Rima project study was the Food and Agriculture Organisation (FAO): it was begun in 1962 and finished in 1968 at a cost of US $2.88 m. Although the terms of reference of the study were broad, in practice the team's conception of development in the river basin was in terms of a series of discrete irrigation schemes (Adams 1983). Seven irrigation projects in Northern Nigeria were analysed and despite the problems encountered with these pilot schemes the FAO concluded 'the projects have shown that economic yields are possible under irrigation' (FAO 1969); they proceeded to prepare detailed proposals for irrigation schemes in the basin.

The regime of the Sokoto and Rima rivers is strongly seasonal (Gill 1974), with 70% of runoff in the two months of August and September (FAO 1969). The basic elements of the FAO's proposals were therefore to control flooding in the wide rice-growing fadamas of the lower Rima (where in some years as little as 25% of the 50–80000 ha planted were harvested) by building dams in the basin headwaters. The water stored in these dams could then be used for irrigation in the upper basin. The benefits expected from these upstream dams were manifold (FAO 1969):

192

a) The area in the floodplain subject to an uncontrolled flooding during the rainy season and on which rice only is grown will have regulated flooding.

b) The fluctuation of flood levels will be minimised and the level of inundation stabilised. This will enable rice to be grown on the upstream portions of the floodplain and will also permit the growing of improved varieties of rice.

c) In the reclaimed areas of the floodplain and on suitable terrace soils, it will be possible to practise agriculture under irrigation throughout the year.

d) There will be a constant supply of water in the river downstream of the reservoirs to meet industrial and domestic needs.

e) Hydro-electric power could possibly be developed for small scale industries.

f) A fishing industry could be developed in the reservoirs and main rivers.

g) A more stable river flow would aid navigation.

Upland areas were not seen by the FAO team to hold great promise for agricultural development, but attention was focussed on terrace and floodplain soils. About 200,000 ha of irrigable non-flooded land and a further 600,000 ha of partly irrigable floodplain and low terrace land were identified (FAO 1969). In the long-range plan four headwaters' reservoirs, Bakolori on the Sokoto, Yarkofoji on the tributary Bobo River nearby, Yautabaki on the Gagare River and Zobe on the Bunsuru, and a reservoir on the Rima floodplain were envisaged to supply a total of 93,000 ha of irrigated land at a cost (1967 prices) of N47 m for 1.73×10^9 m³ of storage (FAO 1969). Some of the irrigated land was upland terrace, some was to be contained in seven polders within flood bunds on the wide lower Rima floodplain.

The FAO recommended a phased development of the Sokoto Rima basin, starting with a scheme of 12,000 ha near Talata Mafara on the Sokoto River. Even on this first phase project they advocated a slow and cautious approach 'because of the large capital investment required for development at Talata Mafara in the Sokoto Valley, and because of the need for confirmation of existing crop yields, the lack of experience in farming under irrigation and the shortage of trained management, administrative and supporting staff' (FAO 1969). They therefore proposed a two-stage scheme. The Bobo Scheme (1300 ha gross) was to be based on a small reservoir of 69×10^6 m³ on the River Bobo irrigated by pump (terrace land) and gravity. Development was expected to take 4 years. The second stage Talata Mafara scheme was to follow at a later date – a further 10,800 ha (gross) of terrace and floodplain land adjacent to the smaller scheme served by a large (446×10^6 m³) reservoir on the Sokoto at Bakolori and a downstream diversion dam. Water was to be supplied by gravity.

In the period following the completion of the FAO report, work on large-scale irrigation schemes proceeded on three fronts in Nigeria. The first development was in North Eastern State (now Kano State) where the

Kano River Project was begun in 1969 following a study by the United States Department of the Interior Bureau of Reclamation. In Sokoto itself a Sokoto Rima Basin Development Ad-hoc Committee was established, and in 1971 the Federal Military Government invited tenders from consulting engineers for design work at Talata Mafara. A contract for comprehensive studies and design was let in July 1972 to an Italian group (Tasso 1978) which began fieldwork in the 1972–73 dry season and completed a report by March 1974 (Impresit 1974).

Meanwhile irrigation feasibility studies were begun on the clay plains around Lake Chad in June 1971 following development of a 400 ha pilot project by the State Government in 1970. The South Chad Irrigation Project (SCIP) feasibility studies were reviewed in 1973, and in August of that year the Chad Basin and Sokoto Rima Basin Development Authorities were set up by Federal Decree. Design for SCIP phase 1 began before the end of 1973, and construction began in 1976. The SRBDA took the decision to implement the Bakolori Project (as the Talata Mafara scheme had come to be called) in January 1974 (Impresit 1974) and construction of the whole scheme – following a streamlined project route to minimise delay in construction (Tasso 1978) – began in the middle of that year.

The Bakolori Project was developed rapidly: the Designer's plan was to complete construction by 1981, within 6 years, compared to 15–20 years

Figure 68. The Bakolori dam on the River Sokoto, Nigeria, inaugurated in 1978. It supplies water to the 30,000 ha irrigation scheme on downstream floodplain and terrace land.

in similar projects elsewhere (Tasso 1978). The project was also greatly expanded over the FAO's conception, the irrigated area being 30,000 ha gross (75,000 acres, or 2.5 times the FAO's plan) and the idea of a two-stage approach and a dam on the River Bobo were abandoned. Design changes also included a long supply canal from the dam to the irrigable terrace and floodplain soils, and a pipe bridge across the River Sokoto to command the right bank (Figure 68).

The proposed cropping pattern at Bakolori was dominated by cash crops, less than a quarter of the area being designated for subsistence crops. Seventeen per cent of it was for commercially grown sugar cane (this was at a period when sugar cane seemed an excellent investment), and groundnuts, cotton, tomatoes (a processing factory was planned) commercial foodgrains (particularly wheat to meet escalating domestic demands) and fodder crops for a major livestock feedlot were envisaged. These crops, as well as supposed downstream flood control benefits and returns from a fishery in the reservoir formed the basis of the economic viability of the planned scheme. These plans have not been realised in a number of respects, but the scheme was duly inaugurated officially in December 1978. Completion of the irrigation area (23,500 ha net) is still, however, continuing (1982) as are experiments to determine suitable cropping patterns and modes of production and management.

At SCIP, construction of Phase I (gross 32,000 ha, net 20,000 ha) is complete and Phase II was due for completion in 1982 (a further 38,000 ha gross, 27,000 ha net). Construction of Phase III (36,000 ha gross) has yet to begin (*West African Technical Review* 1981a). Water is supplied by a long (30 km) intake channel reaching out into the southern section of Lake Chad and pumped into the main supply canal and thence into feeder

Table 26. Irrigated areas, Nigeria 1980 (Nwa & Martins 1982).

Basin Development Authority	Total area proposed (ha)	Areas irrigated December 1980
Sokoto-Rima	108,800	5,200
Hadejia-Jama'are River	75,009	7,009
Chad	157,500	2,000
Upper Benue River	309,700	110
Lower Benue River	130,750	677
Cross River	724,900	na
Anambra-Imo River	5,000	na
Niger River	243,200	448
Ogun-Oshun River	242,300	128
Benin-Owena River	na	na
Niger Delta	2,500	24
Sub-total	1,999,659	15,596
Commercial projects	47,200	6,978
State Government projects	na	8,132
Total	2,046,859	30,706

canals. Long-term plans are for mechanised agriculture, intensive livestock production and agro-industries. Power for pumps is at present supplied by diesel generators, but there are plans to link in to the NEPA grid.

The three major irrigation schemes in northern Nigeria have been followed by a number of others in each of the 11 River Basin Development Authorities established in 1976, for example the Baga Polder in Borno State (CBDA), and the Savanna Sugar Project in Gongola State (run initially by the Commonwealth Development Corporation). In 1979 it was estimated that just over 200,000 ha of irrigation was planned (Nosworthy 1979), but this is already a major underestimate. Nwa and Martins (1982) suggest over 30,000 ha was actually being irrigated in Nigeria by the end of 1980 and the 11 RBDAs have plans for about 2 m ha irrigation (Table 26). However, few schemes are yet operational and a number show signs of failing to live up to the expectations with which they were begun. The budgetary allocations in the 4th National Development Plan suggest that after a period of intense focus on irrigation, government investment is turning away from major projects towards dryland agriculture in the form of state-wide integrated agricultural development projects funded jointly with the World Bank, and smaller-scale developments.

7.4.5 *Irrigation on the Niger and Senegal rivers*

Informal use of the natural flooding regime of the Niger is of great age. Formal development on any scale dates back to 1919 when the Office du Niger was conceived and plans developed for the irrigation of 1 million hectares to grow cotton and rice in the Inland Delta of the Niger in Mali. After small-scale experimental schemes, the Office du Niger was founded to develop the area in 1932. Population settlement and land development was initially rapid (Table 27). The Markala (Sansanding) Barrage was completed in 1947 to supply water to different sectors of the irrigated area via the Canal du Sahel and the Canal du Macina (Figure 69). By 1962 when the Mali government took over the Office, 37,000 people were producing over 40,000 tonnes of rice and 7000 tonnes of seed cotton from

Table 27. Development of the Office du Niger (Burton 1975).

	Area developed for irrigation (ha)	Population settled
1948	22,536	na
1951	na	21,000
1955	35,958	26,000
1958	42,100	32,000
1964	49,636	33,000
1972	55,655	na

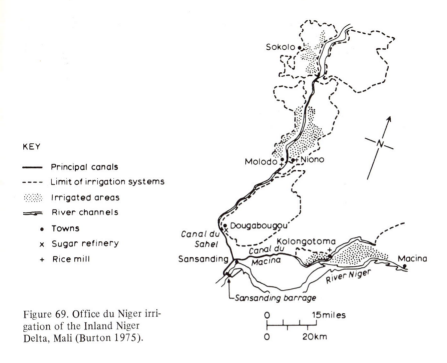

Figure 69. Office du Niger irrigation of the Inland Niger
Delta, Mali (Burton 1975).

18,000 ha of irrigated land (Burton 1975). Development costs up to 1960
amounted to $175 m.

The area developed by the Office du Niger falls far short of their
original target of 1 million hectares, and is also small compared to the
areas under less completely controlled forms of water use in the Delta:
some 130,000 ha of land has been developed by the Service de
L'agriculture in the Delta, comprising 50,000 ha in the lacustrine delta,
23,000 ha in the live delta and a further 32,000 ha west of Mopti. An
additional area of about 13,000 ha above Tanani was developed in 1967,
and there are plans for the development of a total of 60,000 ha of irrigated
terrace and basin along the Niger further downstream in Niger (Burton
1975).

A major objective of Mali's 1974–1978 Five Year Plan was to meet
basic foodgrain needs in the country, but in the year 1978–79 there was an
estimated shortfall of over 80,000 tons of grain (Club du Sahel 1979a).
The vagaries of rainfall are such that irrigation continues to be a major
element in Mali's development plans, but in 1979 no more than 47,000 ha
was under full water control, 39,000 ha of it under the Office du Niger.
Nonetheless, irrigation development continues, first in the extension of
the area of controlled irrigation, for example in the Ségou and Mopti
Rice Projects (34,000 and 41,000 ha respectively) and second in a
programme with World Bank help to rehabilitate the Office du Niger's

197

developed land: over 13,000 ha were left fallow in 1977/78 because of drainage problems (caused by failures of maintenance) and other problems such as the invasion of wild rice (Club du Sahel 1979a).

Although most of the plans made have yet to come to fruition, the Senegal River is the focus of the most extensive integrated river control project in West Africa. It is being planned by the Organisation pour la Mise en Valeur du Fleuve Sénégal (OMVS). This was established in 1972 by Mali, Mauretania and Senegal with assistance from the FAO, the United Nations Development Fund, the World Bank and the European Development Fund. The OMVS inherited a long legacy of planning for the river, evolving through the colonial Mission d'Etude du Fleuve Sénégal, established 1953, the Mission d'Aménagement du Sénégal, 1938, and the Inter-State Committee, which involved Guinea also, 1963–68, and the Organisation des Etats Riverains du Senegal, 1968–72 (OMVS 1981).

The OMVS aims at 'using the river's resources for the economic and social betterment of those living along its banks and of the population in the neighbouring regions' (OMVS 1981). The ambitious plan is to regulate the flow of the Senegal to 300 m^3 per second at Bakel, to make a navigable waterway up to Kayes in Mali, to produce 4000 kw of HEP, and to irrigate up to 375,000 ha (*West African Technical Review* 1978b). The total estimated cost of the work is escalating rapidly: recent estimates

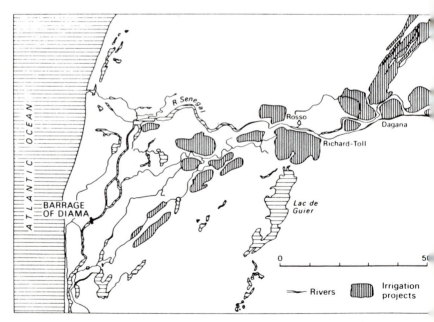

Figure 70. Irrigation on the lower Senegal River (Club du Sahel/CILSS 1979).

are US $750 m (Watt 1981), US $867 m (OMVS 1981) and US $1000 m (*New Civil Engineer International* 1982).

A series of dams are planned. The first is the 1.5 km wide Diama Barrage near St. Louis which will reduce saltwater intrusion in periods of low river flow, will ensure that depressions and lakes along the river are filled, and retain water to increase the possibility of irrigation (Figure 70). The barrage alone should make possible 42,000 ha of irrigation. Initially it will store $250 \times 10^6 m^3$, covering an area of 235 km². In 1978 completion of Diama was expected in 1982 (*New Civil Engineer International* 1978), but despite the injection of large amounts of Arab aid money development was delayed until 1984, and probably 1987 (OMVS 1981). Finance, 40% of it French, was finally fixed in June 1979 (*International Construction* 1979), and a 'symbolic cornerstone' laid in December of that year (OMVS 1981). The contract for construction (worth US $156 m) has been won by a French consortium (*New Civil Engineer International* 1982), and work is scheduled to continue over 6 years (1980–86 inclusive, OMVS 1981). It is likely that there will be further slippage in this timetable.

The second stage in the control of the Senegal is the construction of the 11×10^9 m³ Manantali Dam on the Bafing River in Mali (Figure 71). This will provide 800 GWh of HEP per year and a regulated artificial flood of 2500 m³ sec^{-1} (*New Civil Engineer* 1978). The reservoir will cover some 477 km² and flood 10,000 people in 15 villages (OMVS 1981). Originally the Manantali Dam was due for completion in 1985, but in 1981 work was being scheduled to last 8 years until 1988 and the possibility of further delays was accepted. The estimated cost of the Dam in 1981 was US $670 m (1980 prices), the main sources of finance being West Germany, Kuwait and Saudi Arabia in that order (OMVS 1981).

The countries in the Senegal basin have so far failed to keep up with their own targets for irrigation development. Guidelines drawn up in 1974 aimed for increases of between 6 and 7000 ha per year in the basin between 1977 and 1980, and these were not achieved. In Senegal for example the 5th Plan (1977–81) allocated half the agricultural budget to irrigation, but the Société d'Aménagement et d'Exploitation des Terrains du Delta (SAED) had by 1979 only managed 200 ha out of their 5400 ha target (Club du Sahel 1979b). This failure to meet irrigation targets is of long standing. The SAED's 'Operation des 30,000 ha' for the decade 1965–75 having achieved little more than 9600 ha of rice of which only 2800 ha were under full water control, and the settlement of 8000 out of a target of 40,000 people (Gallais & Sidikou 1978). This failure stands in contrast to other developments in the area (Bradley 1981).

Despite this past low achievement, plans for the future are ambitious (Table 28), with 41,000 ha of irrigation planned by 1990, most of it in Mauretania (21,480 ha, 52%) and Senegal (17,000 ha, 41%). The two dams will make traditional practices of flood-recession farming (covering an estimated 130,000 ha at present) more or less impossible, so irrigation by pumping from the river will be essential. Most of this will be by diesel since HEP will be too costly for most of the length of the river (Watt

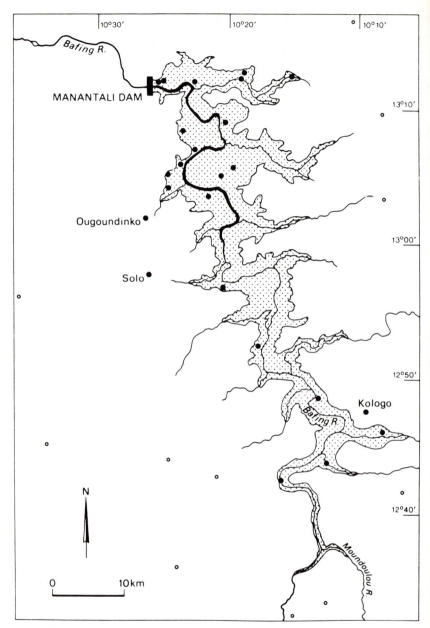

Figure 71. The Manantali dam on the upper Senegal River (Club du Sahel/CILSS 1979).

Table 28. Programme of irrigation development in the Senegal River Basin 1981-90 (OMVS 1981).

	Small perimeters (ha)	Large perimeters Under way 1981	New	Annual rate (ha)
1981	1780	1675	–	3455
1982	1805	1660	–	3465
1983	1990	1410	–	3400
1984	1600	400	1150	3150
1985	1250	800	2500	3780
1986	75	600	400	3850
1987	–	600	5100	4600
1988	–	–	5100	5100
1989	–	–	5100	5100
1990	–	–	5100	5100
Total	9175	6945	24880	41000

1981). Initial developments will focus on village-level schemes (perimeters), but 'because of their very nature they do not fit well into the organised development programs planned by the states' (OMVS 1981). The small schemes will be abandoned after 1986 in favour of larger projects; after 1984 the area under these should rise by over 5000 ha per year.

The wholesale environmental transformation of the Senegal has its proponents (Amin (1974) said it could be 'a really integrated agro-industrial self-sufficient and independent development') but there are severe critics also. The environmental impacts of the dams have been studied (Lubin 1977, Gannet et al. 1980), and doubts about the effects on migratory fish, on disease and on indigenous agriculture have been expressed as well as more fundamental doubts about the whole history and direction of development in the valley (Adams 1977). It remains to be seen how far the intended development will be pursued, with what impact and with what success.

7.5 PUTTING DAMS INTO PERSPECTIVE

The phrase 'environmental side-effects' in the context of development activity is frequently used pejoratively to refer to what are perceived to be harmful side-effects of development. Yet the very purpose of a dam is to exert an effect on the environment by interfering with the natural hydrological cycle, albeit in a controlled and predictable way: a dam for flood control is designed to transform the natural flood hydrograph by storage of peak flows; irrigation or water supply dams do the same, storing water at periods of high discharge for later use. In both cases there is severe environmental transformation consequent on impoundment and the altered pattern of downstream discharge. The effects of the dam on the environment are inevitable: the difficult question comes over whether

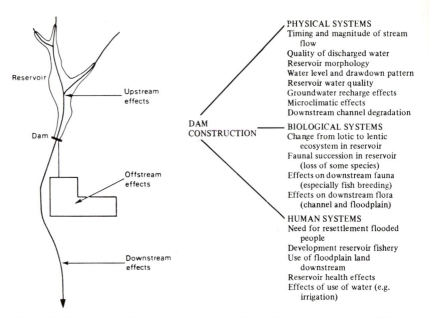

Figure 72. The physical, biological and human effects of dam construction on different environments.

they are to be judged in aggregate beneficial or harmful.

The engineer's or hydrologists's concern with dams is principally to maximise the effectiveness (safety and predictability) with which they fulfill these functions of changing the volume and timing of discharge. Unfortunately, the ramifications of the dam's effects on the environment are far greater than this. Park (1981) in his review of man's impacts on fluvial landforms and processes cites the growing alarm over 'the extent to which, and the speed with which, human impacts in one part of the environment can trigger off serious if not irreversible changes in other parts of the environment'. These effects are often remote from the original impact in space and delayed in time, and as a result are very difficult to comprehend, define and control. The environmental effects of dams are of just this kind.

The effects of a dam can be looked at in simplistic systems terms (Figure 72). Dam construction affects first physical systems: the timing and magnitude of discharge downstream, water quality (turbidity, dissolved load), the development of the lacustrine environment behind the dam, effects on evaporation, groundwater recharge and even geotechnical stability. Secondary effects occur on biological systems: changes in micro and macro-flora and fauna occur in the new reservoir and in downstream areas where flooding regimes are changed or to which water from the reservoir is supplied (e.g. irrigation schemes). Tertiary effects on human

202

systems include responses to the new lake environment, to changes in agricultural potential or fisheries opportunities in the river downstream, as well as knock-on effects remote from the reservoir, for example among distant users of hydro-electricity.

The approach adopted here is to examine the effects of the major West African dams on the two major environments most directly concerned: upstream effects in the newly formed reservoir and downstream effects in riverine areas below the dam. Effects on a third environment—offstream effects on areas served by water from the reservoir, are also important, but are not considered here.

7.6 UPSTREAM EFFECTS OF WEST AFRICAN DAMS

7.6.1 *The reservoir environment*

The closing of a dam brings about the transformation of a lotic (flowing water) into a lentic (still water) environment. Although similar in a number of respects to lakes, reservoirs are sufficiently different to be best regarded as distinct freshwater ecosystem (Baxter 1977). Part of the reason for this is their unique morphology–often an extended dendritic shoreline, a deep point at the downstream end (where the dam is built) often with resultant discharge of 'bottom water' from the hypolimnion which in its turn affects the movement of currents and the prevalence of stratification, and the pattern of annual or seasonal drawdown and exposure of large areas of foreshore. Ecologically, new reservoirs are subject to rapid succession as the lotic benthos dies out and is replaced by lentic communities, and planktonic and littoral species arrive (Baxter 1977). Their management can induce a state of interrupted succession (pulse stability) (Odum 1969) in certain environments such as the drawdown.

The differences between reservoirs and established lakes have attracted the attention of ecologists who have tended to use them as vast open-air laboratories for research. The reservoirs at Kainji and Akosombo are among those studied in some detail prior to, and to a lesser extent following, their inundation in the 1960s. At Kainji, construction of the dam began in February 1964, and research by the University of Ife in Nigeria and Liverpool in England began in 1965 with the help of the Niger Dam Authority (Imevbore 1969). This work followed a United Nations Special Fund mission under E.B. Worthington looking at Man-made Lakes in Nigeria, Ghana and the United Arab Republic (Mabogunje 1973). A first report of research was produced rapidly (White 1965). The Nigerian Institute of Social and Economic Research became involved in the investigations, and sponsored the publication of two volumes of pre-impoundment studies, on ecology (Visser 1970) and on socio-economic conditions (Mabogunje 1973). Research has continued at the Kainji Lake Research Institute at New Bussa (Imevbore & Adegoke 1975). Similar research, initially through the FAO, has been done on Volta lake.

The limnology of new reservoirs is controlled partly by the chemistry, turbidity and temperature of the inflowing water and precipitation, and partly by the incorporation of material from the inundated area. Both the Volta and Kainji dams inundated extensively wooded savanna terrain, and only at Kainji was any vegetation clearance carried out, 37,000 ha being cut and burned (Jenness 1973). Above Kainji, river discharge is at its minimum and dissolved solids at their most concentrated, about 80 micromhos, in June (page 84). At this period the lake is thermally stratified (March-May) (page 81), but with the arrival of the White Flood in August the stratification is destroyed.

The concentration of dissolved solids in the river above the reservoir falls with the arrival of the White Flood in September and October when the conductivity of the lake water varies between 40 and 60 μmhos (Imevbore 1975). Its waters are turbid (Secchi Disc disappears 2.5 m depth Imevbore 1975) although the silt load of the Niger prior to impoundment was small, about 250ppm (0.5 kgm^{-3}, Imevbore 1970); clays derived locally from the reservoir area are probably responsible for the increased turbidity. A diverse benthic fauna has developed at Kainji, and an extension of the zooplankton communities, but there have been no major infestations of algae or surface macrophytes as have occurred at other African reservoirs such as Kariba.

The Volta reservoir developed somewhat differently from that at Kainji, partly because it filled gradually over a period of seven years (1964–71), and initial stratification led to deoxygenation at depth as flooded vegetation decayed (Biswas 1966). The first benthic colonists were chironimid larvae (McLachlan 1974), typical first arrivals in deoxygenated temperate impoundments. The burrowing nymph of the mayfly *Povilla adusta* became abundant in the standing trees (Petr 1970 and page 124), providing an important source of food for the changing fish communities. The Volta lake is low in nutrients and the phytoplankton crop is correspondingly low (Baxter 1977).

Fish and fisheries have been important at both Volta and Kainji. In both, an initial phase of high productivity and fish catches occurred associated with abundant benthic organisms feeding on the flooded vegetation and the release of nutrients from the same source. This was followed by a decline in fish numbers and catches. On impoundment the composition of the fish fauna in both reservoirs changed. Mormyrids (bottom feeders) virtually disappeared, perhaps because of deoxygenation at depth. Cichlids became more common in the southern parts of Volta but not at Kainji, perhaps because of the effects of the drawdown regime on breeding (Lowe McConnell 1975 and pages 114–125). *Tilapia* species became important in both reservoirs, as did the predatory Nile Perch (*Lates niloticus* and *Hydrocynus* spp).

The reservoir fishery has been an important element in the economic development of the reservoir in the case of both Kainji and Volta. There were some 5500 fishermen among the 50,000 evacuees at Kainji (Jennes· 1973), and a number of these have been able to adapt to the new dee water fishing opportunities offered by the lake. A number of others whose fishing downstream was disrupted by the dam have also moved to the lake at Kainji. The same pattern is recorded even more strongly at Volta where over 20,000 fishermen were counted in 1976, in almost 1500 major villages (Coppola & Agadazi 1976), the majority coming from downstream areas. The annual catch is estimated to be about 38,000 tonnes at Volta (Hart 1980), far higher than the 18,000 tonnes estimated before inundation (Preparatory Commission 1956). The success of the fisheries at Volta and Kainji has led to inflated estimates of potential yields from other smaller reservoirs in West Africa, sometimes based on sketchy ecological logic.

An important aspect of the development of tropical reservoir environments is their effect on disease vectors. Studies on this question began early at Kainji (Boyo 1962): the Disease Vector Control Unit was established in April 1961 and vector surveys began in the same year (Walsh & Millnik 1970). Control measures against onchocerciasis and malaria during the construction period were intensive (pages 277-282). DDT was applied by hand at 0.33-2ppm for 30 minutes every 10 days around the dam and on the Obi River, as well as being sprayed round the construction camp (Imevbore 1975). Onchocerciasis virtually died out following inundation, but the incidence of schistosomiasis, transmitted by littoral snail vectors, increased dramatically. Thirty one per cent of a sample of 1656 evacuees at Kainji in 1972 suffered from the disease (Imevbore 1975). A similar pattern of changing disease incidence has been recorded at Volta (Paperna 1970, Obeng 1975 and pages 308-309).

7.6.2 Resettlement of reservoir evacuees

The benefits generated by dam projects are generally enjoyed in locations remote from the dam itself for example in offstream irrigation areas or urban centres where hydro-electricity is consumed. Those living on the site of a dam or in the area to be inundated by the reservoir, however, bear a large measure of the costs of the project. Reviews of resettlement projects judge them severely: 'the literature suggests that most reservoir-related resettlements have been badly planned and inadequately financed, and that most evacuees have become at least temporarily and in many cases permanently worse-off as a result, both economically and socially' (Lightfoot 1978).

All the major dam projects in West Africa have involved major forced resettlement of river valley populations. The numbers involved in some of the larger projects are indicated in Table 29. Some of these projects (notably again Kainji and Volta) have been planned with great care and executed at considerable cost, and a large body of data exists concerning the methods adopted, although there has been far less solid appraisal of their success.

The problem of the population living in reservoir areas is generally tackled several years after engineering feasibility studies, and frequently after decisions have been taken to commence construction. It has been

Table 29. Population displaced by some major West African dams.

Dam	Population
Kossou (Ivory Coast)	85,000
Volta (Ghana)	84,000
Kainji (Nigeria)	50,000
Dadin Kowa, Nigeria	30,000
Kiri (Nigeria)	19,000
Bakolori (Nigeria)	15,000
Tiga (Nigeria)	13,000
Challawa Gorge (Nigeria)	12,000
Kpong (Ghana)	5,500
Jebba (Nigeria)	4,000

known for action to be neglected until after construction has actually begun. By that time it is far too late to hope to solve the difficulties of resettlement adequately: 'planning for the engineering process of construction follows well-known lines, by and large, and if setbacks occur they can be made up by the application of more resources. The same sort of solution is usually not possible with people, and successful resettlement cannot be achieved without a considerable amount of preliminary study, detailed multi-departmental planning, allocation of executive authority and adequate resources and preparation of people for the move' (Black 1975). Such careful planning is much more easily advocated than achieved. The vast gulf in practice between the efficient, materialistic and swift decision-making of engineering construction and the less clear-cut and more delicate procedures of the social sciences necessarily central to resettlement has been often lamented, but rarely crossed (Hamnett 1970, Ingersoll 1968, Scudder 1980).

The most frequent response to the short time schedule allowed by dam construction timetables and the intractable and politically delicate nature of reservoir resettlement has been paternalistic and not participatory planning (Lightfoot 1979): 'the assumption among planners that, as a result of their education and expertise, they can understand and manage the interests of the farmers better than the farmers do for themselves'. This is certainly true of the major West African schemes.

7.6.2.1 *Resettlement at Kainji*. At Kainji about 44,000 people in 203 villages and the towns of Yelwa and Bussa were inundated by the 1200 km^2 lake (Wilson 1975, & Adeniyi 1976). Almost 15,000 ha of farmland were flooded. The dam was a national project, and government agreed to pay for resettlement, but this was made the task of the Northern Region Ministry of Economic Planning (Negedu 1973). In June 1961 the Niger Dams Regional Committee was established to advise the Ministry with members representing the various other Ministries affected, the three Provinces concerned (Ilorin, Sokoto and Niger) and local authorities. In 1962 the Niger Dams Resettlement Authority was established at Federal level, and the first staff were posted to Bussa (Negedu 1973). After the military take-over in 1966 resettlement became the responsibility of the office of the Secretary to the Military Government in Kaduna, and the Niger Dams Authority was reconstituted as a sub-committee of the Niger Dams Project. When States were created out of the Regions in 1967, the Kainji Dam area was split between North-Western and Kwara States.

Initial resettlement policy laid down by the Government of the Northern Region was that with the exception of Bussa town, compensation should be in cash for buildings lost and people should be allowed to settle where they wished and clear their own farm land with advice only from the Ministry of Agriculture. Resettlement surveys began in late 1962 and resettlement began on this principle in 1963. By the end of the following year 2338 people in 18 villages around the dam site had been compensated and moved (Oyedipe 1973, Negedu 1973).

In November 1964 this resettlement policy was reversed, and the Niger Resettlement authority began to build houses for evacuees and as far as possible to group villages together. Reasons for this change included a desire to quicken the pace of resettlement (which characteristically was slower than the tight timetable of dam construction allowed), the lack of water at some sites selected by evacuees and the use of compensation money for purposes other than house construction (Negedu 1973).

A firm of architects were contracted 'to produce a housing and resettlement design which would be acceptable to the people of the area so that they would move willingly into the new accommodation without coercion and with the minimum of stress' (*West African Technical Review* 1978a). They classified settlements in terms of shadow patterns (using aerial and ground photographs) into what were termed urban, semi-urban, rural and semi-rural settlements (Atkinson 1973). On this basis 212 new settlements were laid out, huts being constructed of sandcrete block walls and curved self-supporting asbestos cement roofs (*West African Technical Review* 1978a). By August 1968 a total of 41,654 people from 239 settlements had been resettled in 141 new settlements. Sixty three per cent of the hamlets (49 per cent of the population) had been regrouped (Oyedipe 1973, Table 30).

An interesting, but not untypical, problem facing the resettlement at Kainji was the effects of the reservoir which were felt differently in the three Emirates affected: of the 43,700 people to be resettled over 30,000 were in Yauri Emirate of Sokoto Province, and only 12,000 in Borgo

Table 30. Population resettlement at Kainji (Oyedipe 1973).

	No. settlements Before	After	Population	No. compounds
Cash compensation policy	17	11	2,349	242
Building compensation policy	222	130	41,654	4,390
Total	239	141	44,003	4,390

Emirate (Ilorin Province) and 1000 in Kontagora emirate (Niger Province). In 1963 it was estimated that fully 9700 ha of cultivated land in Yauri emirate would be flooded, compared to 5000 ha in the other two (Negedu 1973). It was decided at an early stage to attempt to resettle people within their own Emirate, and a committee was established in 1962 to look into Yauri Emirate's problem. Soil surveys were done by the Institute of Agricultural Research at Ahmadu Bello University in Yauri and neighbouring Kontagora and revealed a land shortfall in Yauri: eventually Kontagora Emirate agreed to offer some 932 km^2 of land to its less fortunate neighbour (Negedu 1973).

The eventual resettlement policy evolved at Kainji consisted of the provision of replacement private dwellings (with the consequent inflexibility this implies for later extension), replacement of all community buildings, cash compensation for farmlands and economic trees, the allocation of new farmland and the provision of agricultural extension services (Oyedipe 1973). Tax relief was also granted for two years, underwritten by the resettlement authorities.

It has been claimed that there was 95% acceptance of the resettlement (*West African Technical Review* 1978a); but not all were satisfied. One reason for this might have been the inflation of hopes caused by over-zealous use of public relations tapes by the Emirs. The main direct causes of complaint were the unsuitability of village locations, sometimes too far from the lake for fishing or on swampy ground; the way houses were constructed – leaking roofs, the poor thermal properties of sandcrete buildings ('cold cement bunkers' now replaced old brazier-warmed beds) and the lack of provision for kitchens (Oyedipe 1973).

There seem to have been fewer complaints about farmland, although it gave lower yields than the old flooded land and a major occupation among the valley-bottom Gungawa, onion growing, could not be carried out. It seems that those resettled under the initial cash-compensation policy felt hard done by (Oyedipe 1973), and certainly the loss of floodplain grasslands was a major blow to Fulani pastoralists, but the provision made for food aid was not required (Negedu 1973).

As is the case in a number of resettlement schemes, there is quite complete information on what was done at Kainji, but little in the way of retrospective assessment. Overall, the resettlement has been recorded as a success for detailed centralised planning: although it is faintly ironic in the light of all the work done that despite the reservoir demarcation survey 'unfortunately during a contour line location . . . months after the lake had formed, they came across some resettlement villages below the 472-foot contour and one of them was actually below the 465-foot contour (the flood line)' (Negedu 1973). This perhaps indicates something of the way in which the real world can evade the grip of even the best laid plans approached in this way.

7.6.2.2 *Resettlement at Volta.* The resettlement exercise at Volta is probably even better documented than that at Kainji (Chambers 1970,

208

Hart 1980). The lake covers some 8500 km^2 and affected about 80,000 people living in 739 villages: 1% of the population of Ghana. Concern for resettlement dates back to the work of the Preparatory Commission in the 1950s (Preparatory Commission 1956), who recommended self-help resettlement with cash compensation: an approach subsequently shown to be effective in subsequent studies elsewhere, such as Thailand (Lightfoot 1978).

The Preparatory Commission recommended detailed studies, but owing to the uncertainty following their report over the future of the whole project, nothing was done until 1961 when the construction contract was awarded (Kalitsi 1970). The first staff were appointed in 1961, but it was not until May 1962, 9 months after the start of dam construction, that resettlement work began to get off the ground in any effective way. A Resettlement Officer was appointed to coordinate an eclectic Working Party consisting of officers from every relevant Government Department and Ministry, as well as the Volta River Authority (VRA) and academic institutions (Kalitsi 1970).

The Working Party met weekly, and its recommendations were approved by the chief executive of the VRA. It was a curious organisation, for although the Resettlement Officer was seen as carrying executive responsibility, he had no actual powers beyond persuasion to get work done by the officers of the various Government Departments. However, the Working Party was an ingenious solution to the three key problems with the resettlement: the need for haste (impoundment was initially expected in two years in 1964), the lack of money available under the 1961 Volta River Development Act all expenditure on resettlement over £3.5 m had to be borne by Government – the Working Party neatly ensured their involvement) and the hesitation of the VRA to tackle the resettlement alone (Kalitsi 1970).

The Working Party adopted three guiding principles for resettlement (Kalitsi 1965):

1. To use resettlement as an opportunity to enhance the social, cultural and physical conditions of the people.

2. To improve their system of agriculture to enable them to effect the transition from subsistence to cash economy.

3. To plan and locate the settlements in a rational manner so that the flood victims as well as others in the Volta Lake Basin Area can derive maximum benefits from the changes involved.

The general approach was thus initially similar at Volta to that at Kainji, but greater stress was laid on general development of the lake area, and in particular the transformation of agriculture.

The Working Party abandoned the principle of cash compensation and self-help housing at an early stage because the element of coercion and the lack of time available mitigated against its viability, and proposed construction by direct labour of houses at a standard minimum level of 2 rooms, a cooking porch and a sitting porch with concrete foundations, aluminium roof and landcrete walls (Kalitsi 1965). These 'core houses' were to be built in permanent villages provided with certain minimum community facilities (water supply, schools, markets etc.) and at a later date they could be extended by self-help if assistance was provided in the form of advice and materials (Danby 1970).

A Volta Basin Plan was drawn up by the Division of Town and Country Planning in June 1962 with the assistance of the United Nations Regional Planning Mission, followed by a series of Area Plans and the process of resettlement site selection (Huszar 1970). The element of more or less forced modernisation was important, especially in agriculture. The resettlement was seen as 'a unique opportunity to wean an appreciable proportion of Ghana's farmers from the wasteful fragmented and shifting system of agriculture to a settled and improved pattern of farming' (Nicholas 1970). Land was to be cleared and reallocated to evacuees for mechanical cultivation of food and tree crops.

A series of surveys was begun in 1961 and 1962 to provide the data base for resettlement. The best topographic maps available were at 1: 50,000 scale and showed only 50 foot contours. A reservoir demarcation survey was therefore begun in April 1961. Progress was slow: by the end of 1962 only about 436 km had been covered and when work was eventually abandoned a year later with only 3122 km completed it was decided 'to take a calculated risk on the balance' (Kalitsi 1970). By that time the exhaustive social survey and property evaluation exercise were complete: a pilot social survey had been done in mid-1961 and on the basis of this and experience gained by the Department of Social Welfare and Community Development in the Tema Harbour resettlement a full survey was designed and conducted between July and October 1962 (Butcher 1970).

An integral part of this social survey was a series of questions designed to encourage evacuees to consider amalgamation with neighbouring villages. This is quite a common feature of resettlement projects, serving to increase the ease and reduce the cost with which village services can be provided, but the steps taken to involve the people in the process at Volta were exceptional. The positive and negative preferences of each village were recorded, and acceptable amalgamation configurations worked out. At the end of consultation, 72 sites had been chosen by the people, of which 27 were rejected by the VRA for technical reasons. Some of these rejections themselves were not acceptable to the villagers (Table 31). The figure eventually reached was 52 new villages (Amarteifio 1970).

Bush clearance for village sites began in 1962 with commercial labour, at a slow pace. Heavy plant was brought in the following year, but even so by the end of 1964 only 6000 ha had been cleared. House construction was also initially slow. Firm decisions on the exact nature of the housing to be built were not taken until 1963, and by the end of that year only 3400 houses had been built in 10 settlements. A year later over 11,000 houses had been completed (Kalitsi 1970). Agricultural development was even slower, with only 8 new farms established by the end of 1964. Impoundment, however, waited for no man: 200 villages and 15,000

210

Table 31. The selection of sites for resettlement villages, Volta River Project (Amarteifio 1970).

No. sites selected by people and accepted readily by VRA	18
No. sites selected by people and accepted by VRA with slight shift	8
Sites selected by VRA and accepted readily by people	6
Sites selected by people and forced on VRA	15
Sites selected by VRA and forced on to people	5
Final total no. sites selected	52

people were affected by flooding in 1963, and inspired by this 1106 families (out of 15,000) were resettled by the end of that year. By the end of 1964 over 10,000 families were established in 44 settlements.

Since the Volta resettlement, probably to a greater extent even than Kainji, has been used so often as a model for subsequent resettlement projects, it is worth questioning closely its degree of success. Again, there is little information on evaluation compared to that on planning. What there is shows up three areas of concern among evacuees: the environment of the new settlements, livelihoods and compensation.

Studies at New Mpamu (1700 settlers) in 1965 recorded that almost 50% of interviewees were 'enthusiastic' about their new houses, and 67% said their house plot sizes were 'just right' (Tamakloe 1968). By contrast, in New Grube (665 settlers) 'there was much actual overcrowding and a pervasive lack of privacy' in the new houses (Lumsden 1975). Hart (1980) discusses the fact that of the 11,985 houses built by 1970 only 6282 were complete, the rest remaining unfinished. Part of the problem was the enforcement of building regulations which discouraged ad-hoc construction with local materials, which was the only feasible way for a family to extend the minimal core house. There were also, as at Kainji, complaints about the poor thermal properties of the core houses which may have contributed to the lack of interest in completing them.

More serious for the evacuees was the problem of finding a new livelihood. It was estimated during planning that about 42,000 ha of land would be needed to support the evacuees. This was to be allocated in small plots and used for mechanised farming, but even in 1970 the principles under which this was to be done had not been established: 'the system of land tenure is still under active consideration and no final decision has been taken yet' (Nicholas 1970). Hart (1980) points out that to call the form of production contemplated 'cooperative farming' was misleading. Furthermore, he catalogues the way the scheme failed to meet its own targets: by 1967 only some 3000 ha had been cleared of which only 2500 ha were cropped, over half of that manually. In 1968 only 52% of the 9600 adult male farmers in the settlements could farm at all and food relief had been necessary for four years. Land shortage was reported as a major cause of stress among evacuees in Krachi District (Lumsden 1975).

211

Eventually a system of manual land clearance on the 'food for work' principle was begun, but by 1972 the total area cleared was still only 6680 ha (Hart 1980). Fortunately, the fishery on the lake proved very productive, and many erstwhile farmers turned to this activity: there had been 2000 fishermen in the Volta Basin before the lake formed, but after it there were as many as 12,000 fishermen representing a population of 60,000 in 1000 villages (Hart 1980).

The third element in judging the success or otherwise of resettlement is the question of compensation: its acceptability and its sufficiency and effectiveness in meeting the losses of evacuees. The situation over compensation at Volta is far from clear. According to Sagoe (1970) compensation was payable to the owners of all land below the 280 foot contour, although the majority of this was uncultivated and hence 'only a nominal compensation, if at all necessary, can be paid'. Compensation was also payable for crops and trees, and for buildings. However, 'compensation for buildings will, as a rule, be used either in full or in part set-off against the cost of the 'nuclear' or 'core' houses being provided in the new townships'; furthermore, 'the buildings affected by the flooding are not very substantial or valuable so that their degree of subsidisation by the Government on the core house is very high' (Sagoe 1970).

What this meant in practice was that although on paper compensation was payable on private houses, in practice the money was earmarked for core house construction instead – and as described above, these were far from sufficient final dwellings to replace those lost. Hart (1980) examines the problems of the 9000 people who opted to go elsewhere rather than undergo resettlement. The land under the lake was only acquired officially in 1974, and by 1976 (fourteen years after resettlement began) no compensation had been paid to those in the 'host' communities whose lands had been taken for resettlement villages. Clearly, as far as compensation goes at least, the Volta resettlement can hardly be classed as an unequivocal success.

Socially the lack of livelihoods and the nature of the new settlements gave rise to considerable tension: 'the men did very little . . . they complained that they had no farms of their own to cultivate and their resources were being depleted. They spent most of their time drinking palm wine and akpeteshie (local gin) and frequently got into arguments and fights' (Tamakloe 1968). Similar problems were reported by Lumsden from a different area: 72% of household heads thought there was more fighting and quarrelling than before resettlement, and 98% thought there was more drinking than before resettlement (Lumsden 1975). These are all evidence of what Scudder (1975) describes as the psychological stress of resettlement, and certainly call into question the success of the Volta Resettlement.

Perhaps the most eloquent commentary on the scheme's success is the number of people who abandoned the resettlement villages. In 1968 only 25,900 people out of the 67,500 relocated in resettlement villages were still present. Over half the original settlers had moved within 4 years, to be replaced by large numbers of outsiders, many of them downstream fishermen themselves displaced from downstream areas, and better able to exploit the fishing opportunities in the lake (Colaris 1971). Population mobility of this scale is not unheard of in reservoir resettlement projects, but does not speak well of their effectiveness.

7.6.2.3 *Resettlement elsewhere in West Africa.* The experiences of resettlement at Kainji and Volta, as well as those at Aswan and Kariba over a similar period, have provided a broad base of experience on which the large numbers of subsequent schemes should have been able to build. It is certainly true that similar problems have been encountered on a number of dam projects in West Africa, and in many cases similar solutions have been worked out and attempted. However, the lack of in-depth evaluation studies may have meant that problems have had to be re-solved each time. This is particularly so since no resettlement in West Africa has been written up in anything like the detail of the two discussed above. Nonetheless, their experiences are valuable.

In Kano State of Nigeria, the Water Resources and Engineering Construction Agency (WRECA) resettlement section has undertaken resettlement work for a number of dams. A Resettlement Committee was established in 1977 consisting of members of relevant State Ministries, the Emirate Council and WRECA itself. Initially full cash compensation was being paid for economic trees and buildings and replacement farmland was reallocated (for example at Tiga and Jakara Dams), but problems arose where spare land was short or of poor quality, and in subsequent dams (e.g. Kafin Chiri and Challawa Gorge dams) limited cash compensation was paid for farmlands (te Velde 1978). Detailed enumeration of compensatable items was carried out, and compensation was carefully phased in an attempt to maximise its effectiveness in meeting the evacuees' resettlement expenses, and not consumer durables or consumables. Basic village facilities were provided, some by the Local Government Authority, and attention was paid to the question of rehabilitation in displaced communities, especially where land was in short supply. Study of Tiga Dam resettlement villages showed the twin problems overwhelmingly the most significant for farmers were land clearance (95%) and lack of money (91%), but only 20% of respondents claimed they had not received some kind of agricultural support (Voh 1982).

The resettlement at Kiri Dam on the Gongola River in Gongola State Nigeria has apparently been less successful. The dam supplies the Savanna Sugar Estate, which has itself had teething problems, and lies 25 km upstream of the Gongola/Benue confluence. The dam which was closed in the wet season of 1981, will cover about 130 km^2 and flood 18,000 people in 40 settlements when full (Olaniyan 1981). These settlements are recognised administratively as 14 villages, and have been relocated in 4 resettlement centres at which village services have been provided. Compensation has been paid for economic trees, improvements to land and household buildings and structures. Evacuees were allocated a house plot in the resettlement centres, but were left to build their own houses. This 'site and service' approach has been used successfully in Nigeria in small-scale and voluntary housing improvement projects, but its applicability to reservoir resettlement has been questioned (Olaniyan 1981). Particular problems with it are the cost of building materials and the shortage of skilled labour in the face of the extremely short timespan for house construction allowed by the dam construction schedule.

At Kiri disputes over compensation and consequent failure to evacuate according to plan seem to have occurred. These occurrences are perhaps indicative of a change in attitude to reservoir resettlement, at least in Nigeria, since the days of Kainji and Volta. Attention is now sharply focused on the question of compensation for losses incurred by evacuees. The issue is ripe for politicisation and the rather heavy-handed paternalistic planning of the earlier schemes may become increasingly inappropriate.

At the same time, in some recent schemes the whole question of resettlement has been dealt with in what seems to be a rather casual fashion: arguments about compensation, water supply for resettlement villages and new farmland by the 12,000 people displaced by the Bakolori Dam in Sokoto State of Nigeria in 1978 flared on for several years (Wallace 1979), but despite repeated visits and appeals by the River Basin Development Authority General Manager, State Governor and even the Sultan, there was eventually a situation of protracted civil disobedience in 1980 which ended in considerable violence. The cost of the disturbances greatly exceeded the resettlement budget at N 40 m.

Sokoto State has now established a Ministry of Resettlement, and it is claimed that care has been taken in subsequent dams in the river basin to ensure that resettlement goes more smoothly. However even in other parts of Nigeria reservoir construction is still causing difficulties over the question of resettlement. One example of this is the Jebba Dam on the Niger downstream of Kainji, where the construction contract was awarded in January 1979, but arrangements for the resettlement of the 4000 people from the reservoir area were still not decided in mid-1981 (*West African Technical Review* 1981b). It seems that the lessons of the early resettlement projects have not been learned; a major reason for this is that in-depth evaluations of past projects have not been carried out.

7.6.3 *Farming in the reservoir drawdown*

The drawdown zone of a reservoir is that area exposed between the annual high and low water positions, exposed seasonally with water use. Whereas the costs of resettlement, both personal and institutional, can be reckoned a loss to be set against the benefits of dam construction, drawdown agriculture represents one of the few opportunities, besides fishing, actually created by a reservoir. It has been widely recognised that the potential productivity of agriculture in drawdown areas is high: figures from the Volta Lake show a gross income from drawdown farms to be 1.4 times that of upland farms per unit area (FAO 1975b). As such, the drawdown can go some way to replace fertile floodplain land flooded.

In some reservoir projects there has been a presumption against cultivation of the drawdown. In early projects on the Mekong for example, it was forbidden because of fears of public health, of increased erosion and resultant reservoir sedimentation, and also for fears of claims by farmers against the dam authority if fluctuations in reservoir storage level caused crop damage (Ross-Sheriff 1979). Land was therefore purchased up to 1.5 m above the expected high water level. However, later projects on the Mekong recognised both the importance of drawdown farming to evacuees and the impossibility of policing it to prevent illicit use. As a result a policy of renting small (4 ha) plots to farmers was adopted. Rents were paid after harvest, and were not payable if crops were lost.

Land tenure arrangements have not been worked out in this degree of detail in the case of West African dams, but use of the drawdown has been considered in several cases, for example at Kainji (FAO 1975b), Volta (Nuamah ms.) and dams in Kano State of Nigeria (te Velde 1978). Problems arise at Volta because of the shortage of suitable drawdown land and the extortionate, sometimes illegal, rents paid for plots. In Kano State this situation was avoided by allocating 30 m wide strips annually: thus also neatly getting over the problem that the extent of the drawdown will vary from one year to the next in a fashion difficult to predict.

In most reservoirs not all the drawdown area has been taken up for agriculture. At Volta, for example, only 6000 ha of drawdown was cultivated, representing only 10% of the available area. One reason for this was the unsuitability of some soils. Detailed soil capability surveys were carried out at Kainji to investigate this; even so, the cultivation of the drawdown at Kainji is limited to areas immediately round the villages. Reasons for not cultivating larger areas were said to be that people had no need to do so, that most people were mainly fishermen and only farmed for subsistence, unfamiliarity with the lakeshore environment and ignorance of the best farming conditions, lack of capital and lack of access to much of the drawdown (FAO 1974).

Agronomic research was carried out at both Volta and Kainji into suitable crops for the drawdown. Work at Kainji (FAO 1974) suggested the possibility of cropping on both the rising and falling water because of the asynchrony of high river flows and reservoir level and rainfall. One rotation experiment was with deepwater rice followed by cucurbits. There have been problems, however, in converting such research knowledge into practice: at Volta the drawdown was excluded from the agricultural extension programme. Scudder (1980) stresses the importance of crop and cropping advice if farmers are to make the most of the drawdown. Both advice and credit are also important if simple methods of water control such as hand pumps are to be introduced.

The drawdown area of reservoirs is already used productively in an ad-hoc fashion in a number of cases. With appropriate development it could attain considerable importance. Scudder (1980) suggests the coordinated development of the drawdown and downstream floodplain areas by the use of controlled reservoir discharge to give a predictable pattern of drawdown and a simulated downstream flood (see the next section). The loss this would entail in alternative (and more conventional) uses of water would be small, and the number of people who might be supported by the drawdown if properly developed in this way would be significant: for example Scudder suggests perhaps 5-10,000 families might be supported on the drawdown at Kossou in the Ivory Coast.

7.7 DOWNSTREAM EFFECTS OF DAMS

7.7.1 *Discharge and geomorphology*

The effects of dams on downstream channel geomorphology have attracted increasing attention in recent years (e.g. Gregory & Park 1974, Buma & Day 1977, Petts 1979), partly because they are some of the simpler aspects of downstream effects and partly because in mid-latitude countries where so much research effort is concentrated, they are amongst the most significant. The effects are twofold, patterns of both sediment and water transport being transformed in regulated rivers. Sediment load can be changed dramatically by dam construction (e.g. reduced to some 9% of former levels at the Gardiner Dam on the Saskatchewan River, Canada) and for a considerable distance downstream of the reservoir: the effects of the Kubyshevsky Reservoir on the Volga River, for example, being observable for 1000 km. Immediately downstream of dams the release of water low in sediment can trigger off channel degradation (Beckinsale 1972, Park 1981); further downstream the effects may be more complicated (Petts 1979).

There are a number of studies recording these effects from mid-latitude rivers, using both direct observation (Buma & Day 1977, Graf 1980, Borland & Miller 1960) or alternative methods (Gregory & Park 1974, Petts 1979). However, there have been fewer studies of the effects of tropical dams. One exception is a study based on a computer model of the Wabo hydro-electric dam on the Parari River in Papua New Guinea. The river carries a very large sediment load (57×10^6 tonnes per year) but the sediment concentrations are not excessive (Pickup 1980). The study predicted some bed degradation but fairly rapid adjustment to a new equilibrium after dam construction and consequent permanent changes in the river's sediment load.

A study of the Kano River in Nigeria (Olofin 1979) gives a good idea of the typical effects of a dam on the strongly seasonal rivers of the West African savanna. The Tiga Dam, closed 1973, transformed the river from a seasonal to a perennial regime, and also reduced mean annual discharge to 40% of its former value (Henry 1981). The reduction in the wet season floods was most severely marked: further downstream in the Hadejia

Table 32. Percentage reduction in discharge between Kowara (Niger River, upstream of Kainji reservoir) and Kainji stations 1970-76 (Sagua 1978a).

	Year	Aug.-Oct.	Nov.-Dec.	Jan.-March	Apr.-July
	1970	20%	15%	−1%	−97%
	1971	31%	33%	4%	−83%
(Drought year)	1972	167%	45%	−2%	−489%
(Drought year)	1973	100%	37%	3%	−554%
	1974	20%	23%	6%	−227%
	1975	44%	18%	4%	−560%
	1976*	38%	54%	13%	−299%
Average	1970-1976	60%	32%	2%	−337%

* 1976 was a low-flow year.

floodplain, the floods experienced following dam construction were consistently lower later in the season and shorter than before (Stock 1978). A similar curtailment of flood peaks was observed in the Sokoto River in northwest Nigeria below the Bakolori Dam (Adams 1983). In the case of the Kano River the reduced flows were accompanied by reduced sediment loads, changed sediment deposition patterns and the stabilisation of the floodplain by vegetation growth (Olofin 1979).

Sagua (1978a) examined the effects of the Kainji Dam on the flow of the Niger River during the years of the Sahel drought in the early 1970s. Peak flows at the height of the White Flood (September and October) in the whole of the post-impoundment period (1970-76) were on average only about 75% of the peak rates in 1960 (taken as the base year). The lowest years of flows were those at the height of the drought (1972 and 1973) (Table 32), but although the reduction in floods was most acute in these years, there was an overall reduction of 60% in discharge over the period 1970-76 (Table 32). There was a corresponding augmentation of dry season flow: in 1973 the flow at Jebba was actually the reverse of the natural pattern, with a fall in river level during the normal peak months of September and October (Sagua 1978b).

The rate of water demand for power generation at Kainji increased sharply in 1976 when two new turbines were commissioned, and discharge actually exceeded inflow in that year: the water regime of the dam in the drought period was a major factor in the decision not to go ahead with the installation of further turbines at Kainji (Reiss 1980). Even meeting the needs of the generating capacity installed at present has a considerable effect on other users of the river in downstream areas.

7.7.2 Downstream ecosystems

Relatively few studies of the effects of dams on ecosystems below dams have been done in West Africa, although elsewhere in Africa there are more data (Davies 1979). Studies have been particularly intensive on the Nile, where the effects of the Sennar, Roseires and Aswan Dams on

217

plankton in particular have been studied in detail (Hammerton 1972, Rzoska 1976), and the question of the Aswan Dam's trapping of sediment and reduction of discharge have been a source of controversy since the late 1960s (Kassas 1972, Hafez & Shenovda 1978, Kashef 1981). The Zambezi system, with major dams at Kafue, Kariba and Cabora Bassa, has also been extensively studied, and concern for downstream fluvial and wetland ecosystems expressed (e.g. Davies 1975, Davies et al. 1975, Rees 1978, Tinley 1975).

In West Africa, the discharge of deoxygenated water from the hypolimnion at Kainji has been highlighted as being potentially significant in downstream areas since the river is otherwise low in minerals and plant nutrients (Davies 1979), and the question of control of *Simulium damnosum* (Waddy 1973) must surely have a considerable significance for downstream uses for which water quality is important. Hall and Pople (1968) describe the effects of the moderated flow regime of the Volta on the growth of submerged aquatic macrophytes *Potomegeton octandrus* and *Vallisneria aethiopica* due to the lack of wet season scour, and the consequent increase in herbivorous fish species (e.g. *Tilapia*). However, this work aside, most of the few studies done in West Africa have concentrated on the significance of downstream ecological change for economic activities, particularly artisanal fisheries and riparian farming.

7.7.3 Downstream fisheries

The effects of dams on anadromous (longitudinally migrating) fish are well established, largely because of the commercial importance of mid-latitude game fisheries (e.g. Hayes 1953, Pyefinch 1966, Beiringen & Ebel 1970, Fraser 1972, Hellawell 1976), and measures to offset the adverse effects of dams, such as hatcheries and fish passes, are well established. Few fish in tropical rivers exhibit anadromesis, but for those like the eels of East and Central Africa major dams without fish passes seem to be equally disastrous, although the evidence is somewhat in dispute (Davies 1979).

In recent years considerable research has gone into the ecology of fish of floodplain rivers, particularly in Africa (Lowe-McConnell 1975 and this volume 5.3, Northcote 1978, Welcomme 1979) their adaptation to the natural flood regime, and hence their responses to its transformation by dams. They can be divided roughly into those which avoid desiccated floodplain conditions by moving into deeper water (the so-called "whitefish") and those with resistance to deoxygenated conditions ("blackfish") (Welcomme 1979).

In general, as the river starts to flood there is a flush of nutrients from organic matter in the inundated areas which leads to a bloom of algae and zooplankton and in their turn of aquatic invertebrates. Typically, the fish make short distance upstream migrations and move into these productive inundated areas to feed and breed. As the floodwaters fall they move back

218

to the river, or are caught in floodplain pools. There is high mortality at this period both from stranding, predation and fishing which is frequently begun after the end of the wet season farming period in the drying floodplain pools.

The pattern of response by fish to seasonal changes in discharge is still, despite a considerable amount of research, little understood. However, the significance of dam construction and its transformation of discharge is considerable: the triggers to seasonal movement are altered, and the whole complex interlocking pattern of the floodplain ecosystem is disrupted. Floodplain inundation is reduced, many pools are never filled and groundwater recharge is reduced, so those areas which are flooded dry out very quickly. The few studies of fisheries of dammed rivers in West Africa reveal a markedly adverse effect on fish populations downstream (pages 114–125).

Studies below Kainji in the immediately post-impoundment period demonstrated significantly reduced fish catches. They fell from 20 tonnes to 12.4 tonnes between 1967 and 1969 (Lelek & El Zarka 1973). Adeniyi (1973) reported problems for fishermen in the clearer water below Kainji in that fish were apparently able to see and avoid nets; also productive pools and swamps previously inundated were now dry. An interview with the Sarkin Ruwa (head fisherman) of three settlements gave an estimate of between 47% and 73% decrease in catch per crew before and after inundation. Furthermore, there had been a considerable reduction in both the number of seasonal migrant fishermen and the duration of their stay in 1969 compared to years before the dam due to reduced catches (Table 33). A number of full-time fishermen had given up and moved into full-time farming.

A similar pattern of declining fisheries following impoundment has been recorded elsewhere in Nigeria, in the Hadejia floodplain (Stock 1978) and the Sokoto (Adams 1983). However, in contrast to these studies it must be noted that work on the Niger immediately downstream of the spillway at Faku showed a favourable change in species composition in which commercially more important species (*Centropomidae* and *Bagridae*) became more common (Sagua 1978b). Overall, the conclusion of this particular work was that a viable fishery had been established in the dam area, in contrast with that further downstream. A further indication of this is a report of game fishing at the dam tail-race (Otobo 1978).

Table 33. Change in length of stay of fishermen at Katcha village following Kainji impoundment (Adeniyi 1973).

	No. fishermen	Length of stay (months)			
		0-1	1-2	3	Over 3
1967/8	132	6	22	86	18
1968/9	73	42	19	7	15

A unique and well-documented case of the significance of dams on estuarine ecosystems is that of the fishery based on the clam *Egeria radiata* in the Volta estuary. In 1963 some 1-2000 women were employed (Lawson 1963), fishing for the adult clams which lived in submerged sandbanks feeding on particulate organic matter in the water (Purchon 1963). In *Egeria*, spawning is triggered by a rise in salinity corresponding with declining river flow. Impoundment during dam construction meant that the critical 1% salinity zone moved inland for 30-50 km, but the *Egeria* fishery experienced a slight boom in the shallower waters (Hilton & Kowu-Tsri 1970).

Subsequently the steady discharge of 500 m^3 sec^{-1} pushed the fishing within 10 km of the river mouth and canoes were once more necessary for the fishery (Hilton & Kuwo-Tsri 1970). Studies in 1975 and 1976 connected with the Kpong Dam suggested that saltwater incursion might increase with the new dam, as well as highlighting problems of substrate suitability and pollution (Enwin & de Graft-Johnson 1977). The tale of the *Egeria* fishery is clearly far from ended (see page 245).

7.7.4 *Riparian agriculture*

The traditional practices of flood recession agriculture in the floodplains of West Africa have been described above. Dam construction and the resulting reduction in both overall discharge and particularly peak flows, has had a significant adverse impact on this practice in a number of cases. The effects are both direct and indirect: the proportion of the floodplain which is inundated and hence available for recession agriculture is reduced and floodplain depressions where cultivation can continue longest are no longer filled; furthermore, the reduced flooding reduces groundwater recharge in the wet season and hastens the drainage and desiccation of the floodplain once the rains are finished.

A number of rather cursory studies show the significance of these effects in West Africa. Adeniyi's (1973) study of three settlements below Kainji showed that between 44% and 70% of fadama acreage had gone out of production (Table 34). Yields of swamp rice also fell in Rabba, which was the hardest hit village, although at the same time the number of farmers actually increased because of the simultaneous failure of the fishing.

Table 34. Decrease in fadama cultivation downstream of Kainji Dam following impoundment (Adeniyi 1973).

Village	Population (1973)	Fadama area (ha) 1967/8	Fadama area (ha) 1968/9	Fadama lost ha	Fadama lost %
Rabba	2139	200	60	140	70
Muregi	3053	1100	600	500	45
Katcha	6939	650	300	350	54

Stock's study of the Hadejia floodplain where flooding in 1976 was severely reduced by the Tiga Dam showed that crop failure in Guri District surpassed that of the drought years: ironically the area had attracted numbers of migrants from more severely drought-stricken areas to the north during the worst drought years (Stock 1978). A loss compared to previous years of 90% in residual soil moisture vegetables and 75% in shadouf-irrigated vegetables was estimated in the area. The same pattern of reduced floodplain agricultural production has been reported higher in the same river basin (Wallace 1979), and in the Sokoto floodplain by Adams (1983). Hilton and Kwo-Tsri (1970) described the same kind of adverse effects of the Akosombo Dam on the intensive agriculture of the Lower Volta, and there are similar fears expressed of extensive effects on other river systems, notably the Senegal (*New Civil Engineer International* 1978). Even if the initial disruption to cultivation of the changed floodplain hydrology is discounted the continued inadequacies of some floodplain soils for dryland crops (because they become waterlogged with heavy rain, thus killing dryland crops like millet but not allowing the cultivation of more water-demanding varieties of sorghum and rice) means that the deterioration of these areas may persist. To remedy this, remedial development in the form of agricultural extension and the use of small pumps to draw on the perennial river flow will be necessary.

7.8 CONCLUSION

It is relatively easy to amass evidence that describes the adverse environmental effects of dams, but more difficult to balance these with their beneficial effects. Biswas & Biswas (1976) write "there is no doubt that the primary effects of the vast majority of dams around the world has been beneficial. Equally, however, there is no doubt that many of these dams have contributed to unanticipated secondary effects, many of which could have been eliminated by a proper planning process". But does such a planning process exist? Standard forms of appraisal and economic evaluation of the costs and benefits of projects have been shown repeatedly to fail to deal adequately with environmental and social effects. "Since the costs and benefits of changes in fisheries, floodplain land use, erosion control, navigation and health conditions are regional or local or more easily measured in social or economic terms, they are virtually precluded from a significant place in the feasibility level analysis of hydroelectric power projects. Only resettlement costs are routinely included in the analysis, and they tend to be underestimated" (Stein & Johnson 1979). One possible policy instrument to deal with the environmental side-effects of projects is environmental impact assessment, but even this has its severe problems (Chapman 1981, Adams 1982).

The comment often made that people planning development, dam builders no less than others, can learn from their mistakes. Thus studies of the less beneficial effects of past dams will help prevent such phenomena in the future: "The first great African impoundments were genuine novelties; nothing like them had ever existed before, and there was no basis in experience on which to predict their consequences. Subsequent tropical impoundments will not be novelties and their effects should be predictable, in their broad outlines, from earlier experience" (Baxter 1977), and "there are new opportunities to avoid the environmental mistakes of the past in the construction of large dams" (Stein & Johnson 1979). It is questionable whether this learning process is, in fact, at all well developed among those designing and commissioning dams, for several reasons.

There have been a few ideas which would make a radical redirection of the traditional concepts of dam design and function and more rational use of the floodplain's natural resources possible; ideas like Scudder's concept of planning dam releases to maximise the opportunities for drawdown agriculture on the reservoir margin, and for riparian flood recession agriculture downstream with a guaranteed controlled flood (Scudder 1980). Such suggestions, those exhibiting elements of holistic appraisal, opportunity orientation and creative lateral thinking in development (Chambers 1978), have been few and far between, and when they have appeared they have tended to come from the environmental and social sciences and the halls of academia and tended to be remote from the world of practical development politics and commercial interests.

To an extent this is only to be expected: the business and political leopards concerned with the lucrative tasks of dam building cannot be expected to change their spots without a little encouragement. However, the remoteness of the new approaches to developments like dams means that they are rarely stated clearly, understood properly or given serious attention. This problem is exacerbated by the lack of adequate retrospective studies of projects. Ashby (1980) commends Hart's book on the Volta River Project because it is just such a study. Without them it is unlikely that the mistakes of the past will even be recognised by those likely to repeat them, let alone learned from. There is a need, then, for more detailed study of the dams of West Africa, both in the form of restrospective studies of past projects and – more urgently – continuous monitoring of the plethora of schemes being implemented at the present time. The potential for productive multi-disciplinary research is enormous.

As it stands at the moment, different disciplines tend to make radically different judgements of dam projects: "it is not exactly unusual to find a major hydro project hailed as a technological triumph by engineers, accepted in terms of economic efficiency by economists but seriously questioned as to its desirability by sociologists and environmentalists" (Biswas & Biswas 1976). Ultimately, the obvious question of whether a particular dam should have been built is an empty one. It was answered for the Owen Falls Dam in Uganda thus: "first, such questions are unprofitable since what is done cannot be undone. Secondly, if one wants to bring about economic development it is almost always better to do something rather than do nothing and the Owen Falls Dam at the time did not appear to be competing for funds with other projects. Nothing was left undone because the dam was built, and the funds used for building it might never have been available for other purposes anyhow" (Elkan & Wilson 1968).

Thus although it is possible to interpret retrospective studies as means of lambasting dam builders of the past, this is of little value. They will have to be responsibly and constructively designed, forward looking and set against the realities of the contractural and development world if they are to have the slightest influence on the conception and design of dam projects in the future, or for that matter if they are to be of any use to those involved in such schemes. The rate at which new dams are being constructed in West Africa and the productivity of the natural ecosystems into which they are placed and which they affect, must make them a high priority for such research in many disciplines.

7.9 REFERENCES

Adams, A. 1977. The Senegal River Valley: what kind of change? *Review of African Political Economy* 10: 33–59.

Adams, W.M. 1982. A whole new ball game: EIA in developing countries. *ECOS* 3: 30–35.

Adams, W.M. 1983. Downstream impact of river control: Sokoto Valley, Nigeria. Ph.D. thesis Univ. Cambridge.

Adams, W.M. & A.T. Grove, (eds.) 1984. *Irrigation in tropical Africa*. Cambridge African Monographs Nr 3. Cambridge: African Studies Centre.

Adeniyi, E.O. 1973. Downstream impact of the Kainji Dam. In A.L. Mabogunje (ed.), *Kainji Lake Studies 2*. Ibadan: NISER.

Adeniyi, E.O. 1976. The Kainji Dam: an exercise in regional development planning. *Regional Studies* 10: 233-243.

Akintola, F. 1978. Mineral & Energy Reserves. In J.S. Oguntoyinbo, O.U. Areola & M. Filani (eds.), *A Geography of Nigerian Development*. Ibadan; Heineman Educational Books (Nigeria) Ltd.

Amarteifio, G.W. 1970. Social Welfare. In R. Chambers (ed.), *The Volta Resettlement Experience*. London: Pall Mall.

Amin, S. 1974. *Modern Migrations in Western Africa*. London: OUP.

Ashby, E. 1980. Retrospective environmental impact assessment, *Nature* 288: 28-9.

Atkinson, J.R. 1973. Resettlement programme in the Kainji Lake Region. In A.L. Mobogunje (ed.) *Kainji Lake Studies 2*. Ibadan: NISER.

Ayoade, J.O. & Oyebande, B.L. 1978. Water resources. In J.S., Oguntoyinbo, O.U. Areola & M. Filani (eds.), *A Geography of Nigerian Development*. Ibadan: Heineman Educational Books (Nigeria) Ltd.

Baxter, R.M. 1977. Environmental effects of dams and impoundments. *Ann. Rev. Ecol. Syst.* 8: 255-83.

Beckinsale, R.P. 1972. The effect upon new channels of sudden changes in sediment load. *Acta Geographica Debrecina* 10: 181-86.

Beiringen, K.T. & W.F. Ebel 1970. Effects of John Day Dam on dissolved nitrogen concentrations and salmon in the Columbia River, 1968. *Trans. Am. Fish. Soc.* 99: 664-71.

Biswas, S. 1966. Oxygen and phytoplankton changes in the newly forming Volta Lake in Ghana. *Nature* 209: 218-19.

223

Biswas, A.K. & M.R. Biswas 1976. Hydropower and the environment. *Water Power & Dam Construction.* May: 40–43.

Black, R.H. 1975. Human ecological factors of significance. In N.F. Stanley & M.P. Alpers (eds.), *Man-made lakes and human health.* London: Academic Press.

Borland, W.M. & C.R. Miller 1960. Sediment problems of the Lower Colorado River. *Proc. Am. Soc. Civ. Eng. J. Hydraulics Div.* 86: 61–87.

Boyo, A.E. 1962. Medical problems of Niger Dam Project. *Proc. Sci. Ass. Nigeria* 5: 54.

Bradley P.N. 1981. Agricultural development planning in the Senegal valley. In E.S. Simpson (ed.) *The rural-agricultural sector.* Dept. Geography Univ. Newcastle upon Tyne.

Buma, P.G. & J.G. Day 1977. Channel morphology below reservoir storage projects. *Environmental Conserv.* 4: 279.

Bunton, J. 1979. Ivory Coast. *Construction News Magazine* 5: 30–31.

Burton, M.A. 1975. The Niger River as a resource for future development in Mali and Niger. M.Sc. Dissertation. Univ. Southampton.

Butcher. D.A.P. 1970. The Social Survey. In R. Chambers (ed.), *The Volta Resettlement Experience.* London: Pall Mall.

Chambers, R. (ed.). 1970. *The Volta Resettlement Experience.* London: Pall Mall.

Chambers, R. 1978. Identifying research priorities in water development. *Water Supply and Management* 2: 389–398.

Chapman, K. 1981. Issues in environmental impact assessment. *Progress in Human Geography* 5: 190–210.

Clark, W.M. & F.M. Hutchinson 1948. The possibilities of expanding the production of rice in the British West Africa Colonies. *Report of British West African Rice Mission.* London: HMSO.

Club du Sahel. 1979a. *Development of irrigated agriculture in Mali: General overview and prospects.* Permanent Interstate Committee for drought control in the Sahel.

Club du Sahel. 1979b. *Development of irrigated agriculture in Senegal: General overview and prospects.* Permanent Interstate Committee for drought control in the Sahel.

Colaris, J.C. 1971. *Socio-economic and demographic survey of Volta Lake: Interim report to the Government of Ghana.* Volta Lake Research Project, Akosombo, Ghana.

Coppola, S.R. 1976. In K. Agadazi. Frame surveys at Volta Lake (Ghana) *Volta Lake Research and Development Project.* Rome: FAO.

Danby, M. 1970. House design. In R. Chambers (ed.), *The Volta Resettlement Experience.* London: Pall Mall.

Davies, B.R. 1975. They pulled the plug out of the Lower Zambezi. *Afri. Wildlife* 29: 26-7.

Davies, B.R. 1979. Stream regulation in Africa: a review. In J.V. Ward & J.A. Stanford (eds.), *The Ecology of Regulated Streams.* New York: Plenum Press.

Davies, R.B., A. Hall & P.B.N. Jackson 1975. Some ecological aspects of the Cabora Bassa Dam: *Biol. Conserv.* 8: 184–201.

Des Bouvrie, C. & J.R. Rydzewski 1977. Irrigation. In C.I.A. Leakey & J.B. Wills (eds.), *Food Crops of the Lowland Tropics.* London: OUP.

Elkan, W. & G.G. Wilson 1968. The Impact of the Owen Falls Hydro-electric Project on the economy of Uganda. In W.M. Warren & N. Rubin (eds.), *Dams in Africa: An interdisciplinary study of man-made lakes in Africa.* London: Frank Cass.

Elliot, R.A. 1973. The TVA Experience 1933–71. In W.C. Ackerman, G.F. White & E.B. Worthington (eds.), *Man-made Lakes: the problems and environmental effects.* Am. Geographical Union, Geophys. Monograph.

Enwin, M.A. & K.A.A. de Graft-Johnson 1977. Studies on the ecology of *Egeria radiata* (*Lamark*) in the Lower Volta Estuary. *Inst. Aquatic Biology* 74.

FAO. 1966. *Agricultural development in Nigeria 1965.* Rome: FAO.

FAO. 1969. *Soil & Water Resources Survey of the Sokoto Valley, Nigeria.* Rome: UNDP (FAO/SF – 67/NIR 3).

FAO. 1974. *Kainji Lake drawdown, soil and land evaluation.* Rome: FAO.

FAO. 1975a. *Kainji Lake Research Project Agricultural Potential.* Rome: FAO.

FAO. 1975b. *The status of agriculture at the Volta lake (Results of a statistical survey).* Rome: FAO.

Faniran, A. 1972. River basins as planning units. In K.M. Barbour (ed.), *Planning for Nigeria: a Geographical Perspective*. Ibadan Univ. Press.

Faniran, A. 1980. On the definition of planning regions: the case for river basins in developing countries. *Singapore J. Trop. Geog.* 1: 9–16.

Farouk, D. 1971. *Dry season fadama cultivation around Kano*. B.A. dissertation in Geography. Ahmadu Bello University, Nigeria.

Finer, H. 1944. *The T.V.A. – Lessons for International Application*. Montreal: ILO.

Fraser, J.C. 1972. *Regulated stream discharge for fish and other aquatic resources – An annoted bibliography*. Rome: FAO. (*Fish. Tech. Pap. 112*).

Gallais, J. 1967. *Le Delta Interieur du Niger: Etude de géographie regionale*. Dakar: Institut Fondamental d'Afrique Noire.

Gallais, J. & A.H. Sidikou 1978. *Traditional strategies, modern decision-making and management of natural resources in the Sudan Sahel, in Management of natural resources in Africa: traditional strategies and modern decision-making*. Paris: UNESCO (MAB Technical Note 9).

Gannet, Flemming, Cordry & Carpenter Inc. 1980. *Assessment of Environmental Effects of Proposed Developments in the Senegal River Basin*. Dakar: OMVS.

Gill, M.A. 1974. Hydrological characteristics of the Sokoto Rima Basin. *Savanna* 3: 61–76.

Graf, W.L. 1980. The effect of dam closure on downstream rapids. *Water Resources Research* 16: 129–136.

Gregory, K.J. & C.C. Park 1974. Adjustment of river channel capacity downstream of a reservoir. *Water Resources Research*. 10: 870–3.

Hafez, M. & W.K. Shenovda 1978. *The environmental impacts of the Aswan High Dam, Water Development & Management*. Proc. UN Water Conference, Argentina. New York: Pergamon.

Hall, J.B. & W. Pople 1968. Recent vegetation changes in the Lower Volta River. *Ghana J. Sci.* 8: 24–29.

Hammerton, D. 1972. The Nile River – a case history. In R.T. Oglesby, C.A. Carson, J.A. Mann (eds.), *River Ecology & Man*. London: Academic Press.

Hamnett, I. 1970. A social scientist among technicians. *IDS Bulletin 3: 24–9*.

Harrison Church, R.J. 1961. Problems of the development of the dry zone of West Africa. *Geogr. J.* 127: 187–204.

Hart, D. 1980. *The Volta River Project. A Case Study in Politics & Technology*. Edinburgh Univ. Press.

Hayes, F.R. 1953. Artificial freshets and other factors controlling the ascent of population of Atlantic Salmon in the Lettavre River, Nova Scotia. *Bull Fish. Res. Bd. Can.* 99: 1–47.

Hellawell, J.M. 1976. River management and the migrational behaviour of salmonids. *Fish. Mgmt.* 7: 56–60.

Henry, K.A. 1981. Engineering aspects of the Hadejia River Land Use & Water Resource Study. *Water International* 6: 65–70.

Hilton, T.E. & J.Y. Kowu-Tsri 1970. The impact of the Volta scheme on the Lower Volta floodplains. *J. Trop. Geog.* 30: 29–37.

Huszar, L. 1970. Resettlement planning. In R. Chambers (ed.), *The Volta Resettlement Experience*. London: Pall Mall.

Iliasu, S. 1980. Developing Nigeria's Water Resources. *New Nigerian* 4 July: 5, 9, 10; 5 July: 5.

Imevbore, A.M.A. 1969. Biological research in the Kainji Lake Basin, In C.E. Obeng (ed.). *Man-Made Lakes*. Accra.

Imevbore, A.M.A. 1970. Some general features of the Kainji river basin. In S.A. Visser (ed.), *Ecology*. Ibadan: NISER (Kainji Lake Studies 1).

Imevbore, A.M.A. & D.S. Adegoke (eds.) 1975. *The ecology of Lake Kainji: The transition from river to lake*. Ile-Ife: University of Ife Press.

Impresit 1974. *Bakolori project: first phase of the Sokoto-Rima basin development, final report*. Milan/Rome.

Ingersoll, J. 1968. Mekong River Basin Development. Anthropology in a new setting. *Anthropology Quarterly* 41: 147–167.

International Construction 1979. OMVS need a few dollars more. Sept. 3.

225

Ipinmidun, W.B. 1970. The agricultural development of fadama with particular reference to Bomo fadama. *Nigerian Agricultural Journal* 7: 152-163.

Jenness, J. 1973. Fishing and the fishermen of the Kainji Lake Basin. In A.L. Mabogunje (ed.), *Kainji Lake Studies 2*. Ibadan.

Kalitsi, E.A.K. 1970. The organisation of resettlement. In R. Chambers (ed.), *The Volta resettlement experience*. London: Pall Mall.

Kashef, Abdel-Aziz. 1981. Technical and ecological impacts of the High Aswan Dam. *J. Hydrol.* 53: 73-84.

Kassas, M. 1972. Impact of river control schemes on the shoreline of the Nile delta. In M. Taghi Farver & J.P. Milton (eds.), *The Careless Technology*. Doubleday.

Lawson, R.M. 1963. The economic organisation of the Egeria fishing industry on the River Volta. *Proc. Malac. Soc. Lond.* 35: 273-87.

Lanning, G., & M. Mueller 1979. *Africa undermined: Mining companies and the Underdevelopment of Africa*. Harmondsworth: Penguin Books.

Lelek, A. & El Zarka, S. 1973. Ecological comparison of the pre-impoundment and post-impoundment fish faunas of the River Niger and Kainji Lake, Nigeria. In W.C. Ackerman G.F. White & E.B. Worthington (eds.), Man-made lakes: the problems and environmental effects. *Am. Geophys. Union, Geophys. Monograph.*

Lightfoot, R.P. 1978. The costs of resettling reservoir evacuees in Northeast Thailand. *J. Trop. Geog.* 47: 65.

Lightfoot, R.P. 1979. Alternative resettlement strategies in Thailand: lessons from experience. In L.A.P. Gosling (ed.), *Population Resettlement in the Mekong river basin*. Chapel Hill N.C.: Univ. Carolina Press.

Lilienthal, D.E. 1943. *T.V.A. Democracy on the March*. New York: Harper & Row.

Lowe-McConnell, R.H. 1975. *Fish Communities of Tropical Freshwaters*. London: Longmans.

Lubin, S. 1977. Environmental impact of the Senegal River Basin Project. *Kidma* 3: 36-39.

Lumsden, P. 1975. Towards a systems model of stress: feedback from an anthropological study of the impact of Ghana's Volta River Project. In I. Sarason & C. Spiel (eds.) *Stress and Anxiety* 2. Washington: Hemisphere.

McLachlan, A.J. 1974. Development of some lake systems in tropical Africa, with special reference to the invertebrates. *Biol. Rev. Cambridge Philos. Soc.* 49: 365-97.

Mabogunje, A.L. (ed.). 1973. Kainji: a Nigerian Man-made Lake. *Kainji Lake Studies* 2. Ibadan; NISER.

Moxon, J. 1969. *Volta: Man's Greatest Lake*. London; André Deutsch.

Mustafa, S. 1980. On water resources development in Nigeria. *New Nigerian*, 10 Sept.

Mustafa, S. 1982. On water resources development in Nigeria and prospects of drought. *New Nigerian*, 28 Jan.: 12.

Negedu, A.A. 1973. The administrative problem of resettlement in the Kainji Lake Basin. In A.L. Mabogunje (ed.), *Kainji Lake Studies* 2: Ibadan: NISER.

New Civil Engineer International 1978. Arab Cash floats W. African Dam scheme. Oct: 28

New Civil Engineer International 1982. Rural revival in Senegal. April: 22-23.

Nolfi, J.R. 1981. Alternative Energy Application in Nigeria. *West African Technical Review*. Aug: 63-66.

Nicholas, N.S.O. 1970. Resettlement agriculture. In R. Chambers (ed.), *The Volta Resettlement Experience*. London: Pall Mall.

Northcote, T.G. 1978. Migratory strategies and production in fresh-water fishes. In S.D. Gosling (ed.), *Ecology of Freshwater Fish Production*. Oxford: Blackwell.

Nosworthy, M. 1979. The changing face of irrigation in Nigeria. *West African Materials & Equipment*. March: 19-22.

Nuamah, G.E.A. (undated MS). *Volta Lake: Some factors that inhibit agricultural production in the drawdown*. Rome: FAO.

Nwa, E.U. & B. Martins 1982. Irrigation Development in Nigeria. *Fourth Afro-Asian regional conference of ICID, Lagos.* 1: 1-19.

Obeng, L.E. 1975. Health problems of the Volta Lake Ecosystem. In N.F. Stanley & M.P. Alpers (eds.), *Man-made lakes and human health*. London: Academic Press.

Odum, E.P. 1969. The strategy of ecosystem development. *Science* 164: 262-70.

226

Olaniyan, J.A.O. 1981. *Some environmental impacts of Kiri Dam on settlements in the Gongola Valley - a preliminary assessment.* Kano: 24th Annual Conf. Nig. Geog. Assoc.

Olofin, E.A. 1979. *The impact of Tiga Dam on the aquatic ecosystem of downstream areas.* ABU Zaria: Seminar Paper, Department of Geography.

O.M.V.S. 1981. The development of the Senegal River. *Marchées tropicaux* (17 April).

Otobo, F.O. 1978. Game fishing at the Kainji Dam site. *Nigerian Field* 43: 83–85.

Overton, D.J.B. 1976. The Magician's Bargain: some thoughts and comments on hydroelectric and similar development schemes. *Antipode* 8: 33–45.

Oyedipe, F.P.A. 1973. Problems of socio-economic adjustment of resettlers. In A.L. Mabogunje (ed.) *Kainji Lake Studies* 2. Ibadan: NISER.

Palmer-Jones, R. 1981. How not to learn from pilot irrigation projects: the Nigerian experience. *Water Supply and Management* 5: 81–105.

Paperna, I. 1970. Study of the outbreak of schistosomiasis in the newly formed Volta Lake. *Tropen. med. Parasitol.* 21: 411–427.

Park, C.C. 1981. Man, river systems and environmental impacts. *Progress in Physical Geography* 5: 1–31.

Petr, T. 1970. Macroinvertebrates of flooded trees in the man-made Volta Lake (Ghana) with special reference to the burrowing mayfly, *Povilla adusta* Navas. *Hydrobiologica* 36: 373–98.

Petts, G. 1979. Complex response of river channel morphology subsequent to reservoir construction. *Progress in Physical Geography* 3: 329–62.

Pickup, G. 1980. Hydrologic and sediment modelling studies in the environmental impact assessment of a major tropical dam project. *Earth Surface Processes* 5: 61–75.

Preparatory Commission 1956. *The Volta River Project.* London: HMSO.

Purchon, R.D. 1963. A note on the biology of *Egira radiata (Bivalina, Donacidae). Proc. Malac. Soc. Lond.* 35: 251–71.

Pyefinch, K.A. 1966. Hydro-electric schemes in Scotland. Biological Problems and effects on salmonid fishes. In R.H. Lowe-McConnell (ed.), *Man-made Lakes.* London: Academic Press.

Rees, W.A. 1978. The ecology of the Kafue Lechwe as affected by the Kafue gorge hydroelectric scheme. *J. Appl. Ecol.* 15–20.

River Basin Development Authorities Decree 1979. Decree 87, 28th September 1979, A 683–689.

Ross-Sheriff, B.A. 1979. Reservoir edge resettlement. In L.A.D. Gosling (ed.), *Population Resettlement in the Mekong River Basin.* Chapel Hill N.C.: Univ. Carolina Dept. Geog.

Rzóska, J. 1976. (ed.) *The Nile: Biology of an Ancient River.* (Monographicae Biologicae 29). The Hague: Junk.

Sagoe, K.A. 1970. Valuation, acquisition and compensation for purposes of resettlement. In R. Chambers (ed.), *The Volta Resettlement Experience.* London: Pall Mall.

Sagua, V.O. 1978a. Flood control of the River Niger at Kainji Dam, Nigeria, and its use during drought conditions in the period 1970–76. In G. Jan van Apeldoon (ed.), *The Aftermath of the 1972–74 drought in Nigeria.* CSER ABU, Zaria.

Sagua, V.O. 1978b. The effect of Kainji Dam, Nigeria, upon fish production in the River Niger below the Dam at Faku. In R.A. Welcomme (ed.), *Symposium on River and Floodplain fishes in Africa, Burundi.* CIFA Tech. Paper 5).

Scudder, T. 1980. River basin development and local initiative in African savanna environments. In D.R. Harris (ed.), *Human ecology in savanna environments.* London: Academic Press.

Smith, S.R. 1968. Outline Programme for Hydroelectric Development in West Africa to 1980. In W.M. Warren & N. Rubin (eds.), *Dams in Africa: an inter-disciplinary study of man-made lakes in Africa.* London: Frank Cass.

Stein, R.E. & B. Johnson 1979. *Banking on the Biosphere? Environmental Procedures and Practices of Nine Multilateral Aid Agencies.* New York: Lexington Press.

Stock, R.F. 1978. The impact of the decline of the Hadeijia river floods in Hadeijia Emirate. In G. Jan van Apeldoorn (ed.), *The Aftermath of the 1972–74 Drought in Nigeria.* ABU Zaria: CSER.

Tamakloe, M.A. 1968. New Mpamu: Case Study of a Volta River Authority resettlement town. *Ghana Jnl. Agric. Sci.* 1: 45–51.

Tasso, E. 1978. *The Bakolori Project: a new approach to the implementation of large*

227

development projects. Text of informal discussion at ICE London following paper by Tasso reported in *New Civil Engineer,* 3 March and 16 March.

te Velde, P. 1978. *Resettlement of people displaced by dam construction projects in Kano State, Nigeria.* Kano: WRECA.

Tinley, K.L. 1975. Death knell for Gongorosa? *African Wildlife* 29: 25.

Turner, B. 1977. The Fadama lands of Northern Nigeria: their classification, spatial variation, present and potential use. Unpublished Ph.D. thesis, London University.

Visser, S.A. (ed.) 1970. Kainji: a Nigerian man-made lake. *Kainji Lake Studies* 1. *Ecology.* Ibadan: NISER.

Voh, J. 1982. Strategies for improving agricultural production among farms displaced by a man-made lake: the case of Tiga Dam in Kano State of Nigeria. *Proc. Fourth Afro-Asian Regional Conference of ICID.* 28: 353–365.

Waddy, B.B. 1973. Health problems of man-made lakes: anticipation and realisation, Nigeria & Kossou, Ivory Coast. In N.L. Ackerman, G.F. White, & E.B. Worthington (eds.), Man-made lakes: their problems and environmental effects. *Am. Geophys. Union. Geophys. Monograph.*

Wallace, T. 1979. Agriculture Projects & Land in Northern Nigeria. *Rev. African Political Economy* 17: 59–70

Walsh, J.F. & Millnik, J.J. 1970. Freshwater snails of the Kainji Lake with special reference to the transmission of schistosomiasis. In S.A. Visser, Ecology. *Kainji Lake Studies* 1. Ibadan: NISER.

Watt, S.B. 1981. Peripheral problems in the Senegal Valley. In Saha, S.K. & C.J. Barrow (eds.), *River Basin Planning: Theory & Practice.* Chichester: Wiley.

Welcomme, R.L. 1979. *Fisheries Ecology of Floodplain Rivers.* London: Longman.

West Africa 1981. ECOWAS Energy 3358: 2918–2920.

West African Technical Review 1978a. Re-settlement at Kainji. Jan.: 87–93.

West African Technical Review 1978b. Harnessing the Senegal. August: 51.

West African Technical Review 1981a. Irrigating Borno State: South Chad Irrigation Project transforming the region. June: 83–97.

West African Technical Review 1981b. Jebba: more power from the Niger. Aug.: 183–191.

White, F. (ed.) 1965. *The first scientific report of the Kainji Biological Research Team.* Liverpool: KBRT.

Wilson, E.B. 1975. Resettlement communities in the Kainji Lake basin. In A.M.A. Imevbore & O.S. Adegoke (eds.), *The ecology of Lake Kainji.* Ile-Ife; University of Ife Press.

World Bank 1981. *Accelerated development in sub-Sahara Africa: an agenda for action.* IBRD. Washington.

N.G.CHISHOLM
African Studies Centre, Free School Lane, Cambridge

J.M.GROVE
Girton College, Cambridge

The Lower Volta

8.1 THE VOLTA BASIN

The Volta basin, occupying most of Burkina Faso (formerly Upper Volta) and Ghana, is largely covered in savanna and yields few valuable minerals or exportable crops. Burkina Faso is one of the poorest countries in the world and Ghana is remarkable in that its GNP per head has been declining ever since 1963. The headwaters of the river are the scene of a campaign against river blindness and receive attention in Chapter 10. The lower basin in south-east Ghana is occupied in part by the lake behind the Akosombo Dam. The more prosperous part of Ghana, where most of the cocoa is grown and gold, diamonds and other minerals have been mined, lies outside the Volta basin in the south-west of the country.

The main Volta tributaries, the Black Volta and White Volta, rise on crystalline rocks where frequent rapids favour the breeding of *Simulium damnosum* flies the vectors of river blindness. The rivers enter the region of Palaeozoic sandstones and shales that underlie much of east-central Ghana. The river downstream of the confluence has been flooded by the Volta lake into which the Oti and Afram rivers also flow. The lower river, below the Akosombo Dam, emerges from a gorge in the Akwapim Hills and traverses a series of rock bars to reach the sea by a single channel cutting across the western part of an ancient delta of the Volta (Figure 73).

8.2 VOLTA DISCHARGE

The Volta river has not provided easy access to the interior; for much of the year even small craft could penetrate little more than 100 km upstream to a point near Akuse; upstream lay the Kpong and Senchi rapids and the gorge where the dam has been built.

Before dam construction the flow of the river was extremely variable, scarcely more than a trickle in the dry season, with flood peaks varying enormously from year to year; in 1957 the peak discharge at Senchi

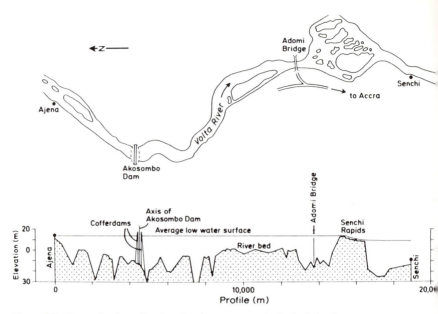

Figure 73. Akosombo dam site, showing the uneven rocky bed of the river.

reached 320,000m³ sec⁻¹ and the next year, 1958, the highest flow
recorded was only 80,000m³ sec⁻¹. The total annual discharge in 1963/64,
when the foundations of the dam were being laid, exceeded 93×10^9 m³
whereas in 1958/9 it was only 11×10^9 m³ (Fig. 74). In spite of its great
storage capacity, the dam is unable to even out the variations of discharge
from one decade to another; from the 1970s into the 1980s the mean level
of the lake has fallen and flow through the turbines has been reduced.

8.3 THE VOLTA DELTA AND LOWER RIVER

The seaward side of the Volta delta is a complex of lagoons and barrier
beaches with extensive plains extending northwards to an old cliff line
(Fig. 75). The hydrology of the delta and the activities of its Anlo
inhabitants are scarcely affected by the Volta River itself. The lagoons are
fed by small rivers rising east of the lower Volta and they fill or dry up
according to cumulative departures from the mean of the local rainfall. In
wet periods, lagoon fishing is actively pursued; when the floors of the
lagoons are exposed, salt is gathered and, in the past, was traded long
distances up the river to the interior. On the coastal sandbars maize,
cassava and other rainfed crops are grown and in particular sites between
the sandbars and at the edges of the lagoons two or three crops a year of
shallots and other crops are grown with irrigation.

230

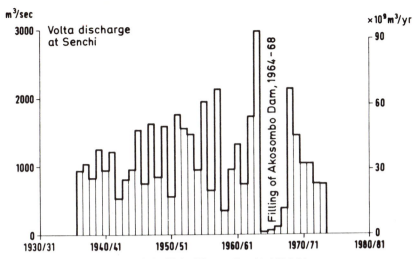

Figure 74. Annual discharge of the Volta River at Senchi, 1936-74.

The main purpose of the Volta dam is to generate electricity, most of which is used for converting alumina into aluminium at a plant at Tema, but the lake impounded by the dam has also provided a new and important fishery for Ewe who have migrated upstream from the lower river. Below the dam the location of a clam fishery has been shifted downstream as a result of the dam evening out discharge through the year.

8.4 IRRIGATION IN THE VOLTA DELTA

Irrigated beds on the coastal sand barrier are aligned along the narrow hollows between the individual sand bars fronting the delta and at the lagoon edge between Keta and Anyanyui (Grove, 1966). They are watered from shallow wells tapping a freshwater aquifer that rests on salty water beneath. A variety of crops such as maize, okro and bananas are grown for local consumption but the main crop is shallots. These are carried out by lorry, crossing the Volta by a bridge at Tefle; the journey to Accra was shortened in 1979 by a new road running across the delta quite close to the left bank of the Volta from Srogboe, near Dzita, to Dabala.

The Anlo are numerous in relation to the land they occupy and, as in other densely populated parts of Africa, the people have been stimulated to acquire new skills both to win a livelihood from the scarce resources of their own environment and to enable them to compete in the urban centres, especially Accra and Tema, to which many of them have emigrated.

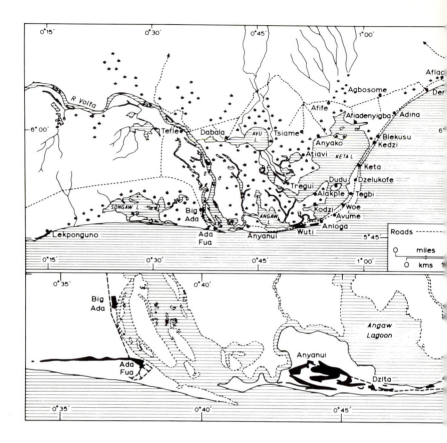

8.4.1 *Shallot growing*

The shallots are grown on rectangular beds arranged in neat rows separated by paths and drainage ditches, with the white concrete tops of wells showing through the bright green of carefully tended crops (Figure 76).

In the decades around 1900 the main source of cash in the Anloga area was copra. About 1930 the local coconut-palms were affected by a disease which greatly reduced yields and has persisted to the present day. At the same time sugar prices were low and so many farmers turned their attention to shallots. A coast road had been opened with a ferry across the Volta mouth to Ada, and Accra offered a ready market. Demand for shallots turned out to be high and there was little or no local competition. Conditions for expansion and intensification of production were exploited, and the Anlo, with little or no European advice and encouragement, improved their techniques. Production now relies on skilled methods of cultivation and the intensive application of labour and

232

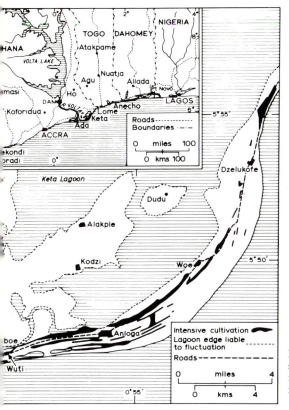

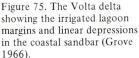

Figure 75. The Volta delta showing the irrigated lagoon margins and linear depressions in the coastal sandbar (Grove 1966).

capital. Skills are learnt by children helping their parents on family land and this accumulated knowledge seems to be a major factor accounting for the area's exclusive position in production.

The following description is based on a survey conducted by Chisholm (1983) in May 1982 which brought up to date the results of fieldwork in 1966 and 1967 by J.M. Grove and M. James. The techniques and physical determinants of cultivation merit detailed description in order to demonstrate the complexity of the system as it has developed indigenously. The system is adaptive rather than static, varying according to physical conditions and adapting to the national economic recession that has affected Ghana since 1963 and since the 1970s several other countries in West Africa.

The beds on which the shallots are grown vary in size but generally range between 1½ and 3 m in width, and between 4 and 30 m in length; modal dimensions are about 2 m by 10 m. Beds on the lagoon side are raised by sand being laboriously carried from the coastal foredunes whereas some inter-ridge depression beds have been extended by

233

Figure 76. Shallot beds separated by ditches running down to Keta lagoon.

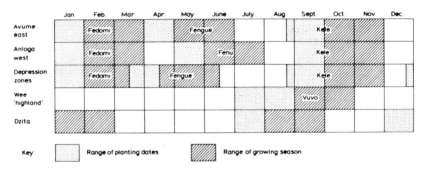

Figure 77. Shallot cropping seasons in the Volta delta.

excavation; a number of large farmers have recently hired bulldozers for this purpose. In both cases the level of groundwater at different seasons is critical. Wells about 2 to 4 m deep are dug and lined with concrete rings to provide a means of dry season irrigation, care being taken not to risk tapping salt water at a greater depth.

Cultivation practice depends on location and season (Figure 77). Generally four shallot cropping seasons are recognised, with as many as three shallot crops being taken in a year in some locations, in others only one. In all areas intercropping occurs. At the height of the dry season, in January, beds are weeded, cleaned and dug with short-handled hoes. They are then watered for 3 to 5 days after which manure and usually artificial fertilizer are applied and watering repeated for another 5 to 7 days. Manure is then dug in and beds levelled prior to sowing. In the dry season watering is needed throughout the eight-week growing period and so more labour is required than at other seasons. First weeding, normally

234

Figure 78. Shallots being planted during the rains; the sides of the beds being protected by corn stalks.

two weeks after sowing, is now usually followed by a top-dressing of chemical fertilizer and then weeding is repeated 3 or 4 more times. The harvested shallots are left on the beds for nearly a week to dry and are then carried home for separating into bulbs for sale and those to be set aside for sowing the next crop but one.

For wet season cultivation, involving sowing in April, furrows are dug between the beds to drain surplus water down to the lagoon, and sides of beds are reinforced with corn stalks and lagoonside grasses (Figure 78). Irrigation at this season may not be necessary and in the second half of the year is usually no more than supplementary.

Shallot farmers face many hazards from natural events and economic circumstances and have developed various forms of risk insurance adapted to local environmental conditions. On the lagoon edge, an area of higher loamy soils west of Anloga on an older set of sandbars, is distinguishable from lower, sandy soils to the east developed on a later sandbar. A third zone is formed by a strip of relatively high ground rising to the south of the lagoonside beds, and a fourth comprises linear depressions between the sand ridges. In every zone except the third a dry season crop, *fedomi*, is grown with the aid of continuous watering; the higher ground would require too much irrigation. In every zone except the third, pre-monsoon and summer, *kele*, crops can also be taken. In the third zone alone shallots are sown in July/August after the main rains at a time when the other zones are usually flooded and sowing is delayed until September. In the Dzita area where shallots have been grown only in the last thirty years conditions are not quite the same; and the growing seasons are from December-February and June-July.

235

Planting time is not solely a function of physical conditions. Planting dates are chosen by community leaders, usually large farmers, with a view to preventing the spread of pests, notably *yoe* which attacks shallots nearing maturity and reduces bulb growth. Planting outside the stipulated periods normally invokes strong community sanctions. However in 1982 the planting time around Anloga for the pre-monsoon crop was extended into June to allow planting by those delayed by unusually heavy early rains. It is possible that the gradual adoption of chemical pesticides, some really intended for the treatment of cocoa aphids and none specifically against *yoe*, is allowing greater flexibility in the timing of cropping.

Chemical fertilizers, first introduced by the Ministry of Agriculture in 1966, are now very widely used by shallot-growers. Dried fish manure previously used as a top dressing has now become too expensive to be economic. Fish manure is less inclined to scorch the crop than artificial fertilisers, especially if they are applied by inexperienced farmers; furthermore, bulbs grown on chemicals are said to deteriorate more rapidly in storage than those grown on organic manures. Manures other than fish continue to be used, cow, fowl and bat dung being applied before sowing. These are also expensive. Cow dung, of which about one bag is needed for every two beds, is usually obtained from kraals established on old Volta distributary channels forming strips of higher ground north of the lagoons. The price in 1982, at the unofficial rate of exchange then current, was about $1.00 per bag; fowl dung was about 50% more expensive and bat droppings up to about $6 per bag. In comparison, subsidised chemical fertilisers (NPK 15: 15: 15), applied at a rate of one bag per 30 to 50 beds, cost about $1.50 per bag. No farmers are known to use chemicals as a complete substitute for organic manures; nonetheless, widespread annoyance at the shortage of NPK in 1982 indicated general acceptance of its beneficial effect on yields.

'Seed' may be resown for anything from 3 to 10 years before declining yields induce the grower to obtain new planting material. This comes from Agu, a town about 70 km north of Lomé in Togo. It is very expensive, about $ 20 per tin, with three tins needed to plant one modal bed. Some farmers send their own shallots to Agu where they are grown for seed without irrigation or manuring, usually intercropped with yams. The origin of the Agu connection is uncertain; the town was a focal point of Ewe migration and had a shrine of regional importance, but how it became a supplier of shallot seed for Anlo of the Volta delta is a mystery.

8.4.2 *Other irrigated crops*

Anlo shallot farmers also grow maize, cassava and vegetables for home consumption and put tomatoes, peppers, okro and garden eggs on the market. These are all planted as intercrops about a month after the shallots to prevent overshading and are harvested before the next crop of shallots is planted. Maize can be grown in most seasons; a two month variety is grown with the dry season fedomi shallots. Peppers and tomatoes give highest yields in *vuvo* and *kele* but fetch much higher prices if they are sown in *kele* and harvested in the November-December period of short supply. The production of commercial crops seems to have expanded in recent years but for the most part only as a supplement to shallot production, except in the case of poorer farmers who cannot afford the high inputs demanded by shallots.

8.4.3 *Limiting factors*

8.4.3.1 *Capital.* Shortage of capital is probably the main limiting factor at any one time. Land and labour can both be obtained but only at a price. Shortage of capital is most pronounced after major floods which not only cause immediate crop losses but also result in high soil salinity damaging lagoon-side beds for two or three years. After severe floods in 1963 large farmers turned to market women for loans. Formal methods of financing are not favoured by many small farmers who are concerned about losing control of their land. In any case bank credit has hitherto been sparse and unreliable, bank officials not trusting illiterate farmers and the latter baulking at strict collateral requirements. Since 1979 attempts to meet some of these problems have been made through the Dzelukope Rural Bank, a branch of the Bank of Ghana, with provision of loans being based on accurate assessment of production needs and involving farm inspections.

8.4.3.2 *Labour.* The second main cost component in shallot cultivation is labour. Demand for labour varies within each household depending on the use made of family labour. There is no necessary correlation between household size and use of family labour. Some members of a family may have their own beds or be engaged in other activities, especially fishing. If family labour is inadequate then wage labour has to be sought at rates that will attract people away from lagoon fishing. *Fidodo*, the traditional form of mutual labour cooperation (Grove 1966) disappeared from the area about a decade ago because of difficulties in determining labour shares and the costs of transporting labourers to and from their homes. Wages are determined by bargaining, with leading farmers setting the trend. Current rates are equivalent to about $ 1.50 for a 7-hour day. Labour costs are at a maximum for watering in the dry season when individual farmers may pay for a hundred man-days of labour or more. Having planted seed, applied fertilizers and paid for watering they may then lose their crop as a result of flooding by early heavy rains.

Cultivation is rarely prevented by labour scarcity. Contract arrangements guaranteeing a secure supply have been made by certain large farmers for one season at a time. They normally require the employee to work at agreed times but do not prevent him from working elsewhere for someone else or on his own or rented beds. A kinship or lineage relationship is often involved in such arrangements or a labourer may expect his employer to provide loans or rent him beds in the future.

In contrast to many other parts of Ghana, most of the shallot cultivation is done by the men. Women are almost exclusively responsible for head-loading sand and manure and also for cleaning the bulbs after harvest. They are also the traders, having developed an elaborate network of largely kin-based relationships to handle all stages of marketing. Attempts to establish cooperative marketing have foundered on resistance from the formidable existing network and on the individualistic attitude of farmers who wish to exploit market opportunities for their own benefit. In the 1960s and 1970s efforts to regulate marketing to even out price variations failed on this basis. Such control would not be easy anyway because of the limited storage space of most farmers and the need to sell some shallots even at a low price to satisfy immediate requirements, pay labour costs and repay debts.

8.4.3.3 *Land tenure*. The apparently family-based nature of cultivation should not obscure the importance of community structures, above all the clan. Every individual belongs to one of fifteen clans and all land is held by one or other of the clans. A clan is made up of lineages, each descended patrilineally from a particular ancestor, and decisions about control over land are made by lineage leaders representing the clan (Benneh 1971).

Allocation of land rights is of basic importance within a community of this kind, where population densities are high and agriculture is increasingly commercialised. Original tenurial systems have been modified but land is still held by usufructuary right. On the death of a household head the land he held is distributed amongst his wives and children; sons get larger shares than daughters and in recent years there has been a tendency for shares of land inherited by the women to diminish and for them to be compensated in cash or otherwise. Cases of buying and selling of land were beginning to become known in the early 1950s but have since become very rare, possibly because of the security land offers in times of economic instability.

Land distribution is very uneven, with some individuals holding over a thousand irrigated beds and others less than ten; a holding of 0.2 ha is not at all unusual in Anloga. Inequalities derive originally from usufructuary rights obtained at the time of settlement when some clan leaders obtained more land than others. Subsequent distribution has been influenced by inheritance patterns. However, various procedures have evolved that allow use of the land to be shared in a more rational manner, by renting, mortgage and other arrangements.

There are two distinct rental systems, one a short-term fixed rent system, *bodada*, the other a longer-term share-crop system, *dame*. Under *bodada*, beds are hired out for only one season at fixed rents, varying in 1982 over a range of $1 to $3 depending on size and location. Under *dame* the duration of tenure varies but may persist for over a decade: this system seems to be increasingly favoured both by landholder and tenant since the greater security encourages increasingly intensive production. Proceeds from marketed shallots are shared equally, after deducting the tenants operating costs.

238

Another system, *fame*, operates in cases where farmers with surplus seed sow it in the beds of individuals who, for one reason or another, lack it. These individuals cultivate the beds and two thirds of the crop goes to the provider of the seeds.

The possibility of obtaining the use of beds by such means as these introduces a valuable flexibility into the system, enabling individuals to arrange to cultivate in several different areas thus reducing vulnerability to flood, drought, or burning by salt spray, which can simultaneously affect crops only a few hundreds of metres apart as was observed in May 1982. Shallot farmers are evidently 'gamblers' rather than 'conservative peasants'. Those who suffered flood damage in May 1982 had sown depression beds intending to harvest early and take advantage of very high prices (up to about US $70 for a 45 kg bundle, the usual price in 1982 being about $40). But heavy rains fell unusually early and the shallot beds were waterlogged.

A system called *woba* allows a landholder to mortgage his irrigated beds in return for a cash loan, the beds being returned when the loan is repaid. It provides immediate cash that may be required as a result of crop damage, or is needed to provide capital for investment in more land, or it may be used to finance a fishing concern. Anlo sea fishermen usually have some land which may be mortgaged to raise capital or can be rented out if members of the family are not wanting to farm it themselves. The system allows young farmers to procure land for their own use, but there is a tendency for *woba* to promote inequality of operational holdings simply because large farmers have capital to lend. They take no interest, the returns from cultivation being seen as adequate recompense. In the last few years arrangements have been made by which in return for a sum of money, land is handed over for a fixed period of years, thus providing security for both parties in a time of inflation.

Underlying all these arrangements there seems to be a recognition of the individual's need to exercise some choice amongst a range of options according to the circumstances in which he finds himself. The traditional tenure system has proved itself to be flexible and so far has served the community and the individual well.

8.4.4.4 *Possibilities for extension of shallot growing*. Specialisation in shallot cultivation continues to be a logical way of meeting local needs within a setting of national economic recession. Subsistence needs are partly met by maize, cassava and vegetables intercropped with the shallots and also grown as rainfed crops on the crests of the sandbars. Additional maize is bought with cash from the sale of shallots. The prices of the two have risen almost in parallel (Table 35) and farmers have been able to continue purchasing maize even in times of national or regional scarcity.

Opportunities seem to exist for extending the area under shallots. In the last two decades, bulldozers have been used near Anloga to widen the irrigated areas in the inter-ridge depressions. Between 1930 and the 1960s,

Table 35. Ghana national average wholesale prices of maize and shallots in cedis, 1970-81.

	1970	1971	1972	1973	1974	1975	1976	1977	1978	1979	1980	1981
Maize (100 kg bag)	12	12	17	18	20	25	57	119	134	172	413	711
Shallot (45 kg bundle)	13	11	12	18	23	32	48	127	206	278	418	830

shallot cultivation spread westwards from Anloga towards Dzita. On the northern side of the Keta lagoon several Anlo villages producing irrigated sugar-cane, bananas and vegetables for sale all have historical connections with Anloga. A few individuals there are known to have been growing shallots in 1967 and it is possible that with experience and diffusion of skills, the importance of the crop will increase outside the Anloga area. Other areas that would appear to be physically suitable for shallot growing lie west of the Volta in that part of the delta occupied by the Adangme.

The system described in the preceding pages appears as a contradiction of stereotypes of African rural communities: the Anlo are innovative rather than conservative, with land tenure practices permissive rather than restrictive and farms employing risk-bearing rather than risk-averse strategies. In the Volta delta, producers are the experts; extension workers are the learners (see Adams & Grove 1984).

To what extent is irrigation in the Volta delta unique? Techniques have been developed there indigenously to suit specific environments, but such adaptation is not uncharacteristic of many African, especially riparian communities. The land tenure system has evolved in such a way as to permit an individual to take risks without catastrophic consequences, but tenure systems commonly do respond to such needs. The environment is peculiar, but comparable conditions probably occur along other parts of the coast and in the river valleys of West Africa. The concentration of effort on a particular cash crop for the domestic market in preference to subsistence production is a rarer phenomenon and has allowed greater independence to the producer than is the case when an export crop is grown. Hard work is rewarded and within an unequal community institutional arrangements allow the small man to grow bigger and the big man to diminish. In view of the relative prosperity of the people involved and the stability of their society, in spite of natural hazards and economic stresses, some notice might well be taken of their example when large-scale, exogenous irrigation development schemes are being planned.

8.5 THE VOLTA RIVER PROJECT

The Volta River Project carried out between 1962 and 1967 involved damming the river at Akosombo about 100 km from its mouth thereby creating a huge lake to provide a head of water for generating electricity and also to even out extremely variable flow. The dam rising 80 m above the river bed has a clay core, 40 m thick at the base, covered with a thick layer of rock. It was completed within the planned period and also within cost estimates in spite of the occurrence of an exceptional flood in 1963 at a critical stage in construction (Moxon 1969). Within a few years 4000 million KWh of electricity were being generated annually, two thirds of it being used by the Volta Aluminium Company Limited (Valco) at Tema in a smelter converting alumina imported from America into aluminium. The rest of the electricity is distributed to urban consumers in Accra-Tema and other towns in southern Ghana and also in Togo and Benin. The project is generally considered to be far and away the most successful industrial enterprise in Ghana.

8.5.1 *Preparations for the project*

An assessment of the project has been made by Hart (1980) as "a case study in politics and technology" in which he attempts to compare the costs and benefits arising from the scheme. Having considered the effects upon industry and the macro-economy plus 'side-effects' he comes to the conclusion that the overall benefit to Ghana has been limited.

Early interest in harnessing the Volta envisaged generation of electricity for the manufacture of aluminium from local bauxite. in the years following World War II the United Kingdom government was attracted by the opportunity to procure a Sterling Area supply of aluminium. Largely as a result of this a study of the economic value to the Gold Coast of the development of the Volta basin was made between 1949 and 1951 by the consulting engineers, Sir William Halcrow and Partners. Their report (Government of Gold Coast 1952) recommended a dam 80 m high to be built at Ajena, a power plant with a capacity of 564,000 KW, and an aluminium smelter at Kpong about 16 km downstream. New railways would be built for the transport of bauxite from the Aya-Yenahin area and a new port constructed at Tema (Jackson 1964). A Preparatory Commission was then set up in 1953 by the Gold Coast government to examine the project more closely. Headed by Sir Robert Jackson, it was assisted in its investigations by a number of experts with international reputations. As Jackson has written, they covered "the coordination of all the technical aspects of the project, the implications of the new railways, communications and logistics, materials and manpower, the planning and design of townships at Ajena and Kpong, living conditions in the new communities, recruitment and employment of labour, and human factors. The effects of the dam and lake in the area which would be inundated had to be analysed carefully as well as those of the dam on riparian communities living downstream. The impact of the lake on health and sanitation involved very detailed surveys, and evaporation, inland water transport and lake ports, together with a wide range of problems related to agriculture, irrigation, fisheries and forests all had to be investigated thoroughly. The financial and economic implications of the project were analysed – both internally and externally – and the Commission sought the best available advice in trying to assess the future world demand for aluminium and the probable cost of energy generated by nuclear power stations."

Jackson (1964) drew special attention to certain aspects of the Commission's work amongst which we may note:

a) More attention was paid to people than to any other problem. It was felt that men even more than machines would be the key to success and every scrap of knowledge available in Ghana and in countries with roughly similar climates was recorded that might lead to the best conditions for work and the achievement of the highest levels of productivity.

b) A major operation was carried out to ascertain the exact conditions of people living in the area to be inundated, and those who would be affected downstream from the dam. This work went on for some years and so too did investigations into problems of health and sanitation, not only those arising from the creation of the new lake, but also in the new communities. Malaria, bilharzia, trypanosomiasis and other diseases were investigated especially onchocersiasis."

After the publication of the report at the end of 1955 (Preparatory Commission 1956) the project hung fire, though work had already begun on the construction of a harbour at Tema. There were various reasons for a decline of interest on the part of overseas investors. The Tanganyika Groundnuts Scheme was still fresh in peoples' minds. Oil refineries had recently been nationalised in Iran and the policies of the government of Ghana, which gained its independence early in 1957, were socialist. By this time too there was no longer a world shortage of aluminium and the cost estimates that had been made by the Preparatory Commission were high, too high for potential participants. The Aluminium Company of Canada, Alcan, which had been involved in discussions at an early stage was prepared to pay only a very low price for the electricity; the United Kingdom government looked towards the World Bank as the main source for financial support. Nkrumah, the President of newly independent Ghana for whom the Volta River Project seemed to provide the key to Ghana's industrialisation and transition to a modern industrial state, now found himself in a weak bargaining position.

In 1958 Nkrumah approached President Eisenhower and it was eventually agreed that the engineering aspects of the scheme should be reassessed by Kaiser Company of California. The Reassessment Report (Kaiser 1959) recommended a dam at Akosombo, a short distance downstream of the site originally chosen at Ajena, where a gravity dam could be built with modern, large-scale earth-moving equipment in four years instead of taking seven years as had originally been intended; this would shorten the time before the investment would produce an income. Furthermore, in order to keep down capital costs the smelter was to be at Tema, using bauxite from Kibi though it was later agreed that imported alumina would be used initially.

242

In 1951 Impregilo started work building the dam and power plant; in September 1965 the first commercial power became available and by 1967 the smelter was operating. A second smaller hydroelectric dam at Kpong, 20 m high, was completed in 1980 to supplement power from Akosombo especially in periods when repair work to the generating units limits output. This has helped to make up for the reduced power output resulting from persistently low rainfall totals and river discharge in recent years.

8.5.2 Costs and benefits

To finance the Project the Ghana Government made a loan of $100 million, about half the cost of the dam and power plant, to the Volta River Authority (VRA). (This money had been accumulated in the 1950s by the Cocoa Marketing Board paying prices to cocoa producers well below those on the world market.) The other $100 million came as loans from the World Bank, the US, Canadian and UK governments. The smelter was financed through the Kaiser and Reynolds aluminium companies by American banks with guarantees from the US government. The interest charges were to be paid and the loans repaid by the income derived by the VRA from sales of electricity. Ghana paid for Tema harbour construction and for the electricity distribution network.

The benefits to Ghana in cash have not been great. Until 1977 Valco was able to import alumina and other needs free of customs duty and until 1979 it paid no company tax. Starting in 1980 however, in addition to paying $26 million for electricity and handing over $15 million in taxes to the Ghana Government, it contributed $9 million out of profits towards a fund for social development. The Project provides about 9000 Ghanaians with well-paid jobs. Urban dwellers are provided with electricity and though prices for it are not low it saves Ghana several tens of millions of dollars annually that would otherwise go on oil imports.

The price Valco pays for the huge amount of electricity it consumes is low and although the company has complained about failures in electricity supplies from time to time that have caused aluminium pots to freeze, thereby reducing production and increasing costs, it has been able to produce aluminium profitably at a time of low world prices. So far it has shown no signs of being interested in using Ghanaian bauxite to produce alumina; integrated plants are vulnerable to nationalisation and are extremely rare in Third World countries and the Kaiser company has been under no obligation to provide one. The optimistic hopes and ambitions of the politicians of the 1950s and 1960s are unlikely to be realised for a long time to come.

The side-effects of the dam are more difficult to assess than the monetary returns. The lake interrupts communications between agricultural producers in the north-east of Ghana and their markets in Kumasi though small cargo boats on the lake were carrying over 20,000 tons and nearly 30,000 passengers annually in the 1970s, and roads constructed along the east side of the lake have improved access to some eastern border areas.

The most costly side-effects have been those borne by the people who were displaced by the lake; in particular resettlement has proved to be a much more difficult and delicate operation than building the dam (see 7.6, 2.2).

Some health hazards around the lake have been reduced, others have greatly increased. Many sites where *Simulium damnosum* used to breed, the flies that transmit river blindness, have been flooded. But schistosomiasis is much more prevalent than was formerly the case. Before Akosombo was built the prevalence of urinary schistosomiasis around the area later impounded was quite low but within a year of the lake reaching its maximum level, in 1968, very high prevalence rates were being recorded in lakeside communities. Over the years the VRA has reduced its services to resettlement villages, water supply points have been neglected, and increasing numbers of people have come to depend on lake water with consequent greater risks of infection (see pages 308–309).

Downstream of the dam, reduced sediment load and greater light penetration has been accompanied by enhanced growth of aquatic weeds and the arrival of *Bulinus* snails resulting in intense transmission of schistosomiasis. In the Ada area, which was once envisaged as a tourist haven, the river estuary is occupied by freshwater throughout the year allowing bilharzia to be transmitted where formerly it was absent.

Storage of water behind the Akosombo Dam and evening out of the discharge of the river downstream seemed to offer opportunities for irrigation in the coastal region where mean annual rainfall is less than 1000 mm. The F.A.O. reported on a survey of the lower Volta River floodplain in 1963 and concluded that 25000 ha could be developed to produce rice and sugar-cane if irrigation water were to be provided and low-lying land were to be adequately drained. Two years later a report by Kaiser Engineering proposed irrigating a much larger area extending over the grassy plains towards Accra. The topography is gently rolling rather than flat, with heavy, cracking clay soils and the difficulties of water distribution and mechanical cultivation would be considerable.

An agricultural development corporation, sponsored by the Ghana Government has obtained the use of 8000 ha of floodplain on the left bank of the river downstream of Kpong in an area occupied by the Torgome Ewe. It was intended originally to grow cotton for a local textile factory but the chief crop at present is maize. On the right bank Osoduku farmers are growing sugar-cane to supply a factory nearby. When the Kpong dam was under construction, Impregilo established a small farm of 6 ha to supply the expatriate workforce with meat, poultry and eggs. Following this example, the VRA is considering the possibility of irrigating 155 ha in the same general area to produce rice, maize, plantains and vegetables. Certainly there would seem to be opportunities for irrigation agriculture in the area extending from the Akuse area towards the coast, using pumps and canals, in an area where reduction of flood peaks on the lower river has restricted flood farming on riverside lands.

8.6 CLAM FISHING

The fishing or 'picking' of clams, *Egeria radiata*, on the lower Volta downstream of Torgome has been described by Lawson (1972) as having provided an aggregate yield of £100,000 in 1954 when it was the main occupation of between one and two thousand women. The Tongo women dive from canoes to collect the clams from beds about 2 m under water. They also establish clam farms by transplanting small individuals to sites where they will grow better. Harvesting is controlled by taboos strictly enforced; in Mepe, for example, women can pick clams on only 3 days in the week and there is a 2 month closed season. The clams are extracted from their shells, smoked, and find a ready market in Akuse and Accra. The shells are used in poultry food and also for making terrazzo floor covering.

The location of the fishery is determined by the need for a short period of high salinity to ensure satisfactory breeding. The critical salinity boundary formerly restricted the fishery to the reach above Tefle. When the dam was constructed and storage was complete, dry season discharge through the turbines held the salinity boundary to within a few kilometres of the river mouth throughout the year (Figure 79). The main clam beds accordingly shifted 20 km downstream and now extend from Tefle down to Agrave, within 10 km of the sea. The women migrate downstream to harvest the new beds and they also collect young clams and take them upriver, transplanting them near their homes in the Alabohya-Mlefi reach of the river. Yields do not seem to have fallen, prices remain high and the women involved are able to maintain a considerable degree of domestic independence as a result of their incomes from clam picking and trading.

8.7 LAKE FISHING

Before the completion of the Akosombo Dam, fishing in the Volta upstream of the Ajena gorge was of little importance. Some Tongu Ewe who spent most of the year farming and fishing in the Battor-Mepe area, would spend a month or two fishing above the gorge living in temporary camps and return home in August. After the closure of the dam in 1964, fishing expeditions to the lake found catches were extremely good and by 1968 landings are estimated to have reached 60,000 tons annually. There was a great rush of people to exploit the new resource, most of them Tongu Ewe, and by 1975 though annual landings had declined to about 40,000 tons, about 12,000 fishermen were settled around the lake.

The fishermen use boats with outboard motors and imported nylon nets. The industry remains family-based, the large sums of money for

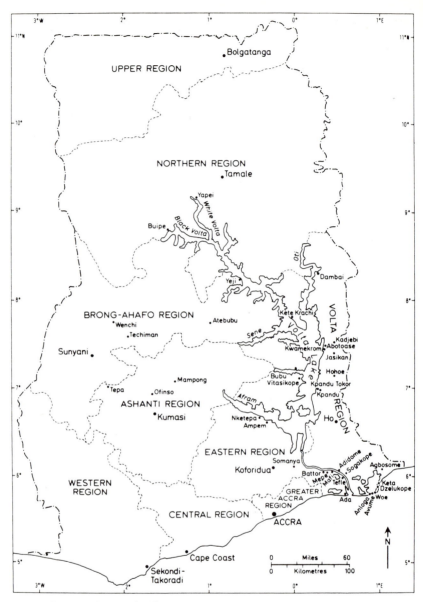

Figure 79. The Volta Lake in Ghana.

246

equipment being borrowed from traders, especially fish traders, who thereby ensure a regular supply of fish for their own activities. A high proportion of the catch is smoked in the small settlements on the shores of the inlets west of the lake and is then carried to large markets that have grown up near the road on the east side of the lake (Figure 80).

8.7.1 The fish trade

Attempts at developing cooperatives and development banks have so far failed. Most fishermen value the secure outlet and access to funds provided by the traders with whom they deal. Traders get a guaranteed supply from their creditors which is vital in a trade where rapid turnover of capital is a characteristic. Large numbers of petty traders, including fishermen's wives, also participate but their profits are small in comparison to those of the large traders.

At local markets that have sprung up near the fishing settlements, foodstuffs such as maize, cassava, tomatoes and vegetables are exchanged for fish. At Bubu Vitasikope the market was overseen by the chief fisherman or his son. Trading starts at an appointed time and exchange is made by placing fish on a certain quantity of (for example) oil-palm nuts, the relative quantities then being haggled over until both parties are satisfied or else one withdraws his offer.

Even at the wholesale assembly markets on the east side of the lake barter also takes place between traders and producers. At these markets fish is bulked into larger consignments and then taken by road to Accra, Kumasi and other large towns. A large basket of fish cost about $ 100 in 1982; and wealthier traders will buy a number of baskets each market day.

Most of the traders, but not all, are Ewes. At the local markets they recognise a Queen Mother who settles disputes between them. Some depend on intermediaries, often women relatives, who bring fish to them from the fishing settlements on the west side of the lake. Some obtain their supplies largely through providing nets to fishermen to whom they may or may not be related.

Net prices are high, around $ 300 for 'a bundle' about 90 m long and a fisherman may need up to five bundles of various mesh, all of which need to be replaced every 2 or 3 years. A boat with a life expectancy of 5–10 years cost almost $3000 in 1981, even before the engine and running costs were considered, so capital requirements are high.

The local fishing and trading communities have responded rapidly to economic opportunity, elaborating a marketing network and raising the necessary capital. Difficulties in procuring imported nets and outboard engines, on account of the country's shortage of foreign exchange, have been the main factors limiting expansion of the industry. The state of fish stocks and the potential sustainable catch are uncertain because fisheries research and monitoring are inadequate and deteriorating as a result of the national economic situation.

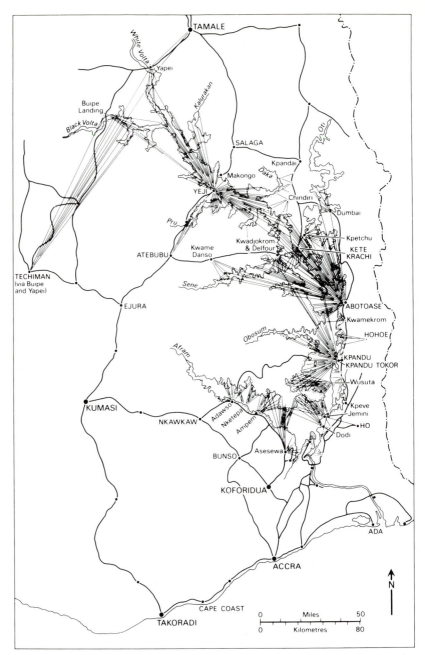

Figure 80. Fishing settlements and markets to which the fish are taken around the Volta lake.

248

8.7.2 *Lakeshore settlement*

Fishermen now occupy their workplace, the lake and lakeshore, for most of the year; but 'home' is still the family house on clan land below the dam. Fishermen and their families still return to their homes around July-August and also for funerals. On the lakeshore they still live in temporary mud houses while their houses at home are in comparison well-built with cement blocks and metal roofs even though they are unoccupied for much of the year. Youngsters are sent back home for schooling to stay with grandparents, though a number of new communities have set up elementary schools often staffed by teachers who have returned from the towns on account of excessive living costs.

In the new fishing settlements a chief fisherman represents the community in dealings with the local chief. He may attempt to extract rent for the increasing areas of land being used by the Ewe for cultivation not only on the mud exposed as the lake recedes towards the end of the year but also upslope on the higher 'landward' side. Ewe from Adidome District on the lower Volta, where cattle are widely owned, are beginning to keep herds on lakeside grazing. Various cottage industries are emerging with lakeside reeds being dried and woven into mats and mechanised mills used to process cassava and maize. The Krobo and other local people are beginning to take more interest in fishing but there still remains much interchange of forest products for fish.

Social services and local road networks are scarcely developed on the west side of the lake. Government activity in these areas has been limited and medical services to cope with schistosomiasis and other water-borne diseases are generally lacking.

8.8 THE INFORMAL SECTOR ON THE LOWER VOLTA

In the years that have elapsed since the construction of the Akosombo Dam, Ghana has reaped considerable benefits from the generation of electricity it has made possible and investment in the Project has probably been of greater long term benefit than expenditure on a similar scale in other sectors of the economy. Amongst the returns the fishing industry on the lake is of outstanding importance. When we add to this the clam 'picking', which does not seem to have suffered markedly from the Dam, and irrigated production of shallots in the Volta Delta, it would seem likely that the "informal sector" on the lower Volta contributes as much towards the national economy as does the Volta River Project itself.

8.9 REFERENCES

Adams, W.M. & A.T. Grove, (eds.) 1984. *Irrigation in tropical Africa*. Cambridge African Monographs Nr. 3. Cambridge: African Studies Centre.
Benneh, G. 1971. Land tenure and sabala farming systems in the Anlo area of Ghana. *Research Review, University of Ghana* 7: 74-94.

Chisholm, N.G. 1983. *Response of some rural communities in South-East Ghana to economic recession 1982.* Cambridge African Monographs Number 2; Cambridge: African Studies Centre.

Government of the Gold Coast 1952. *Development of the Volta River Basin.* Accra.

Grove, J.M. 1966. Some aspects of the economy of the Volta Delta (Ghana). *Bull de l'Inst. Fondamental d'Afrique Noire* 28 (Ser B): 381–432.

Hart, D. 1980 *The Volta River Project: a case study in politics and technology.* Edinburgh: Edinburgh University Press.

Jackson, R.G.A. 1964. The Volta River Project. *Progress (Unilever)* 4: 146–61.

Kaiser, H. J. & Co. 1959. Reassessment Report on the Volta River Project for the Government of Ghana. Oakland, California.

Lawson, R.M. 1972. *The changing economy of the Lower Volta, 1954-67; a study in the dynamics of rural economic growth.* London: Oxford University Press.

Moxon, J. 1969. *Volta: Man's Greatest Lake.* London: Andre Deutsch.

Preparatory Commission 1956. *The Volta River Project* London: HMSO.

250

Part Three
River associated diseases: Their ecology and control

D.H.MOLYNEUX
Department of Biological Sciences, University of Salford

9

Trypanosomiasis: Sleeping sickness

'The long history of West African civilisation is . . . . the history of the evolution of human societies along paths that have enabled them to avoid frequent periodical decimation by trypanosomiasis' (Ford 1971).

9.1 HUMAN TRYPANOSOMIASIS

9.1.1 *The organisms involved*

African human trypanosomiasis exists in two forms. An acute disease known as Rhodesian sleeping sickness and a chronic disease Gambian or West African sleeping sickness. Both forms of disease are caused by microscopic parasitic protozoa, trypanosomes, belonging to the genus *Trypanosoma*. The biological names are *Trypanosoma brucei rhodesiense* causing acute Rhodesian sleeping sickness and *T.b. gambiense* which causes the chronic disease. These parasites cannot be distinguished by morphological means but may by their biochemical characteristics.

These infections are transmitted to man by the bite of the tsetse (genus *Glossina*); there are twenty-two species of tsetse but not all transmit human sleeping sickness. Tsetse species are restricted to a variety of different habitats in Sub-Saharan Africa. They are limited by the higher temperatures and absence of shade in the northern limits of distribution and by low temperature at the southern end of the range. *Glossina* are different from other flies (Diptera) as the females do not lay eggs but incubate the larvae within a uterus (larviparous). The larva develops over a period of approximately 12 days after the fertilised egg has been deposited in the uterus. The female after this period of 'pregnancy' deposits the larva (larviposition) in a suitable habitat (usually in shady humid conditions with friable soil) where the larva burrows rapidly and pupariates. A black barrel-shaped puparium remains in the soil whilst the adult fly develops within the puparium. The emergence of the adult usually takes place after approximately 30 days but the time taken to emerge is dependent on temperature and in the colder seasons may be up to 60 days. Sleeping sickness in West Africa is transmitted by the riverine species *G. palpalis* and *G. tachinoides* whereas the acute form is usually transmitted by savanna inhabiting species of tsetse of the *G. morsitans* group. A complex cycle of development occurs in the tsetse which acquires the parasites from the blood of its host during a bloodmeal. Tsetse are obligatory haematophagous insects and must take a bloodmeal every 2–3 days; both sexes take blood. When the trypanosomes have completed their cycle of development after 15–30 days (depending on temperature), infective forms are found in the salivary glands of the fly and these parasites are transmitted to man or an animal host during the act of feeding. The infection rates in wild caught flies, however, are very low (0.03–0.04%) as tsetse usually need to take their first bloodmeal from an infected host if they are to become infected and physiological barriers exist in flies which inhibit trypanosome development.

Glossina also transmit pathogenic trypanosomes to livestock. Animal trypanosomiasis throughout the tsetse belts of Africa is of serious concern to the Food and Agricultural Organisation; it has been described as the only disease that has impeded the development of a whole continent (see 9.2.).

9.1.2 *Disease status and effects*

Most recent estimates suggest 20,000 new cases of Human Trypanosomiasis occur every year in Sub-Saharan Africa. Forty-five million people are reported to be at risk. However, both these figures are likely to be underestimates due to the absence of surveillance and serious epidemics at present occurring in Uganda. In West Africa however, the situation varies from one of low endemicity to areas where serious epidemics are occurring (Figures 82–84). Recent figures suggest that there is a resurgence of disease in many foci of West and Central Africa (WHO 1977). However, only a small proportion perhaps 10% of the population at risk are under surveillance and many cases are likely to remain undetected.

Sleeping sickness in man is almost inevitably fatal unless treated. A lesion known as a chancre is occasionally observed at the site of the bite of an infected fly. In the early stages of the disease a recurrent fever, headaches, pains in joints and reproductive abnormalities, such as impotence, ammenorrhoea and infertility occur. There is enlargement of cervical lymph glands and a state of general malaise, reversal of sleep patterns, loss of weight and pruritus (itching). Invasion of the central nervous system which takes place after a varying period of time is accompanied by a different type of symptom such as personality changes, psychotic behaviour, mania and coma. Some patients become violent or conversely show a happy unresponsive expression. Such symptomatology and inevitable death if the disease is not treated create fear in rural communities. The disease has caused depopulation through death, desertion and migration from river valley communities with the abandonment of farms and settlements through

254

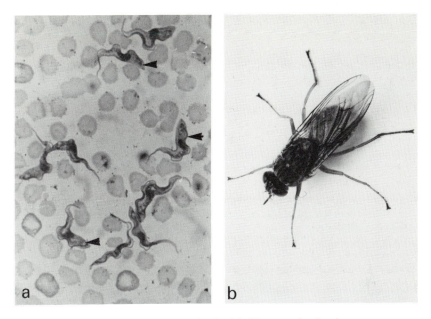

Figure 81. a) Blood film of mouse stained with Giemsa stain showing trypnosomes (arrowed) of the type which causes sleeping sickness in man amongst red blood cells (Magnification 2400 times).

b) A tsétse fly (*Glossina morsitans*) which transmits sleeping sickness to man by its bite. Note the wings folded over the abdomen in characteristic appearance and proboscis at anterior end (magnification 12 times life size).

fear of the disease. Sleeping sickness has been recognised in West Africa since the days of slave trading; one of the principal clinical signs of the early stage of the disease-enlarged cervical lymph glands (Winterbottoms sign) – resulted in potential slaves with this condition being rejected for shipment.

Sleeping sickness is believed to have first reached Nigeria in epidemic form in the early 1920s and from then it spread westwards throughout all the countries encircled by the Niger and its tributaries. It is believed that this devastating epidemic killed many thousands of people; the size of the problem can be envisaged by the finding of 90,000 out of 400,000 examined were infected. These epidemics are believed to have spread from the outbreak in the Congo (now Zaire) during the early part of the century and decimated populations in Central Africa, as far north as Cameroon where Jamot had organised an anti-trypanosomiasis organisation responsible for case finding and treatment. Although the British later formed a similar team it is likely that this was too late, as in the Chad Basin 18,000 cases were treated between 1930-1935 and the epidemic died out. As Duggan (1970) suggests this was probably due to

255

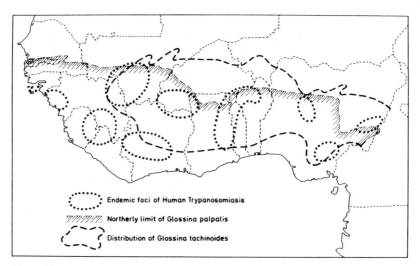

Figure 82. Human trypanosomiasis foci and *Glossina* distribution in West Africa.

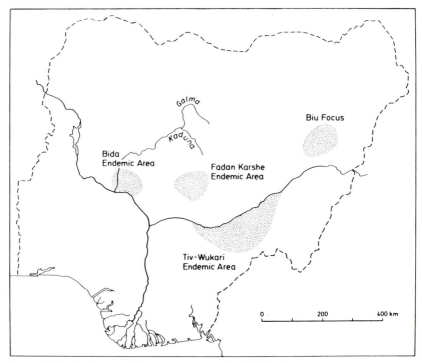

Figure 83. Endemic areas of human trypanosomiasis in Nigeria.

256

migration from those settlements which remained viable away from the rivers. Duggan pinpoints the permanent source and point for spread of infection throughout Central Nigeria as the Kaduna and Galma rivers (Figure 83); over the ten year period (1930–1940) 300,000 people were treated by mobile teams and at fixed treatment centres. Similarly in Ghana the disease spread as a result of association with rivers due to the presence of the fly and their use as lines of population movement. As colonisation progressed however, an outward movement of disease spread began (Morris 1946). Morris however, considers that sleeping sickness spread along the Black Volta as early as 1870–1880 and in 1905 was prevalent within 1 or 2 miles of the river as far as the northern bend in Upper Volta. Depopulation of the most severely affected area through death and emigration indicate that in the Lawra and Wa areas of north-western Ghana there was a 24 and 34% decrease respectively in the population over the 8 year period 1931–1939. The infection rates in these areas being between 6 and 7% over areas of 500–800 km²; in some

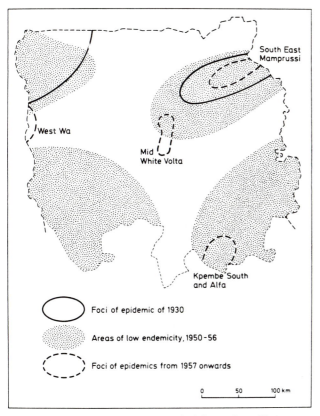

Figure 84. Foci of human trypanosomiasis in northern Ghana.

257

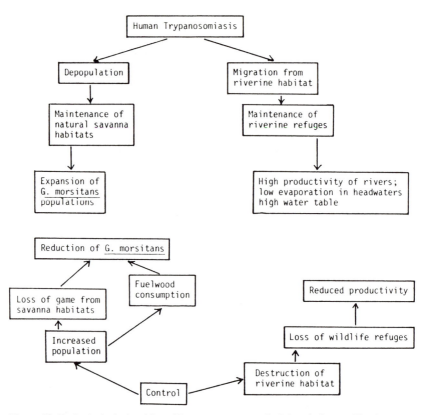

Figure 85. Ecological relationships of human trypanosomiasis in relation to *Glossina* control and the effect of the disease.

villages 30% of the population were infected. Similar patterns with resultant depopulation was seen in the areas to the East of the Black Volta in Upper Volta and Ivory Coast and in North-east Ghana around Mamprussi (Figure 84).

Evacuation of river valleys has a variety of consequences. The disease is distributed to other communities; abandonment is accompanied by movement of livestock and population into less fertile areas nearer headwaters and watersheds where a denser population settles on land agriculturally less suitable for sustaining the pressure of over-farming. This results in absence of grazing and rapid depletion of water sources in the dry season – with consequent nutritional and disease problems in cattle as well as increased erosion, decreased yield and exhaustion of the soil. These interactions are summarised in Figure 85.

Depopulation will increase game animal populations consequent on abandonment of land and with an increase in *G. morsitans* fly belts (in

258

West Africa, *G. morsitans submorsitans*); *G. morsitans* populations are not usually associated with areas where the population exceeds 40 km^{-2}, as this fly is largely dependent on game animals for their food. Thus development of a livestock industry is severely handicapped by the levels of trypanosomiasis challenge which results from such a situation (see Section 9.2).

However where sleeping sickness has forced populations to settle in areas distant from rivers which are thus relatively safe from sleeping sickness (and onchocerciasis) the populations reach 650 per square kilometre in areas of the Northern Guinea Savannas. In such areas the pressure on the land resource is so intense as to have reduced riverine vegetation also to a degree where even residual pockets of *Glossina* can no longer survive. The importance of activities which deplete the savanna woodland and riparian vegetation resources has been emphasised recently with reference to Nigeria by Onyiah (1978) and Jordan (1979). Around Kaduna both *G.p. palpalis* and *G. morsitans submorsitans* habitats have been destroyed by fuelwood collection (including from riparian woodland) as well as increased agricultural activities as a result of population pressure.

Against this background it is clear that sleeping sickness has had profound effects throughout the Niger Basin both in Anglophone and Francophone territories; these effects still reflected in the distribution of the population today, result from the desertion of fertile river valleys and settlement on higher ground distant from areas of riverine vegetation. Sleeping sickness could be regarded as the major factor in depopulation this century comparable to slaving in the last (Ford 1971); in addition its association with rivers has on the one hand prevented their exploitation through migration and desertion but on the other has contributed to the preservation of riverine habitats. The maintenance of the riverine habitat is important for the hydrobiology of the river systems as the dense fringing vegetational cover provides a habitat for a variety of faunal groups, contributes to the nutrient levels in the watercourses themselves, thus increasing fish productivity, and maintains the water for longer periods during the dry season as compared with those areas where riverine vegetation has been removed and the converse applies. Removal of riverine vegetation will thus increase the likelihood of erosion, produce increased evaporation and markedly reduce the contribution to the nutrient cycle of the system (Figure 85). Onchocerciasis (Walsh, J.F., Chapter 10) has been less of a factor in causing the initial movement away from rivers but acts as a means of preventing resettlement in these fertile areas. This may reduce the likelihood of epidemics of sleeping sickness recurring; however *Simulium* control, as in the Onchocerciasis Control Programme in the Volta Basin, if it results in resettlement where *Glossina* populations exist (as they will almost certainly do) then epidemics of sleeping sickness in resettled populations could pose major public health problems and undermine development programmes.

9.1.3 *Epidemiology*

Sleeping sickness in the Niger basin is found in well defined endemic foci; these foci have been known as residual or hardcore foci and are shown on the map (Figure 81), (de Raadt & Seed 1975). Within these so-called foci (the French term 'foyer' seems more appropriate) there appears to be a persistent low level endemicity as well as a capacity for epidemics to arise (revivify is the French expression) (Janssens 1971). Janssens emphasises that certain localities are involved consistently in human trypanosomiasis outbreaks; the levels of endemicity in such foci are also consistently higher than in the surrounding areas; Scott (1957; 1959) demonstrated a three to twelve-fold increase in incidence in epidemics in north-east Ghana and the contribution of the foci to the epidemic was much higher than the rest of the district; the incidence was far higher in the centre of the focal outbreak and rates of infection diminished towards the periphery.

Several theories have been evoked to explain the maintenance of these foci of infection (Janssens 1971, Molyneux *et al*. 1979, Molyneux 1980). They can be summarised briefly as changes in virulence of the parasites, the existence of human carriers and animal reservoirs (it is now recognised wild and domestic animals are infected with parasites biochemically identical to those infecting man with the chronic disease; Gibson *et al*. 1978, Mehlitz *et al*. 1982); or less precise suggestions such as "microclimatic or ecosystem factors" or "new man fly-trypanosome relationships" (Janssens 1971).

What is clear, however, in West Africa is that mobility of human populations has played a most important part in the distribution of trypanosomiasis; the human reservoir, particularly in the early stages of the disease, cannot be under-estimated as a source of new infections through migration into fly infested areas, for traditional seasonal activities and through movements, also perhaps seasonal, in response to availability of employment or the prospect of resettlement (Prothero 1963).

Transmission of human trypanosomiasis in West Africa is regarded as most likely to occur in the Northern Guinea and Sudan Savanna zones at the end of the dry season where man and flies congregate around the available sources of water where (for *Glossina*) food is readily available and the humidity is highest, temperature lowest and shade is available. Hence the disease is associated with watercourses particularly those where water is available at the end of the hot dry season. Similarly sacred groves (Forêt sacré) where dense vegetation is preserved provide suitable habitats adjacent to villages; man-made fly habitats such as mango, cocoa and coffee plantations may also pose a disease hazard (Finelle 1980).

Man-fly contact is considered to be intense and personal in this situation (Nash 1978). This classical concept is applicable in the drier parts of the savanna but is difficult to reconcile with the prevailing climatic situation in the foci which are active at present in West Africa for example, in the pre-forest zones of Ivory Coast (Vavoua, Bouaflé) and

Cameroun (Fontem & Bafia). It is clear in these more humid zones that man-fly contact is less intense (Page & MacDonald, 1959) but despite this transmission is occurring.

There is clear evidence that sleeping sickness existed in West Africa prior to the intervention of the colonial powers (Morris 1946; Duggan 1962). Ford (1971) has outlined the Pax Brittannica theory for the origins of the destructive epidemics which occurred during the first half of the twentieth century. The pacification of the residents of the area of the Niger and its neighbours resulted in the movement of people away from the concentrations of populations such as walled towns or other communities established for the purpose of defence against slave-raiding. Thus settlements were established adjacent to riverine *Glossina* habitats, which for the purpose of agriculture were the most fertile and provided permanent water sources for domestic purposes. Pagan tribes, which were the principle sufferers from slave rading had retreated to safer terrain such as the Plateau and its escarpments around Jos and Bauchi (McLetchie 1948, Duggan 1962, Ford 1971). With colonisation the inhabitants of both the refuge areas and the walled towns had greater freedom of movement and thus greater risk of exposure to fly. The greater freedom of movement with increased capacity to travel circulated parasites and spread the infection.

Ford (1971) believed that other explanations for the sleeping sickness epidemics in Nigeria must be found besides the Pax Brittanica theory. He suggests the role of animal reservoirs of infection requires alternative consideration suggesting a role for the bushbuck and incriminating cattle as a source of infection although the situation may differ in the different epidemic zones in Nigeria. Ford (1971) has identified two zones of foci – one centred on the Chad river system, the other on the Niger-Benue; the former epidemic zone he believed to have originated from northward migratory movement of labourers associated with the development of roads and rail systems from the Niger-Benue primordial focus where the milder form of the disease appears to originate. It has been suggested by Duggan (1962) that the source of the more acute human infection observed in north-eastern areas of Nigeria may be the result of acquisition by man of parasites from bushbuck via *G. tachinoides*.

9.1.4 *Sleeping sickness control and treatment*

Human sleeping sickness in West Africa has been controlled by a combination of techniques. Active case finding and treatment has played a vital role in controlling epidemics. Case finding has relied on medical surveillance teams and their capacity to diagnose the disease. Diagnosis depends on the finding of parasites in the body; usually a lymph gland biopsy is performed on persons who have enlarged cervical (neck) lymph glands. The material is then expressed onto a microscope slide and teams of microscopists attempt to find parasites. Blood film examination is also carried out but this is even less sensitive unless concentration techniques are employed such as filtration through cellulose or centrifugation. The latter techniques however are not used on a wide scale and thus those currently in use by the mobile rural health teams are insensitive and thus cannot be expected to detect all cases. In addition not all the population is sampled due to absenteeism at the time of the survey particularly during planting and harvesting periods; a variable but important proportion of cases are therefore undetected and remain capable of infecting flies. A patient who is detected as positive in the blood must have an examination of his cerebrospinal fluid (CSF) by lumbar puncture to determine if the infection has invaded the brain. This is essential to determine the type of treatment. Attempts to improve diagnosis using immunodiagnostic techniques are under development specifically for field use. These techniques are designed for simplicity and to speed up diagnostic procedures. It is hoped that kits of immunodiagnostic reagents will be made available to mobile teams. Such kits utilising simple agglutination tests – stained and fixed parasites being agglutinated together in the presence of antibody (Magnus *et al.* 1978)—could be performed using blood from a finger prick and permitting a result to be obtained during the time the team is in the village. This is important as suspects detected centrally by other serological techniques are often not retraced if a team leaves a village and returns later (1–2 weeks) to find them for more intensive parasitological examination.

Treatment using currently available drugs is dangerous and involves hospitalisation of cases for approximately 4 weeks. The drug of choice for the advanced disease when the central nervous system is involved has been the arsenical Melarsoprol (Mel B), which must be given under strict medical supervision due to the need for impeccable intravenous injection techniques and because it carries a mortality of up to 10% due to a reactive encephalopathy. Three, 3-day courses of Mel B are usually given, separated by approximately a week. A course of cortico-steroids is also given initially. Two drugs, Suramin and Pentamidine, are available for treatment of the disease in the early stages and remove parasites from the blood. They are however not effective against the parasite in the central nervous system. Suramin and Pentamidine are given prior to Mel B. Suramin is the drug of choice for the early stage disease and must be used in areas where Pentamidine is used prophylactically. Whilst receiving treatment it is essential for sleeping sickness patients to have a vitamin and protein rich diet to raise their general level of health. Occasionally patients relapse after courses of Mel B and a further longer course is required possibly at higher dose levels. The danger of relapse necessitates patient follow up; this should be ideally every 6 months after treatment for 2 years. The need for follow up places a heavy burden on the transport resources of the public health authorities. Relapse cases may indicate initial inadequate dosing and could result in drug-resistant fly-transmissible parasites in circulation in the human population.

Pentamidine has been used extensively as a prophylactic in early campaigns against the disease particularly in French speaking countries.

Injections were required every 6 months. However, pentamidine resistance has been identified in some areas and thus pentamidine prophylaxis has been largely discontinued except in regions where the risk is very high e.g. tin mining areas or in railway construction. There is however, the danger pentamidine may mask the early symptoms of the disease reducing parasitaemia thus delaying detection until the disease has reached the advanced stage.

The need for long hospitalisation of sleeping sickness patients for treatment implies a considerable pressure on hospital beds and staff resources which could otherwise be used for other perhaps more acute problems. A less toxic drug more easily adminstered could help solve this problem. Control strategies have thus been based on case finding by diagnosis followed by compulsory treatment, prophylaxis in some areas and on vector control activities. The strategy of case finding, treating and prophylaxis has been employed in the former French territories whereas in Nigeria and Ghana a much stronger emphasis was placed on the need to reduce populations of *Glossina* initially by bush clearing along watercourses adjacent to villages but later with the advent of DDT by the use of insecticidal control techniques. Morris (1946) argues strongly in favour of the inclusion of vector control in the overall approach. However, it is clear that an integrated strategy is necessary which responds to the local situation and the maximum human and financial resources available.

Early methods of vector control of sleeping sickness involved attempts to reduce populations of *Glossina* by destruction of the riverine fly habitats and by fly catching. Clearing of riverine vegetation was successful in many areas of the Northern Guinea Savana zones in Ghana and Nigeria. With the advent of insecticides, particularly the chlorinated hydrocarbons (DDT and Dieldrin), ground spraying of fly resting sites was carried out using knapsack spraying equipment. This type of spraying has been the major *Glossina* control technique in Northern Nigeria since the eradication campaign directed against animal trypanosomiasis began in early 1950s (Davies 1964). This campaign is believed to have had a major effect on sleeping sickness in those parts of Nigeria cleared of flies.

Passive methods of vector control of sleeping sickness have involved the use of DDT impregnated traps in Ghana (Morris 1950) and more recently the use of Deltamethrin – a synthetic pyrethroid impregnated into the material of a biconical tsetse trap (Challier & Laveissiere 1973). Field trials with these impregnated traps have been successful in reducing riverine *Glossina tachinoides* populations over 99% (Laveissiere & Couret 1980). Such techniques it is hoped will be of value in self-help control activities designed to reduce fly populations and thus transmission around villages and in plantations.

Aerial applications of insecticides as residual and non-residual (sequential application) application have been used for the control of animal trypanosomiasis. Again in Nigeria residual applications by helicopter (of DDT, Dieldrin, Endosulfan and the synthetic pyrethroids)

263

to riverine forest and savanna woodland drainage lines have eradicated *Glossina* from many northern areas and have probably contributed to the reduction in recorded cases of sleeping sickness. However, there has been concern about the environmental consequences of application of residual insecticides and the non-target organism populations have been severely affected, particularly fish in watercourses contaminated with Endosulfan, crustacea in rivers contaminated with pyrethroids and cold blooded vertebrates and insectivorous birds when DDT and Dieldrin are applied (Koeman *et al.* 1980). However, in most cases long-term effects are not significant and reinvasion from adjacent unsprayed habitats occurs and should be planned for.

In association with the need to reduce the dosages of insecticides applied and the need to evolve techniques suitable for non-residual applications by helicopter, Molyneux *et al.* (1978) described the development of such techniques for control by non-residual low dosage applications to denser riverine forest habitats where resettlement may occur as a result of the Onchocerciasis Control Programme controlling *Simulium* in the river valleys of the Volta Basin. These techniques were evolved to ensure that a rapid response could be mounted should epidemic human trypanosomiasis occur; the objectives being to reduce transmission providing time for surveillance teams to survey, diagnose and treat those infected, whilst the use of non-residual techniques reduced environmental damage caused when residual doses were used (Koeman *et al.* 1980).

Despite the efficacy of vector control in reducing fly populations its use in endemic situations is not likely to be cost effective. In epidemics it could make an important contribution to breaking transmission. However, the mainstay of human trypanosomiasis control in West Africa is the mobile field team operating at the rural periphery. These teams may be responsible for diagnosis of sleeping sickness only or the diagnosis of sleeping sickness may be a part of the responsibility of polyvalent health teams. Thus the maintenance of the efficiency of such teams through provision of transport and diagnostic facilities remains essential for the prevention of epidemic sleeping sickness by early case detection and treatment. The problems at present are the financial constraints on governments which reduce facilities and operating potential of mobile teams with the resultant danger of resurgence of epidemics.

It cannot be too strongly emphasised that the dangers of sleeping sickness do not rest on its current impact in areas of low endemicity. Sleeping sickness has the potential in many areas to become the major threat to the health and development of these communities. A reduction in the maintenance of the control activities of mobile teams, through political unrest and the consequent civil disorder as demonstrated in Zaire in the 1960s and Uganda in the late 1970s until the present (in addition to vegetational and ecological changes in Uganda) illustrate the potentially disastrous consequences such a lack of vigilance could have. It is therefore of vital importance to maintain the mobile teams in the rural

264

periphery so that their expertise in sleeping sickness diagnosis remains available and so that new diagnostic tools can increase diagnostic efficiency. Above all it is necessary to ensure resources of fuel and transport are adequate. This requires a recognition by the responsible authorities of the importance of the problem.

9.2 ANIMAL TRYPANOSOMIASIS

Through the range of its distribution *Glossina* acts as a vector of trypanosomiasis of livestock, particularly of cattle. Infections are acquired directly or indirectly from game animals. However the present paucity of game animals in West Africa outside the National Parks suggest that maintenance of cattle trypanosomes is now as a result of flies feeding on infected livestock. Three trypanosome species cause disease in cattle; these are *T. vivax, T. congolense* and *T. brucei*, the last of these is closely related to the organisms causing the human disease. The pattern of livestock development in West Africa is largely determined by presence of trypanosomiasis and for economic returns trypanosomiasis control is essential through chemotherapy, vector control or through the maintenance of trypanotolerant cattle. This last, involving raising the smaller dwarf West African Shorthorn breeds of N'dama, Baoulé and Muturu particularly in the forest and preforest zones together with small ruminants and pigs enables at least some effects of trypanosomiasis to be alleviated. These dwarf breeds, however, are not favoured by the traditional Fulani (Peulh) livestock owners of the Sahelian and Sudan zones, the larger Zebu being their favoured animal. The Zebu is more susceptible to trypanosomiasis. Its exposure to 'challenge' by tsetse is reduced by transhumance whereby herds migrate north as the rains move north and then, as the dry season advances and the fly populations diminish, the herds move south to better grazing. This traditional activity allowed Fulani cattle herders to reduce the levels of challenge or trypanosomiasis risk to which their cattle are exposed. Although trypanosomiasis does occur in the trypano-tolerant as well as susceptible breeds none of these qualities is absolute. Tolerance depends on maintenance of a constant challenge of parasites but this tolerance can be broken down by heavy challenge or stress and the response of cattle to trypanosome infection is dependent on the number of infected fly bites received both in N'dama and Zebu.

Drugs are available for the treatment of animal trypanosomiasis but there is widespread resistance to some of them and no new trypanocide has been marketed recently nor are new ones likely to be available in the foreseeable future. Berenil and Samorin are the most widely used compounds as there is no evidence of cross resistance between them. However side effects can be a problem (e.g. Berenil is fatal for camels). Lack of availability, expense and underdosing (which provokes resistance) are problems associated with the use of chemotherapy for trypanosomiasis control. Chemoprophylaxis using Samorin can be employed to protect cattle on trek to markets if they pass through areas of heavy challenge. However, most cattle reared in the northern parts of West Africa, north of the belt of *Glossina* distribution, are now transported to southern markets by lorry.

A vector eradication programme has played a major role in the development of the livestock industry in northern Nigeria. This programme was based initially on ground spray application of DDT and Dieldrin to specific resting sites (Davies 1964) and most recently by helicopter application of these insecticides (Spielberger *et al.* 1979) as well as Endosulfan. This programme has eradicated *Glossina* from many areas of northern Nigeria over a 25 year period allowing effective development of a livestock industry in parallel with other agricultural systems. These campaigns began in the north-eastern part of Nigeria in the river systems draining the Chad basin and moved south-west into the Guinea Savanna zones. However it is here that problems of insecticide application in more humid habitats are found and at present an experimental approach using sterile males is being considered for tsetse control.

The economic benefits of tsetse eradication in terms of an increase in production and an economic return on investment have been recently stressed. It must however be emphasised that it is necessary to adopt long-term programmes with eradication as the objective, for control is likely to be a continuing commitment which may not necessarily be economic. Vector control and other trypanosomiasis control activities are now viewed by FAO as important adjuvants to rural development in Africa and rational utilisation of the land. It is clear that in some areas tsetse control would for different reasons be an entirely inappropriate option e.g. in mountainous or hilly areas, national parks and densely forested areas. Thus the trend is to emphasise the need for an economic return on investment from any tsetse or trypanosomiasis control activity which must be seen as just one component in an integrated plan for development; without such an approach ad hoc activities will be uneconomic and irrelevant.

9.3 REFERENCES

Challier, A. & C. Laveissière 1973. Un nouveau piège pour la capture des glossines (*Glossina: Diptera, Muscidae*): déscription et essais sur le terrain. *Cah. ORSTOM sér. Ent. méd. Parasit.* 11: 251–262.
Davies, H. 1964. Eradication of tsetse in the Chad River systems of Northern Nigeria. *J. Appl. Ecol.* 1: 387–403.
de Raadt, P. & J.R. Seed 1977. Trypanosomes causing disease of man in Africa. In J.P. Kreir (ed.), *Parasitic Protozoa* (Volume I). London: Academic Press.
Duggan, A.J. 1962. A survey of sleeping sickness in Northern Nigeria from earliest times to the present day. *Trans. R. Soc. trop. Med. Hyg.* 56: 439–480.
Duggan, A.J. 1970. An historical perspective. In H.W. Mulligan & W.H. Potts (eds.), *The African Trypanosomiases*. London: George Allen & Unwin.
Finelle, P. 1980. Répercussions des programmes d'aménagement hydraulique et rural sur

l'épidémiologie et l'épizootiologie des trypanosomiases. *Insect Sci. Appl.* 1: 95–98.

Ford, J. 1971. *The role of the Trypanosomiases in the African ecology.* Oxford: Clarendon.

Gibson, W., D. Mehlitz, S.M. Lanham. & D.D. Godfrey, 1978. The identification of *Trypanosoma brucei gambiense* in Liberian pigs and dogs by isoenzymes and resistance to human plasma. *Tropenmed, Parasit.* 29: 335–345.

Jordan, A.M. 1979. Trypanosomiasis control and land use in Africa. *Outlook on Agriculture* 10: 123–129.

Janssens, P.G. 1971. Review of the sleeping sickness situation *Tropenmed. Parasit.* 22: 213–224.

Koeman, J., F. Balk & W. Takken 1980. The environmental impact of tsetse control operations: a report on present knowledge. *FAO Animal Production and Health Paper* 7 (Rev. 1). Rome: FAO.

Laveissière, C. & D. Couret 1980. Traps impregnated with insecticide for the control of riverine tsetse flies. *Trans. R. Soc. trop. Med. Hyg.* 74: 264–265.

Magnus, E., T. Vervoort & N. Van Miervenne 1978. A card-agglutination test with stained trypanosomes (CATT) for the serological diagnosis of *T.b. gambiense* trypanosomiasis. *Ann. Soc. belge Med. trop.* 58: 169–175.

McLetchie, J.L. 1948. The control of sleeping sickness in Nigeria. *Trans. R. Soc. trop. Med. Hyg.* 41: 445–470.

Mehlitz, D., U. Zillman, C.M. Scott & D.G. Godfrey 1982. Epidemiological studies on the animal reservoir of gambiense sleeping sickness. Part III. Characteristics of *Trypanozoon* stocks by isoenzymes and sensitivity to human serum. *Tropenmed. Parasit.* 33: 113–118.

Molyneux, D.H. 1980. Animal reservoirs and residual foci of *Trypanosoma brucei gambiense* sleeping sickness in West Africa. *Insect Sci. Appl.* 1: 59–63.

Molyneux, D.H., D.A.T. Baldry. & C.P. Fairhurst 1979. Tsetse movement in wind fields: possible epidemiological and entomological implications for trypanosomiasis and its control. *Acta tropica* 34: 53–65.

Molyneux. D.H., D.A.T. Baldry, P. De Raadt C.W. Lee & J. Hamon 1978. Helicopter application of insecticides for the control of riverine *Glossina* vectors of African human trypanosomiasis in the Moist Savannah Zones. *Ann. Soc. belge Med. trop.* 58: 185–203.

Morris, K.R.S. 1946. The control of trypanosomiasis by entomological means. *Bull. ent. Res.* 37: 210–246.

Morris, M.G. 1950. The persistence of toxicity in DDT-impregnated hessian and its use on tsetse traps. *Bull. ent. Res.* 41: 259–288.

Nash, T.A.M. 1978. A review of mainly entomological research which has aided the understanding of human trypanosomiasis and its control. *Medical Entomology Centenery Symposium Proceedings, London, November 1977.*

Onyiah, J.A. 1978. Fluctuations in numbers and eventual collapse of a *Glossina palpalis* (R-D) population in Anara Forest Reserve of Nigeria. *Acta trop.* 35: 253–261.

Page, W.A. & W.A. MacDonald 1959. An assessment of the degree of man-fly contact exhibited by *Glossina palpalis* at water holes in northern and southern Nigeria. *Ann. trop. Med. Parasit.* 53: 162.

Prothero, M. 1963. Population mobility and Trypanosomiasis in Africa. *Bull. Org. Mond. Santé: Bull. Wld. Hlth. Org.* 28: 615–626.

Scott, D. 1957. The epidemiology of human trypanosomiasis in Ashanti (Ghana). *J. trop. Med. Hyg.* 60: 205–215.

Scott, D. 1959. Human trypanosomiasis in Northern Ghana, 1950–6. An epidemiological review. *W. Afr. med. J.* 8: 165–184.

Spielberger, U., B.K. Na' Isa, K. Koch & A. Manno 1979. Field trials with the synthetic pyrethroids permethrin, cypermethrin and decamethrin against *Glossina* (*Diptera: Glossinidae*) in Nigeria, *Bull. Ent. Res.* 69: 667–689.

World Health Organisation 1977. The African Trypanosomiases. Report of a Joint WHO Expert Committee and FAO Expert Consultation on the African Trypanosomiases. Rome: FAO.

267

J.F. WALSH
Department of Biological Sciences, University of Salford

10

Onchocerciasis: River Blindness

10.1 INTRODUCTION

Onchocerciasis or 'River Blindness' is a parasitic disease of man which occurs widely in tropical Africa with a small related focus in North Yemen and adjacent areas of Saudi Arabia. It also occurs in parts of central and northern South America. Some 30 million people are thought to be victims of the disease. It is caused by a filarial worm, *Onchocerca volvulus*, which passes its mature, sexually reproducing stage in the human host, and is transmitted from person to person by bloodsucking flies. It is not thought that there are any significant animal reservoirs of this disease, though it has been recorded from a lowland gorilla *Gorilla gorilla* and can be experimentally transmitted to chimpanzees *Pan troglodytes*. Closely related species of *Onchocerca* are found in cattle and large wild herbivores. Many West African cattle harbour three different species of *Onchocerca*, segregated in various parts of their bodies, without any noticeable ill effects.

In humans the adult female worm may grow to a size of 50 cm and remain reproductively active for at least 11 years and possibly as long as 18 years, the precise maximum length of fecund life being at present undetermined. Such a worm, if fertilised by the smaller male (20–40 cm long) produces countless minute offspring, called microfilaria, about 300 microns in length. These microfilariae cannot themselves develop further or reproduce unless they are taken up by a suitable blackfly of the genus *Simulium*.

Although the encystment of bundles of adult worms of both sexes may cause unsightly nodules the clinical manifestations of the disease are caused by the microfilariae. Each of these probably survives for only a few months, though maximum survival time may be as much as 30 months. The deaths of these microfilariae and their subsequent disintegrations cause extensive inflammatory reactions in the superficial tissues where they swarm in the intercellular fluid, including that of the eyes. In their extreme form such reactions can cause lesions of the eye tissues and lead to irreversible blindness. Onchocercal blindness usually arises when parasite loads are very high, and then only after a lengthy period of infection. Thus it is unusual to find people under 20 years of age blinded by this disease. In addition, to those who have become completely blinded, many more people suffer from lesser visual impairments.

Apart from blindness the disease causes a severe itching which ultimately results in serious skin lesions and depigmentation with loss of elasticity, and an ageing effect. Itching may be so severe that sleeping is virtually impossible. It is also likely that the presence of heavy *O. volvulus* infection is directly debilitating, but this has not been adequately quantified. There is evidence for reduced body weight among onchocerciasis (non-blind) victims who may eventually develop an extreme form of wasting desease. Mortality among the blind may be as much as four times as high as for non-blind individuals of the same age and in the same community (Commission Report 1981).

The disease is transmitted from person to person by the bite of a bloodsucking blackfly (*Diptera: Simulidae*) of the aptly named *Simulium damnosum* species complex. There are about ten extremely similar species in West Africa, in some cases only distinguishable by study of the salivary gland chromosomes of the larval stages, which until 1975 were united under the name *S. damnosum* (Vajime & Dunbar 1975). Developmental stages of these flies are found in the fast flowing reaches of rivers and large streams. It is this association of the fly with rivers that has given rise to the common English name for the disease of River Blindness.

The female *S. damnosum* cannot mature her eggs without obtaining a bloodmeal from a warm-blooded vertebrate, which for many fly populations is by preference, man. Following the blood feed the fertilised female matures her egg batch, which may number as many as 900, in 2 or 3 days. She usually deposits these on vegetation trailing in, or emerging from, the waters of a rapid, where the current speed is between 1 and 2 m sec^{-1} at the water surface. The female is capable of completely submerging in a fast current to lay eggs, and this she sometimes does on the concrete walls bounding the spillways of small barrages. Eggs are also laid on natural rock substrates, but this seems to be relatively uncommon behaviour in *S. damnosum* from West Africa.

At prevailing West African temperatures the eggs hatch within 48 hours into minute larvae. After an initial short downstream migration floating in the current while attached to a silken thread spun by themselves, the larvae become fixed to a suitable plant or rocky substrate in fast flowing water, by means of an anal sucker and circlet of hooks. They henceforth lead an essentially sessile existence obtaining their nourishment by filtering particulate materials such as bacteria, unicellular algae (diatoms) and possibly colloidal materials, from the passing water current, by means of elegantly adapted mouthparts.

The larva grows rapidly, moults seven times in as many days, spins a shoeshaped cocoon, again attached to the substrate, usually that on which it has lived its larval life, and pupates. After two or three days the adult

270

emerges, rises to the surface on a bubble of gas and flies up to the vegetation bordering the breeding site.

On the day following emergence the female takes a meal of nectar, mates and seeks a bloodmeal. The male does not take blood, subsisting solely on nectar, and thus plays no direct role in the transmission of disease. If a recently emerged female obtains blood from a person infected with onchocerciasis, microfilariae are ingested with the blood. These undergo development in the vector, but do not multiply there. Indeed usually only one or two of the many microfilariae which may have been imbibed successfully develop and become themselves capable of transmission. This development takes from six to eight days, and changes the asexual microfilaria into an infective larva which is capable of becoming a sexually mature adult in the human host. However, this development in the fly is completed only by the time of the third bloodmeal. Thus unless a fly survives the laying of two batches of eggs it does not function as a vector.

Although adult females are tied to water for breeding purposes those of savanna populations, at least, are capable of travelling great distances probably with the aid of winds (Garms et al. 1979; Walsh et al. 1981). This is presumably an adaptation to life in temporary habitats. Especially north of 10° N most rivers are only suitable as breeding sites in the wet season, and even further south the suitability of the majority of savanna breeding sites is markedly seasonal. Given this ability, which includes active uninterrupted flight for at least 3 hours (R. Cooter, pers. comm.), man-biting may occur at considerable distances from rivers.

However, older flies especially, and these are the ones likely to be harbouring the infective parasitic larvae, have a strong tendency to bite fairly close to their oviposition sites (Le Berre 1966, Duke 1975). Thus although the infections may be found in a section of the human population over wide areas, it is only near to rivers, with suitable breeding places for the vector, that a very high proportion of the human population has the disease, and where the intensity of transmission and infection is such that high blindness rates and other severe reactions result in the disease being a major socio-economic factor.

10.2 THE DISTRIBUTION OF ONCHOCERCIASIS IN WEST AFRICA

Onchocerciasis is extremely widespread in the well watered savanna and forested areas of West Africa. Important foci of the disease occur along all major river valleys wherever rapids are a prominent feature of the river geomorphology. Thus areas where the Niger, Senegal and Volta river systems flow over the outcropping Pre-Cambrian basement complex provide ideal breeding grounds for *S. damnosum*. Areas of sedimentary rocks such as that traversed by the Benue river are generally much less suitable. In the north the vector population, and consequently the disease, is limited by the lack of suitable breeding sites arising from the sandy nature of the river beds caused by the presence of ancient dune systems, rather than by the severity of climate though, of course, lack of water eventually becomes a limiting factor (Figure 86).

Thus it is a consequence of geomorphology, rather than of climate that the main belt of onchocerciasis reaches its northern limit at about 12° N. Where fast flowing rocky streams occur, as in the Dogon country of eastern Mali, or where man has provided such conditions by his civil engineering works, as at the barrage across the Niger, at Markala, *S. damnosum* breeding, and thus transmission of onchocerciasis, may occur at more northerly latitudes.

In the south, onchocerciasis occurs widely in the forest, until the coastal plain, with its extremely sluggish streams and rivers is reached. However, in the West African forest regions the epidemiology of onchocerciasis differs from that of the savanna (Prost et al. 1980). Different strains of the parasite, of less pathogenicity to the eye (Duke & Anderson 1972), and different members of the vector complex, occur (Vajime & Quillévéré 1978). Although prevalence of infection may be high onchocercal blindness is usually not a socio-economic problem.

10.3 PREVALENCE AND ECONOMIC IMPORTANCE OF ONCHOCERCIASIS

It is extremely difficult to determine the numbers of people at risk from onchocerciasis in the Niger River Basin and West Africa as a whole, but there has been a number of studies which gives some indication of the size of the problem. The World Health Organisation produced a feasibility study in 1973 concerning the control of onchocerciasis in an area of 654,000 km[2] centred on the savanna region of the Volta Basin and encompassing parts of seven countries. In this region 10 million people were thought to be living, 1 million of them being infected with onchocerciasis and 100,000 blind as a result of the disease (WHO 1973). Recently (WHO 1981) a similar study has been produced for a project on onchocerciasis control in the savannas of Senegal, Western Mali, Guinea Bissau, Guinea and Sierra Leone. The area encompassed is 430,000 km[2] with a population of 5,930,000 people of whom 3,200,000 are considered to be exposed to real risk of infection, and 1 million are onchocerciasis victims, 34,000 of them blind. In Nigeria it has been estimated that biting *Simulium damnosum* may occur in 320,000 km[2] of the savanna zone (Crosskey 1981). How many people are at risk in this zone is not known. It has been estimated that there may be 30–40,000 people blind from onchocerciasis in the old political region of Northern Nigeria, with about as many others suffering from severe visual handicap (WHO 1978).

These figures for Nigeria certainly underestimate the full scale of the problem there, and the other estimates give incomplete coverage of the rest of the subcontinent. It is therefore likely that about 200,000 persons are blind from the disease and many more than 4 million are suffering lesser effects in West Africa at the present time.

It is clear that with such a scale of blindness, onchocerciasis, even if it caused no other effects, would present a serious problem. In fact many of the non-blind sufferers undoubtedly have impairment or the debilitating effects of high parasite loads. However, the most serious social consequences of onchocerciasis arise from its focal distribution. In communities which are located close to major breeding places of the vector, and which are not shielded from the full ravages of the attacks of the flies by other communities, the prevalence rate of infection may exceed 66%. More than 4% of the population may be blind, and a further 6% have major visual impairment. Parasite loads, with consequent itching, severe skin damage including depigmentation, and debility are prominent features. In such communities overall blindness rates may exceed 10%. In the Kita areas of the Senegal river headwaters, a maximum of 18.3% blind persons has been observed (WHO 1981). In Nigeria, in the Niger valley villages with 11% overall blindness rates have been recorded during very thorough, whole community surveys. In the Oli valley close to the Kainji dam, there were 21 (16%) blind people in a village of 130 people, and 15% of a small community in the lower reaches of the nearby Kontagora valley were also blind (Walsh 1970).

Blindness from onchocerciasis is essentially restricted to adults, and as men are more prone to contract the disease in its severe form, blindness rates among them considerably exceed these already horrifying totals. Budden (1956) showed that in heavily infected communities with a standardised blindness rate of 57 per 1,000, approximately 17% of the male population over 30 years of age was blind.

Although it seems obvious that such blindness rates must have serious socio-economic consequences there are very few studies which give adequate data. It is clear that in West Africa savanna river valleys with major S. damnosum breeding sites are frequently under-populated, even where soil fertility is high. This was certainly the case in the lower Kontagora valley, before the start of the Kainji Dam project (Walsh 1970). Waddy (1969) has pointed out that in northern Ghana rural land settlement is densest on the watersheds and least in the river valleys, a situation giving rise to over-cropping and erosion in the uplands. This he attributed to the ravages of onchocerciasis. Hunter (1966) working in northern Ghana in the Red Volta valley developed a hypothesis of cyclical advance and retreat of the cultivated area and settlments. As settlements approached the river, blindness and other manifestations of onchocerciasis built up until the community was forced to retreat. Hunter envisaged this cyclical pattern as taking several generations.

Bradley (1972, 1976) carried out a most detailed study concerning the social and economic effects of onchocerciasis on land settlements in the Middle Hawal Valley, Nigeria. He compared 8 lowland villages where onchocerciasis was hyper-endemic (prevalence > 66%) with two upland hypo-endemic villages (prevalence < 34%). He demonstrated that the

273

lowland population was more mobile, and that remains of deserted settlements were much more numerous in the lowlands. He concluded that onchocerciasis predisposed towards the failure of settlements and was probably the primary, though never the sole, cause of desertion. Severe onchocerciasis in the community enhanced the already strong tendency for fit young people to migrate to the big towns from which they do not return. Visually impaired people were shown to be poorer than those unimpaired in the same communities, while in non-onchocercal villages yields of cash crops (groundnuts, cotton, rice) were many times larger than in infected villages. Visual impairment tended to restrict farming to within 1 km of the homestead where all efforts had to be concentrated on producing staple food crops.

The importance of onchocerciasis in deterring settlement is vividly illustrated by the case of the village of St Pierre in Upper Volta. In 1963 a group of 50 more or less onchocerciasis-free people established themselves in a fertile valley, within a few hundred metres of an important *S. damnosum* breeding site. After only 5 years 90% of the community had onchocerciasis, with 30% showing signs of severe ocular involvement. By 1972 the settlement had been abandoned (Rolland 1972). This experience supports Bradley's (1976) contention that 'although onchocerciasis is responsible for some out-movement, its principle effect seems to be in deterring in-movement'.

Thus the severity of onchocerciasis with its widespread but focal nature has almost certainly exerted a substantial effect on the land settlement of the relatively well watered savannas, especially between 8° and 11° N. Figures given by WHO (1981) for land occupancy levels of 35 persons per km^2 in hyperendemic onchocerciasis areas compared with 50 in hypoendemic areas are suggestive. It is perhaps not coincidental that most of the major *S. damnosum* breeding foci in Nigeria (Crosskey, 1981) lie within the 'Middle Belt' which has a lower than average population (Buchanan & Pugh 1955). Though as Glover and Aitchison (1970) state 'on touring around the country one often hears that people have moved away from a certain area because of river blindness' they were unable to procure detailed information. Further work on the lines of the study by Bradley (1976) is urgently required.

The effects of onchocerciasis, therefore are malign not only for the direct human suffering caused but also because of the resulting maldistribution of population which is especially well seen in the middle reaches of the Volta River basin. Fertile valleys are at times under-populated, or even deserted, with human populations crowded on to the watersheds. This pattern of settlement may result in serious deterioration in soil conditions. It is probable that small tributary streams in heavily populated upland areas become more deeply gullied, and hence rocky, following a succession of flash floods, consequent on the removal of riverine trees and other vegetation. Such streams are thus more suitable as wet season breeding places for *S. damnosum* and the disease situation worsens.

The justification for the Onchocerciasis Control Programme in the Volta River Basin, at present under execution by the WHO, was based largely on the argument that removal of this obstacle to development would open up much currently underutilised, well-watered, valley land. This, however, undoubtedly oversimplifies the situation and the justification currently being put forward for the proposed onchocerciasis control scheme for the Senegambian region is based more directly on eliminating the cause of blindness in 34,000 people, improving the general health of the communities, and of moving towards WHO's stated goal of 'Health for All by the Year 2000'. Nevertheless the likely beneficial impact of the control schemes on the proposed development of some 350,000 hectares of good agricultural land is not overlooked.

10.4 THE EFFECTS OF RECENT LARGE SCALE RIVER MANAGEMENT SCHEMES

Recent engineering works to control the major rivers of West Africa for irrigation purposes and the generation of hydro-electricity have profoundly altered the patterns of disease hazards associated with the rivers. The diseases themselves, especially onchocerciasis, have in turn posed problems for the dam builders. As regards onchocerciasis the impoundments of large lakes have been highly beneficial. Flooding has greatly reduced the available breeding habitat of the vector fly. Indeed it was partly the impoundment of the 8,800 km^2 Volta Lake behind the Akosombo Dam in 1964 which led interested specialists to believe that onchocerciasis control might be achieved by means of vector control in the interior savannas of the Volta Basin.

More important in terms of the elimination of vector breeding sites was the impoundment of Lake Kainji in 1968. This much smaller Lake (1,250 km^2) eliminated breeding which occurred throughout the Niger river channel from Kainji to Foge island, in particular in the immensely productive Bussa rapids. With the formation of this lake *S. damnosum* breeding in the Niger, north of Kainji, became confined to a small rapid a few km north of Yelwa, until one reaches the man-made breeding site of Markala barrage in Mali.

The Kossou Dam has also played a useful part in the control of onchocerciasis in the Ivory Coast, and the Kpong Dam has eliminated those rapids which remained on the Volta downstream of the Akosombo Dam. The Jebba Dam on the Niger and the Shiroro Gorge Dam on the Kaduna river should also have major beneficial effects in reducing onchocerciasis in those valleys. Of far greater potential benefit than these dams is the proposed but indefinitely postponed, barrage across the Black Volta at Bui Gorge, Ghana. This would eliminate by far the largest complex of *S. damnosum* breeding sites in the West African savanna. An action which alone would probably reduce onchocerciasis to below the hyperendemic level through most of northern Ghana.

Apart from the flooding of breeding sites, dam construction may greatly modify *S. damnosum* breeding downstream. At Kainji during the first year of hydro-electric generation the experimental fluctuation of spillway discharges allowed a marked alteration of water levels in the relatively narrow run off channel. The result was that no *S. damnosum* bred in the Niger downstream of the dam for several km to Awuru (Walsh 1970), a situation which has continued.

However, the building of dams is not always an advantage from the point of view of the control of onchocerciasis. Most small barrages and some larger ones tend to worsen the situation. Below Akosombo Dam. *S. damnosum* breeding was intense in the uncontrolled Kpong rapids prior to the impoundment of the Kpong reservoir. It is possible that regulated steady water flow from the penstock channels had in fact improved breeding conditions for *S. damnosum* below the barrage. Below Kossou Dam, on the Bandama river, regulated discharge rates may also have favoured intensified breeding of *S. damnosum*. In northern Cameroun the Lagdo barrage, which is currently being constructed across the Benue river, is situated in a region of low onchocerciasis prevalence. The creation of a spillway and the regular flow through the penstock channels are likely to greatly increase the *S. damnosum* breeding potential of the river below the barrage, while the lake only floods insignificant breeding areas.

In northern Ghana and central Upper Volta there are over 200 small irrigation dams, many with uncontrolled concrete spillways. Usually there is no spillage from such dams, but in a good wet season many spill for 8 to 12 weeks, the spillways and run-off channels providing ideal breeding sites for *S. damnosum*. Often they provide breeding sites in otherwise geologically unsuitable valleys. In northern areas these barrages together with such man-made structures as causeways and bridges may provide an opportunity for the vector, and ultimately the disease, to extend its range. All the breeding sites of *S. damnosum* in the White Volta valley, north of Ouagadougou are provided by manmade structures. On occasion the same problem arises with a large barrage. The Markala dam across the Niger in the inland floodplain region in Mali provides the only *S. damnosum* breeding site in the area and is enormously productive. It will be of interest to see whether the recent large scale development in the Sokoto valley, and the future dam building in the Gongola valley result in a worsening of the onchocerciasis situation in these areas which hitherto have been generally unsuited to vector breeding.

10.5 THE IMPACT OF ONCHOCERCIASIS ON LARGE SCALE DEVELOPMENT SCHEMES

Following experience at the Owen Falls Dam (Uganda) Balfour-Beatty, one of the Joint Constultant Engineers to the Niger Dams Authority at

276

Kainji, took advice from the late Dr B B Waddy of the Ross Institute. They concluded that vector-borne diseases, especially onchocerciasis, posed a threat to the satisfactory conduct of construction work, as did the possibility of extremely high levels of man-biting by blackflies. Apart from the problems likely to arise should highly skilled senior staff, or worse their families, contract a disease, however trivially, of such emotive power as onchocerciasis, the authorities were afraid that the large itinerant indigenous labour force might spread onchocerciasis to areas of the country hitherto free from the disease where any small construction works on dams, bridges and causeways were for the first time providing suitable conditions for *S. damnosum* breeding.

As a result of these considerations a vector-borne disease control unit was organised at Kainji which operated throughout the dam construction period. It is difficult to evaluate the cost effectiveness of such preventive action but, at Kainji, where *Simulium* control operations extending over 13,000 km² were carried out, it is believed that no personnel contracted onchocerciasis either at the dam site or in the construction township during the 1964 to 1968 construction period. That this satisfactory conclusion was at least partly attributable to the vector control activities is likely, given the high onchocerciasis infection rates among indigenous riverine communities in Borgu, and the extremely high *Simulium* biting rates (Walsh 1970).

During the feasibility studies three expatriates from a small investigation group had contracted the disease after only a few months exposure in the area. Furthermore, in August 1968 in the Borgu district flies were so numerous that 3,350 per hour were recorded landing on the bare legs of a man wearing a skirt-trap (Walsh 1970). At such levels of fly abundance work on high scaffolding, etc., becomes extremely hazardous. If such levels had been reached at the dam site itself, during the construction phase it is likely that workers would have found conditions intolerable, apart from the safety aspect, and a work stoppage would have been inevitable. Without control there is little doubt that such a problem would have arisen in August 1965 and possibly on other occasions. The economic loss from even 2 days of lost construction time would have exceeded the total expenditure on vector control, throughout the life of the project.

Following the example at Kainji, the Volta River Authority responsible for the Akosombo development took advice from the Joint Consultant Engineers, and set up their own *Simulium* control operation. At both sites limited control still continues in the vicinity of the barrages to protect the communities which have settled there. Additional proof that the Nigerian authorities consider the vector control operations are necessary is provided by the fact that the Electricity Corporation of Nigeria has organised *Simulium* control operations in connection with the recently started Shiroro gorge hydro-electric project on the Kaduna river.

277

10.6 CONTROL OF ONCHOCERCIASIS

A disease such as onchocerciasis can be brought under control either by the direct treatment of sufferers using drugs or by the physical separation of the human and insect hosts of the parasite, or by interrupting the chain of transmission by the elimination of the vector fly.

Only two drugs are at all suitable for the treatment of the human host, diethylcarbamezine (DEC) which is highly active against the microfilariae but does not destroy the adult worms, and suramin which kills the adult worms but has only a limited effect on the microfilaria. Unfortunately both drugs are of limited value in that they have fairly high inherent toxicities and in addition, may cause severe allergic reactions. With both treatment extends over several weeks. In the case of suramin, the drug is applied by a weekly injection for about six weeks, while DEC is taken daily in tablet form for several weeks, the dose rapidly being increased. Severe allergic reactions are commonplace and patients frequently fail to undergo the full, effective, course of treatment. Thus while neither drug is suitable for 'mass campaign' application by mobile teams occasionally visiting isolated peasant communities, they can be used to cure individuals who are in a position regularly to attend a properly staffed medical centre.

In Central America adult worms which frequently occur in palpable nodules on the scalps and upper parts of the body, are surgically removed. This nodulectomy undoubtedly reduces the incidence of eye lesions by cutting down the supply of microfilariae in the neighbourhood of the eye, but does not effectively reduce transmission (Duke 1971). Nodulectomy is not carried out on a large scale in West Africa where most nodules are on the lower parts of the body and many are inpalpable.

The disease can also be brought under control by physically separating man from fly. In West Africa, at least, one of the main aims of control is to allow the settlement of uninhabitated, but often fertile, river valleys; accordingly, breaking the man-fly link by the removal of man from the habitat of the fly is not normally an acceptable solution.

However, recently it was necessary as a matter of urgency to resettle Chadian refugees in a reasonably well-watered area of northern Cameroun. Unfortunately all potential reception areas proved to lie within onchocerciasis transmission zones. A compromise solution was suggested based on the proclivity of the older flies for biting very close to their breeding sites, and the fact that transmission, though widespread, did not appear to be intensive or to be leading to elevated blindness rates. The resettlement area was surveyed and zones a few kilometres distant from potential *S. damnosum* breeding sites determined (Walsh 1982). It is to be hoped that sufficient groundwater can be found in such zones to reduce the contact of the settlers with the riverine habitats favoured by the flies (see below).

Large scale control of onchocerciasis thus depends mainly on the control of populations of the transmitting flies. We know little of the population dynamics of any *Simulium* species. However, the basic details of the life-cycle of *S. damnosum* are known. If we assume a generation time (from egg to egg) of 21 days, that each female fly lays a single egg batch of 400 eggs, a half destined to yield female flies, and that there is no mortality, then one egg will give rise to 40,000 egg-laying females in 63 days. This is by no means an exceptional rate of fecundity for an insect.

The only *S. damnosum* population not subjected to an important level of invasion, or to interference by man, which has been studied for a lengthy period is located in the forested Volta Region of eastern Ghana. Over a four year period, this population proved to be remarkably stable with a maximum month to month increase of only 1.4 fold. Thus instead of 40,000 females produced from one egg (given no mortality) after 63 days the maximum production observed was two females. This population was reduced to an average of less than one fly biting man per day in August 1981, following two months of treatment of the (breeding) river with insecticide. It rose to nearly nine flies per day after one month without insecticidal control, an 11.3 fold increase. Thus after 63 days one egg could be expected to give rise to about 130 female flies, instead of the theoretically possible 40,000 female flies.

Clearly such populations are held down by a series of abiotic and biotic mortality factors. The most conspicuous controlling factor, at least for savanna populations, is the water regime. Sharp changes in water level are inimical to *S. damnosum*. Spates result in the washing away of egg masses and larvae, the churning up of rocks and boulders of the stream bottom and the destruction of vegetation, on which eggs, larvae and pupae are attached. Possibly flies which may not be able to emerge successfully through several metres of water are drowned. Such spates are a regular wet season feature of most rivers and streams in the savanna regions, even influencing rivers as large as the Niger itself. Rapid declines in water level also have adverse effects, eggs and pupae become stranded and dehydrated, larvae are forced to detach and drift in the current where they are very vulnerable to predation by fish. In the dry season many rivers and streams cease to flow entirely and others are much reduced in size. This greatly diminishes the number of potential breeding places for *S. damnosum*. For example, in the WHO Onchocerciasis Control Programme area it is estimated that while there are over 23,000 km of river suitable for *Simulium* breeding during the wet season, this is reduced to less than 8,000 km in March, a reduction of nearly two-thirds in riverine length with a far greater reduction in volume of water discharged.

The relative long-term stability of *S. damnosum* populations, however, must rest with the operation of density dependent (biotic) factors. About these very little is known, though a wide variety of parasites and predators which attack *S. damnosum* has been identified. Among those which have been studied in some detail are the mermithid worms (*Nematoda*) which parasitise *Simulium* larvae, and in some cases certainly exert a powerful controlling effect on larval populations. Hopes that these worms could be used as biological agents in control campaigns have not so far materialised and must await the development of *in vitro* mass production techniques. It is against this background of natural control that vector population reduction to limit the transmission of onchocerciasis must be carried out.

Currently we know too little about the behaviour of adult *S. damnosum* to plan a large scale attack on this stage of the life-cycle. Small isolated populations are likely to yield to this type of approach and the 'trapping-out' technique have yet to be tried against *S. damnosum*. Our lack of knowledge of the resting sites of the adult flies and their wide dispersal and low concentration has so far precluded the use of residual insecticides. Nevertheless, there is little doubt that adulticides will be brought into use against *S. damnosum* especially in restricted areas at known oviposition sites where despite good control of larval populations, biting flies remain numerous owing to the infiltration of adult migrants from nearby untreated rivers.

10.6.1 *Reducing man-fly contact*

There are several basic ways in which man-fly contact can be reduced, in the absence of direct reduction in the populations of either, or both, species. For the individual there is the possibility of dressing to avoid the bites of the vector or of using repellents. Repellents are not really a practical proposition in tropical climates. Exposure to fly bites pre-supposes activity out-of-doors, and such activity in *S. damnosum* habitats inevitably leads to a high rate of perspiration. Thus repellent application is required not less than once every two hours.

In savanna areas, less so in the forest, *S. damnosum* has a strong tendency to bite below the knee. The wearing of long trousers and solid footwear with socks confers a considerable degree of protection as *S. damnosum*, unlike the tsetse fly, does not bite through fabrics. Farmers frequently work wearing long trousers and some sort of footware but usually there is exposed skin as no socks are worn and footwear is most often of the sandal type. Some workers protect themselves adequately but this is usually in response to the nuisance of very high biting rates rather than to a fear of infection. The wearing of suitable footware and socks should be encouraged. In any case it is likely to increase in communities which become more affluent.

Communities can also avoid excessive man-fly contact in several ways. Ideally no village should be sited beside a major breeding rapid. Even with good insecticidal control such breeding places attract flies moving through the area. A displacement of as little as 5 km confers a considerable degree of protection and even 1 or 2 km displacement from a minor breeding site is valuable. As already mentioned this approach is being applied in the northern Cameroun resettlement.

The provision of domestic water supply points, greatly to be desired for the control of many other diseases, would help to lessen the dependence of the community on the river and thus should greatly reduce man-fly contact.

Probably the women and very young children would reap most benefit. The reduction of onchocerciasis transmission during early childhood may well prove to be the single most worthwhile effect of any control campaign which falls short of interrupting transmission.

Despite these useful local solutions to the problem of onchocerciasis transmission in West Africa the only regularly applied, large scale method of controlling onchocerciasis has been the use of insecticide to kill the larval stages of the vector fly. The reasons for choosing the larval stages of the vector as the target for control operations are that:

a) They are concentrated in very limited habitats in fast flowing rivers and large streams (in contrast to the adults which are widely dispersed);

b) They are relatively small, filter feeding animals which are especially sensitive to very small quantities of insecticide.

In fact the first attempt to control *S. damnosum* in West Africa (Taufflieb 1955) was made against the adult stages in the Mayo Kebbi valley, Chad. This campaign failed for various reasons and all subsequent large scale control operations have been aimed at the larvae of *S. damnosum*.

The first carefully monitored control study was made at Abuja, Northern Nigeria from 1955 to 1961 in an area of 3120 km^2. DDT was applied from 10 treatment points on 4 rivers, once weekly for a period of 12 weeks each wet season. Results were assessed by the direct observation of the effects of insecticide treatment on larval populations and by the regular standardised capture of adults biting man (Davies *et al.* 1962). This study was carried out to determine the feasibility, and cost, of a limited control programme undertaken within an area not isolated from other uncontrolled areas from which flies could readily invade. Control resulted in about a 90% reduction in biting flies but transmission was not interrupted (Davies 1968). Whether this reduction in biting fly populations greatly influenced the occurrence of onchocercal blindness has not been established (Rodgers 1973).

In 1961 control of *S. damnosum* populations, again using DDT as a larvicide, commenced in the area surrounding the site of the proposed Dam at Kainji on the Niger river. The aim, which was attained, was to protect the work force and their families, as mentioned earlier (Walsh 1970).

During the 1960's the entomologists of ORSTOM carried out a series of control operations in the rivers of S W Upper Volta, E Mali and N Ivory Coast using DDT as a larvicide. These operations were funded by the Fonds Européen Developpement (FED). Experiments on treatment technique and with ways of assessing the impact of larval control measures were conducted (Le Berre *et al.* 1965, Le Berre 1968).

In the Farako district of the Sikasso arondissement (Mali) control began in October 1962 and continued until March 1964. There were interruptions in 1964 and 1965 but since January 1966 the control campaign has continued uninterrupted (since February 1975 under the aegis of the OCP). It is probable that in the early years there was about

80% reduction in biting fly populations, followed by almost complete absence of transmission since 1975 when application of insecticide by helicopter was introduced. This entomological control has led to the reduction of onchocerciasis to a level at which it is no longer a public health problem and at which the disease appears to be dying out (Prost 1977). By 1976 the occurrence of microfilariae in the eye, and consequently the risk of blindness had been greatly reduced (Thylefors & Rolland 1977).

In 1968 USAID together with OCCGE and WHO sponsored a meeting on the feasibility of onchocerciasis control (WHO 1969). The meeting concluded that control of the disease was technically feasible and depended on the reduction of *S. damnosum* populations by means of larvicides applied by aircraft. This meeting led to the establishment of a mission to report on the setting up of an onchocerciasis control programme in the Volta River Basin. The mission reported (WHO 1973) in December 1973 to a group of seven participating West African countries, interested International Agencies (IBRD, FAO, UNDP, WHO), and a number of potential donor organisations and governments. It was agreed to set up a Special Onchocerciasis Fund administered by the World Bank (IBRD) to pay for an Onchocerciasis Control Programme in the Volta River Basin areas for which WHO agreed to act as executing agency. This Programme (the OCP) came into being in January 1974 and began control operations in early 1975.

10.7 THE ONCHOCERCIASIS CONTROL PROGRAMME IN THE VOLTA RIVER BASIN AREA

10.7.1 *Management structures and funding*

General supervision of the policies to be adopted in planning and executing the OCP rests with the seven participating West African countries, a group of about a dozen donor agencies and governments, and the four responsible International Agencies which meet annually as the Joint Programme Committee (JCP). WHO which acts as the executing agency, meets about four times a year with the other responsible agencies (FAO, IBRD and UNDP) in the Committee of Sponsoring Agencies (CSA). In each participating country there is a statutory National Onchocerciasis Committee which usually consists of eight to twelve members from the ministries most actively concerned. The chairman and executive officers of each of these committees meet together annually. This meeting of the National Onchocerciasis Committees is attended by the Programme Director and his senior staff.

To provide intellectual and scientific support the WHO and JPC are advised by an Expert Advisory Committee (EAC) which comprises a group of twelve eminent entomologists, medical doctors and socio-economists experienced in relevant disciplines, meeting at least once annually to consider the progress of the OCP. An additional statutory committee is the Ecological Group, consisting of five experts in the fields of hydrobiology and toxicology. They also meet at least once a year to consider all matters pertaining to environmental protection. At least one member of the EG also sits on the EAC and representatives of both groups may attend the JPC. Both committees submit annual written reports to the JPC, through the CSA.

In addition to these statutory bodies, informal working groups are convened by WHO from time to time. In these meetings WHO obtains the advice of foremost experts on subjects of importance for the satisfactory execution of the Programme. The EAC is usually represented on such working groups, and may indeed request that they be set up to consider relevant problems.

The World Bank (IBRD) has responsibility for obtaining funds for the programme. The first funding phase covered the six year period 1974-1979, the budget for which, allowing for inflation, was estimated in 1973 to be $53 million. This money was obtained from a group of sixteen donor countries and agencies. Actual expenditure was $53.6 million. In 1978 the WHO carried out an internal evaluation of the programme and made recommendations concerning the activities and costing of the second funding phase. Total costs for the six year period 1980-85 were estimated as $130 million. Considering the worsening international financial climate this request for funding received a very favourable response with pledges of substantial long term support forthcoming. However in 1978 the donors did not feel able to incorporate the Nigerian National Onchocerciasis Control Programme within the pre-existing OCP and the proposed programme in the Senegambia Basin was treated as a separate scheme. By December 1981 the budget for the 1980-85 period had been revised to $109.5 million. However firm pledges from the donors for the whole of this amount have not so far been forthcoming.

10.7.2 Aims and duration of OCP

The basic aim of the Programme is to reduce the vector fly population to a level at which the transmission of the disease is interrupted or, at least, to one at which the parasite is only sustained at a very low level in the human population. It has been stated that it is sufficient to reduce the impact of onchocerciasis to a sufficiently low level that it no longer represents either a public health problem or an obstacle to socio-economic development (WHO 1978). However, in these circumstances which may imply a prevalence rate over 20% it is difficult to see how vector control activities ever could be safely curtailed in the absence of drugs to control the parasites.

Owing to the great length of reproductive life of *O.volvulus*, trasmission needs to be greatly curtailed for somewhere between 11 and 18 years. Should control cease earlier a reservoir of reproductively active parasites would remain in people infected before control was implemented. Given the great migratory ability of the vector there is little doubt that the whole zone formerly controlled, virtually irrespective of its size, would be recolonized by the vector. This would occur probably during the first post-control wet season, in numbers equalling the pre-control populations. Indeed numbers might be higher than in pre-control conditions, should some of the parasites or predators normally preying on the *S. damnosum* population have been eliminated during the insecticiding campaign.

10.7.3 *The OCP area*

The strategy of the OCP is firmly based on the lessons learnt during the FED campaign and of those at Kainji and Abuja. The sole means of control to date, is the weekly application of larvicide to the rivers which are suitable for breeding *S. damnosum*. To reduce the likelihood of reinfestation from adjacent untreated areas the scale of operations greatly exceeds that of any previous blackfly control campaign. The area originally chosen consisted of 654,000 km² of the Guinea and Sudan savannas in seven West African countries, Mali, Ivory Coast, Upper Volta, Ghana, Togo, Benin and Niger. The whole savanna portion of the Volta River basin is included. The northern boundary of the OCP is the natural northern limit of the vector fly and the disease. To west and east the boundaries of the scheme are political and have no ecological merit. They are the Ivory Coast frontier with Guinea and the Benin frontier with Nigeria. To the south the boundary was set at what was then considered

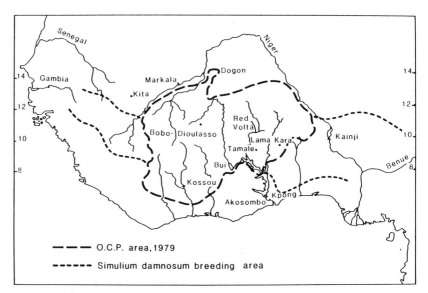

Figure 86. *Simulium damnosum* breeding areas and OCP (Onchocersiasis Control Pro-gramme) area in 1979.

284

to be the southern limit of the savanna (severe) form of the disease. Following new evidence about the distribution and migration of savanna forms of the fly this boundary has been moved farther south in Ivory Coast to incorporate the Baoulé gap. This added 110,000 km^2 to the area covered by the Programme (Fig. 86). An additional extension southward in Ghana, Togo and Benin covering 100,000 km^2 is intended.

10.7.4 Entomological evaluation

Before undertaking the control campaign an entomological evaluation network had to be established. This at present consists of 25 laboratories (sub-sectors) scattered throughout the seven countries of the Programme area. From each laboratory three or four teams using all-terrain vehicles, carry out regular series of weekly visits to potential breeding rivers to check for the presence of the immature stages of *S. damnosum* and to read the river gauges. In addition two-man teams make a series of 11 hour catches of flies coming to bite, using themselves as bait. In an average wet season month, flies are caught at just over 300 different locations, at most of which one full day catch is made each week.

Flies so caught are either preserved directly in 80% ethanol for possible taxonomic studies or are kept alive in ice boxes, transported to the laboratory and dissected as soon as possible. It is possible by examining their ovaries to determine whether they are old enough to have taken a previous bloodmeal, and if so, a check for the presence of the developmental stages of *O. volvulus* the causative organism of onchocerciasis is made. In addition the presence of other filarial worms, and organisms such as mermithid worms, which may be pathogenic to the flies, is recorded.

10.7.5 Control activities

10.7.5.1 *The choice of insecticide.* Any insecticide intended for use in *Simulium* control programmes at the present day
a) must have a very low toxicity to vertebrate animals, especially fish
b) must have a low persistence in the environment
c) must not accumulate in the food chain, and
d) should have a relatively low toxicity to aquatic invertebrate organisms while being active against *Simulium* larvae at low concentrations.

This is asking a great deal, and such an insecticide is likely to be hard to find and expensive. Very careful consideration was given and numerous field trials were carried out, before it was decided to use an emulsifiable concentrate of temephos, an organo-phosphorus compound, in the OCP campaign. This material, as formulated by Procida, proved satisfactory on all counts as well as retaining its effectiveness after prolonged storage in the harsh conditions of tropical Africa. It is of course, many times more expensive than DDT which, though highly suitable on most counts, had to be rejected owing to its persistence in the environment and greater toxicity to non-target organisms.

10.7.5.2 *Methods of applying insecticide.* Experience of control in the much smaller areas covered by the FED campaign and that at Kainji had shown convincingly that to operate on the scale proposed for the OCP would require the use of aircraft both for survey work and for the weekly application of larvicide. Trials carried out in 1973 and 1974 indicated that while the larger more open rivers could be treated using slow-flying fixed-wing aeroplanes, for the smaller and more wooded streams helicopters would be essential. These would also be invaluable for prospecting new areas and for checking the efficacy of control activities.

It was estimated that the control campaign would eventually require the services of at least two fixed-wing aircraft and six to eight helicopters. Initially consideration was given to the purchase and operation of aircraft by WHO but it was wisely decided to put this work out to international tender thereby obtaining the services of an experienced aerial contractor with an international reputation. To ensure the selection of a satisfactory contractor an extremely demanding contract was drawn up.

10.7.5.3 *Aerial operations.* The aerial operation has to be geared to the biology of *S. damnosum.* As the insecticide only kills the larval stages and has no effect on the eggs or pupae of *S. damnosum* the length of larval life determines the frequency of application of insecticide. In West African conditions, with water temperatures usually between 24 and 32°C, the larval stages may be completed in 8 or 9 days, sometimes even less. Therefore, it was decided that insecticide should be applied on a weekly basis where needed.

Treatments began in February 1975 in SW Upper Volta, E Mali and NE Ivory Coast, and spread to central Upper Volta and N Ghana in 1976, and to Mali, east of Bamako and N Togo, N Benin, E Upper Volta and the Niger Republic west of the Niger river in 1977. During 1978 and 1979 control was extended into southern Ivory Coast. The scale of operations (Table 36) can be appreciated from the annual totals of hours flown and

Table 36. Flight hours and insecticide use for whole Onchocerciasis Control Programme area.

Year	Hours flown Helicopter	Fixed wing	Insecticide dispensed (litres)
1974	144	104	3570
1975	2783	541	76000
1976	4265	614	129950
1977	5358	1026	155620
1978	5356	1204	215880
1979	5504	1371	263380
1980	5752	1056	184520
1981	6186	1008	221950*
1982	5655	955	402000*

* In addition to temephos, includes chlorphoxim and *Bacillus thuringiensis* H14.

286

quantities of insecticide used. This aerial operation which at maximum has resulted in the insecticide treatment of about 18000 km of river per week during the wet season and about 7500 km per week during the dry season is a major logistic exercise. Both the helicopters and fixed-wing aeroplanes so far used (Bell Jet Ranger 206B, and Hughes 500 C helicopter and the Pilatus Porter PC6 fixed-wing aircraft) have endurances of about 2½ hours. This means that a refuelling stop must be made about once every two hours.

To avoid excessive, and costly, ferry flying the aircraft fleet is split into halves. One half is based at Bobo-Dioulasso in SW Upper Volta and the other at Lama Kara in Togo. In addition there are over 100 fuel and insecticide dumps scattered over the OCP area. The stocking of these dumps is a carefully planned exercise. Many are in extremely isolated places served by roads which become impassable soon after the first rains fall. Should stocks run out at any such landing site, which cannot be re-provisioned during the wet season, expensive ferry flights may be necessary for refuelling and loading with insecticide.

During the life of the Programme techniques for applying the insecticide have been improved and the amount of control work has been reduced at the heart of the area. The continual increase in activity shown in Table 36 reflects the increasing responsibilities of the Programme. That control per unit area has been reduced is shown by the figures for the Phase II area which covers most of northern Ghana and Central Upper Volta (see Table 37). The number of flying hours required to achieve a satisfactory result has steadily declined since the start of operations in 1976. The amount of insecticide used, has also declined, though erratically. This latter feature is inevitable given the sharp differences in rainfall and run-off from one year to the next.

The aerial operation is not a routine exercise repeated unchanged week after week. In fact each week the rivers to be treated are determined on the basis of the entomological and hydrological information obtained by the 25 sub-sectors. Each is linked by radio to the HQ of the Programme in Ouagadougou, and to the two aerial operation bases. Each weekend the Sub-Sectors pass their information concerning active breeding of S.

Table 37. Flight hours and insecticide use in Phase 2 of the Onchocerciasis Control Programme.

Year	Hours flown Helicopter	Fixed wing	Insecticide dispensed (litres)
1976	1410	224	33611
1977	859	200	17524
1978	614	223	18634
1979	569	179	21346
1980	452	55	9609
1981	383	97	12358
1982	338	41	10198

damnosum, the numbers and ages of biting flies and river discharge levels to the HQ and aerial operation bases. Using this information, and the interpretations of the evaluation staff, the aerial operations staff of the Programme prepare flight plans giving details of insecticide treatments and on Monday afternoons brief the contractors' pilots. On Tuesday the treatment aircraft set out on what is usually a three or four day circuit of treatment flights. In the wet season treatment is relatively simple, though the rivers to be treated are numerous. Insecticide is dropped into rivers at a rate of about 0.05 parts per million based on a ten minute period of discharge and is distributed and carried up to 50 km by the rapidly flowing waters of the larger rivers. In the dry season river discharge levels are very low and each breeding rapid has to be treated individually with the insecticide carefully distributed across the width of the stream. Dosage rates are then usually double those effective in the wet season.

10.7.6 *Results of OCP*

10.7.6.1 *Entomological evaluation.* The results of this insecticide campaign are assessed qualitatively by the examination of the treated rivers for the presence of aquatic stages of the vector and quantitatively by standardised catches of biting flies a sample of which are dissected to investigate the proportion carrying infective stages of the parasite.

Details of these entomological methods and results are given by Walsh et al. (1979). In brief it can be stated that to date control over approximately 80% of the original Programme area has been such that transmission of the disease appears virtually to have ceased. Difficulties in the other 20% of the area arise from the invasion from surrounding uncontrolled savanna areas of disease carrying flies. This has affected parts of Ivory Coast, Mali, Togo and Benin.

10.7.6.2 *Problems of migration.* Although the Programme was planned in the knowledge that *S. damnosum* was a highly migratory insect it was assumed that maximum movement of individual insects would be of the order of 150 km and that the flies involved would be predominantly recently emerged individuals (WHO 1973). There would, in effect, be making an 'exodus flight' before taking their first bloodmeal. They would thus be capable of repopulating a cleared area but would not introduce the disease from outside. In the event migratory movements by savanna fly populations covered much greater distances. There is strong circumstantial evidence for substantial numbers of flies travelling 400 km with the aid of prevailing winds, and for smaller numbers travelling at least 600 km from their breeding places (Walsh et al. 1981).

Of greater epidemiological importance, than the distance travelled, is the fact that the flies involved are older parous individuals. It is now clear that flies continue their movements after having taken one or more bloodmeals and becoming infected with *O. volvulus*. Thus the cleared area is not just repopulated by flies but also by the parasite (Garms et al.

288

1979). Fortunately these older flies tend to seek bloodmeals very close to their oviposition sites (S.Λ. Sowah pers. comm.). So that even in reinvaded areas onchocerciasis seems to be declining in most communities.

10.7.6.3 *The problems of resistance.* In the Ivory Coast a more serious problem has arisen in the southern extension added to the original area. This is the occurrence of resistance to temephos in the forest populations of *S. damnosum.* This resistance first became noticeable in March 1980 in the lower Bandama river south of the Taabo dam. Resistance soon spread to other river systems in Ivory Coast and temephos was replaced by chlorphoxim, another organophosphorus compound, in this area. However, by mid-1981 resistance to chlorphoxim was noted. By December this resistance to chlorphoxim had spread throughout the area already demonstrating temephos resistance and chlorphoxim was withdrawn from use. Laboratory tests have shown that populations of *S. damnosum* resistant to both temephos and chlorphoxim are also resistant to several other organo-phosphorus insecticides.

From February 1981 a formulation of *Bacillus thuringiensis* serotype H14 produced by Sandoz has been used on a small scale. This material should class as an 'insecticide of biological origin' rather than as a 'bio-control agent'. It is used in the same manner as a conventional insecticide, being applied afresh each week, and having no capacity to propagate itself in the environment. Its great advantage is that the toxin is remarkably specific and seems to have little or no effect on most orders of insects and none on other classes of animals. Unfortunately, at present, the formulation contains 1% only of toxin. Treatment rates are accordingly high at 1.5 to 1.6 ppm (against the temephos rate of 0.1 ppm). This poses a major logistic problem for the aerial operations team, for during the wet season some river treatments would require quantities of insecticide not far short of the maximum payload for the helicopter. In addition the cost of such large quantities of formulation would be prohibitive.

10.7.6.4 *Epidemiological evaluation of OCP.* The initial evaluation of the OCP had to be entomological, not only in order to provide data on which to manage the day to day operations but also to provide a short-term method of assessing the validity of the Programme for participating and donor countries, and agencies. This is because with a disease such as onchocerciasis, the causative organism of which is so long lived, changes in the epidemiological situation consequent on alterations in the level of transmission need some time to become apparent. Nevertheless the ultimate aim of the Programme is disease control, not insect control per se.

To make an assessment of the level of disease control the Programme has an Epidemiological Evaluation Unit staffed by Medical Parasitologists and Ophthalmologists. Before control commenced in each area the populations of certain villages were examined for the presence of *O. volvulus.* Where present, an estimate of the parasite load of each individual was made by counting the microfilariae in a skin biopsy. In all, over 100000 people in 425 villages have been examined in a pre-control survey. About 17% of these people were given a detailed ophthalmological examination. Of the villages examined over half have been revisited since control began, some on several occasions.

Of paramount importance in determining the rate of transmission is the fate of children born since the start of vector control. Of 88 villages in the Phase I and II areas (controlled since 1975 and 1976) which have recently been resurveyed 30 (34%) had no children under five infected with onchocerciasis either before or after vector control operations began. In 50 (57%) villages the prevalence rate had been reduced to zero; and the remaining 8 (9%) villages the prevalence rate had fallen, though some transmission must have occurred since the start of the control operations.

In the population as a whole the overall prevalence rates also appear to be falling as does the parasite load. From six villages which were revisited in 1980, 1098 people over the age of 5 years had been given detailed eye examinations in 1975. During the re-survey 940 people were so examined. In this short period (5 years of vector control) there had been an overall reduction of 28% in the prevalence of ocular onchocerciasis (OPC data provided at the Expert Advisory Committee meeting in October 1981).

10.7.7 *Environmental aspects of the OCP*

Uncontrolled onchocerciasis has a major environmental impact. It reduces the pressure of human populations in many riverine areas. In some valleys it may possibly result in a total lack of human settlement. It is probable that the settlement pattern in Northern Guinea Savanna areas usually reflects the action of a complex mosaic of factors, political, agricultural and medical. Onchocerciasis may play a by no means negligible role, though historically both sleeping sickness and cerebospinal meningitis have been at least as important.

The effect of vector control is to drastically alter the current settlement pattern. This will most likely lead to dispersal of upland populations with possible improvement in soil conditions. However, at the same time it will increase the carrying capacity of the land with the increased human population more closely associated with medium sized savanna rivers. This is likely to result in riverine forest degradation, increased speed of run off and gulley erosion. The flow period of rivers denuded of riverine forest is reduced and the complete drying up of surface waters becomes more common. The amount of food material falling into the rivers from the canopy forest is reduced, as are the chances of dry season survival of many aquatic organisms. In the long term the aquatic environment becomes impoverished and fish catches inevitably drop, even in the absence of over-fishing. These are long term changes and depend on local development initiatives. There is little or nothing that the OCP can do to influence the course of these events.

The OCP affects the aquatic environment in a direct and obvious way by deliberately introducing insecticide into the riverine habitat. This activity has been monitored very carefully by teams of independent hydrobiologists in several of the participating countries who regularly carry out a standardized sampling programme to obtain quantitative data on the invertebrate and fish populations (Lévêque et al. 1977). The data are stored in the WHO HQ computer and have been subjected to sophisticated analysis by biologists at Salford University, UK and by ORSTOM hydrobiologists. The Ecological Group has regularly reviewed the data and the analyses made.

As already mentioned the choice of temephos as the operational insecticide was made after many field trials. It has proved to be an exceptional insecticide and the Ecological Group in its 1981 report, was able to conclude that (1) the effects of temephos on the invertebrate fauna were ecologically acceptable, (2) although there may have been some reduction in invertebrate organisms at *S. damnosum* breeding sites no disequilibrium occurred under normal application conditions, (3) there was little evidence of disappearance of invertebrate species, and (4) no fish mortality or any other notable change in fish populations had been recorded after temephos applications.

Unfortunately chlorphoxim appeared to have a much greater impact on the invertebrate fauna at least in the dry season. However, its limited use during the 1981 wet season, following the development of resistance to temephos in several Ivory Coast rivers, led to no marked deterioration of the habitat. The use of *Bacillus thuringiensis* H14 holds out the prospect of even more selective elimination of the target species than is achieved by temephos.

It is intended that the regular monitoring of the aquatic environment will continue throughout the life of the OCP, with particular attention being paid to the long-term health of the fish populations, and to the environmental screening of new insecticides which may be developed for operational use.

10.7.8 *Conclusions arising from the OCP*

There is little doubt that the vector control operations are bringing about a regression of onchocerciasis, and if they can be maintained for a further 6–10 years (which should be possible given adequate effective insecticides) will result in the elimination of onchocerciasis from a very large area of West Africa. However, the problem of reinvasion, especially by infected flies, from uncontrolled areas remains to be solved. Owing to doubts, arising from this problem, about the long term situation, in 1979 the Director General of WHO established an Independent Commission chaired by Dr C E Gordon Smith, Dean of the London School of Hygiene & Tropical Medicine. The Commission reported that to date the Programme had been successful and should be continued. However, given the problem of reinvasion, the Commission felt that maintenance of the present Programme boundaries would be difficult or impossible in the long term. It concluded that the Programme would have to expand westwards, the direction from which the principle reinvasion is occurring.

10.8 THE FUTURE OF ONCHOCERCIASIS CONTROL IN AFRICA

At present the OCP in the Volta River Basin covers an area of 764,000 km^2. Extension into a further 100,000 km^2 of southern Ghana, Togo and Benin is planned and costed, and awaits the availability of a satisfactory operational alternative insecticide to temephos. The JPC has asked the Director of the OCP to provide concrete operational plans and costings for a proposed extension of control activities into Western Mali, Guinea, Senegal and the savanna zone of Sierra Leone. The area covered by this 'Senegambia' scheme is 430,000 km^2. In the east the government of the Federal Republic of Nigeria has decided on a strategy for onchocerciasis control and is currently seeking to recruit the necessary expertise internationally. This programme can be expected to cover an area of about 600,000 km^2.

In the United Republic of Cameroun ORSTOM entomologists are carrying out preliminary investigations in the Vina-Pende-Logone Basin, with a view to the development of an onchocerciasis control programme embracing parts of Chad and the Central African Republic, as well as Cameroun.

All these programmes ought to be attainable at a lower cost per unit area covered than that of the OCP, providing account is taken of the lessons learnt in the last few years. However, more time should have been given to assess the true impact of the OCP in the Volta River Basin. Unfortunately there is little doubt that many of the same mistakes will be repeated owing to the fact that technical considerations count for little in comparison with political considerations.

Nevertheless the control of onchocerciasis in contiguous programmes covering over 1,800,000 km^2 offers a tremendous challenge and equivalent opportunity for altering patterns of rural development in the river valleys of the Guinea and Sudan Savanna zones of West Africa.

10.9 REFERENCES

Bradley, A.K. 1972. The effects of disease on rural economy, social structure and settlement. Unpublished mimeographed document, WHO/ONCHO/72.93.

Bradley, A.K. 1976. Effects of onchocerciasis on settlement in the Middle Hawal Valley, Nigeria. *Trans. R. Soc. trop. Med. Hyg.* 70: 225–229.

Buchanan, K.M. & J.C. Pugh 1951. *Land and people in Nigeria*. London; University of London Press.

Budden, F.H. 1956. The epidemiology of onchocerciasis in Northern Nigeria. *Trans. R. Soc. trop. Med. Hyg.* 50: 366–378.

Crosskey, R.W. 1981. A review of *Simulium damnosum* s. l. and human onchocerciasis in Nigeria, with special reference to geographical distribution and the development of a Nigerian Control Campaign. *Tropenmed. Parasit.* 32: 2–16.

Davies, J.B., R.W. Crosskey, M.R.L. Johnston. & M.E. Crosskey 1962. The control of *Simulium damnosum* at Abuja, Northern Nigeria. *Bull. Wld Hlth Org.* 27: 491–510.

Davies, J.B. 1968. The *Simulium* control scheme at Abuja, Northern Nigeria, and its effect on the prevalence of Onchocerciasis in the area. *Bull. Wld Hlth Org.* 39: 187–207.

Duke, B.O.L. 1971. Onchocerciasis. *Brit. Med. Bull.* 28: 66–71.

Duke, B.O.L. 1975. The differential dispersal of nulliparous and parous *Simulium damnosum*. *Tropenmed. Parasit.* 26: 88–97.

Duke, B.O.L. & J. Anderson 1972. A comparison of the lesions produced in the cornea of the rabbit eye by microfilariae of the forest and Sudan-Savanna strains of *Onchocerca volvulus* from Cameroun. *Tropenmed. Parasit.* 23: 354–368.

Garms, R., J.F. Walsh & J.B. Davies 1979. Studies on the reinvasion of the Onchocerciasis Control Programme in the Volta River Basin by *Simulium damnosum* s. 1. with empahsis on the South-Western areas. *Tropenmed. Parasit.* 30: 345–362.

Glover, P.E. & P.J. Aitchison 1970. Some causes of depopulation in Northern Nigeria. *Nigerian Field.* 35: 12–28.

Hunter, J.M. 1966. River blindness in Nangodi, Northern Ghana: a hypothesis of cyclical advance and retreat. *Geogr. Rev.* 56: 398–416.

Le Berre, R. 1966. Contribution à l'étude biologique et écologique de *Simulium damnosum* Theobald, 1903 (*Diptera, Simuliidae*). *Mémoires ORSTOM.* 17.

Le Berre, R. 1968. Bilan sommaire pour 1967 de lutte contre le vecteur de l'onchocercose. *Méd. Afr. Noire.* 15: 71–72.

Le Berre, R., M. Ovazza. & E. Juge 1965. Resultats d'une campagne larvicide contre *Simulium damnosum* Theobald (*Diptera, Simuliidae*) en Afrique de l'ouest. *Proc. XII Cong. Ent. London 1964* (Section 12).

Lévêque, C., M. Odei & M. Pugh Thomas 1977. The Onchocerciasis Control Programme and the monitoring of its effect on the riverine biology of the Volta River Basin. In F.H. Perring & K. Mellanby, (eds.), *Ecological Effects of Pesticides.* Linnean Society Symp. Series 5. London: Academic Press.

Prost, A. 1977. Situation dans un foyer d'Onchocercose du Mali apréz treize ans de controle anti- Simulidien. I. Aspects parasitologiques. *Ann. Soc. belge Med. trop.* 57: 569–575.

Prost, A., A. Rougemont & M.S. Omar 1980. Caractères épidémiologiques, cliniques et biologiques des onchocercoses de savane et de forêt en Afrique occidentale. *An. Parasit. Hum. Comp.* 55: 347–355.

Rodgers, F.C. 1973. The *Simulium* control scheme at Abuja, North Nigeria, and its effect on the prevalence of ocular onchocerciasis. *Trans R. Soc. trop. Med. Hyg.* 67: 225–237.

Rolland, A. 1972. Onchocerciasis in the village of Saint Pierre: an unhappy experience of repopulation in an uncontrolled endemic area. *Trans. R. Soc. trop. Med. Hyg.* 66: 913–915.

Taufflieb, R. 1955. Une campagne de lutte contre *Simulium damnosum* au Mayo Kebbi. *Bull. Soc. Path. exot.* 48: 564–576.

Thylefors, B. & A. Rolland 1977. Situation dans un foyer d'Onchocercose du Mali aprez treize ans de controle anti- Simulidien. 2 Aspects oculaires. *Ann. Soc. belge. Med. trop.* 57: 577–582.

Vajime, C.G. & R.W. Dunbar 1975. Chromosomal identification of eight species of the subgenus *Edwardsellum* near and including *Simulium (Edwardsellum) damnosum* Theobald *(Diptera: Simuliidae).* *Tropenmed Parasit.* 26: 111–138.

Vajime, C. & D. Quillévéré, 1978. The distribution of the *Simulium damnosum* complex in West Africa with particular reference to the Onchocerciasis Control Programme area. *Tropenmed. Parasit.* 29: 473–482.

Waddy, B.B. 1969. Prospects for the control of onchocerciasis in Africa with special reference to the Volta River Basin. *Bull. Wld Hlth Org.* 40: 843–858.

Walsh, J.F. 1970. The control of *Simulium damnosum* in the River Niger and its tributaries in relation to the Kainji Lake Research Project, covering the period 1961–1969. Unpublished mimeographed document. WHO/PD/70.4.

Walsh, J.F. 1982. Enquiry into the transmission of onchocerciasis in the proposed refugee resettlement area of the Poli Arrondissement (North Cameroon) with suggestions on the siting of villages. Unpublished mimeographed report to the United Nations High Commissioner for Refugees.

Walsh, J.F., J.B. Davies & R. Le Berre 1979. Entomological aspects of the first five years of the Onchocerciasis Control Programme in the Volta River Basin. *Tropenmed. Parasit.* 30: 328–344.

Walsh, J.F., J.B. Davies & R. Garms 1981. Further studies on the reinvasion of the Onchocerciasis Control Programme by *Simulium damonsum* s.l.: the effects of an extension of control activities into Southern Ivory Coast during 1979. *Tropenmed. Parasit.* 32: 269–273.

WHO 1969. Joint USAID/OCCGE/WHO Technical Meeting on the feasibility of Onchocerciasis control. Tunis, 1–8 July, 1968, Report. Unpublished mimeographed document, WHO/ONCHO/69. 75.

WHO 1973. Onchocerciasis control in the Volta River Basin area. Report of the Preparatory Assistance Mission to the Governments of Dahomey, Ghana, Ivory Coast, Mali, Niger, Togo and Upper Volta. Unpublished mimeographed document, WHO/OCP/73.1.

WHO 1978. Onchocerciasis Control Programme in the Volta River Basin Area. Evaluation Report Part I. Unpublished mimeographed document WHO/OCP/78.2.

WHO 1981. Senegambia Project. Onchocerciasis control in Guinea-Bissau, Mali, Senegal and Sierra Leone. Unpublished mimeographed document WHO/VBC/81.2.

D.S.BROWN
*Experimental Taxonomy Unit, British Museum
(Natural History), London*

C.A. WRIGHT†
†*Deceased 19th June 1983*

11

Schistosomiasis: Bilharzia

11.1 INTRODUCTION

Some 500 million people in 73 countries are estimated to be exposed to infection with schistosomiasis or bilharziasis (Iarotski & Davis 1981). This is the most closely water-related of all the major parasitic diseases. People can become infected only through direct physical contact with water and the parasite's life cycle can be completed only if its eggs subsequently fall into water. Schistosomiasis is common in the Niger basin and is found in every country within the West African region. The main courses of large rivers are not usually major sources of this disease, but waters sustained by them, through seasonal flooding, impoundment and extraction for irrigation, may be important transmission sites. Schistosomiasis is essentially an infection of rural and agricultural communities where the way of life encourages the contamination of inland waters with human excreta. Infection is readily acquired by fishermen, peasant farmers and agricultural workers in their daily work, women while washing clothes and drawing water, and by children while playing and swimming.

Schistosomes belong to the group of parasitic worms known as blood-flukes (members of the order Digenea). Like most other Digeneans they have two kinds of host in their life cycle, a definitive host (a vertebrate animal) and an intermediate host (a mollusc). Schistosomes use certain freshwater snails as their intermediate hosts.

Schistosomiasis of man occurs in Africa and the Middle East, the Neotropical region (Brazil, Venezuela, Surinam and certain Caribbean islands), and in the Far East (China, the Phillipines, Indonesia, with limited foci recently reported in the Mekong basin and in Malaya). The passing of bloody urine, an early indication of urinary schistosomiasis, is so common in boys about the age of puberty that it is accepted as part of their normal development in some African communities. Infected people are rarely killed by schistosomiasis, but it has varied and important effects on health and was selected by the World Health Organisation (WHO) for attention under the current Special Programme for Research and Training in Tropical Diseases.

In comparison with the winged insect vectors of trypanosomiasis and onchocerciasis, a snail harbouring schistosome larvae is sedentary. Thus transmission is highly focal; the carrier, in a literal sense, is man, and it is instructive to consider urinary schistosomiasis in Africa as a disease of snails carried by small boys (Wright 1981). There is no known reservoir of schistosomiasis of man in any non-human vertebrate in West Africa (though perhaps *S. curassoni* does exist as a zoonosis, see Section 11.2.2). Thus one obstacle to control presented by certain other diseases is lacking, but daunting problems are posed by the large reservoir of sub-clinical infections in man and the variety of the transmission sites, which range from small seasonally-filled pools to great man-made lakes. The advent of new, safe and efficacious schistosomicidal drugs has greatly improved prospects for effective chemotherapy in large communities of people (Webbe 1981). However, there is no immediate prospect of effective long-term control of schistosomiasis in West Africa, or elsewhere in the continent. On the contrary, it appears that prevalence and intensity of infection are generally increasing.

11.2 THE ORGANISMS INVOLVED

11.2.1 *Outline of the life cycle*

Adult schistosome worms are either male or female, unlike most other flukes which are hermaphrodite. Mature paired worms live in the blood vessels surrounding, according to species, either the intestine or the bladder of their definitive hosts. The life span of the worms is thought to be usually between three and eight years (though there are reports of 20 – 30 years). The eggs have a spine and work their way through the wall of the blood vessel, then through the tissues of the intestine or bladder and eventually are voided in either the host's faeces or urine. The egg is ready to hatch if it falls into water. Hatching will not occur in sea-water, though it can take place in dilute brackish water. The ciliated larva which emerges is known as a miracidium, and swims free in the water though it does not feed (Figure 87). A miracidium has a maximum swimming life of 12 to 24 hours, but it is in the first few hours that it appears to be most successful in locating and penetrating a snail suitable to serve as the intermediate host. The micracidium responds to light and temperature in ways which tend to bring it into the vicinity of a potential host, and the final stages of host-finding depend on responses to substances diffusing from the snail. Within the snail, the larva metamorphoses into a mother sporocyst, a sac-like organism from which daughter sporocysts eventually are liberated and migrate to the snail's digestive gland. Here the daughter sporocysts grow and each one produces a large number of another larval stage, the cercaria, which consists of a small body and a much larger muscular forked tail. Cercariae migrate through the snail's tissues to emerge into the water where they, like the miracidium, have a free-swimming life of

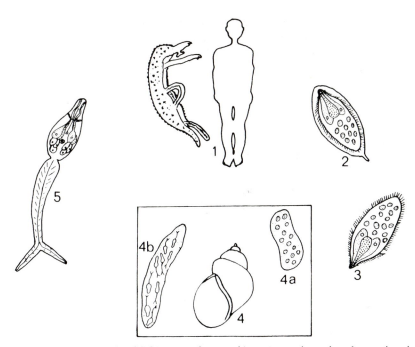

Figure 87. The life cycle of *Schistosoma haematobium*. Approximate lengths are given in brackets. 1: Paired adult worms (15 mm) live in man, the definitive host. 2: Egg (0.15 mm). 3: Miracidium. 4: Shell of freshwater snail (*Bulinus*) the intermediate host. 4a,b: Mother sporocyst and daughter sporocyst. 5: Cercaria (0.35 mm). From Wright (1981).

about one day. Cercariae of schistosomes infecting man are mostly shed from snails during the early afternoon, when water-contact activities by people tend to be high (Tayo et al. 1980). The time between penetration of a snail by a miracidium and emergence of the first cercariae is about one month, and thereafter cercariae continue to be shed throughout the life of the snail, which may continue for many months. Because of multiplication of the parasite within the snail, a single successful miracidium may produce several thousands of cercariae.

Cercariae do not need to be ingested by the vertebrate host, and invasion may occur anywhere on its surface, since the larvae are equipped to penetrate through unbroken skin. Soon after penetration by many schistosome cercariae a person may suffer from an irritating rash (though a similar 'cercarial dermatitis' can be produced by other kinds of trematode larvae which do not continue their development within the human body). On penetration the forked cercarial tail is shed and the parasites, now known as schistosomula, migrate through the circulatory and lymphatic systems to the lungs and thence to the liver, where they remain for some weeks, growing to maturity and pairing. Paired worms migrate to the veins of their final site, egg laying begins and the life cycle is complete. The time from cercarial penetration of the host until egg laying begins is about 2 – 3 months. It is commonly observed that most infected people carry few worms and only a small proportion are heavily infected; this phenomenon may be turned to advantage in strategies for disease control (see 11.5).

11.2.2 *Schistosoma species in West Africa*

There are two main schistosome parasites of man in West Africa. *S. mansoni* adults live in the intestinal blood vessels; the eggs have a pronounced postero-lateral spine and the larvae develop in snails of the genus *Biomphalaria*. This is the only schistosome parasite of man found in the Neotropics, to where it appears to have been introduced from Africa in the course of the slave-trade. *S. haematobium* adults (Figure 88) live in blood vessels surrounding the bladder, the eggs have a terminal spine and the larvae develop in snails of the genus *Bulinus*. Different strains of

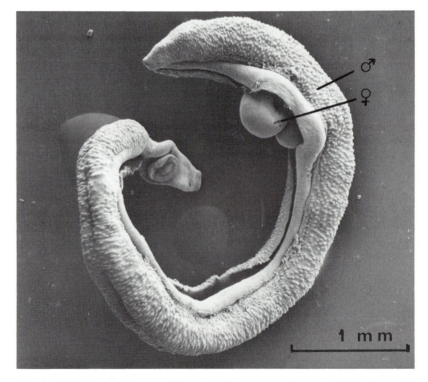

Figure 88. Paired mature worms of *S. haematobium*, somewhat contracted by preparation for the scanning electron microscope. A loop of the female is seen protruding from the ventral fold of the male.

298

this parasite are recognisable (see following section). *S. bovis* adults live in the intestinal blood vessels of cattle; the larvae develop in *Bulinus*. Also found in cattle, sheep and goats is *S. curassoni*, recently recognised as distinct from *S. bovis* and possibly infective to man (Southgate *et al.* 1984). *S. intercalatum*, which resembles *S. haematobium* but lives in the intestinal blood vessels of man, occurs in Zaire, Gabon and Cameroun, but has not been recorded with certainty in West Africa proper.

11.2.3. *Snails carrying schistosomes in West Africa*

From an approximate total of 60 species of freshwater snail found in West Africa, probably not more than 8 are intermediate hosts for schistosomes (Brown 1980). *Biomphalaria* is represented in West Africa by the species *B. camerunensis* and *B. pfeifferi*, of which the latter is by far the most abundant and widespread, and is the major intermediate host for *S. mansoni* (see Figure 89).

Relationships between *S. haematobium* and *Bulinus* are more complex, for there are representatives of three species-groups of these snails in West Africa and each group plays a part in the transmission of urinary schistosomiasis.

1. *B. forskali* group. *B. senegalensis* is widespread in the sahelian zone and is a proven host in the Gambia. *B. camerunensis* is restricted to southwest Cameroun, where it is a host in certain crater lakes. *B. forskali* itself, though found practically throughout West Africa, has not been proved to carry *S. haematobium*.

2. *B. africanus* group. *B. globosus* is a widespread and important host; *B. jousseaumei* has a comparatively restricted distribution and is reported to be a host in The Gambia and Upper Casamance.

3. *B. truncatus/tropicus* complex. Snails reported as *B. truncatus*, *B. rohlfsi* or *B. truncatus rohlfsi* are hosts in certain parts of West Africa. Possibly all belong to one species, *B. truncatus*, which probably should also include snails identified as *B. guernei*.

Experiments with *S. haematobium* have shown that isolates from communities where transmission is by *B. rohlfsi* do not develop so well in *B. globosus*, and *vice versa*. Thus the parasite has evolved strains differently adapted to different host snails, and differences in the distribution and ecology of these snails can play an important part in determining local patterns of disease transmission. There is some evidence that the strain carried by *B. rohlfsi* is more pathogenic to man (Cowper 1963, Wright & Knowles 1972).

B. forskali is the only known intermediate host for *S. intercalatum* in Cameroun. The discovery of natural hybridisation between this parasite and *S. haematobium* at Loum led to a series of experiments (Wright & Southgate 1976), in which hybrid miracidia were found to be infective to both *B. forskali* and to *B. rohlfsi* (the host snail for *S. haematobium* in the same locality). It has been suggested that the natural hybridisation was facilitated by clearance of forest which led to the establishment of *S.*

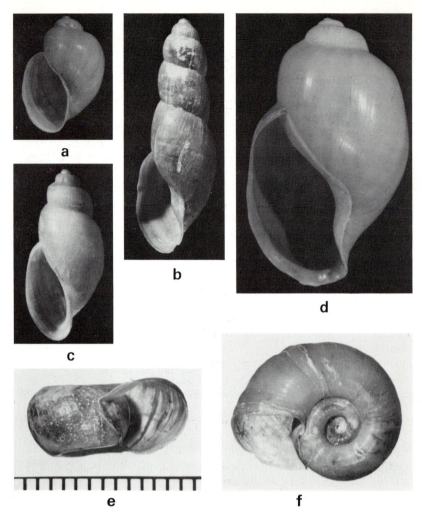

Figure 89. Shells of some freshwater snails (family Planorbidae) which are hosts for schistosomes in West Africa: a) *Bulinus rohlfsi*; b) *B.senegalensis*; c) *B.camerunensis*; d) *B.globosus*; e) and f) *Biomphalaria pfeifferi.* A millimetre scale indicates the magnification for a, d, e and f: Magnification of b and c is 50 per cent greater.

haematobium and its host snail in a transmission site where previously only *S. intercalatum* had occurred. This explanation introduces the consideration that new strains of *S. haematobium*, possibly with unusual ranges of compatibility with snails, might arise elsewhere in West Africa as a consequence of interbreeding between previously isolated strains, brought into contact through the activities of people and their movements.

300

Certain aspects of the biology of *Biomphalaria* and *Bulinus* are of particular relevance to understanding the success of their schistosome parasites. Since individual snails are hermaphrodite and can self-fertilise, they are well suited to colonise new habitats and rapidly to build up new populations. High fecundity and rapid growth rate allow an explosive increase in population density under suitable conditions. Moreover, these snails can survive the disappearance of surface water for periods of several months, by a period of dormancy known as aestivation. Thus, snails are able to live in seasonally filled waterbodies in savanna where few other species of freshwater mollusc are found. For disease control, it is significant that an immature schistosome infection can be carried by an aestivating snail from one transmission season until the next (Hira & Muller 1966, Hira 1968).

11.3 HISTORY AND STATUS OF THE DISEASE

11.3.1 *History*

The first schistosome to be described was *S. haematobium*, discovered in Cairo during an autopsy by the German surgeon Theodor Bilharz in 1851. There is evidence that this infection occurred in people in ancient Egypt (Farooq 1973), though possibly both *S. haematobium* and *S. mansoni* evolved with early hominids in the plateau areas of East Africa (Wright 1969). There are nineteenth century reports relating to the urinary infection in West Africa (Nachtigal 1881, Eyles 1887), and thus it appears that the disease has a long history in the region. According to legend, the Fulani tribe of northern Nigeria brought schistosomiasis with them during their migration from the upper Nile basin (Blair 1956).

The schistosome life cycle in Africa was not understood until 1915 when the British parasitologist R.T. Leiper reported on his investigations in Egypt. His discovery of the development of *S. haematobium* and *S. mansoni* in snails stimulated a spate of similar investigations in tropical Africa. Early studies showed *Bulinus globosus* to be an intermediate host for *S. haematobium* in Sierra Leone (Blacklock & Thompson 1924, Gordon et al. 1934), and *Biomphalaria pfeifferi* to transmit *S. mansoni* in French Guinea (Vogel 1932). Further major discoveries were that *Bulinus senegalensis* is a host for *S. haematobium* in the Gambia (McCullough & Duke 1954, Smithers 1956), and that two strains of this parasite are distinguishable in Ghana (McCullough 1959, Paperna 1968a), one adapted to *B. globosus* and the other adapted to *B. rohlfsi*.

Little attention was given to schistosomiasis as a public health problem in West Africa until after the Second World War. This is understandable in view of the need to devote available funds and personnel to combating more urgent threats such as malaria and trypanosomiasis. During the past 30 years, an increasing interest in schistosomiasis in Africa as a whole has been fostered by the WHO. One reason for this heightened interest was an appreciation of the potential for increased transmission of the disease in planned major dams and man-made lakes. The largest of these in Africa, Lake Volta in Ghana was filled in 1968 and has been the subject of an outstanding series of investigations sponsored by the Ghanaian authorities, United Nations Development Programme (UNDP) and WHO. In the period 1971–79, a major longitudinal study of the medical importance of urinary schistosomiasis formed part of the Malumfashi Endemic Diseases Research Project in Northern Nigeria (Pugh, Bell & Gilles 1980). Knowledge of distribution of schistosomiasis and intermediate hosts in French-speaking countries has been greatly advanced since 1969 by the Organisation de Coordination et de Coopération pour Lutte contre les Grandes Endémies (OCCGE) (Moreau et al. 1980, Sellin et al. 1980).

11.3.2 *Prevalence*

Reported frequencies or prevalences of infected people indicate that *S. haematobium* is much commoner in West Africa than *S. mansoni*. However, the latter parasite, causing intestinal schistosomiasis, is the less readily diagnosable. It may be calculated from estimates given by Gaud (1955) for 13 countries in West Africa, that out of a total population of 36 millions about 6 millions were infected with *S. haematobium*, but only 206 thousand cases of *S. mansoni* were estimated to occur in the larger population of 41 millions from 8 countries for which data were available. For Upper Volta, McMullen & Francotte (1962) estimated that 50% of the population, or over 1.6 million people, were infected at some period of their lives. Probably these figures underestimate present levels of prevalence but later authors have been deterred from making such calculations by the formidable sources of error. Serological techniques of diagnosis may be expected to detect more infections than direct examination of urine or faeces for eggs, which an infected person may not excrete. One such investigation of 3390 school children in the Senegal river valley in Mauritania, showed over 50% infected with *S. haematobium* and prevalences of over 90% were observed in some localities (Monjour et al. 1981). Examination of 4485 school children in Lagos State of Nigeria showed 13.4% infected with this parasite (Ejezie 1981). Within communities, prevalence is generally age-related, reaching a maximum in children and adolescents and declining over an age of about 20 years. This is of considerable significance in relation to plans for controlling schistosomiasis, since there is a large reservoir of infection in young people, many of whom are lightly infected and do not consider themselves to be ill.

11.3.3 *Medical importance*

The presence of blood in urine is a well known symptom of infection with *S. haematobium*, but this is just one of the very wide variety of effects and pathological changes associated with schistosomiasis. For schistosome infections in general, three disease syndromes are recognisable (Webbe

1981): dermatitis, which results from cercarial penetration of the skin; Katayama fever or acute schistosomiasis which occurs in intense initial infection and usually coincides with the onset of egg laying by the worms; and chronic schistosomiasis, in which lesions in different organs are dependent on the main egg laying sites. The major parasite factor responsible for chronic disease is the egg, which produces a granulotomous response in the host. Large granulomas around eggs cause destruction of tissue, causing pathological changes of an importance depending on both the intensity of infection and the intensity of the host's response. It appears that *S. mansoni* infection tends to cause more serious medical consequences than *S. haematobium*.

Though schistosomiasis can seriously disable and kill individuals, its degree of public health importance is not easy to determine. A statement made some years ago is still relevant. 'In most areas of endemic schistosomiasis there is not only a high degree of undernourishment and malnutrition in the community, but also a multiplicity of parasitic infections, which make it extremely difficult to differentiate the consequences of the several conditions involved' (Farooq 1963). In an area of low endemicity, the public health importance of *S. haematobium* may be not so much actual as potential, in view of an upward trend in the intensity of transmission (Pugh, Bell & Gilles 1980). There have been attempts to quantify any reduction in working capacity in infected people (e.g. Collins 1976), though some reservations about such analyses have been expressed by an economist (Adreano 1982).

11.3.4 *Distribution in West Africa*

11.3.4.1 *General considerations.* Schistosomiasis is common in the Niger basin (3.4.2) and occurs in all countries making up the West African region (Gaud 1955, Blair 1956, Odei 1961, W.H. Wright 1973, Moreau et al. 1980). The geographical range of *S. haematobium* extends northwards into the semi-arid Sahel zone. *S. mansoni* is less widespread and is not yet reported from Mauritania, Guinea Bissau and Niger. Schistosomiasis is a disease of savanna rather than of forest Gaud (1955); one reason is that streams and pools within undisturbed forest are not usually favourable habitats for host snails.

Within its broad geographical range, endemic schistosomiasis occurs in foci dependent on the existence of transmission sites (examples are described in 11.4). For some parts of Africa, climatic temperature is believed to play an important part in determining the distribution of schistosomes and their snail hosts. For example, the adverse effect of low temperature may account for the absence of human schistosomiasis from the coolest parts of the East African highlands and of southern Africa (Brown 1978). In West Africa, cool climatic areas associated with highlands do not appear to be sufficiently extensive to produce major discontinuities in the distribution of schistosomiasis. On the other hand, the unfavourable effect of high temperature possibly accounts for the absence of

Biomphalaria from the coastal region of East Africa (Brown et al. 1981) and from parts of West Africa (Sellin et al. 1980). It appears that all potential snail hosts are absent from a coastal zone about 100 km deep in Liberia (Sodeman 1973, Saladin et al. 1980), Guinea (Odei 1961) and Sierra Leone. Suggested reasons are the possibly adverse effects of high temperature and of the relatively low level of dissolved salts in the freshwater habitats (conversely, too high a salinity due to marine influence may also exclude such snails from coastal waters). Whatever factors are involved, they are local in effect, at least for *Bulinus rohlfsi*, which transmits *S. haematobium* in foci near the coast in Ghana and in western Nigeria.

Of surveys of snail distribution in West Africa, the most extensive in geographical coverage was carried out in a central group of French-speaking countries (Bénin, Ivory Coast, Upper Volta, Mali, Niger and Togo) (Sellin ct al. 1980). In this area there is a recognisable northern zone dominated by *B. truncatus*, a southern zone of *B. globosus* and an intermediate area where both species occur. Ecological observations suggested that *B. truncatus* achieves its maximum population density in the hot season, and it seems to be the better adapted of the two snails to the Sahelian climate. *S. haematobium* is able to develop, through the evolution of differently adapted strains, in both species of snail and the parasite's reported distribution corresponds broadly to their combined ranges. However, it is not known exactly to what extent each intermediate host is exploited, especially where both occur. *B. senegalensis* was found only rarely by Sellin et al. (1980) but probably it is widely distributed in the Sahel region, where it may serve as a host for *S. haematobium* as it does in Gambia. *Biomphalaria* has been found only rarely above latitude 14° North in West Africa and its distribution effectively determines the northward extension of *S. mansoni*. However, in part of north-west Ghana the snail is present but not the parasite and there may be considerable potential for the spread of intestinal schistosomiasis in West Africa (Sellin et al. 1980).

When considering the distributions of schistosomes and their snail hosts it is important to appreciate the unstable nature of any described situation. All these snails, with the possible exception of *B. senegalensis*, may benefit from forest clearance and the creation of water impoundments and irrigation systems. Excessive pollution of water exterminates snails, but they occur in high density in the presence of domestic refuse which provides a rich source of food and surfaces for attachment. Thus, in their response to human activities, such snails behave as 'weed' organisms, springing up and flourishing in disturbed environments.

11.3.4.2 *The Niger basin.* Compared with other great African rivers the Niger has a poor snail fauna in terms of endemic species (Brown 1980). A possible explanation is the marked instability in water level, caused by seasonal factors and by longer term changes in climate. The headwaters arise in an area of eastern Guinea where both *S. haematobium* and *S.*

mansoni are reported to be prevalent, but we have seen no details of the transmission sites. On the great northern curve of the Niger through Mali, low to high prevalences of *S. haematobium* are reported for towns situated close to the river, with low prevalences of *S. mansoni* in Bamako and Mopti (Moreau et al. 1980). In the Republic of Niger, *S. mansoni* has not yet been found, though *S. haematobium* is endemic at Tillabery, situated on the Niger river (Moreau et al. 1980). Observations made recently in Niger (Mouchet & Sellin in litt. 1982) indicate the transmission of *S. haematobium* in the Niger river, for example in villages on small islands, and *B. rohlfsi* appears to be the host snail in the riverine foci of infection.

In Nigeria, urinary schistosomiasis is almost universally distributed, with hyperendemic areas including Ibadan, Abeokuta, Ondo, Epé, Katsina, Sokoto, Kano and Zaria (Cowper 1963, 1973). *S. mansoni* is comparatively uncommon and found mainly in the north and west. *B. globosus* is the most frequently reported intermediate host for *S. haematobium*, though *B. rohlfsi* is widespread and is suspected to carry this parasite (Cowper 1973, Okpala 1961). *B. senegalensis* occurs in northern Nigeria and deserves consideration as another intermediate host. One of the early known high-prevalence areas for *S. haematobium* was the Wawa-Pategi region, extending on both sides of the Niger river, where infection was particularly frequent in rice-growing workers (Cowper 1963). Subsequently, the Kainji dam was constructed within this area; its significance for transmission of schistosomiasis is considered below (11.4.4). Special attention has been given to transmission in the urban area of Ibadan (11.4.3), and to some irrigation systems in north-eastern Nigeria (11.4.7).

A longitudinal study of schistosomiasis over a period of eight years was recently completed in the Malumfashi district of Kaduna State, northern Nigeria (Bell & Howells 1973, Pugh et al. 1980). This district lies within the Funtua Agricultural Development Project financed by the World Bank. Most rivers in the area have sand beds and flow only during the rainy season, and many earth dams have been constructed under the Development Project in order to relieve chronic water shortage. *S. haematobium* is transmitted by *B. globosus*. Infection is predominant in men and boys, because these communities are Muslim and the females are obliged to lead retiring lives which allow them comparatively little contact with infective water. *S. mansoni* is much less prevalent, though there is evidence of recent increase. Following the pilot observations in 1971, there was a decline in *S. haematobium* associated with increasing desertification, culminating in the severe Sahel drought of 1973 which eliminated much marshland and greatly reduced the available habitats for snails. By 1976 an increase in the parasite was detected and this was accelerated by the construction in the same year of an earth dam between two villages. This dam was soon colonised by *Biomphalaria* and *B. globosus*, and became much frequented by males from local communities (Tayo & Jewsbury 1978, Tayo et al. 1980). In 1979 prevalence of *S. haematobium* had almost recovered to the level seen before the Sahel drought, and *S. mansoni* also appeared to be more prevalent (Pugh, Burrows & Tayo 1980).

11.4 TRANSMISSION SITES

Here we describe some transmission sites chosen to illustrate the diversity of ecological conditions in which schistosomes maintain their life cycles.

11.4.1 *Floodplains*

There is a high prevalence of urinary schistosomiasis amongst Mauritanian people living in the valley of the Senegal river and its tributaries (Monjour et al. 1981). The alluvial valleys are regularly inundated by seasonal rises in the river water, and while the flooded areas slowly dry out the people plant crops ('waalo' cultivation) wherever possible. Cultivation is also practised in rain-filled depressions on dunes bordering the Senegal river ('jeeri' cultivation). The presumed snail host, *Bulinus guernei*, occurs in the collections of water in both types of cultivated area. The people, both sedentary and semi-nomadic, practise agriculture and stock-raising and make frequent contacts with water. Their annual movements, to marshes with livestock and between the 'jeeri' and the 'waalo' also contribute to their high level of infection with schistosomiasis.

11.4.2 *Isolated seasonal pools*

High prevalences of *S. haematobium* in certain villages on the laterite plateau in the Gambia are maintained by transmission in small pools, well described by Duke & McCullough (1954): 'On the plateau, the only water, other than that from the village wells, is confined to small ponds, of which one or more are to be found near every village. Most of these ponds are collections of water in shallow depressions in the laterite rock . . .their water content depends entirely upon rainfall and evaporation and they dry up in a varying number of months, according to their size, after the rains cease. During the rains they are entered daily by the villagers, who continue the practice into the dry season, until the ponds become so muddy and uninviting that they are left entirely to the cattle.' These laterite ponds contain large populations of *Bulinus senegalensis*, proved to serve as the intermediate host. It is significant that 'Laterite pools are not easily found: they are not marked on maps and may remain dry during part of the year. Often they are hidden in the bush, and are found only by enquiring at the villages, the whereabouts of any pools used for washing and bathing. As a result they may be easily overlooked when searching for dangerous transmission sites' (Smithers 1956). Although *B. senegalensis* is the only snail found in most of the laterite pools,

306

presumably because other species cannot tolerate the low concentrations of dissolved salts and long periods of desiccation, it has recently been shown to live also in other kinds of habitat including irrigated rice-fields (Goll 1981).

11.4.3 *Urban areas*

Gross pollution of water and habitat disturbance does eradicate aquatic snails, but they remain sufficiently abundant in some densely populated urban areas to maintain high prevalences of schistosomiasis. In the walled towns of northern Nigeria, snail habitats are formed in water-filled borrow pits, left after the digging out of mud blocks for building; consequently large urban populations are brought into contact with intermediate hosts, despite the provision of purified pipe-water supplies (Blair 1956). In Ibadan, *S. haematobium* is transmitted by *B. globosus* in a variety of sites, including seasonally-filled ponds and pools formed in permanent streams at footbridges and culverts (Muller & Hira 1966, Hira 1969, 1970). It is noteworthy that transmission of schistosomiasis was maintained in Ibadan even though it was observed that nearly all snails in temporary ponds were killed in the dry season, and many of the snails in the streams were washed away during the rainy season. The distribution of snails downstream from a source of severe pollution in a Nigerian river was studied by Smith (1982). The upper limit of the *Bulinus* zone corresponded roughly with the upper limit of the area used for washing and bathing; above this the local people regarded the water as too dirty for these purposes.

11.4.4 *Man-made lakes*

A valuable review of the hydrological and biological aspects of man-made lakes in Africa is provided by Beadle (1981).

11.4.4.1 *Lake Volta.* Area 8800 km². Maximum depth: 80 m. Year of closure: 1964. A dramatic rise in the prevalence of urinary schistosomiasis around Lake Volta occurred within a few years of its formation. A WHO/UNDP project was established in 1971 to study the epidemiology of the disease and to investigate methods for control. Fortunately, the origins and subsequent epidemiology of this outbreak of schistosomiasis are notably well documented in a series of publications (e.g. Odei 1972, 1973, Klumpp & Chu 1980, Scott et al. 1982).

The original population of about 70,000 persons displaced from the impoundment area was re-settled in new townships on or near to the lakeshore. A similar number of people, including many fishing families from lagoons near the lower part of the Volta river, were attracted by rich catches of fish made in the new lake, and settled in scattered communities along the shore. It is presumed that many of these immigrant people brought with them the strain of *S. haematobium* transmitted by *Bulinus rohlfsi* in certain coastal lagoons (11.4.6). Originally, infections with *S. haematobium* were generally light in the part of the river basin destined to be affected by the new lake, but as early as 1969 prevalence levels of 90% were found in children living on the lake shore. In the period 1973–74, total population surveys in the Afram and Pawmpawm branches showed a prevalence of about 73%, and in some communities it was practically impossible to find an uninfected person (Scott et al. 1982). The intermediate host is *B. rohlfsi*, and it is rare for other species of *Bulinus*, and *Biomphalaria*, to be found in Lake Volta.

Although it has so successfully colonised Lake Volta, the snail *B. rohlfsi* was found only rarely in the pre-impoundment area. *B. globosus* was commoner and lived in eastward flowing streams, but apparently is unable to exploit the new lacustrine environment, possibly because it cannot tolerate the wide annual fluctuation in the shoreline caused by the seasonal draw-down in water level. The key to understanding both the success of *B. rohlfsi* and the pattern of disease transmission proved to be the lacustrine vegetation. Dense populations of the snail are associated with luxuriant growths of the submerged plant *Ceratophylum demersum*: possibly its whorls of stiff leaves protect snails and their eggs from predators (Odei 1973). The main transmission season occurs when the water level is high and there is a dense stand of emergent vegetation at the margin, mainly *Polygonum* and grasses. During this period, human contacts with water are concentrated in pocket-shaped clearings in the marginal vegetation, and large snail populations develop in the submerged *Ceratophyllum* growing in the pockets of clear water. During the period of low water, open beaches of mud or sand are exposed and the water contact sites for people are diffused; some transmission still occurs but only where beds of *Ceratophyllum* are growing offshore. A contrary effect has been observed in some localities where extremely heavy growth of the plant interrupted disease transmission, by causing the water to become stagnant, snail populations to decline and the people to change their water contact sites to less polluted points. *Ceratophyllum* grows best in deep stream inlets of the lake, where probably the water is rich in nutrients required by the plant and there is shelter from wave-action (Klumpp & Chu 1980).

11.4.4.2 *Lake Kainji*. Area: 1250 km². Maximum depth: 60 m. Year of closure: 1968. Extensive work was done on the hydrology and biology of the section of the River Niger designed to form the new lake (Imevbore & Adegoke 1975, Beadle 1981), but little detailed information is available about schistosomiasis in this area either before or after closure of the Kainji dam. Both *S. haematobium* and *S. mansoni* were originally widespread in the area extending southwards from Garafini (Cowper 1963) and now occupied by the southern part of the lake, and these parasites are found in communities at or near to the lake shore (Adekolu-John 1979). In 1970, *B. globosus* and *Biomphalaria* were found on the northwest shore of the new lake between Rofia and Ambodhidi (Dazo & Biles 1972), and some snails of each species were obtained naturally infected with schistosomes. *B. rohlfsi* has been reported to occur in Lake Kainji (Bidwell & Clarke, 1977), but we have seen no evidence that the snail is associated with the plant *Ceratophyllum* as is the case in Lake Volta. This plant has been found in Lake Kainji (Imevbore & Adegoke 1975), but apparently it has not become generally common, and other aquatic vegetation is reported to be poorly developed. This has been attributed to several causes, the depletion of nutrients by the rapid flow-through of the water, the large annual draw-down which periodically exposes a large area of the bottom, and the instability of extensive parts of the shoreline due to erosion or to deposition. As Lake Kainji matures, an increase in submerged and emergent vegetation may be expected and would heighten the potential for transmission of schistosomiasis in this lake.

11.4.4.3 *Lake Kossou (in Ivory Coast).* Lake Kossou, like Lake Kainji, appears to have considerable potential for the transmission of schistosomiasis. Both the urinary and intestinal diseases were known in the area before impoundment, and *Bulinus* and *Biomphalaria* were found in the lake before it had reached its full extent (Scott & Chu 1974, Deschiens & Cornu 1976). The occasional presence of *Ceratophyllum* is reported, but in contrast to Lake Volta, *Biomphalaria* became common while all species of *Bulinus* remained rare (Sellin & Simonkovich 1980).

11.4.5 *Crater lakes*

Lakes formed in the craters of extinct volcanoes are a feature of parts of East Africa, but for West Africa the only examples known to us lie in the western region of Cameroun. Urinary schistosomiasis is known to be transmitted in Barombi Mbo lake, where *Bulinus rohlfsi* is the host snail, and in Barombi Kotto lake, where both *B. rohlfsi* and *B. camerunensis* are hosts (Duke & Moore 1976). These lakes are situated at altitudes of 300 m and 110 m respectively in the district of Kumba. The isolation of the villages within these two craters encouraged an attempt to eradicate schistosomiasis (see 11.5).

11.4.6 *Coastal lagoons*

On either side of the lower Volta River lie complexes of lagoons and creeks, the upper ones of fresh water, the lower ones increasing in salinity towards the river mouth. The transmission of *S. haematobium* was studied before and after construction of the Akosombo dam, which resulted in control of flooding which had fed the lagoons annually (McCullough 1956, Paperna 1968b). Prevalence of the parasite was high in local communities living close to lagoons inhabited by *B. rohlfsi*, the only intermediate host. Prevalences were lower or non-existent in communities situated closer to the Volta River or to saline lagoons. It is interesting that *B. rohlfsi* was closely associated with the plant

Ceratophyllum demersum, for this association later enabled the snail to thrive in the newly formed Volta Lake. The control of flooding resulted in the drying out of small lagoons, but *B. rohlfsi* persisted in the larger lagoons, which were reduced in size but still maintained by rainfall and occasional flooding from the river. Consequently, and contrary to expectation, there was no reduction in the prevalence of schistosomiasis (Paperna 1968b). During the years since these investigations, it is possible that the sustained control of flooding has diminished further these freshwater habitats. On the other hand, the continuous flow of fresh water from the Akosombo turbines has had the effect of pushing the fresh water zone in the river about 20 kms nearer to its mouth, compared with its position in 1963 (Beadle 1981), and some previously saline lagoons could now have fresh water and thus be potential new transmission sites.

11.4.7 *Irrigation systems*

Some major irrigation projects show serious potential for the transmission of schistosomiasis. The snails *B. globosus* and *B. rohlfsi* were found commonly amongst vegetation in main canals, but not in rice-paddies, at Yau in northeast Nigeria (Oxford University Expedition 1971). Specimens of *B. globosus* carrying infections of *S. haematobium* were obtained in 1980–81 in a canal of the South Chad Irrigation Pilot Project at Ngala, northeast Nigeria (Betterton 1984). In an irrigated rice-growing area in the Kou valley, Upper Volta, transmission of schistosomiasis was controlled at a low level, compared with neighbouring villages, by ensuring that the people in new settlements observed strict rules of hygiene (Colette et al. 1977).

11.5 CONTROL

Effective, long term and low cost methods for controlling schistosomiasis are lacking (Hoffman et al. 1979, Webbe 1981). For this reason and also because the public health importance of schistosomiasis has been realised comparatively recently, its control has lagged behind that of other parasitic diseases. Estimates of the economic cost of schistosomiasis may persuade health authorities to commit more funds to its control, but it is difficult to achieve satisfactory benefit/cost ratios of control programmes for any of the major parasitic diseases (Adreano 1982). Already in 1976, the government of Ghana had allocated 8.8% of the national health budget to control of schistosomiasis (Iarotski & Davis 1981).

As vaccines against schistosomiasis are unlikely to become available for some years, the major control methods used on a world-wide scale are biological control, water supply, sanitation, health education, agricultural engineering, treatment of people with schistosomicidal drugs and the use of molluscicides to kill snails (Hoffman et al. 1979). Each method suffers from limitations and a combination of methods should be applied in each

310

project. Biological control of snails has barely entered the stage of field trials in Africa (McCullough 1981); field work in Ibadan formed part of a recent study of the American snail *Helisoma* as a potential competitor of local intermediate hosts (Tait 1982). The provision of sanitation and supplies of pure water would bring health benefits additional to reducing infection with schistosomiasis, but these services cannot be expected in most rural areas. An important but sometimes neglected requirement of sanitary facilities is that they must be attractive to people and easy to maintain in good order at low cost. Agricultural engineers can design irrigation systems to minimise potential transmission sites, and workers' villages can be sited to reduce water contact, but there remains the problem of reservoirs of infection in areas surrounding such projects. Both schistosomicides and molluscicides are widely used, but they are not one hundred per cent effective and are costly to use in mass treatments. A major advance in chemotherapy is the drug Praziquantel (Biltricide) which is highly effective against both *S. haematobium* and *S. mansoni* when given in a single oral dose. Possibly the cost of chemotherapy could be substantially reduced, while still achieving significant reduction of disease, through the selective treatment of heavily infected individuals and high-risk groups, since a relatively few people with high worm burdens are responsible for most of the egg output. Molluscicides suffer from the environmental disadvantage that they are toxic to other organisms including fish; various methods have been proposed to improve their effectiveness and specificity, including the use of slow-release formulations and snail attractants, but these are still in the experimental stage.

In West Africa, many investigators have recommended methods for controlling schistosomiasis in local situations, based on knowledge of the precise location of transmission sites, seasonal variation in intensity of transmission related to changes in the abundance of snails, and of the habits of the people in making contact with contaminated water. Actual attempts at disease control mostly have been small in scale, and ineffective in the long term. For example, ten years after a costly programme of mollusciciding at Monguel in Mauritania, schistosomiasis was diagnosed in 90% of the schoolchildren (Monjour et al. 1981).

Two major control programmes in West Africa, in southwest Cameroun and on the shore of Lake Volta in Ghana, illustrate the difficulties in the way of long term control of schistosomiasis. A total of about 1400 people associated with the Barombi crater lakes, Cameroun, were treated with a schistosomicide (Ambilhar) and at the same time a molluscicide (Frescon ®) was applied to the lakes (Duke & Moore 1976). The technical difficulty in applying molluscicide in adequate concentration down to a depth of 1.5 m was overcome by means of an applicator tube attached to a pump in a boat. Transmission of *S. haematobium* by *B. rohlfsi* declined to below a detectable level, but became evident again during two years of post-control observations. The continued incidence of snail infections was due to residual eggs still being passed by people after chemotherapy. *B. camerunensis* also transmitted this parasite (though possibly a different strain) and continued to do so until the interval between molluscicide applications had been reduced from 6 to 2 weeks, when the snail population was greatly reduced. However, the reproductive potential of *B. camerunensis* was so high that the survivors re-established the population, after mollusciciding was finished, in only four weeks. From these results, it was concluded that the 'break-point' in the transmission of *S. haematobium* was so low as to be practically synonymous with total eradication. The cost of the entire programme was estimated to be nearly US dollars 10 per person protected per annum, a sum about three times the total estimated expenditure per head of the population on all health and social services for the year 1974-75.

At Lake Volta, a three-year programme of control of *S. haematobium* in selected parts of the southwest shore covered a total population of 15,000 people (Chu, Klumpp & Kofi 1981, Chu, Vanderburg & Klumpp 1981). A combination of focal application of molluscicide (niclosamide), removal of the plant *Ceratophyllum* and selective chemotherapy (with metrifonate) reduced prevalence of infection by 72% in an area of low endemicity and 40% in an area of high endemicity. Reduction in intensity of infection, as shown by the drop in numbers of eggs passed in urine, was about equal in the two areas at about 78%. The close association between the intermediate host *B. rohlfsi* and *Ceratophyllum* suggested that removal of this plant should be an effective means of snail control. However, this was found to be practicable only in areas where the plant grew in light density (Klumpp & Chu 1980). Removal of heavier growths by hand or with rakes was time-consuming and expensive, control by herbicides proved to be ineffective, and mechanical removal was impracticable because of the numerous tree stumps projecting from the lake bottom. Where *Ceratophyllum* was difficult to remove, molluscicide was applied in areas of water cordoned off from the open lake by a plastic curtain. For effective control chemotherapy had to be extended beyond. the original project area to include villages up to 5 kms away from the lake, as their inhabitants depended on the lake for their water during most the year. The costs of mollusciciding and manual removal of *Ceratophyllum* amounted to US dollars 1.09 per person per year (1973-78). It was concluded (Chu, Vanderburg & Klumpp 1981) that such methods are not sufficient to stop transmission, though they gave good results in the short-term control of intensity of infection; permanent control would require the virtual eradication of schistosomiasis in a wide zone along the lake shore.

It has recently been demonstrated in Nigeria that people intensely infected with *S. haematobium* can be readily detected by means of standard urinalysis reagent strips, in place of the inconvenient counting of eggs by microscopy (Pugh, Bell & Gilles 1980). The investigators suggest, that by using urinalysis strips in conjunction with single oral dose drugs, selective chemotherapy programmes could be executed at low cost by junior staff.

312

11.6 PROSPECTS

Immediate prospects for controlling schistosomiasis in West Africa are not encouraging. There is likely to be a continuing increase in prevalence and intensity of infection, and the disease is likely to become established in new endemic areas. In existing endemic areas, transmission tends to be augmented by the creation of new habitats for snails through forest clearance and the impoundment of water. Increasing density of human population results in more crowded water contact sites and increasing pollution, that up to a certain level is favourable for snails. The establishment of new endemic foci of infection is favoured by the high capacity of snails for dispersal and colonisation of new habitats, and by the increasing mobility of people aided by modern means of transportation. Sellin et al. (1980) observed in the region of Bobo Dioulasso, the replacement of *S. haematobium* by *S. mansoni*, and considered this to be part of a general northwards spread by this parasite. The increasing dispersal of parasites could possibly have significant effects on the relationships between *S. haematobium* and both its intermediate and definitive hosts. In West Africa, this parasite exists in at least two strains, differing in their most compatible host snail and possibly in their pathogenicity in man. Increasing contacts between such strains could possibly lead to the origin of parasites with new genetic constitutions and unusual combinations of biological characteristics. Existing methods of control can substantially reduce the prevalence and intensity of schistosomiasis, but one may apply to West Africa the general conclusion of Hoffman et al. (1979): 'Without further development of measures that would be effective, of long duration and low cost, schistosomiasis will remain a major public health problem in most endemic areas'.

11.7 ACKNOWLEDGEMENTS

We are indebted to F. Mouchet and B. Sellin for permission to refer to unpublished observations. Photographs of shells and worms were prepared in the British Museum (Natural History) by the Photographic Unit and the Electronmicroscopy Unit: the shell pictures have been previously published (Brown, 1980). We thank V.R. Southgate for helpful comments during the preparation of this article.

11.8 REFERENCES

*Important contributions published while this article was in press and therefore not cited in the text.

Adekolu-John, E.O. 1979. A communication of health and development in the Kainji Lake area of Nigeria. *Acta tropica* 36: 91–102.

Adreano, R. 1982. Economic impact studies on parasitic diseases: a select review of research since 1973. In, *Proceedings and abstracts, Fifth International Congress of Parasitology* 2: 77–89.

Beadle, L.C. 1981. *The inland waters of tropical Africa*. London & New York: Longman.

Bell, D.R. & R.E. Howells 1973. The Malumfashi pilot survey. 1: Introduction, malaria and urinary schistosomiasis. *Ann. trop. Med. Parasit.* 67: 1–14.

Betterton, C. 1984. Ecological studies on the snail hosts of schistosomiasis in the South Chad Irrigation Project Area, Bornu State, northern Nigeria. *J. arid Envir.* 7: 43–57.

Bidwell, A. & N.V. Clarke 1977. The invertebrate fauna of Lake Kainji, Nigeria. *Nigerian Field* 42: 104–110.

Blacklock, D.B. & M.G. Thompson 1924. Human schistosomiasis due to *S. haematobium* in Sierra Leone. *Ann. trop. Med. Parasit.* 18: 211–234.

Blair, D.M. 1956. Bilharziasis survey in British West and East Africa, Nyasaland and the Rhodesias. *Bull. Wld Hlth Org.* 15: 203–73.

Brown, D.S. 1978. Freshwater molluscs. In M.J. Werger (ed.) *Biogeography and ecology of southern Africa*, The Hague: Junk.

Brown, D.S. 1980. *Freshwater snails of Africa and their medical importance*. London: Taylor & Francis.

Brown, D.S., J.E. Jelnes, G.K. Kinoti, & J. Ouma 1981. Distribution in Kenya of intermediate hosts for schistosomiasis. *Trop. geogr. Med.* 33: 95–103.

*Chaine, J.P. & E.A. Malek 1983. Urinary schistosomiasis in the Sahelian region of the Senegal river basin. *Trop. geogr. Med.* 35: 249–256.

Chu, K.Y., R.K. Klumpp, & D.Y. Kofi 1981. Results of three years of cercarial transmission control in the Volta Lake. *Bull. Wld Hlth Org.* 59: 549–54.

Chu, K.Y., J.A. Vanderburg & R.K. Klumpp 1981. Transmission dynamics of miracidia of *S. haematobium* in the Volta Lake. *Bull. Wld Hlth Org.* 59: 555–60.

Colette, J., G. Garrigue & B. Sellin 1977. Etude parasitologie sérologique et epidémiologique d'une zone rizicole Africaine à haut risque d'extension Bilharzienne. *Médicine tropicale* 37: 521–529.

Collins, K.J. 1976. Physiological performance and work capacity of Sudanese cane cutters with *S. mansoni* infection. *Am. J. trop. Med. Hyg.* 25: 410–21.

Cowper, S.G. 1963. Schistosomiasis in Nigeria. *Ann. trop. Med. Parsit.* 57: 307–322.

Cowper, S.G. 1973. Bilharziasis (schistosomiasis) in Nigeria. *Trop. Geogr. Med.* 25: 105–118.

Dazo, B.C. & J.E. Biles 1972. Schistosomiasis in the Kainji Lake area, Nigeria. Report on survey made in October-December 1970. Unpublished report/Schisto '72.21. Geneva: World Health Organisation.

Deschiens, R. & M. Cornu 1976. Commentaires écologiques et épidémiologiques concernant les bilharzioses et le lac de retenue de Kossou (Côte d'Ivoire). *Bull. Soc. Path. exot.* 38: 163–69.

Duke, B.O.L. & F.S. McCullough 1954. Schistosomiasis in the Gambia. 2: The epidemiology and distribution of urinary schistosomiasis. *Ann. trop. Med. Parasit.* 48: 287–299.

Duke, B.O.L. & P.J. Moore 1976. The use of a molluscicide in conjunction with chemotherapy to control *Schistosoma haematobium* at the Barombi Lake foci in Cameroon. Parts 1–3. *Tropenmed. Parasit.* 27: 297–313, 489–508.

Ejezie, G.C. 1981. The parasitic disease of school children in Lagos State, Nigeria. *Acta tropica* 38: 79–84.

Eyles, C.H. 1887. Bilharzia haematobium in West Africa. *Lancet* 2: 659.

Farooq, M. 1963. A possible approach to the evaluation of the economic burden imposed on a community by schistosomiasis. *Ann. trop. Med. Parasit.* 57: 323–331.

Farooq, M. 1973. Historical development. In N. Ansari (ed.), *Epidemiology and control of schistosomiasis*: 1–16. Basel: Karger.

Gaud, J. 1955. Les bilharzioses en Afrique occidentale et en Afrique centrale. *Bull. Wld. Hlth Org.* 13: 209–258.

Goll, P.H. 1981. Mixed population of *Bulinus senegalensis* and *B. forskali* in the Gambia. *Trans. Roy. Soc. trop. Med. Hy* 75: 576–78.

*Goll, P.H., H.A. Wilkins & T.F. de C. Marshall 1984. Dynamics of *Schistosoma haematobium* infection in a Gambian community. 2. The effects on transmission of the control of *Bulinus senegalensis* by the use of niclosamide. *Trans. Roy. Soc. trop. Med. Hyg.* 78: 222–226.

Gordon, R.M., T.H. Davey & H. Peaston 1934. The transmission of human bilharziasis in Sierra Leone, with an account of the life-cycle of the schistosomes concerned, *S. mansoni* and *S. haematobium. Ann. trop. Med. Parasit.* 28: 323–414.

Hira, P.R. 1968. Studies on the capability of the snail transmitting urinary schistosomiasis in Western Nigeria to survive dry conditions. *West Afr. med. J.* 17: 153–160.

Hira, P.R. 1969. Aspects of the transmission of *S. haematobium* in Ibadan, Nigeria. *West Afr. med. J* 18: 28–32.

Hira, P.R. 1970. Aspects of the spread and control of schistosomiasis in Ibadan, Nigeria. *West Afr. med. J.* 19: 180.

Hira, P.R. & R. Muller 1966. Studies on the ecology of snails transmitting urinary schistosomiasis in Western Nigeria. *Ann. trop. Med. Parasit.* 60: 198–211.

Hoffman, D.B., J.S. Lehman, V.C. Scott, K.S. Warren & G. Webbe 1979. Control of schistosomiasis. Report of a workshop. *Am. J. trop. Med. Hyg.* 28: 249–59.

Iarotski, L.S. & A. Davis 1981. The schistosomiasis problem in the world: results of a W.H.O. questionnaire survey. *Bull. Wld Hlth Org.* 59: 115–27.

Imevbore, A.M. & O.S. Adegoke 1975. *The ecology of Lake Kainji.* Nigeria: Ife University Press.

Klumpp, R.K. & K.Y. Chu 1980. Importance of the aquatic weed *Ceratophyllum* to transmission of *Schistosoma haematobium* in the Volta Lake, Ghana. *Bull. Wld Hlth Org.* 58: 791–98.

Leiper, R.T. 1915. Report on the results of the bilharzia mission in Egypt, 1915. 1. Transmission. *J. Roy. Army med. Corps* 25: 1–55.

McCullough, F.S. 1956. Transmission of *S. haematobium* by *Bulinus* sp. in the Ke district of the Gold Coast. *Trans. Roy. Soc. trop. Med. Hyg.* 50: 449–57.

McCullough, F.S. 1959. The susceptibility or resistance of *Bulinus (Physopsis) globosus* and *B. (Bulinus) truncatus rohlfsi* to two strains of *S. haematobium* in Ghana. *Bull. Wld. Hlth Org.* 20: 75–85.

McCullough, F.S. 1981. Biological control of the snail intermediate hosts of human *Schistosoma* spp.: a review of its present status and future prospects. *Acta tropica* 38: 5–13.

McCullough, F.S. & B.O.L. Duke 1954. Schistosomiasis in the Gambia. 1. Observations on the potential snail vectors of *S. haematobium* and *S. mansoni. Ann. trop. Med. Parasit.* 48: 277–86.

McMullen, D.B. & J. Francotte 1962. Report on a preliminary survey by the W.H.O. bilharziasis advisory team in Upper Volta. *Bull. Wld Hlth Org.* 27: 5–24.

Monjour, L., G. Niel, A. Mogahed, M. Sidatt & M. Gentilini 1981. Répartition géographique de la bilharziose dans la vallée du fleuve Sénégal. *Ann. Soc. belge Med. trop.* 61: 453–60.

Moreau, J.P., C. Boudin, J. Trotobas & J. Roux 1980. Répartition des schistosomiases dans les pays Francophones de l'Afrique de l'ouest. *Médecine tropicale* 40: 23–30.

Nachtigal, G. 1881. *Sahara und Sudan: Ergebnisse sechsjahriger Reisen in Afrika* Berlin: Reprinted Akademische Druck und Verlagsanstalt, Graz, Austria, (1967), Band 2, 465.

Odei, M.A. 1961. A review of the distribution and snail hosts of Bilharziasis in West Africa. *J. trop. Med. Hyg.* 64: 27–41, 64–68, 88–97.

Odei, M.A. 1972. Some preliminary observations on the distribution of bilharzia host snails in the Volta Lake. *Bull. Inst. fond. Afr. noire* 34; 534–43.

Odei, M.A. 1973. Observations on some weeds of malacological importance in the Volta Lake. *Bull. Inst. fond. Afr. noire* 35: 57–66.

Okpala, I. 1961. Studies on *S. haematobium* infection in school children in Epé, Western Nigeria. *West Afr. med. J.* 10: 402–412.

Oxford University Expedition to Nigeria 1971. *Bull. Oxf. Univ. Explor. Club* 20 (Special series 1): 1–95.

Paperna, I. 1968a. Susceptibility of *Bulinus (Physopsis) globosus* and *B. truncatus rohlfsi* from different localities in Ghana to different local strains of *S. haematobium. Ann. trop. Med. Parasit.* 62: 13–26.

315

Paperna, I. 1968b. Studies on the transmission of schistosomiasis in Ghana, 3: notes on the ecology and distribution of *Bulinus truncatus rohlfsi* and *Biomphalaria pfeifferi* in the lower Volta basin. *Ghana med. J.* 7: 139–45.

Pugh, R.H.N., D.R. Bell & H.M. Gilles 1980. Malumfashi Endemic Diseases Project, 15. The potential medical importance of bilharzia in northern Nigeria: a suggested rapid, cheap and effective solution for control of *S. haematobium* infection. *Ann. trop. Med. Parasit.* 74: 597–613.

Pugh, R.H.N., J.W. Burrows & M.A. Tayo 1980. Malumfashi Endemic Diseases Research Project, 14. Increasing schistosomi transmission. *Ann. trop. Med. Parasit.* 74: 569–70.

Saladin, B., K. Saladin, E. Dennis & A. Degremont 1980. Preliminary epidemiological survey of schistosomiasis in central and southern Liberia. *Acta tropica* 37: 53–62.

*Saladin, B., K. Saladin, B. Holzer, E. Dennis, A. Hanson & A. Degremont 1983. A pilot control trial of schistosomiasis in Central Liberia by mass chemotherapy of target populations, combined with focal application of molluscicide. *Acta tropica* 40: 271–295.

Scott, D. & K.Y. Chu 1974. Research in the epidemiology and methodology of control of schistosomiasis in man-made lakes. Unpublished Report/MPD/74.7. Geneva: World Health Organisation.

Scott, D., K. Senker & E.C. England 1982. Epidemiology of human *S. haematobium* infection around Volta Lake, Ghana, 1973–75. *Bull. Wld Hlth Org.* 60: 89–100.

Sellin, B. & E. Simonkovich 1980. *Les mollusques hôtes intermediaires des schistosomes sur le site du Barrage de Kossou.* Report No. 7.360/Doc. Techn. O.C.C.G.E.

Sellin, B., E. Simonkovich & J. Roux 1980. Etude de la répartition des mollusques hôtes intermédiaires des schistosomes en Afrique de l'ouest. *Médecine tropicale* 40: 31–39.

Smith, V.G.F. 1982. Distribution of snails of medical and veterinary importance in an organically polluted watercourse in Nigeria. *Ann. trop. Med. Parasit.* 76: 539–46.

Smithers, S.R. 1956. On the ecology of schistosome vectors in the Gambia, with evidence of their role in transmission. *Trans. Roy. Soc. trop. Med. Hyg.* 50: 354–65.

Sodeman, W.A. 1973. The distribution of schistosome vector snails in central Liberia. *Ann. trop. Med. Parasit.* 67: 357–60.

Southgate, V.R., D. Rollinson & J. Vercruysse 1984. *Schistosoma curassoni* Brumpt, 1931, a little known parasite from Senegal. *Trans. Roy. Soc. trop. Med. Hyg.* (in press).

Tait, A.I. 1982. Field and laboratory studies on the biological control of *Biomphalaria pfeifferi* (Krauss): a snail intermediate host of schistosomiasis. U.K.: PhD Thesis, University of Sussex.

Tayo, M.A. & J.M. Jewsbury 1978. Malumfashi Endemic Diseases Project, 4. Changes in snail populations following the construction of a small dam. *Ann. trop. Med. Parasit.* 72: 483–87.

Tayo, M.A., R.H.N. Pugh & A.K. Bradley 1980. Malumfashi Endemic Diseases Research Project, 11. Water-contact activities in a schistosomiasis study area. *Ann. trop. Med. Parasit.* 74: 347–54.

*Thomas, J.D. & A.I. Tait 1984. Control of the snail hosts of schistosomiasis by environmental manipulation: a field and laboratory appraisal in the Ibadan area, Nigeria. *Phil. Trans. Roy. Soc. Lond.* B 305: 201–253.

Vogel, H. 1932. Beitrage zur epidemiologie de schistosomiasis in Liberia und Franzosisch-Guinea. *Arch. f. Schiffs-u. Trop.-Hyg.* 36: 108.

Webbe, G. 1981. The six diseases of W.H.O. Schistosomiasis: some advances. *British med. J.* 283: 1104–1106.

*Wilkins, H.A., P.H. Goll, T.F. de C. Marshall & P.J. Moore 1984. Dynamics of *Schistosoma haematobium* infection in a Gambian community. 1. The pattern of human infection in the study area. 3. Acquisition and loss of infection. *Trans. Roy. trop. Med. Hyg.* 78: 216–221, 227–232.

Wright, C.A. 1969. The ecology of African schistosomiasis. In J.P. Garlick, & R.W.J. Keay (eds.), *Human ecology in the tropics.* London: Pergamon Press.

Wright, C.A. 1981. The schistosomes. *Biologist* 28: 99–108.

Wright, C.A. & R.J. Knowles 1972. Studies on *S. haematobium* in the laboratory. 3. Strains from Iran, Mauritius and Ghana. *Trans. Roy. Soc. trop. Med. Hyg.* 66: 108–118.

Wright, C.A. & V.R. Southgate 1976. Hybridization of schistosomes and some of its implications. In Taylor, A.E. & R. Muller (eds.), *Genetic aspects of host-parasite relationships.* Oxford: Blackwell.

Wright, W.H. 1973. Geographical distribution of schistosomes and their snail hosts. In N. Ansari (ed.), *Epidemiology and control of schistosomiasis.* Basel: Karger.

Authors cited

319

320

321

Place names

Subject index

329